JUDAISM FOR THE WORLD

JUDAISM FOR THE WORLD

Reflections on God, Life, and Love

ARTHUR GREEN

Yale
UNIVERSITY PRESS
New Haven and London

Published with assistance from the Mary Cady Tew Memorial Fund.

Yale University Press books may be purchased in quantity for educational, business, or promotional use. For information, please email sales.press@yale.edu (U.S. office) or sales@yaleup.co.uk (U.K. office).

Set in Janson type by Newgen North America, Austin, Texas.
Printed in the United States of America.

Library of Congress Control Number: 2020933184
ISBN 978-0-300-24998-9 (hardcover : alk. paper)

A catalogue record for this book is available from the British Library.

This paper meets the requirements of ANSI/NISO Z39.48-1992 (Permanence of Paper).

10 9 8 7 6 5 4 3 2 1

To my ḥaverim *from our years together in Havurat Shalom*
1968–1975
In enduring friendship
כי עזה כמות אהבה

Contents

To the Reader

Welcome! The volume before you is a collection of essays, short teachings, insights, and readings of Jewish sources that have occurred to me after more than half a century as a Jewish seeker and teacher of Torah. These pieces are offered as a way of bringing you along on my own religious journey. Rather than providing "answers" to the great spiritual questions with which I've grappled for so long, they are my way of sharing something of the feeling-tone of my own inner life and some ways I read the tradition that I have so long been privileged to teach.

I am an old guy now. The roots of my own journey go back even farther than the late 1960s, when spiritual quest first began to appear on the radar screen of an entire generation. Over the course of those years, I have taught Judaism, especially its mystical stream, to three generations of future rabbis and scholars. But I have also stood by, watching sadly, as three generations of Jewish seekers, in much larger numbers, have turned away from our native tradition and sought to sink spiritual roots elsewhere, primarily in gardens nurtured by teachings flowing from the East. I always carry such seekers in my heart when I write, partly because I feel myself to be one of them. Even though I did not make the journey eastward, I shared their sense of disappointment with the Judaism that we had once been taught. Fortunately, I was led early into the hasidic and mystical path, and that saved Judaism for me. But my heart still goes out to the many other Jewish seekers who were not given that opportunity. It is partly for them that I write.

A parallel group of readers I have in mind are seekers who do not come from any sort of Jewish roots, including Jews-by-Choice, others considering the path of conversion, curious non-Jewish seekers, and those of Jewish ancestry whose families are already so fully assimilated that they have lost any sense of meaningful Jewish identity. I have had the privilege of meeting many people coming from each of these groups, and I have taught quite a few of them. Each of these has found a way to Torah through a remarkable and unique personal journey. I treasure these students, and believe there are many more like them. If you are one of them, consider this a personal invitation.

In titling this book *Judaism for the World*, I am making a very specific claim, one that is obvious to me but needs to be stated clearly. I understand religion as a set of tools for the purpose of cultivating interiority, the life of the spirit. By this I mean an inward journey that leads one precisely toward self-transcendence, to an awareness of the universal Self in whose presence we exist. All the external forms of the tradition—study, practice, prayer, poetry, music, celebration, rites marking the cycles of lives and the sacred year, and all the rest—are there in order to awaken a spirit that lies dormant within us, an inner self waiting to be called forth. The purpose of all true religion, including Judaism, is to help us discover and cultivate that divine spark, and then to build a society and civilization that recognize and treasure that spark in each human being. In the language of Judaism, both "soul" and "image of God" are used to designate it. Both of these terms are rooted in the opening narrative of Genesis, the tale of Adam and Eve in the Garden of Eden. By definition, then, they apply to all humanity.

This truth does not belong to Jews alone. I take it as my personal task to spread this understanding of religion as widely as I can. But I believe that is our collective mission as well. When we agreed to be called a "kingdom of priests" at the foot of Mount Sinai (Ex. 19:6), we committed ourselves to share the teachings we received there with all of humanity. In some of the dark ages of Jewish history (and there were many), voices arose that tried to apply terms like "divine soul" and "image of God" to Jews alone. They found it hard to believe that those who slaughtered and exiled us so mercilessly could be truly human, bearers of souls just as holy as our own. It is no surprise that ethnic and religious persecution should have given rise to xenophobia, the fear and hatred of outsiders. It is also no surprise that these claims should have gotten a new hearing in the years following the Holocaust. Brought out into the light, however, such narrowing views need to be seen for what they are: a violation of our Torah's truth. "Why was Adam created singly?" asks the Talmud. "So that no person could ever say to another: 'My father is greater than yours'" (M. Sanhedrin 4:5).

Since religion is primarily addressed to this essential divine-human spirit, rather than to the rational mind, I understand its truth to dwell in an inner realm closer to art than to science. Religion has nothing it can *prove;* it can only *witness.* It is meant to be evocative, soul-awakening. Accordingly, I ask that you read what I place before you here as testimony, perhaps even as a work of art. You may find some parts of it surprisingly personal and revealing; it could not be otherwise. But it is also a reading of Torah, *my language for that inward journey,* as I have come to live and understand it over the course of a long lifetime, one filled with many blessings. I welcome you to come and read along with me, as I might welcome you to listen to my music or to view my set of paintings. I hope you enjoy this book and derive meaning from it, in your own way. But I hope for more than that. If my teachings speak to you, whoever you are and wherever you come from, I hope they will inspire you to create your own readings and understandings of this tradition. They will surely be different from mine, just as each of us is a unique human being. All our life experiences are there with us as we approach the world of Torah.

The language in which I write is very deeply and particularly Jewish. Although this book is presented in English and offered to "the world," reaching beyond borders, I consider it to be an entirely Jewish book, and I look forward to offering it also in a Hebrew version. I have not watered down its Jewish content in reaching out to you. It is important to me that I speak to you *from within* the tradition of Judaism and Jewish mysticism. There may be concepts you encounter here that sound familiar from the study of other religions, or even from works of Western philosophy. Yes, I believe that truth is one, to be found in many places. But it is important to me that most of my insights grow out of my study of classical Jewish sources, especially those of the mystical tradition, and I seek to present them to you in a language derived directly from their own. Some readers, especially those new to Judaism and its forms of self-expression, may struggle here and there. Please stick with me; I promise you great reward. I have taken care to translate all the Hebrew terms, and there is also a glossary at the end of the volume. For those readers who are beginners to Judaism's spiritual language, I recommend my book *These Are the Words: A Vocabulary of Jewish Spiritual Life,* which you might even want to hold alongside this one as you read.

I write in this way because there is another addressee toward whom this book, and all my work, is turned. That is the tradition itself, both the beloved works I study, most written in the distant past, and those who live today and see themselves as their heirs, the ones who hold fast to Torah. I love this tradition and its language, and want to see it live again, inspiring new generations of seekers. It cannot do that, I believe, so long as it is stuck in the clutches of certain premodern conceptions, including both literalism and exclusivism. I am trying, in short, to pull the Jewish mystical tradition, often kicking and screaming, into the twenty-first century. As a tough old guy, I can abide some of those kicks and screams. In this, I stand firmly in the tradition of the neo-hasidic masters who have come before me.

Intentionally, there is no central "argument" to this volume, no progression of thought from one essay to the next. Each is meant to be read on its own, and to invite your contemplation. Because of that, you will find some overlap of themes among them; I think it valuable to say important things more than once. I hope there will grow in the reader a sense of what my pathway to the great questions of life is all about, and how I draw on Jewish sources to respond to them. Although I still regard myself primarily as a seeker, seventy-eight years into this earthly journey, the truth is that I have developed an approach, both to the tradition and to life itself, that seems to work for me. I hope to share much of that in the course of this volume. Perhaps some of my insights will be useful to you in the course of your own journey as well.

The three sections of this book, "Soul," "Year," and "World," are based on a triad first identified in the ancient tract *Sefer Yetsirah*, "The Book of Creation." They signify, according to many later interpreters, the three realms in which divinity is manifest in the world. The historian of religion would call them sacred space, sacred time, and sacred person. The kabbalist, thinking cosmologically, would always begin discussing them from above, starting with "World." In deference to our existential age, I begin the book with "Soul." Here I share much of my own religious journey with you, as openly as I can. This section concludes with the essay "Judaism as a Path of Love," at once a scholarly reflection on this often unseen element in Jewish teachings and my own statement of what it has meant to live all these years as a devotee of that Judaism. "Year" offers a series of reflections on the Jewish calendar, thoughts to which you might want to turn as each season comes along, perhaps even to stimulate conversation across your own Shabbat or holiday table. "World" opens with some essays on Creation, both mythically and scientifically—in true postmodern union—and then reflects on what it has meant to me to live in this created world, as a human being and more specifically as a contemporary Jew. But all three—soul, year, and world—are fully present throughout these teachings.

Welcome along! I hope you enjoy the journey.

Acknowledgments

Earlier versions of several of these essays appeared in various publications, including *Tikkun, Raʿayonot,* and the *Reconstructionist.* All of those have been significantly rewritten for this volume. "How I Pray" appeared first in Hebrew in the Israeli edition of *Radical Judaism.* "Judaism as a Path of Love" also appears in *Be-Ron Yaḥad: Essays in Honor of Nehemia Polen* (Boston: Academic, 2019).

This volume was originally suggested to me by my student and friend Ariel Evan Mayse, who also offered comments on a number of the essays. I am most grateful to him. David Maayan served as first reader and editorial assistant for this entire project, and deserves much credit and gratitude for helping me bring it to fruition. I am also grateful to Jennifer Banks and the staff at Yale University Press for their warm acceptance of these offerings as a follow-up to my *Radical Judaism* (2010).

Soul

THOUGHTS ON THE INWARD JOURNEY

Neo-Hasidism

A JUDAISM FOR MONISTS

THERE IS ONLY ONE. That is the great truth of mysticism, found within and reaching beyond all religions. That One embraces, surrounds, and fills all the infinitely varied forms that existence has taken and ever will take. We call that truth out twice daily in reciting *Shema' Yisra'el*, "Hear, O Israel." "Y-H-W-H is One" means that there is none other.[1] Our daily experience of variety, separate identity, and alienation of self from other renders an incomplete and ultimately misleading picture of reality. "You were One before the world was created; You are One since the world was created."[2] Unchanged, eternal; worldly existence covers over the reality of that deeper truth, but human consciousness is so constructed as to permit glimpses of it to shine through. The one Being is clothed within each being. For reasons we do not begin to understand, that One dressed itself in this "coat of many colors" called the universe, and on this planet entered into the endless dance of variety and multiplicity that we call evolution. It is present within each unique form of existence that has come to be in the universe, and yet remains One, in and through them all.

Responding to the utter elusiveness of that inner (and outer) One, spiritual teachers around the world have approached it by saying only what it is not, or by naming it *ayin*, the primal Naught. This *via negativa* has been especially attractive to the mystics, who see existence as bearing a great secret. "Being is Naught, and Naught is being," say the kabbalists;

the *ayin*, or Naught, is true being, and that which we thought was being, *yesh*, is truly naught. It is captured, as it were, by the name revealed to Moses, when he asks what to call the One who has sent him on his mission. "I am Y-H-W-H" (Ex. 6:2), he is told, offering an impossible quasi-nominal form of the verb "to be," probably best rendered as "Is-Was-Will Be." But the One can never be "captured" by the finite human mind; it had already been liberated even from that name in a prior verse (Ex. 3:14), where the voice says, "I shall be whatever I shall be." If you think you've "got" Me by naming Me "Is-Was-Will Be," I will fly out of that nominal box and become a verb again! Elusiveness is uncompromised by revelation. The One is a *dynamis*, not a static entity.

This glimpse of a monist or panentheist worldview, one that sees God in all, the One manifest in each of the many, but the mystery ever beyond our grasp, lies deeply veiled within Judaism—and so too within Christianity and Islam—behind the mask of religious personalism, faith in a personified deity who created this world as a humanlike act of will, rules over history, guides each person's fate, and promises redemption. But awareness of this all-pervasive spiritual presence that fills the world is never completely absent from the Western faith traditions. "Behold, He stands behind our wall, peering through the windows, gazing through the cracks" (Cant. 2:9). The One is ever "peering through" the mask of multiplicity behind which it is hidden, an invitation for us to peer behind that mask as well. The ancient rabbis referred to God as "the place of the world," meaning that there is no place devoid of God's presence, that the world exists *within* the One.[3] "God" came to refer to an abstract and elusive entity that preceded and underlay all existence. This sense of abstract divine oneness underlies both of the most significant theological constructions of medieval Jewry: Moses Maimonides' *Guide for the Perplexed* and the *Zohar*. It peers through most boldly in the teachings of some of the early hasidic masters, who sought to turn the subtle mystical insights of a learned elite into a religious revival that could inspire the masses.

Judaism urgently needs a renewal of that revival. In this era, when conventional notions of God, faith, and religious living have failed to speak to so many, it is time for this monistic face within Judaism to step out of the closet. The simplistic either/or of personified theism versus atheism ("Do you believe in God, the Old Fellow in the sky, or not?"), often encapsulated in the inability of so many Jews to say *barukh atah Adonai* ("Blessed are You, O Lord"), has been an unnecessary barrier that has kept two or three generations of seekers at arm's length from their tradition. The "I

don't believe in God" of so many Jews (and other Westerners) is often
really "I don't believe in the God of my childhood fantasy, and I've been
given nothing to take its place." Yet it turns out that our need to reach for a
truth beyond that of God as cosmic parent or potentate has a long history
within Jewish tradition itself. When Maimonides (1135–1205), the tower-
ing figure of classical Jewish philosophy, insisted on purifying the notion
of God of all anthropomorphisms, he sought to step beyond the ancient
faith legacy he had received, reconstituting Judaism in a philosophical
mode. God represented a truth that remains eternally beyond our grasp,
best reached by the pathway of denying all that God is not, stripping away
all but essential truth. Only the philosopher, starkly committed to that
negative path, could hope to perceive a glimmer of the truth. A highly
philosophical reinterpretation of Torah was offered to buttress that faith,
and to root it in the praxis of Judaism.[4]

    The first kabbalists, coming a century later, grappled with the same
issue of the inadequacy of the seemingly naïve religious personalism inherited from the biblical/rabbinic tradition. They came at solving it from
the opposite direction, however, seeking to hyper-stimulate rather than
to restrict the religious imagination. Instead of denying all this-worldly
images of God, they embraced them, but expanded them beyond all limit.
Surely God is a Father and a King. But so too is Y-H-W-H a Queen, a
Bride, a River, a Well, an Ocean, a Lake, a Tree, and a Mountain. Almost
every noun of scripture was taken as a potential symbolic description of
some aspect of the deity. God is the Tabernacle, the Holy of Holies, Jerusalem, and Mount Sinai; the Myrtle Branch, the Sabbath, and the Tree of
Life. Thus the kabbalists described the dynamic, ever-changing Godhead,
behind which lay the infinite and utterly indescribable mystery called only
eyn sof, "the Endless." Having so many images forces one to believe that
all are symbolically true but none is to be taken literally or posited as ultimate truth; all of them flow forth from an endless mystery that transcends
them as it brings them forth, ever using and renewing them to reach out
toward the limited human mind. They serve as a symbolic language that
becomes a portal through which to receive glimpses of the truth beyond.
The kabbalists say quite clearly that the personal God-figure is "born"
out of the womb of mystery, serving as a bridge to reach out to the finite
human mind.[5] We tend to view that figure as a projection coming from
our side, our way of reaching toward that mysterious One. They see it as
the One's way of reaching forth, extending Itself to approach the naïve and
limited human mind. But the mystic understands that the cosmos is a hall

of mirrors, one that can be opened from either end. As the God-figure is a "projection" from our world, so too may we be a self-projection of the mysterious One. The "awakening," as the kabbalists call it, may come from "above" or "below."

For the past two hundred years, Judaism as presented in the West has been denuded of this mystical tradition. At the turn of the nineteenth century, a new notion was proposed, something entirely alien to all of Judaism's prior history. The first modern Jewish historians, active in that era, called forth a "mainstream Judaism," a term that had not previously existed, and cannot even be translated into proper Hebrew.[6] This "mainstream" was defined in various ways by Orthodox and Reform spokesmen. They agreed, however, on the negative side of it. "Mainstream Judaism" existed in large part in order to exclude the mystical tradition, along with anything else that seemed like an embarrassment to a Jewry that sought to have its faith accepted as liberal and rational by those well-meaning liberal and rational Christians who had first welcomed us as equal human beings and citizens. As we emerged from the ghetto, one imposed both from within and without, mystical Judaism was considered too odd, too exclusivist (as indeed it often was), and too alienating to others. In the name of progress, it therefore needed to be set aside. Judaism was the religion of the prophets (for the Reform), the Talmudic legislators (for the Orthodox), and of Maimonides' enlightened spirit, reread as referring to the "enlightenment" of a very different era.[7] As this very Western notion of "enlightenment" moved eastward, contention around the place of mysticism went with it, leaving Kabbalah and Hasidism the legacy of old-style Jews, later seen as "ultra-Orthodox," alone, while "modern" Jews rejected them.

These European models passed over into American Jewish life as well. A general ignorance of Jewish sources, as well as the Hebrew language itself, characterized most of American Jewry throughout the twentieth century. This combined with a lack of theological sophistication in the immigrant and post-immigrant generations. Very little of the profundity of Jewish teaching was passed on. Later American Jewish generations knew and were taught nothing of mystical—or philosophical—Judaism.

Two hundred years later, Jews are scrambling to rediscover the mystical tradition. That effort is under way on all levels, from the most popular (sometimes even commercialized) to the most academic. It is present in books, in film, in music, and in many other forms of contemporary Jewish culture. It is offered by such Orthodox hasidic outreach efforts as Chabad and Breslov, as well as in liberalized versions such as Jewish Renewal or my own neo-hasidic teachings. This has come about partly because of the wide interest in spiritual quest in late twentieth- and twenty-first-century America. Throughout this half century, many of the most profound minds among us have been turned toward the recovery of ancient, long-lost truth, whether from the Yogis, the Tibetan masters, or the kabbalistic sages. This search is very much a part of our society, perhaps in the hope that somewhere in this legacy of wisdom humanity will find a way not to destroy our precious and much-battered world.

But there is also an internal Jewish reason for this renewed interest in the mystical tradition. Although American Jews knew little of the subtleties of Jewish theology, many of them have become highly educated and intellectually sophisticated in a variety of spheres. For some, this extends also to their thinking about spiritual matters. They sensed a certain dead end in nonmystical approaches to Jewish theology. All the essential elements of our religious language are challenged by modernity. How do we celebrate God's Creation in Shabbat each week, while also believing the conclusions of astrophysicists, geologists, and evolutionary biologists about the age of our planet and how we got here? Why do we continue to live by our Torah, if we are no longer literal believers in its divine revelation? What meaning do the *mitsvot*, the ritual forms of Judaism, have if they are not "commanded" by God in the most literal sense? Just what does a post-Holocaust Jew mean by prayer?

Only the mystics seem to offer adequate response to these challenges. They do so by awakening new perspectives, transposing the conversation about them to a different realm of discourse, one that is at once more "inward" and functional. Their question is no longer on the factual or historical plane, but on that of inner awareness and emotional response. One does not need to believe in a traditional idea of Creation to experience and celebrate the divine presence in each new morning. "Receiving the Torah" becomes an opening of heart and mind that can take place in each moment, rather than an ancient event. The origin of the *mitsvot* becomes less important than their role as reminders, stimulating awareness of the One, which is their ultimate goal. Prayer is more about training the heart to open than it is about expecting a response from an external Listener.

Similar challenges face the thinking Christian or Muslim who lives in open encounter with the modern and now postmodern world, and in those traditions, too, a recovery of the mystical approach has begun to take hold. As we approach religious questions today, we should realize that we are privileged to be living at a great moment in the history of world religion. All of us seekers are blessed with a unique opportunity to learn from one another, in a way that was never before as possible. Until the mid-twentieth century, religion was mostly understood to be a "zero-sum game," that is, if mine is true, yours is false. Beginning in the latter half of the twentieth century, two major changes have taken place that have the potential to be transformative, if we give them a chance to do so. First came a self-transformation of Christianity, created in significant part by the recognition of Christian responsibility for the Holocaust. The triumphalist spirit that had dominated Christianity throughout the era of Western conquest and colonialism, a sense that it alone had the salvific truth and needed to impart it to all humanity, was shattered. The carefully wrought doctrinal statements that emerged from Vatican II, both with regard to the Jews and concerning the other religions of humanity, had great repercussions. So too did various parallel statements by Protestant bodies, redefining the evangelical message of the churches to allow for equal and mutually respectful dialogue with the wisdom to be learned from other faith communities. While this transformation has not spread to all of Christendom, especially not to some of the Eastern Orthodox and American evangelical churches, they too cannot ignore its spirit.

A second great blessing—again in potential—of our era is the opportunity for open dialogue between the spiritual traditions of East and West. Aside from the tiny Jewish communities in India, we Jews never had any contact with the religious traditions that arc from the Indus Valley across all of East Asia. Islam had encountered them chiefly in a spirit of competition and confrontation, although there had been important exceptions to that in the past, especially among the Sufis. Christianity had known them only as the religions of those it had sought to convert. Many of its early attempts to understand Eastern religions had been wrought in that context. But now we live in a different era. The postmodern spirit needs to insist that the zero-sum game regarding religion is at an end. Religions acting in competition with one another bear responsibility for many of the most terrible acts of violence and bloodshed in human history. But religions acting together, in common quest for God—or the One, or Being, or the great Nothing—and fulfillment of the divine purpose in existence, can be a great force for good. Humility, a great virtue in all of our teachings, *demands* of us that we be open to learning from one another. "Who is wise?" the ancient rabbis asked.[8] "One who learns from every person." They did not say "from every scholar" or "from every Israelite," but "from every person."

A key part of this emerging dialogue has to be a conversation about what we mean by "God" or "the One," or "the Naught" as our various teachers and traditions have understood it. The religions of the East did not settle on a single personified deity who was the author of all creation and everything that came in its path. They contain great varieties of approaches to the oneness of existence or the unifying spirit of being. Some of these remain quite abstract; others are concretized in a variety of images. We need to be open to exploring with them what we mean by the ultimate truth of existence, including where we might converge and where we differ. Our practices and symbolic languages remain distinct, as they should, but theological conversation across those lines will enrich us all.

This conversation is just beginning. Until now, it has been one-sided and imbalanced. Western religious leaders have often shunned true dialogue with Eastern religions that they dismissed as "pagan" or idolatrous.[9] At the same time, many thousands of Western seekers, having failed to find meaning in their own faiths, have rushed into the only partially understood world of Eastern teachings, often creating Westernized versions of those teachings that Asian practitioners barely recognize as their own. Knowing nothing of the mystical traditions within the Western religions from which they had fled, they sometimes created theologies that sound remarkably like what might have emerged from new readings of Hasidism, Sufism, or Christian monasticism, had history shaped things differently.

Toward a Neo-hasidic Judaism: Essential Teachings

Hasidism is a mystical approach to Judaism based on the teaching and practice of compassion, *ḥesed*. Accompanying Judaism throughout its history, it is a passionate religiosity that inhabits and delights in the traditional forms of religion, but sees them as instrumental toward the higher goal of intimacy or union with God, rather than as ends in themselves. Neo-Hasidism is a Judaism that evokes the key religious teachings of popular eighteenth-century Hasidism, *universalizing* them and seeking to live them out in a context that does not reject either secular learning or life in the open society. In proposing a new Jewish mysticism or a neo-hasidic Judaism for contemporary seekers, I have in mind a rereading of the key teachings of Hasidism that would look something like this:

1. *Shekhinah*. The indwelling presence of Y-H-W-H is to be found everywhere, in each place, moment, and human soul. We need only

to open our eyes to it, to take the time and train ourselves to notice, to pay attention. All of life is filled with opportunities to uncover and uplift sparks of divine light, restoring them to their single Source. "The blessed Holy One needs to be served in every way." It is not only through following the commandments and Torah study that God is worshipped, nor do Jews have a monopoly on religious truth. Everything one does and encounters in life, including our engagement with the physical world, may become a place to discover the One. A religious person is one who seeks *shekhinah*, the Presence, or divine sparks, within each moment and every deed, transforming them into occasions for worship, and restoring the fragmented universe to cosmic wholeness.

2. *'Avodat ha-Shem be-Simḥah*. The purpose of life is the joyous service of Y-H-W-H. We serve God by loving and serving God's creatures, especially the neediest among them. This may begin with those closest to us, but ultimately transcends all borders. In our day, serving God also means an active commitment to preserving the natural world itself, alongside living a life of service to the human community. To serve God is to help enhance the divine image in the world, to treat each person as a unique and precious embodiment of the divine spirit. The life of service is meant to be one of great joy and fulfillment, offering greater and deeper happiness than all the pleasures of the world. But we engage in it not for the sake of that pleasure, but for the good we can do. Be careful of anything that might keep you or distract you from that task, *even if it is dressed up in the garb of religion.*

3. *Kavvanah*. The essence of religious life lies in the link between inward devotion and acts of outer-directed goodness. The inner core of faith serves as a spring that constantly renews our commitment to a life of compassion and generosity of spirit. In our personal religious lives, we struggle to balance the need for spiritual discipline (hence ritual, daily practice) and the danger of routinized religious behavior, a potential barrier to spiritual growth. The commandments of religion are to be followed lovingly, but seen as means rather than ends in themselves, as vessels for the divine light that floods the soul, or as concrete embodiments of the heart's joy and devotion. *Devequt*, true inner attachment to God, is the goal. All of life, including all the precepts of religion, which exemplify a way of living in God's presence, is to serve as a means toward that end.

4. *Yisra'el*. Judaism is the religion of the Jewish people, a community that was collectively called to divine service at Mount Sinai. We believe in that community and are devoted to its rebirth. Sinai (that of the heart, ever re-creating that of the ancient tale) calls us beyond the status of ethnic identity to live as "a kingdom of priests, a holy nation" (Ex. 19:6). Jews have a collective obligation to a life of service, to human dignity, and to spiritual awareness. As liberated slaves and as victims of genocide, we are called especially to witness to their horrors, and to prevent them from occurring anywhere. We welcome newcomers and returnees to our community of covenant, one that always has room to expand. We are also part of a wider *yisra'el*—the term literally refers to those who "struggle with God"—and we celebrate that spiritual identity as well.

5. *Torah*. Our tradition has bequeathed to us great gifts of wise teachings, beginning with the *TaNaKh*, or Hebrew Bible, and embracing vast stores of Jewish lore. These include the learned teachings of Jewish men as well as the daily household practices of Jewish women, in many forms and over many centuries. As we open our hearts to this tradition and engage with it, we hear a mysterious voice, a divine echo, that addresses us from within these practices and teachings. This does not mean we deny the human authorship of the texts or that we find no fault in them. Arguing with the teachings has always been legitimate in Judaism, seen as an act of love, a sign of engagement. Part of the sacred process of Torah is the endless reinterpretation of the texts and traditions as they apply to the lives of Jews in the course of an ever-changing history. As we open ourselves to the texts, they become windows into a trans-verbal eternity, present within ourselves as within the words of Torah. More than an expression of divine will, the Torah in its secret form is our verbal embodiment of wordless divinity. Engagement with Torah, including both study and the fulfillment of its forms, is an actual partaking in the mysterious divine Self, the cosmic One. *Talmud Torah*, the study of Torah, a key value throughout Jewish tradition, is to be transformed into an intense devotional activity focused on opening the pneumatic keys to this inner teaching. The insights that come to us in the course of study, teaching, and interpretation are themselves a divine gift, the ongoing flow of revelation.

6. *Tefilah*. Prayer is the most essential paradigm of devotional experiences. All of life—including but not limited to Torah study and *mitsvot*—should be seen as an extension of the prayer experience,

one that involves the entire self and is offered entirely as a gift to God, just as were the sacrifices of Temple times. This includes both traditional liturgy and new forms of prayer, including use of wordless melody and silence. The act of praying, that of opening and sharing one's heart in the presence of the One, is more basic to Judaism than any prayer book text. Difficulty with traditional language should not cause us to abandon our attempts at the act of prayer.

7. *Middot.* The moral transformation to which our lives should be devoted is one of uplifting and transforming the physical and emotional self to become an ever more perfect vehicle for God's service, partly through creating communities that support these values. The call toward spiritual and moral growth is without limit. This process begins with the key devotional pair of love and fear. We need to purify these in daily life, coming to realize that all true love contains the love of God, or the unselfish love of life itself, shared with all others who live, and the only worthy fear is the great awe at standing in the presence of the One. All other loves and fears derive from these and mask them. The twin facts that each of us is a unique link in the great and ongoing evolutionary journey, and that each of us exists for but an instant in evolutionary time, should bring us to a life of devotion and humility. Judaism is our path for living out our awareness of that universal truth.

Contemporary Speech

What you have just read is a translation of a hasidic Judaism into a language made to work for the contemporary seeker. The living out of this translation is the task that remains before us. If Judaism is going to serve new generations, who continue to be highly educated in a scientific age, we will have to forge a religious language, rooted in the mystical and hasidic tradition, that will speak to us in ways that are both *spiritually profound* and *intellectually honest.* The suppleness of our religious language has great influence on our openness to religious teaching, especially that which by its very nature dwells beyond the reach of full verbal expression. Students of perception have long noted a deep relationship between the subtlety of our language and the range of our ability to experience the world. We "see" only as many gradations of "blue" as we can name; variations more shaded than those described by our language tend to escape our mind's eye. The mycologist who walks through the forest after a rain, armed with a detailed vocabulary for the description of mushrooms, experiences a richness of life in that form that most of us would blithely ignore. So too with the life of the spirit. Those who have a rich language to talk about such subtle (and essentially trans-verbal) matters will be better equipped to open themselves to profound religious experience.

For us, such a language will have to be deeply rooted in the sources of Judaism. Only then will it speak with an authentic Jewish voice. It will have to include such Hebrew terms as elude translation (as I have done here), and it will need to be rich in traditional symbol and metaphor, tokens of that rootedness. But we will also have to both *universalize* and further *de-anthropomorphize* that inherited language. We can no longer place Israel at the center of humanity, seeing God as deriving strength or pleasure from Jewish lives alone. Even universalized, the notion of a God who creates the world for the sake of His own pleasure, as the old hasidic masters saw it, is—and should be—alienating to the contemporary reader. Perhaps we need to restate it this way: *The One is manifest in every creature, and "delights" equally in being present within each form of existence that it enters.* Each creature exists by token of that divine delight. Within our own human community, the One is present within each person and is manifest in every human culture. *Tsaddikim* and *tsaddikot*, "the righteous," exist throughout the world, across all lines of gender, ethnicity, and religious language; we need to learn from all of them. The "pleasure" God takes in human worship needs to be understood in terms of the human goodness and love brought forth in the worshipper and in the religious community. We give to the One through our service to the many.

In order to remain honest in our use of religious language, we will have to maintain a dual relationship to it. We will have to admit that we are both "insiders" and "outsiders" to the world framed by it. Living in an open and diverse religious landscape, we have studied religion critically and comparatively, or we read the works of those who have. We know something about the human origins of religious forms, and about the nature of symbolic language and myth. We recognize both their great power and potential danger when misused. We live in daily awareness of both the physical and social sciences, and the assumptions upon which they operate, so different from the worldview of our premodern ancestors. Without abandoning these parts of our awareness, we also seek to rejuvenate our spiritual lives within a Judaism that has the ring of antiquity and authenticity. To understand this dual relationship to tradition, some basic matters of theology will have to be examined.

Facing the Big Questions

Our Western traditions differ on the question of revelation and scripture. For us Jews, Torah and the Hebrew Bible constitute our sacred text, accompanied by endless rubrics for creative reinterpretation. Christians add the New Testament and the ever-living example of the life of Jesus. Muslims, while walking in the footsteps of the prior Western faiths, revere a new revelation, that of the Qur'an. Each of our traditions revolves around its own sacred narrative—Sinai, the Crucifixion and Resurrection, the Hijra—which it proclaims as the central moment of human history, "the greatest story ever told." But we all have in common a universal notion of Creation; we worship God as the Creator of the universe. That is a bigger story, and forms the basis for all that follows. Therefore, it is to that narrative that we need first to turn.

What do we mean when we say that we believe in Creation? Christians, along with Jews, turn to the opening chapter of Genesis for inspiration. "In the beginning . . ." For us as Jews, that narrative is essential to our religious lives. It climaxes in the Sabbath, the defining ritual form of Judaism. Each week, we raise our wine cup and proclaim: "Heaven and earth were completed, they and all their hosts." Yet most of us are far from being literal believers in the biblical Creation narrative. We accept the scientific accounts of planetary and human origins, though we seek to infuse them with religious meaning.[10]

"In the beginning," therefore, means something beyond the beautifully told *story* of Genesis 1. Before there were many, there was a One. The precedence of that One to the many may not really be temporal, since "time," in any case, has little meaning on the other side of the Big Bang. It means rather that the One underlies the many, now as always, in the same way we might say that silence underlies and "precedes" the many sounds that are to be heard in the course of a great symphony. The symphony begins not with the first note, but with a recognition of the silence out of which it is to emerge, a silence that also will be there—enduring but transformed—in the moment after it. The One is there, in that sense, before each of us began to live, and will be there, too, after we are gone. It is to that One that we bow in awe. It is to that One, as manifest in all its creatures, that we seek to open our heart in love. That is what it means to be a religious person.

In Genesis, that abstraction has been turned into narrative. A narrative takes place within time. It needs to have a beginning point from which all the rest of the story proceeds. Hence "The One underlies the many" becomes "In the beginning God created . . ." Our faith in creation does not have to mean that we believe in the world's origin as proceeding from a willful act, as we humans would understand it, at a specific moment in time. "In the beginning" is our way of saying, "There is a One that underlies the many." We continue to assert our faith that we live in a God-infused and hence "created" world. Nothing is more important to us as religious people, and nothing is of greater moral urgency, in the era in which we live.

Here we have begun to open the doorway to a deceptively simple-seeming question: What does it mean to be a religious human being? What *difference* does it make in our worldview, attitude, or behavior that we choose to call ourselves "religious"? This approach takes a universal human question rather than a uniquely Jewish one as its point of departure. The great Jewish theologies have always sought to deal with universal questions. The *answers* such theologies provide are, of course, rooted in the Jewish tradition and speak the very particular language of Judaism. But the *questions* are those of all humanity.[11]

The theology that emanates from our ground question takes as its starting point humans and the realm of personal religious experience, rather than God and the origins or nature of the cosmos. Our stance is "existential"; that is, it begins with the fact that *we* exist and the fact that humans in a great variety of cultural contexts have reported—in mystical diaries, in poetry, in art, and in many other ways—some sense of the oneness of all being. All of that is part of the reality of the human situation—alongside mortality, suffering, love, joy, and all the rest. But "existential" is also meant in its other sense: life-and-death issues are at stake in this conversation. A religious outlook that does not offer some sense of ultimate meaning and purpose—"Why am I alive? What am I to do with this life?"—is hardly worth the effort. For the seeker, life without engagement in the quest for such ultimate meaning is not worth living.

Our question also presumes an article of faith: that the inner life, a spiritual inner sanctum (*kodesh kodashim*, or "Holy of Holies" in Hebrew) in which a person may seek and find such meaning, is a distinct and irreducible element of human experience. Every human soul is capable of the journey to seek and find that inward "place." It cannot be detected, and certainly cannot be explained away, by brain-wave measurements. Nor is it reducible either to clinical or sociological explanations. This area of human activity can be defined broadly as "spiritual quest," "search for God," or "religious devotion." In contemporary (supposedly "secular") parlance, it is sometimes misidentified as the "search for self." The danger with that terminology is the possibility of solipsism, getting lost within the self, or overinvolvement with feeding the ego, an especially great danger in our day. The language of self-discovery works only insofar as it is understood as leading toward an inner ego-*transcendence*, helping to move the person beyond fulfillment of personal needs and desires. Both the inescapable challenge of mortality and the daily struggles of "Why go on?" lead to the understanding that we need an answer that reaches beyond ourselves. Humanity, at its most noble and profound, has sought to live in the presence of that which transcends us, a quest that simultaneously and paradoxically also makes us most fully human. Although discovered by a turn inward, it quickly leads us beyond the self.

The early hasidic masters, as in other mystical master/disciple traditions, saw themselves as teachers of spiritual wakefulness and awareness. In this they differ from both the rabbi, teacher and judge of proper daily living, and the prior kabbalistic master, transmitter of esoteric lore. The hasidic teachers, at their best, used the tradition and its language as a resource for awakening us to the inner life. They saw this task as the very core of religion, *the cultivation of an awareness that we live in relation to the transcendent, to something larger than ourselves.* The religious life is one lived in constant striving for this awareness and in response to the demands made by it. From this point of view, all the institutions, practices, beliefs, and taboos of religion are centered around that awareness. They are there to awaken us to it and to help us integrate it into our daily lives. Torah, as described above, is a gold mine of both learning and praxis for both of these purposes.

That need for self-transcendence, however, does not necessarily take us toward faith in a God who is separate from the world, who stands over against it and creates, commands, and saves. The One that calls out to us indeed dwells within each soul, as within all that is. There is only One. We exist as a part of that One, as rays of its light, as letters of its Torah. Awareness (*da'at*) is the process of learning to shine, or learning to hear ourselves speak the words that ever create Torah anew.[12]

The value of this way of life exists independently of the traditional theological claims that once buttressed its system of authority. If the forms of Jewish piety were seen as *commanded* by God, a deity who watched, rewarded, and punished, one dared not step beyond their bounds. That belief has disappeared for most Jews in the modern era, a casualty of the secularization of culture, of biblical criticism, of the Holocaust—and lots more. But the postmodern move is a different one. We rediscover that the power of sacred deeds, the call they issue to the Jew who *loves* them and lives on their path, is not diminished by the critical claims of modernity. So too does the possibility of loving engagement with the Torah text not depend on a literalist view of revelation. We *are* Torah, if we learn how to open ourselves to it; that level of self-discovery *is* divine revelation.[13]

Traditionally, every day in the life of a pious Jew is filled with the recitation of blessings. Each of these is ideally an opening of the heart to the eternal Thou, a reaching forth to embrace the transcendent in the intimacy of familiar forms. Restrictions on eating serve as an aid to viewing the dining table as a sacred altar, at which fulfillment of our most basic and animal-like need is transformed into an act of religious devotion and awareness. The confining of sexual activity to the context of a relationship of love and responsibility means that this biological instinct may also be spiritualized, fraught with a love that extends, through the eros of love shared with one's partner, out toward a broader love of God and the created world in which we live. The cycle of life and the cycle of the Jewish year both exist to extend this awareness through the seasons of the year and across the seasons of a human lifetime, offering a combination of cyclical regularity and a rich variety of experience that is highly sensitive to the needs of the human soul.

Tasting Transcendence

The actual experience of transcendence as it exists within divine immanence is *both the beginning and the end* of the search for awareness. Such experience, or at least a sense that it is possible, is the starting point of religion. Without some taste of transcendence, we would not have patience for the great demands that religious discipline makes upon us. "Taste and see that Y-H-W-H is good" (Ps. 34:9). We would not see light at the end of the tunnel had we not known some bit of that light at the outset of our journey. Our search is, on one level, the attempt to make constant, or at least regular, a level of insight that has already existed in moments of spontaneous flash. In biblical language, this is called *le-maʿan tizkeru* ("so that you remember"): you perform the commandments—or live the religious life—so that you remember the "I am the Y-H-W-H your God" (Num. 15:40) that you encountered at a personal Sinai. *We are commanded to re-create by means of disciplinary regimen the awareness given us in rare moments of divine grace.* Realizing that life is studded with such moments is the gift granted in retrospect to the one who has long walked along the path.

What are the moments of such grace in our lives? The truth is that we cannot recount them for anyone but ourselves. They may come in encounters with birth or death, in exhilaration, or in reaction to great trauma. For many, they come primarily in the context of human relations, especially in the shared love and intimacy with a single other, perhaps a spouse or lover, but sometimes also in a moment with a beloved child, parent, or friend. Some experience that special openness of the soul primarily in nature, standing in silent witness to sunrises, sunsets, stars, mountains, and water. The special qualities of light at dawn and dusk seem to evoke such feelings, as those who made these our daily prayer times must have known so well.

Everyone is capable of such experiences, though usually we have not labeled them as "religious." Most often we just let them pass, not digging into them as we might, in order to mine them for the treasures they contain. Moments of awesome awareness that we are connected with something greater and deeper than ourselves are a vital part of what makes us human. Some of us know them mostly because we spend our lives running away from them.

A Vision of God

I have made no claims here for the "existence" of God, that is, for the objective reality of a distinguishable Being or entity that transcends the universe as we generally know it. Our *experience* of transcendence remains in the realm of shared subjectivity, rather than in that of objective or scientific truth. Speaking about the religious reality "in itself," fully aware of the philosophical impossibilities of separating it from recounting our experience, we stumble toward the English word *God*. This term, historically rooted in Nordic paganism, does little to express our personal reality. It also has become so overburdened with childish baggage—both positive and negative—that we find it hard to redeem. Here we are fortunate to be able to return to the Hebrew. Y-H-W-H, in addition to being the Is-Was-Will Be of which we have spoken, is also a word composed of nothing other than breath. Its four letters, Y, H, W, and H, are all formations of the mouth in breathing; there is not a true consonant among them. *While this name cannot be spoken, it can be breathed.* Try it.

Y-H-W-H is, in short, all of being, so unified and concentrated as to become Being, yet as elusive as a passing breath. This is a deity beyond naming, one that fills all names as the soul fills the body, transcending them all as it fills them.[14] *It is none other than the universe, yet it bespeaks a vision of that universe so utterly transformed by integration and unity as to appear to us as indeed "other," a mirror of the universe's underlying and unitive self that bears the name Y-H-W-H, or Universal Self.* It is beyond the experience of our ordinary mind, even beyond articulation in any language except that of mythmaker or poet. Yet it embraces us and the world in which we live, transformed as the core of this transcendent vision.

Such a religious viewpoint is that of mystic and religious naturalist at once. It demands no "leap of faith" as does the transcendent and miracle-working deity of conventional Western theism. Seeing the transcendence or the "otherness" of God as epistemological rather than ontological (a "wholly other" way of knowing, rather than a "wholly other" being), this perspective requires rather a *leap of consciousness*, an openness to considering that there could be a vision of the universe more whole, more beautiful, more perfect than the ordinary well-guarded mind would ever allow. It calls for the sort of mind that can see Eden in our own backyard, that can feel the presence of Sinai on an "ordinary" Tuesday afternoon, or can make almost anywhere into a Promised Land. Not blind faith, but open-eyed *vision* is what such a religion demands; it calls upon us not to *believe* in the prophets, but rather to develop the prophetic consciousness in ourselves.

Directing the Mind in Prayer

All our images and ideas of God are creations of the human mind. The person on the throne, to paraphrase one surprisingly radical hasidic statement, is there because we put Him there.[15] No such God-figure would exist had we not created or projected it.

But we who create "God" do so in response to the completely real presence of divinity within and around us. We have a semi-instinctive sense, given expression in all the world's religions, that there is "something more" to our existence. *We intuit the oneness of being.* We are creatures of a natural world that is itself a multicolored garbing of divine glory. When we come to view that natural world with the eyes of wonder, we see the panoramic unity of all being that the mystic calls Y-H-W-H. We struggle to create a language that makes the mystery accessible to us. In the course of doing so, we humanize it in our image. *This quest, including the projection of our own images onto the divine, is the most ennobling of human activities. We give to the faceless One the gift of our humanity, the greatest offering we have to place upon the altar.* The human need to do so is itself testimony to the reality and irreducibility of religious experience.

I call that mystery "divine" not because of objective knowledge about it, of which I am quite innocent, but because all my attempts to encounter it evoke in me a feeling of an awesome presence, one that can be described only in the language of the sacred. As I stand "outside" my religious vocabulary, I know full well that "God" is a human projection onto the One. But as I seek a level of consciousness beyond that of my prosaic "weekday" language, I know in the depths of my being that saying *Adonai* in prayer (an act of submission, substituting *Adonai* as "My Lord" for Y-H-W-H, the mysterious and unutterable Hebrew name) is as close as I can come to naming and addressing the inexpressible mystery of life.

Our awareness that all images of God are human projections should not keep us from using them. Our search requires a turning inward and a reaching toward psychological depths that cannot be addressed without emotions. The way to God leads through our deepest and even our most pained emotional selves and cannot detour around them.[16]

Since our emotional lives are created and developed through encounters with other humans, we need in some part to approach the inner work of religious transformation by confronting such an "other" in the personhood of God. We realize that in doing this, we are lending a human face to that which has none without us. But only by doing so can we become comfortable addressing the divine universe as a "Thou," becoming engaged with it to the full depth of our human subjectivity. It is chiefly God remade as person whom we can love, at whom we can shout in anger, with whom we can share pain. This God, especially as embodied in the father figure of our prayer book (and the Freudian insight is helpful, even if troubling, here), has to be accepted, contended with, and sometimes surely "killed," in the spirit of the old Buddhist adage. It urgently needs to be balanced with the great mother figure of mystical Judaism, *binah*, the cosmic womb that is ever birthing all existence. But those of us who have rejoiced at the liberation we once felt in the "death" of God (a term that was current in religious thought back in my youth), now, on the far shores of our attempts at atheism, find ourselves still contending with those personal figures, whether male or female. In the process of becoming whole adults, we have allowed ourselves again to love, laugh, and cry with the beloved projected parent of our childhood fantasies. God may indeed be a figment of our imagination. *But our imagination, we should always remember, is itself a figment of divinity.* We create gods because we intuit Y-H-W-H.

Invigorating Our Religious Lives

The Jewishness of this theology lies in its language. Yes, one could use similar ideas, with a few changes and additions, to construct a mystical Christianity, a Sufi Islam, or a Western Buddhism. I encourage the non-Jewish reader to do so! It is the language, points of reference, scriptural roots, and ties to religious discipline and practice that make a theology belong to a particular tradition. I turn to Judaism not because it is the only source of truth, a superior religion, or God's single will, but because it is my own. I have learned to express the universal truth in the language of Jewish tradition. But I know full well—*and I rejoice at the fact*—that it can be described in all the other great religious languages of humanity as well, with whatever differences of nuance are created by those different language systems.

The Judaism to which I relate is that of the tradition in its most whole and authentic form; traditions work best when they are least diluted (see the essay below, "How I Practice Judaism—and Why"). To sign on to this notion, one need not be a fully practicing Jew as today's Orthodoxy would understand the term; but one does have to feel *addressed* and *challenged* by each word of the Torah, by each teaching of the sages. Even our rejections of practice and teaching must emerge from honest engagement. That means facing, rather than avoiding, even that which strikes us as foreign, awkward, or troubling. Our "liberal" views on revelation and theology should not serve as a cloak for cavalier desertion or disdain of our traditions. Serious Judaism means serious engagement with *mitsvot.*

What, then, of change? Is our age no different than those past? Can we expect Jews in today's free and seemingly borderless society, in a history transformed first by modernity, then by the Holocaust, and then again by renewed Jewish statehood and its responsibilities, to live as though they were still in the ghetto-defined past?

Of course not. Change has come, whether we accept it or not. We do best if we make peace with it. Aspects of the religious task of this hour differ from those we have faced before. Seventy years after the Holocaust and the renewal of Jewish statehood, we still stand on the threshold of a new age in Jewish history, and the proper Judaism for that age is only beginning to emerge. It will be reshaped partly in response to the great events of our times and also in view of the great change in Jews' role as full members of an open society and as participants in the general Western culture.

A Judaism appropriate to this age in Jewish history will have to emerge as a joint undertaking of Israeli and diaspora Jews. It will contain within it the new rerootedness in the soil of the Land of Israel and the reborn Hebrew language and culture that are such essential parts of what it means to be an Israeli Jew. These are essential building blocks of the reborn house of Israel, risen out of the ashes of the Holocaust. But it will also need to embrace the truths that we acquired through our long history of living outside the Land, creating a living tradition that locates us as a distinctive people and faith community that finds its place among others, sharing our way of expressing the universal truth and learning as well from the insights of others.

We must never lose sight of the fact that the deeper task of religion is common to all ages and to all humans. Building a life of *da'at*, to be lived in constant awareness of the One within, the One that ever calls us to transcend, transform, and grow—is a demand that does not change with the times. In the divine eternal, all time is One. We live in its presence, as have our ancestors since the dawn of humankind, as will our descendants for as long as we see ourselves as human. The religious language we speak—including the symbols we use—must be deeply rooted in our past, rich enough to excite us and fire our imagination, and contemporary enough to carry us forward into the uncharted future. It must also speak to us in a way that calls upon us, while deeply committed to our unique Jewish path, to live as full participants in the broader community of seekers, those who share our awareness of the great secret: there is only One.

How I Practice Judaism—and Why

The Way Jews Live

I AM A TRADITIONAL—BUT non-Orthodox—Jew. If you like labels (which I generally don't), you may call me a neo-hasidic heterodox traditionalist. Each of those terms will hopefully receive some unpacking in the coming pages.

I am a religious Jew because of my encounter with Hasidism as well as the mystical tradition that preceded it. Without these, I think I would have wandered away from Judaism, partly out of rebellion, partly out of disinterest. The hasidic sources offered me a Judaism characterized by the deep devotional life that I craved, a soulful embrace of a life of service, both to God and to those around me. It did so while allowing room for a subtle and intricate theology, one in which Y-H-W-H was to be understood in abstract and essentially monistic terms, as the ultimate One behind the multiple faces of reality. It is toward that One that my heart is drawn and my inner eye is turned. Hasidism showed me how to read all of Jewish praxis, the *mitsvot* and the *halakhah*, as pathways along that inner journey and as means of expressing and sharing the joys and struggles I encounter on the way.

My Judaism has not been centrally given to the question of authority, nor is it primarily focused on the details of proper observance. In this, I feel myself quite different from many of those who surround me in the community of traditionally observant Jews, who seem to be so remarkably taken up with those matters. This includes both those searching for ever greater stringencies to observe and those looking for proper halakhic justification for loosening up on them. I do not play on that chessboard, in either direction. Sometimes I feel rather lonely and out of place among those who do, especially since they seem quite convinced that this is what Judaism is all about. I live on another planet, as it were. To put it another way, I am mostly an *aggadic-hasidic*, rather than *halakhic*, Jew. It is the devotional content, rather than precise performance, that interests me. Although I am quite traditionally observant, I am well aware of my freedom of decision in choosing to live that way. My inspiration for that choice comes largely from lives and teachings of earlier centuries, especially those of the early hasidic masters. Much of my intellectual life has been devoted to translating those sources and to building bridges between them and the contemporary Jewish seeker.

This great concern for proper performance is hardly a new problem. Detailed concern with the "what" and "how" of religious praxis has been the defining focus of rabbinic Judaism since its first codification in the second-century Mishnah. The Talmud, in both its Palestinian and Babylonian versions, contains much discussion and extension of that code's authority over emerging rabbinic communities during the next several centuries. Views of individuals and schools, along with locally developed styles of practice, needed to be aligned with the original code and various ancillary documents that stemmed from the same early circles, along with the voice of scripture. True, that legal discussion is interrupted on nearly every page by a wide array of aggadic material and all sort of other matters brought along in chains of oral memory (this is part of Talmud study's great charm), but eventually the text does try to get back to the legal structure that underlies it—though often leaving the questions of practical application unresolved.

This intense focus on questions of how to fulfill every detail of what was considered the divine will characterized emerging rabbinic Judaism early enough that it became an object of criticism and derision already in the New Testament, as well as among various Hellenistic authors. While the Jesus movement among Jews, which evolved into Christianity, was not born of a critique of emerging *halakhah*, these polemics seem to indicate that such barbs could serve as effective tools in recruiting new members from within the ranks of Jewry. Had I lived in the second century, I might have been among those listening.

Did everyone (that means all literate males, of course) in the Jewish communities share in this vision of *halakhah* or normative praxis as the prime and defining characteristic of what was to emerge as "Judaism" (a much later term, of course)? Certainly not. The very large Greek-speaking diaspora was by no means part of this consensus. Much of it, in fact, converted rather readily to Christianity in the early centuries of that movement's spread, perhaps partially for this reason. (This was aided, incidentally, by the accepted Greek rendering of *Torah*, "teaching," into the Greek *nomos*, or "law," which Paul played upon, a narrowing that defined Torah in what we might call "strictly halakhic" terms.) But even within the Hebrew-literate communities of Palestine, we know of many Jews, prominent teachers among them, who were more interested in developing *aggadah*, narrative theology and wisdom-based lore, than in working through details of praxis by means of legal argumentation. There were also circles of Jews whose religious lives focused on journeys into the heavens, visions of the divine throne, and singing their way into the angelic chorus. They left us a literature known as *merkavah*, the earliest form of Jewish mysticism. Their works were shunned by later editors and publishers of the rabbinic corpus, hence coming to us only in surviving fragments. But it is anachronistic to dismiss these or others as small or marginal groups. We simply do not know how widespread this practice was. There was much overlapping among these circles, of course. The point is that not everyone was primarily devoted to questions of law. The view of most second- or fourth-century Jews as a people concerned first and foremost with *halakhah* is a projection of the nineteenth-century Lithuanian *yeshiva* culture onto the Palestine of late antiquity.

The role of praxis as defining both Judaism and the Jewish community continued to grow over the centuries. The codes of Alfasi (eleventh century), Maimonides (twelfth), Jacob ben Asher (thirteenth), and Caro (sixteenth) surely reflect that growing consensus, as do the endless volumes of responsa, the curricula of learning in *yeshivot*, and so on. But *halakhah* was studied, up until modern times, alongside other forms of worthwhile literary activity within the tradition: midrash, religious poetry, biblical interpretation, philosophy, and mystical tracts.[1] Its practice was normative, in the sense that it was *the way Jews lived*. Largely, for most Jews, it was as natural as breathing. In that sense, *halakhah* could have been defined as the *pathway of tradition* as well as law. Yes, it was considered binding; it was the way everyone was supposed to live. But it was also the way most people *did* live, just as a matter of course. Medieval Jewish thinkers were much preoccupied with seeking out the meaning of Jewish praxis. The mystics treated the *mitsvot* as true sacraments, ascribing to them infinite meaning and power as rituals that united heaven and earth. Though obligatory, they were infinitely more than "law" in a modern sense.

That changed, of course, once the ghetto, shtetl, and mullah walls broke down, beginning in the eighteenth century. Jewish practice became optional, as lives outside its domain became both available and attractive. Hence "Orthodoxy" emerged (a term, of course, borrowed from the Christian vocabulary) as a movement committed to maintaining and strengthening the remaining observant communities, and to defining authentic Judaism as that committed to halakhic normativity, all other considerations relegated to second place.

I tell you all this history because I can relate to my own Jewish practice only in its context. I understand myself as a surviving Jewish traditionalist. I like to think of myself as one who practices Judaism (yes, I am romanticizing, to be sure) as it was practiced before modernity forced one to decide whether or not one was inside the halakhic camp, whether one was "Orthodox" or something else, presumably heterodox.[2] I practice Judaism, first and foremost, because *that's the way Jews live*, and I seek precisely that sort of simplicity and naturalness in my own religious life. I do not believe in a God who has commanded me to observe specific forms of religious behavior, nor do I consider such behavior legally binding upon all Jews. I do not think that one who violates halakhic norms either will or should be punished. This means, in effect, that *halakhah* (I am speaking here of religious praxis, the realm of "between God and person," not of human moral/ethical norms) is not normative, or is not quite fully "law" for me. If we take the word *halakhah* quite literally, as a way of walking, or a path, I am fully comfortable with it. Such a reading is widely found in the hasidic sources, and has earlier roots as well.[3] The term itself probably originates in a midrashic expansion of *ve-halakhta bi-derakhav*, "You shall walk in His ways" (Deut. 28:9).[4] Yes, I try to walk that path, and do so to a fairly great extent, though in somewhat relaxed fashion. I *love* that way of life, a way of "walking toward God," hence I choose to live it. But once you tell me it is a legal system, one that I *must* observe, either to fulfill God's will or to be defined as a proper Jew, I'm afraid you will find me bolting from the conversation.

Yes, a piece of that reaction is personal history, as it always is. Although raised in a completely nonobservant home, I was drawn to Judaism at a very young age. I loved everything about it, most especially its old-world charm, which I intuited as a countercultural force that could stand up against things I did not like in the values of the American society all around me. I avidly studied both Hebrew and Yiddish, read any Jewish books I could get my hands upon, and began to become increasingly observant. Just at the onset of adolescence, I discovered something called the *Code of Jewish Law*, an English translation of the *Kitzur Shulḥan 'Arukh*, an abbreviation of the Caro code. Not understanding that this work was a product of extremist nineteenth-century Hungarian ultra-Orthodoxy, I tried, with great seriousness and not a little compulsiveness, to observe everything I could. I lived with great guilt over all the many dictates I could not follow, living in my atheist father's strictly nonkosher home, and subject to his rising fury at my turn toward what he considered medieval nonsense.

My break with that sort of observance, coming as I turned eighteen, was my great moment of spiritual liberation. I realized that I had been using religion to hide from life, and I departed from observance completely. When I began to study Hasidism, some two years later (because I remained a seeker), I immediately understood that my release from the bonds of self-imposed oppressive religion was my *yetsi'at mitsrayim*, my "Exodus from Egypt," from personal and spiritual constriction. I began praying again precisely because I was so grateful to Y-H-W-H, the inner spirit within and around us, that had given me the strength to make that break from a compulsive, but essentially false, religiosity.

The path back to Judaism was necessarily a slow and cautious one, as I had been deeply wounded. A consistent pattern of observance was probably the last thing to happen. But now that it has come to be, some fifty years later, I feel a need to explain it—to myself as well as to the reader. Of course, I choose this life of Jewish observance not only as "the way Jews live," but because it gives expression to my own spiritual life and strivings. It is really this that I seek to describe here. I do so in the hope that there are others who might find this useful, a gateway toward a very different sort of Jewish religious living. Its language is very much that of the Jewish mystical and hasidic sources in which I remain so deeply immersed, but read through my own uniquely postmodern lens.

Toward the Sacred Deed

I stand before the mountain, ready to hear God's word. Standing in that place, in that eternal moment, is what it means to be a Jew, part of that "kingdom of priests, holy people" forever gathered at Sinai. Because eternity entered history in that place and time (metaphoric as it may be; don't bother me with the question of literal historicity), it is there forever.

Wherever I am, whenever I stop to listen, the voice from the mountain calls.

Yes, it speaks in my own voice, as it did in Moses's.[5] That's alright. And it doesn't need to say much, just a single word, pronounced in the silence of a speech that is beyond human language. You may hear that word as *anokhi*, "I am," or as Y-H-W-H, the unpronounceable name. It makes no difference. If you tell me that for you it comes out in Sanskrit or in Pali, I will not object. Hear it as you will, as you need to. I hear it in Hebrew. It is, as my teacher the Master of old Chernobyl says, the entire Torah spoken in a single word, that which no human ear could hear, no human mouth could speak.[6]

I am given a lifetime charge of unpacking that word, pouring its flowing oil or liquid light into endless vessels (Kabbalah, I've discovered, is all about mixed metaphors), enough to sustain me throughout my life, and to nourish those around me. I thank God that I live in a tradition that has such rich and beautiful *kelim*, vessels, in which to contain that flow. Those vessels take the form of *mitsvot*, linked to the word *tsavta*, "togetherness."[7] They are meeting places for an intimate rendezvous with the transcendent: deeds, objects, moments in which Eternal Spirit is joined to my own, and where they flow into oneness. The word *mitsvah*, we are taught, contains the name of God in half-revealed and half-hidden form.[8] Divinity is half present and visible in the deed, and we need to draw the other half out of hiding. (Yes, I am aware that I am taking supposedly "secondary" meanings of *mitsvah* and making them primary. I know. This is how it works for me.)

The *mitsvah* is a sacred deed. I want to do it in such a way that it reverberates with all the richness of associations that the generations have planted within it. Those associations never die, but remain implanted within the deed, present to stir the devotion of future generations who recover them. In fulfilling the *mitsvot*, I fortify myself with our collective memory of how these deeds were done by great figures of the past. To find those, I will turn to books, perhaps tales of the hasidic masters, perhaps *kavvanot* or "intentions" recorded by the kabbalists. That is how I will prepare to encounter the *mitsvah*. I do not need to express the intensity of my devotion by extreme concern over getting all the details right. Thank God, I have been doing these things long enough that I feel I know how to do them. How to put my heart into them, how to *really* use them as guideposts along my inner journey, is another matter, one that requires constant growth. That is where I put the effort.

The specific *mitsvot* provided by the Torah are paradigmatic. I understand them both as vessels to contain the light and as teaching tools, ways of showing me how to engage with *all* of life as a series of encounters that embody the divine presence. *Shekhinah ba-ma'arav*, the divine presence that filled the holy Temple, was there to teach us about *shekhinah be-khol makom*, the divine presence to be found everywhere. The love and awe that accompany the performance of a *mitsvah* are there to awaken you to the love and awe that might accompany every deed through life, even the most simple.

We need those paradigms as pointers toward the life of holiness. The *mitsvot* call us out of the realm of the ordinary, redeeming us from the tyranny of boredom. Life cannot be boring if it is filled with spiritual adventure, the quest to find and uplift sparks of divine light, even in the most unlikely places and in the seemingly most mundane moments. The *mitsvot* are beacons to show us how to transform our life into such a journey. Without them, we would not know what holy living means. The fact that they occur both regularly, on a daily basis, and intermittently, throughout the sacred year, provides for us a pattern of devotional discipline that keeps us on our spiritual toes.

Love and awe are the great twin emotions of the Jewish religious life. "Rejoice in trembling," the psalmist says (Ps. 2:11). I open my heart in love and gratitude, while at the same time I tremble in awe at the magnificence of the One in whose presence I seek to stand. *The vulnerability of the open heart only makes the trembling greater; the sense of awe and wonder calls me to open my heart ever more.* The echoing back and forth of these two emotional states, each calling forth greater intensification of the other, takes us back to Sinai. "My soul came forth as He spoke," says the beloved in the Song of Songs.[9] Rabbi Akiva, the great mystic voice within the rabbinic tradition, claimed that the Song was first spoken at Sinai and R. Yehoshua ben Levi applied this verse to the revelation of Torah. "Unify our hearts," we say each morning, just before calling out the *shema'*, "to love and stand in awe of Your name." Holding both of these at once, raising them together to their highest level, stands at the core of the Jewish life of faith, taking us back to the mountain.

Discipline and Law

You might have noticed that the word *discipline* crept into my discussion just above. Yes, I believe that the cultivation of religious life calls for discipline and regularity of commitment. That is how I understand my *halakhah*, choosing a particular and regularly repeated path along which to walk.

Discipline, regularity, commitment . . . but not "law"? Am I kidding myself? Yet I feel there remain some important differences. Discipline is a regimen that I voluntarily take upon myself. I live up to it, or I don't; the responsibility is only to myself. Law is an institution imposed by authority, external or internal, upon a society and its members. If something is law, its violators will be—or at least should be—punished. Part of that punishment occurs in the form of social ostracizing. "She's not fully observant anymore, so she's not one of us." Because law is imposed from without, it is also something with which I will comply just enough to fulfill the obligation.[10] "I pay as little in income tax as the law permits," as a notorious American once said. I do what I need to get by, to stay within the letter of the law. To fulfill the law does not require either love or awe. In fact, it is indifferent to them. What matters to it is only conformity to its norms, measured by proper action. I want a *halakhah* that is much *more* than "Jewish law."

Franz Rosenzweig, taking the word *mitsvah* in its ordinary sense as "commandment," still insisted on the distinction between commandment and law (*Gebot* and *Gesetz* in German). "Commandment" is an act of relationship, one in which the Commander Himself is necessarily and personally present.[11] Law is detached from the living Commander, something that can be looked up in legal codes, in itself remaining emotionally dry. Rosenzweig insisted that a life of Jewish faith was one in which the law constantly had to be brought back to life, transformed again into the face-to-face commandment that stood at its core. The code might tell you *what* to do, but only your heart could tell you *how* to do it.[12]

For Rosenzweig, as well as for my revered teacher Abraham Joshua Heschel, the relationship with God was an essentially personal one. The biblical God who calls and commands, primarily as a token of His love, lay at the heart of their religious lives. My own path is somewhat more complicated in this regard. Following the kabbalists rather than the religious existentialists, I have an abstract notion of the Deity in the deepest inner reaches of my spiritual life. Y-H-W-H is the One that underlies the many, the Endless (*eyn sof*, beyond description) behind the multiple masks of the finite. As a Jew committed to the religious language of our tradition, I choose to personify that One, to relate to it in the second person, through the mask of a personal God. I choose that path of personification because it affirms my own personhood, because it calls upon me to be my own most fully human self. The personal God image serves as a bridge between myself and the mystery beyond.[13] But I do see myself and my needs as the source of that personification.

But when I then say that "God commands" me to follow the *mitsvot*, you would be right in raising an objection: "But isn't this a God of your own creation? If you admit that this personal language is one you choose, are you not projecting your own Commander? And if that is the case, what is the power of such a commanding voice?"

I am a human, a mere mortal. I seek to serve, to devote my life to a higher purpose, to stand before the One. I cannot do that without the language of the personal; I do not know how to enter into relationship other than with a person. My faith, however, is that this need to personify exists because my very human self is created in the divine image, in ways we are not given fully to understand. Is God in my image, or am I in God's? The answer to this question can only be yes. *The mitsvah, calling upon us to step forward with the deed, serves as an embodiment of that relationship, offering a way to crack open that hall of mirrors*, making it all "real" in a moment of performance. In the mystics' language, the deed binds heaven and earth, and the soul of the devotee is drawn in together with them into oneness. To work this "magic" requires deep concentration and commitment, but not the force of external authority, not even a belief in the commandments' literal revelation.

While I continue to resist the word *law*, I know that there is *obligation* emerging from my encounter with the divine. Israel rush forth at Sinai to say, "We will do!" as well as "Let us hear." An encounter with God that does not call me to action remains barren. If such a moment does not cause me to transform my life, it is as though it never happened.

But what is the nature of that call? I hear the One cry out: "Know Me! Be aware! Remember! *Act* and *live* as one who is aware of the oneness of all being!" That is all there in the *anokhi*, the "I am" of Sinai, maybe even in its silent *aleph*. The deep truth of oneness is easily forgotten as we go about the business of this-worldly living. We have to surround ourselves with a series of reminders: on our foreheads and our doorposts, on our calendars and in our daily lives. Yes, I know about the evolving history of religions, including our own. I understand all the specifics of Jewish praxis to be of human origin, developed and constantly evolving over the course of our long history. Many of these forms of praxis were adapted from the majority cultures amid which we Jews lived, beginning in ancient times.

But there is a divine voice behind them, one to which all those forms *are our human response.* I encounter that voice more as a plea than as a command. "Remember! Be aware! Create the forms that will help you along the way! Follow them and live with that awareness!"

The One calls upon us to create religions. We do so in response to our instinctive understanding that we hear the voice of God, a voice that makes demands upon us. Thus, attributing religious obligation to God is not entirely disingenuous. It is indeed the divine voice that has called forth these forms from within the creative reservoir of our people's faith. Yes, religion is all about commitment, including my loving and awe-filled relationship to those forms. In that sense I do indeed feel myself to be *mushba' ve-'omed,* "standing under oath ever since Sinai."[14] But that oath is to remaining open to the word of God and to acting upon it. This includes, but is not limited to, acting in accord with those forms, "the way a Jew lives." The forms themselves have emerged—and continue to emerge—from our collective effort to hear and respond to the divine voice.

The *Shulḥan 'Arukh* is a convenient guide to those forms. "What's wrong with that?" you might ask. The answer lies partly in the facts of codification and the sense of ordinariness that it engenders. The law code is a bit like the Wikipedia of prior generations. Just look it up and act accordingly. Lost in the convenience of that moment are both Rosenzweig's reliving of the personal encounter in "commandment" and awareness of the complex interface between divine imperative and human creativity that I am suggesting here. Responsiveness to the divine call in the language of Judaism is not quite the same as loyalty to the *Shulḥan 'Arukh.*[15]

Over the years, I have had some interesting conversations with Christian friends about this question, especially with Catholics devoted to some form of priesthood or religious life. They too come from a tradition in which authority plays a central role. In their case, that authority is very much alive in the hierarchy of the church. More than once, I have heard such friends say that "commitment to God and commitment to Rome— or to my bishop, or to the order—are not the same thing." My feeling is similar, even though our authority is embodied in books rather than in hierarchical organization. My commitment is to trying to stand in God's presence, to each day struggle to open my heart in prayer, to live aware of the holiness in each person I encounter. I choose to do all of this through the language and forms of Jewish tradition. That cannot be reduced to simply following the *Code of Jewish Law.*

All that I have said here applies chiefly to what our sources define as "*mitsvot* between person and God," the ritual and devotional aspects of religion. When it comes to the other side of the ledger, the "commandments between person and person," I fully accept that the conduct of human affairs does require societally imposed norms. The *halakhah* provides these, and in some areas does so with great sensitivity and insight. While there are realms in which I feel the need for major and bold revision—the areas of women's status and the treatment of sexuality in all its aspects are the most prominent of these—I am far from being an anarchist when it comes to matters of life in human society. Here too, however, I feel that the legalistic approach often gets bogged down within itself, and that the real human being—the *'agunah* and the *mamzer* (the "chained" wife, unable to divorce, and the "illegitimate" child, expelled from the community) are only the most blatant examples—often gets lost in the welter of a trivializing quest for precedents and lack of legislative courage.

Receiving and Re-creating Torah

One of my most beloved hasidic texts, the *Sefat Emet* by R. Yehudah Leib Alter of Ger, offers the following comment on one of the best known of all rabbinic texts, the blessing recited following a reading from the Torah. One blesses Y-H-W-H, "who gave us the Torah of truth, and who implanted eternal life within us." The blessing concludes: "Blessed are You, Y-H-W-H, who gives the Torah." The *Sefat Emet* says that "Torah of truth" refers to the Written Torah, given at Sinai. The "eternal life implanted within us" is the Oral Torah, the power to constantly reinterpret the written text. Only as the two are joined together is the once-given Torah received again. Hence the switch from the past tense, "who gave us the Torah," to the present, "who gives."[16]

Torah is given anew through the process of interpretation. The once-given Torah (I might say "the Torah of tradition") comes alive as the divine word only when it flows through the filter of "eternal life within us." The teaching sounds much like that of Rosenzweig, to which we referred above, but here it is spoken fully from within the language of tradition.

But let us not ignore the radical and innovative implications of this teaching because of its pious garb. Oral Torah, that which is now abbreviated (and usually dismissed) as *TuSHBa'* in Israeli high schools, is not a set of books sitting on the *bet midrash* shelf. Oral Torah is an ongoing, living process. In a certain sense, *we are* the Oral Torah! It is the creativity and soulfulness of each individual, meeting with the wisdom of tradition, that makes for a new moment of divine revelation.

This notion of revelation as a continuous and ongoing process is widely documented in the mystical tradition, and has been discussed by scholars.[17] In Hasidism it takes on special prominence because of the role of the *tsaddik*, who is thought to be a living font of divine teaching. The Yiddish phrase *zogn toireh*, "to speak Torah," is uniquely applied to the hasidic master. The phrase "The *shekhinah* speaks from within his throat," created by the medievals to describe the experience of prophecy, is now used with regard to the *rebbe*'s teaching, sometimes even with reference to enthusiastic hasidic prayer.[18] But here, following a well-known trend within later Polish Hasidism, the *Sefat Emet* seeks to democratize it. It is not just the *tsaddik* who plays an active part in this ongoing revelation of Torah, but everyone who studies and interprets—perhaps even everyone who is called for an *'aliyah* as Torah is read.

What might this mean in the context of our relationship to the *mitsvot* and their observance? The old forms come back to life as they are per-formed anew by each generation; it is we who pour life back into them, as we too are nourished from their ancient wellsprings. For many of us, these forms are newly discovered, making that rebirth even more dra-matic. My great-grandfather, a Gerer *ḥasid* from Zelichow in Poland, could hardly have imagined that his great-grandson, heir to two gener-ations of atheism and assimilation, would practice a Judaism that looks a lot like his, and would even be quoting the teachings of his own master. "The fourth generation shall return here," our father Abraham was once promised (Gen. 15:16).

I cannot explain the power of these ancient forms to renew themselves, becoming so rich with meaning again in the inner lives of such new and very different generations. Nor can I explain the great power they come to have in the lives of my many dear students who have chosen Judaism, without having those ancestral memories to back them up. I can only gaze and reflect upon all this in wonder. As I do, I reexamine my confident as-sertion that "all the specifics of Jewish praxis are of human origin." Yes, of course. I know things about anthropology and the history of religions that I cannot deny. But I also know that lines between the divine and human realms cannot be so neatly drawn, certainly not for one who claims to be a monist. If something of the divine spirit dwells within us, the soul being "a part of God above," surely we would not exclude that soul from having a key role in our own religious creativity, nor in that of prior generations. Who, then, is the creator of the *mitsvot?* But who, also, is their fulfiller? I think of the Talmudic picture of God putting on *tefillin*.[19] I think also of the hasidic reading of "Grant us, Y-H-W-H our God, in love and grace, Your holy Sabbath." We only know *our Shabbos*, says the comment. We are still waiting and hoping to receive Yours.[20]

I can only conclude this essay by quoting my late and much-lamented wife, Kathy, a theologian in her own right. One Friday night, just after the candles were lit and all the pre-Shabbat bustle suddenly came to an end, she took a deep breath and said to me: "Whoever invented Shabbos really did a *mitsvah*!" I submit that theology for your consideration.

How I Pray

Approaching the Question

READERS OF MY WORK are often puzzled by the sort of religious voice they encounter in it. On the one hand, I am speaking out of a rather abstract notion of divinity, Y-H-W-H as the underlying oneness of existence, the "Is-Was-Will Be" of all that is. On the other, I am very much a devotional type, one for whom the inner life of prayer stands at the very center of religious life. Particularly the reader who has a serious life of prayer will somewhere along the way have asked the question: "But can you pray to such a God? What might this theology mean for the life of prayer?" If God is not ultimately "other," but we are a part of the totality of Being called Y-H-W-H, what is the role of prayer? The question is a terribly important one to me as well. I believe that theology is meaningful only if it is a reflection of one's own inner religious life. That life is developed and cultivated by prayer. Religion is born out of our need to pray, to express the full range of our hearts' emotions as we come into God's presence. Theology comes only later, as we reflect upon and try to articulate what we are doing in the course of our religious lives.

Y-H-W-H is with me always. When I say that I am a religious person, that is what I mean. But here prayer encounters a paradox. I say that to pray is to come into the presence of God, a presence that I also know full well is with me everywhere and at every moment. My life as a religious

36

person means that I seek to live in that presence always, to acknowledge and respond to it in everything I do. What, then, can it mean to *come into* that presence, since it is always there?[1] To pray is to choose a particular time and place to *notice* that presence, when I stop everything else I am doing, when I leave behind all the bustle and activity, good as well as bad, that fill my life, and come to God, saying, "Here I am."

Here I am. I have not forgotten. I live in this world as a ray of Your shining light, as a drop in Your ever-flowing stream. I am just usually so caught up in the fast pace of living, rushing from place to place and from one activity to another, that I tend to forget who I really am, what I am really doing here. Exchanges of goods, services, and information seem to fill every hour: I give and take, I pay and consume, I learn and teach. Taking in, giving out—it seems like an endless parade. When I face myself, I know that all this preoccupation with *doing* is somehow an escape, a poor substitute for real living, so busy and yet so empty. Real living means remembering who I am, allowing my heart to well up with love for You, which is to say for all of being, as fully and freely as my lungs fill with air. It means taking the time to stand in awe of the magnificence of life and to wonder at our human ability to love and embrace it.

But now I stop. I leave all the bustle behind. I have no need other than to be here with You. Yes, You. I know that You are both subject and object of that endless love. To paraphrase the RaMBaM, You are the Lover, the Beloved, and the Love itself.[2] You are the deepest Heart of my heart, the One within my innermost in. When everything else is stripped away, You are what remains. But I know very well that You are not just me or mine; my love for You is the very opposite of love for self. You call me to transcend my selfhood and You bind me to every other, to all that is. You are the One who is there in every heart—indeed, in every creature. In You, I am one with each of them, and with the mystery beyond. You tear into me and call me once again to *ahavah* and to *yir'ah*, to love and to awe, both of them at once. I am here to be a lover; Your greatest gift to me is that of the ability to love, to live with a halfway open heart. Living that way can be painful, but I would not even think about giving it up. I just need to keep pushing that doorway open, ever a little bit more, and not to be afraid. As I do, I discover over and over again that giving is receiving, that in You I have all the reward I need, and so much more.

Leaving all my protections and disguises behind, I come before You naked, alone, and vulnerable beyond telling. The same half-open heart that allows me to love also has me trembling. The mountain quakes and my soul quakes with it. I open my mind and heart to the majesty and won-der of existence: a universe vast and ancient far beyond my ability to com-prehend, one in which "infinitesimal" hardly describes the tiny place and moment in which this self exists. I am overwhelmed by wonder, dwarfed by a sense of awe. How do I dare to even think that I am real in this blink of an eye for which I am here?

But now I have the same instinct that we had at the foot of Sinai: I want to make an idol, something to keep me safe, to protect me from the terror of this naked moment. Moses has vanished into the cloud on that mountaintop, and I fear that I have been abandoned. I want a God I can hold onto, one who will reassure me that my life and my struggles are significant after all, that I have not lived through all these years, so filled with both pain and joy, for nothing. Yet I also know that I do not want an idol, a God who will answer all my questions, who will make both moun-tain and soul stop shaking. I want to stand before You as Y-H-W-H, to be there whole and undefended, with love and awe both overflowing, bearing nothing but these. I bring with me much disquiet about the pretenses of my life, the masks I wear, the defensive "shells" I am unable to shed, even in a moment such as this. To really stand before You, I have so much more to leave behind.

Why am I here? What do I want of You? Or, if it is You who have dragged me here once again to the foot of this mountain, what is it You want of me? Why can't we leave each other alone, You and I? I'll go be an intellectual. You go sustain the universe. Enough of this!

No, that doesn't work. I've tried it. I know I'm stuck with You, and I'm afraid, at least for this particular instant in eternity, You're stuck with me as well.

So here I am. Alone and naked, yes, and yet I have brought everything along with me. This is a second paradox of prayer. I come into this mo-ment as a whole self. All my needs are here, all my loves, my fears, my joys and celebrations, my wounded pride, my little victories and defeats in the course of daily living, my beauty and my ugliness, everything to which I am attached—I bring them all to You and cast them at Your feet. Here I am, with all my broken bits of baggage. Do something with them! Help me pick up the pieces and put this package back together again.[3] Give me something to bind up my wounds, so that I can manage to stumble through another day, maybe even a little better—a little more whole and less hurting, please!—than I did yesterday.

Lord of the Universe! I do not believe in You! You, our all-good Maker and Master, You who watch and listen (do you taste, sniff, and touch us as well?), know everything and act for goodness always, You who "support the fallen, heal the sick, release the bound, and keep faith with those who lie in the dust." I do not believe in You. I have seen and tasted too much dust. I read the daily headlines: war, destruction, typhoon, tsunami, earthquake. I have dared to love and watched my loved ones die. Those fool enough to love me will soon watch me die as well. Why? What should I believe? Koheleth said it all. In a world filled with both human evil and nature's indifference to us, how am I supposed to believe in You?

But to whom can I bring the pain of my disbelief if not to You? To whom can I cry out if not to You, the All, Foundation on whom my house is built, Rock upon whom I stand, Sea into whose oblivion I will fall when oblivion becomes my fate? Am I too weak to live without You, without a Someone into whose ear to scream, so that I have to invent You, O terrible plaything of my imagination? There are days when it feels like that. Or am I indeed, as I think on better days, wise enough to have seen beyond the horizons of my daily mind, deep enough to see the Truth of truths, the far shores of the chasm of great emptiness, to recover a truth beyond reality, beyond words.[4] That Truth knows of something I can barely address as "You," but surely cannot call "It." Then I dare to open myself and turn to You, the hope and dream of that place, across the chasm that is none other than the hole in my broken heart (yes, Naḥman, you knew that too!), that gives me life, that allows me to go forward, day after day.

I do not believe in You. But my life is saved, because I do not believe in "believing" either. "Believing" has about it the air of intellectual proposition, a claim that cannot be proven and is therefore a matter of *mere* belief. But You are on the other end of that spectrum of doubt, belief, and certainty. You are "above the line" rather than "below," or vice versa. I do not *believe* in You; I *know* you, a knowing that always bears within it that first occasion of the biblical word for knowing: "Adam *knew* his wife Eve." I know You with an intimacy even beyond that sexual knowing. I know you as I know myself, since this little individual human self is so very obviously a part and a reflection of Universal Self, of the One that underlies and overlays and precedes and follows and surrounds and fills and laughs and cries within all that is/was/will be. That is more than a belief; it is a *knowing*, a message from the root of my contemplative soul, one that I have sought long and hard to escape so many times, but to which I always return. Here's Rabbi Naḥman of Bratslav's version of *The Little Prince:*

> The prince was a wise man; he had a great love for wisdom. He surrounded himself with sages [or perhaps "intellectuals"], and

whoever brought a clever word to him was highly rewarded. . . . The sages of that country, however, became heretics because of their "wisdom," and the prince too was drawn into heresy. . . . But because there was some good in this prince—he was, after all, a well-born and noble person—sometimes he would ask himself "Where am I in the world? What am I doing?" At such times, he would utter a great sigh, moaning over what had become of his life. But as soon as he began to reason again, the "wisdom" of heresy would be strengthened within him. This happened to him over and over again. When he asked himself where he was in the world, he would sigh and moan, but when he regained his reason he was again a heretic.[5]

That's why Rabbi Naḥman is my *rebbe*. Writing more than two hundred years ago, he knew me and described me better than I could describe myself.

My Life of Prayer

The core of my religious life is an experience of fullness, of overwhelming presence. Biblically, it that moment when Moses finished erecting the tabernacle, a dwelling-place for God. Suddenly, once it was completed, he discovered it was so full of divine presence that there was no longer room for him to even enter (Ex. 40:35). I have been blessed to know such moments more than once in my life. Prayer takes me back to them; at its best, it even offers a taste of them.

The world is so filled up with God, so charged within divine energy, that there is no room for me. This little self, next to the Self of the universe? Little ego, with all its wounds and needs? But then, out of the cosmic Nowhere, a voice speaks, using those three most touching words from Moses's journey up the mountain. *Hineh makom iti.* "Here is a place, with Me" (Ex. 33:21). There is room for you in My world. I will move over, reduce My all-filling presence, as it were, to make a space for you. I am overwhelmed with gratitude, touched to the point of heartbreak.

My instinct, both natural and paradoxical, is to reciprocate. *Hineh makom iti.* "Here, there is a place for You, right here in my heart." I will build that *mishkan;* I will become that earthly dwelling-place for God. I can think of nothing better to do with this unearned gift of life. Of course, the tabernacle I build will not be quite like that of Moses. It will not have much by way of gold, silver, or goatskins. It will contain all the inadequacies of the one who is ever seeking to build it, to repair it, to rewash those grimy curtains and repair the holes in the roof. Moses had a collective *mishkan* made by an entire people, each giving the best they had. Mine is just a one-man show. Still, it is what I have to offer. Come in and hover awhile above my holy altar.

There is always room for You in here. Even when I try to keep You out, You know I don't mean it. You who fill the universe always find a way in. The problem is whether there is room for *me* in the tabernacle of my own heart. Sometimes I feel I have lost the key, that the way in is just too complicated to navigate. A sense of alienation, both from God and from my own self, keeps me out. At their best, the words of prayer or the holy deeds of *mitsvot* become such a key. They press against the lock or crack the inner shell in just the right way as to let me in, to let me be in here with You. These ancient keys, gifts of my ancestors' wisdom, I continue to carry in my pocket. I try to keep them polished, working well, free of the rust that comes with age—both their age and mine. To my delight—even surprise—they work pretty often.

True prayer, like great poetry, requires a delicate balancing act between speech and silence. If prayer is *'avodah sheba-lev*, "worship within the heart," how can words ever adequately express what is in our hearts?[6] The fullness of joy and gratitude, so too the emptiness of desolation and abandonment—both these feelings within the heart are equally betrayed by the inadequacy of language to express them. All we can really pray for is that we be up to the task of praying. Then we come to realize that this too—like everything else—is a divine gift. So we have the custom of opening our central prayer, to be recited three times each day, with the psalmist's line: "Lord, open my lips, that my mouth might declare Your praise" (Ps. 51:17). The power to pray, to open my lips and bring words out of silence, is not my own, but comes to me only by the grace of God.

What do I then say? I might have thought that at least the words were my own, the inner silence belonging to God. But the psalmist seems to read things the other way around: I escape my silence only by the gift of words from the One who opens my lips. The hasidic masters, our greatest teachers on the subject of prayer, understood that both the silence and the words are God's. "Lift up your voice like a ram's horn" they quoted in describing the act of prayer. You are nothing more than the horn, a megaphone, we might say, for the voice of God that emerges from within your silence.[7]

I return to that phrase *'avodah sheba-lev*, "worship within the heart."
'Avodah really means service, even "work." It is what an *'eved*, a servant,
does for the master. Yes, it requires submission, but it also demands effort,
sometimes really hard work. It originally meant the transfer of all the pag-
eantry and exhausting effort of Temple service—with its eternal flame, its
sacrifices, blood-gathering, fragrant spices, and all the rest—to the realm
of the human heart. We serve God from within as the priests once served
before the altar.

But what does it mean to "serve God" in our age, one in which the
royal metaphor seems so hopelessly outdated? Is that what I want, to be a
servant before the King? I do not know a God who wants or cares about
ritual forms and mumbled words any more than One who wants a great
parade of dead animals served up upon the altar. And yet I will not let go of
that powerful language, precisely because its call on me is so great. Indeed,
I know that I am here to serve, and that is precisely what I want the power
of prayer to call on me to do.

Did you hear me? "The power of prayer" is its power to call on *me*,
to demand a response *from me*, to make me shape myself into a vessel
for God's service. What is that service? Now as in all times, it is first and
foremost serving God through loving and serving God's creatures. It is
not the God of transcendent mystery who needs us; it is the God present
in every life-form who cries out and says: "See Me! Hear Me! Know Me!
Help Me!" Be aware and be present to the infinite faces of the One that
exist in all people, each a unique divine image. But in our day, it cries out
to me even more loudly to work at protecting this magnificent planet itself, the earthly home of so much richly garbed and varied divine presence.
This is the work, the service, the worship to which I need to be devoted,
that which will call upon me to proclaim with full-throated joy: *ana 'avda
de-kudsha brikh hu*, "I am the servant of the blessed Holy One."

A Voice from the Tradition

Bahya Ibn Pakuda, the eleventh-century Spanish-Jewish moral philosopher, describes the purpose of prayer in this way: "You should know, my
brother, that our intent in prayer is only that our soul long for God and
submit to Him. The soul exalts and praises her Creator; she is grateful to
His name and casts all her burdens upon Him."[8]

Bahya is an interesting figure in defining Jewish prayer. A philosopher
rather than a rabbi, he was the first to advocate *hitbodedut*, or lone medi-

tation, as a Jewish spiritual value, having great impact upon Maimonides and many other Jewish thinkers. He was in fact aware of Sufi practices in the surrounding Muslim culture (he wrote in Arabic) and was deeply impressed by them.

This means that Jewish reflection on the *act* of prayer—as distinct from comments on the *text* of Jewish prayers—almost begins in a context that transcends the boundaries of religious difference. The desire to pray is universal, expressed in an infinite variety of forms across the spectrum of human experience. We usually think of prayer as verbal, but it may be expressed by the heart's silence as well as, sometimes even better than, the mouth's words. The classic rabbinic term for prayer, "service within the heart," tells us that the heart is the essential locus of prayer, the mouth only serving as vehicle for its outward expression. But it also links prayer to earlier forms of ʿavodah (service), including the altar in the wilderness tabernacle and the Jerusalem Temple and thence to the endless variety of sacrificial rites, real and symbolic, found across the spectrum of devotional practice throughout the world. "From east to west, My name is great among the nations; everywhere incense and sacrifices are offered to My name" (Mal. 1:11). The prophet understands clearly that all nations and their religions are worshipping the same One.

Why do we pray? Bahya answers: "Only that our soul long for God and submit to him," paraphrasing the ancient psalmist. We pray *in order to* long for God. That longing is part of prayer's purpose. But we also pray *because* we long for God. Which comes first, the longing or the prayer? Perhaps we should say it this way. We begin to pray because of a longing within our hearts. We sense that something is missing from our lives, a sense of nearness to the ultimate, a feeling that we are in touch with that which most matters. But the purpose of prayer is to stimulate or cultivate that longing, not to quench its thirst and make it fade from view. To pray is to partake of a quest for a glimpse of God's presence, to hear an echo of divine speech. A person on such a quest is not like a questioner who hopes to receive an answer that satisfies, making the question disappear. "Seek His face always," says the psalmist. The quest of prayer is a never-ending one. A moment's glimpse of the transcendent never suffices to quench our thirst, but instead calls us forth to seek further, to long for God with ever greater passion.

At the same time prayer calls upon us to *submit* to God. This is the harder part of devotion for us moderns, the ability to say (in the words of a famous Zohar passage) "I am a servant of the blessed Holy One, before Whom and before whose glorious Torah I bow at all times."[9] Our backs tend to stiffen when we hear that word *bow*, and for good reason. The history of the modern West is deeply tied to the rebellion against religious authority. Both arts and sciences, while nourished by a background of sacred wisdom, came into their own only by breaking the shackles of tradition. For Jews, that transformation came late, as we emerged from a ghetto imposed from within as well as from without.

Yet we discover, here on the far side of modernity, that the need to submit is still with us. However much medicine has lengthened life, we remain mortal and still wonder both why we live and why we are fated to die. Our quest for something that transcends ourselves inevitably leads us to a sense of awe, and from there to submission. As we become aware of the magnificence of our human journey, indeed of the wondrous quality of the evolutionary journey as a whole, we cannot but bow down before it and say: "I am here to serve." That serving means, above all, the transmission of legacy from one generation to the next: genetic, cultural, spiritual—all of them aspects of the same heritage that we carry forward.

"The soul exalts and praises her Creator"—indeed, "she" finds singing praise to be her most natural state. The soul is "she" not only because *neshamah* happens to be a feminine noun in Hebrew, but because in speaking of the soul we are talking about the most vulnerable and delicate inner chamber of our self, that inward place in which we in fact go beyond individual selfhood, catching glimpses of a Self other than our own who also dwells within. It is through "her" openness and receptiveness to that greater Self that we all become united with the One.

"She is grateful and casts all her burdens upon Him." All this happens within a single act of prayer! Yes, gratitude is another way of expressing this emotion so essential to prayer. How grateful I am for all I have been given! But "casting our burdens" takes us to another level. It is the move from gratitude toward acceptance. "I cast my burdens upon You" means that I no longer pray for a particular outcome. I give up all sense of control in the act of prayer. I am not praying for *something*, but only to give myself to You. I have no more burdens. I let go. No ambitions, no desires, naught but that which You will grant me. The burden is Yours now, not mine. Whatever You bring me, I will accept with grace. I will be try to be grateful.

What Prayer Is Not

What, then, is prayer? First let me tell you what prayer is not. Prayer is not simply a conversation with God, one in which you, the pray-er, are on one side of a conversation and doing the speaking, while God is "somewhere else," and is either listening or not. I like to describe this model of prayer, unfortunately that held by most people, through the story of a *hasid* and the telephone.[10]

It seems that our friend the *hasid* is having a very busy afternoon at his business affairs, running all over New York to try to get things done on time. A little after 6 p.m. (it must be early spring or fall), he is dashing through Grand Central Station and he realizes that he has not yet recited *minhah*, the afternoon prayer, and the latest time for doing so is fast approaching. A bit too self-conscious to just stand up against a wall in the busy station and begin to pray, he takes out his telephone, holds it up to his ear and mouth, and starts to recite his prayers. Lots of people are talking into their phones in the middle of Grand Central Station! A few of them are even standing still while doing so. Why not one more?

He begins to pray: "Happy are those who dwell in Your house; they shall forever praise You." At that moment the great station is God's house, and the *hasid*'s prayer may be deeply from the heart. It should not be judged by the too-simple question: "Is there anybody on the other end of the line?" The telephone is irrelevant, only a prop in this great drama of prayer. The relationship between the one who prays and the One who receives prayer is *not* that of the two ends of the telephone.

Many years ago a friend and I were preparing a collection of hasidic teachings on prayer for an anthology that came to be called *Your Word Is Fire*. The brief teaching that stood out above all the others and has remained closest to my heart came from Rabbi Pinhas of Korzec, a close friend of the Ba'al Shem Tov, the central figure of early Hasidism. Rabbi Pinhas simply said: "People think that you pray *to* God, but that is not the case. Rather prayer itself is of the essence of divinity."[11]

Where is God as our friend begins his prayers with the telephone receiver in his hand? All around him, of course, filling that vast hall just as intensely as the ancient tabernacle was filled, when there was so much God in it that Moses himself was unable to enter (Ex. 40:35). And God is in our *hasid*'s heart, just as God is in the hearts of all those other folks on their phones, those talking to sick children at home, those listening to the latest stock quotations, and those cursing out their travel agents for messing up the tickets. If we could only see and hear that busy room from the divine point of view, we would be witnessing a New York City afternoon version of the great symphony, a true chorus of angels! In fact the only difference between the *hasid* and all those around him is that he has stopped to *listen*. He has taken the time to *acknowledge* that he dwells in God's house. God is present in his saying of those words. Hopefully, if he is paying attention to the moment, *he* is present as well.

Prayer, then, is about listening as much as it is about speaking. "Let your ear hear what your mouth is saying!" the rabbis teach regarding the proper way to recite *shemaʿ yisraʾel*. If "prayer itself is of the essence of divinity," the whole process of prayer is a holy one, taking place inside us and around us. In prayer we give voice to the deepest self that lies hidden within us, the spark of divinity that lies within our soul. But that innermost spark, like the highest, primordial Torah, dwells in a realm far beyond words. We give it the gift of language, allowing it to come forth and be present to the world of our conscious selves. But as we say: "Lord, open my lips . . . ," we acknowledge that even the ability to speak the words of prayer is a gift of God. We do not pray alone. God prays through us! We may provide the words, but the divine stirring in the depths of our souls makes the music.

On the face of things, prayer is absurd. Do we really need to communicate with God in human language, by moving our mouths and making sounds in our throats? Is this the way to reach the One who knows our hearts, who indeed *is* our deepest heart? Why language? What place is there for words between us?

But for prayer to be *ours*, to be a vehicle for the soul or the divine within to communicate with us, it has to be in our language. Not because God needs words, but because *we* do. It also has to be in the sort of language that touches us most deeply. As the innermost self, really the Self of God within us, makes itself manifest to us, it needs to reach and "travel" through all our most vulnerable and wounded places. It needs the language that can reach us where we hurt and where we feel true joy. We put it into words so that *we*, our conscious selves, can be part of it, not because God needs those words in order to hear what is in our heart.

Devotion in the Postmodern Mode

It will be clear by now to the reader of these words that their author is not one who holds to a naïve or simplistic theology of prayer. I understand God as the mysterious oneness of being, the force of existence that lies within and behind each creature, the unchanging One that Big Banged itself into the endless dance of variety and multiplicity, the bodiless Self of the universe that has chosen for reason beyond our ken to don the coat of many colors and enter into the forms of all these beings, including us humans.

But what can it mean to pray to such a One? The text of our prayers, formed largely by the conceptual world of the biblical psalmist, seems to be speaking of and to an entirely different sort of God, an entirely personal deity, awesome yet compassionate, who created a world other than *Him*self as an act of love, one to which He is related as loving Creator, Parent, Ruler.

The term most Ashkenazic Jews use for traditional prayer is *davnen*, a word that has long puzzled scholars of the Yiddish language. It has no analogue in German, Hebrew, or Slavic languages, the usual sources of Yiddish. Some have tried to connect it to the Latin *divinus*, others to the English word *dawn*. But I once heard a famous Yiddish scholar suggest that it originally served as a translation of the Hebrew *minḥah*, and that it derives from a Lithuanian word meaning "gift."[12] He claimed that the Jewish *shtetl* storekeeper, in having to explain that it was time for him to recite afternoon *minḥah* prayers, was the source of this translation into the local language. Be the real etymology whatever it is, I have always liked this idea of *davnen* or praying as giving a gift.

After the ancient Temple in Jerusalem was destroyed, prayer replaced the sacrifices that had been offered there. Such sacrifices were indeed a gift. It was no small thing for the farmer to bring a prized animal to the Temple. The gift of words seems paltry by comparison, a gift too easily falsified and costing us nothing at all. But we should remember what lay behind the sacrificial gift. Animal sacrifice replaced human sacrifice at some early point in ancient history, but the memory of that human sacrifice was never totally forgotten. There was a time in ancient Israel when firstborn sons were sacrificed. Both the story of the binding of Isaac and that of the slaying of the Egyptians' firstborn bear echoes of that horror. (In Christianity, in fact, it remained crucial to the central act of worship. The sacrifice was offered by God, but the shedding of human blood was still required for atonement.)[13] But the offering of a son was itself a substitution; you gave that new life instead of giving your own. The sense was that I owe my life to God (or the gods, in earlier times), and God has a right to demand it of me. I ward off that demand, at least for a while, by offering the life of my beloved offspring.

How distant we are from those ancient memories, and how unchanged is our essential situation! Yes, we still owe our lives to the mysterious force of life that is both within us and far beyond our comprehension or control. We are still mortals who one day will have to let go of life, and we still hope to postpone the coming of that day as best we can. But we do not sacrifice our children. Prayer comes in place of sacrifice. In true prayer, we give the only gift we have to offer: ourselves. *Va-ani tefillati*, says the psalmist (69:14), felicitously mistranslated by later hasidic readers as "I *am* my prayer."[14] But we have learned that to give ourselves to God does not mean to climb upon the altar. The prophets long ago taught us a better way. We give ourselves by opening our hearts, by being present to God's presence in our lives, by sharing with others, by generosity toward the needy, among whom God's spirit rests.

Now we see the cycle of prayer in its wholeness, and we can begin to appreciate the comment of Rabbi Pinhas of Korets. I say: "Lord, open my lips." I ask God for the strength to help me pray, to be present within my prayer. What is it that I ask of God? To help me give myself to God! "Help me, O Lord, to give myself to You!" We seek the God deep within to be present as we offer ourselves to the God beyond, the One who is of course in no way separate from the One within. Indeed, "prayer itself is of the essence of divinity."

There is only one more step to go. If I am all I have to give to God, I must allow the same to be true of God as well. All God has to give me is God. The Ba'al Shem Tov read Psalm 102, titled "The Prayer of a Poor Man," as "A Prayer *to* a Poor Man." Come before God as you would to a poor person, he said. Do not expect any gifts, any riches. All God has to give you is God's own self.[15] So too did the hasidic masters read the prophet's words "Blessed is the person who trusts in Y-H-W-H; Y-H-W-H is the object of their trust" (Jer. 17:7). "Why the seeming repetition in this verse?" they asked. "We truly trust in God," they said, "when all we want of God is God."

Sacred speech, in the Jewish conversation, comes in two forms: *Torah u-tefillah*, teaching and prayer. God gives us the words of Torah, a verbal revelation, teaching us how we are to live. That teaching is unpacked and expanded throughout the generations by *talmud torah*, the ongoing process of teaching and interpretation, the very lifeblood of Judaism's existence. We respond by taking the letters of those same words and rearranging them into prayers, which we offer back to God, making for two-way communication. "Make the teachings into prayers!" taught our master R. Naḥman of Bratslav.

How are we going to understand these twin processes in a postmodern rather a premodern mode of thought? God does not "give us" the words of Torah, but God is to be found within them. We are not literal believers in verbal revelation, but we marvel before the power that the ancient teachings have to stir our hearts. This is true of the language of the prayer book as it is true of the Torah itself. For us to "turn Torah into *tefillah*" cannot quite mean taking the words that God gave us and returning them to him in different form. All the words are ours. But we do believe that the breath of life, the inner *ruaḥ*, wind or spirit, that animates those words is a divine gift. In every moment, God breathes life into us as into the first human. That is a moment that has never ceased. We take that breath, use it to sing God's praises, and we return it to its Source. The words are the vessels we use to contain that breath. The Psalms conclude with the verse *Kol ha-Neshamah tehallel Yah*, "Every breath praises God!"

The Purpose of Prayer: Creating Bliss

A pair of young hasidic masters-to-be were engaged in a debate more than two centuries ago across the table of the Maggid, the great preacher of Mezritch. Menaḥem Naḥum, later himself the Maggid of Chernobyl, said that the service of God brought about the greatest of all human pleasures. "Why seek anything else?" he asked. Our lives are filled with pursuit of pleasure, including sex, food, and creature comforts. (How much more comfort we have today than then, he could not have imagined! Yet still we are seeking more.) But these pleasures are all externals, he said. They are made alive, as are we, by the bolt of energy, the life force of divine presence, that surges through them—as through us—in every moment. Without that, they would be dead, quickly losing all their attraction. Why then pursue the outer forms? Instead, seek that life force itself and hold fast to it. That will bring you true pleasure, one that cannot die.

His friend Levi Yizḥak (to become rabbi of Berdichev) had a bit more of their own master's ascetic streak still left within him. "Pleasure?" he asked within some disdain. If it is pleasure you seek, do it for God, not for yourself. As long as you seek your own pleasure, even in this most subtle form, you are still worshipping yourself and your own desire. *Give pleasure to God, not to yourself.* "The blessed Holy One longs for the prayers of the righteous."[16] Offer your words as a gift, however paltry it may be. God takes pleasure in your prayer, greater than the delight offered by the glorious song of all the angels.

God's pleasure? Divine delight? A primitive notion, you might say, one rooted in the most ancient of human attempts at religion. We are

divine playthings, created to give pleasure to the gods. They find us en-
tertaining, with all our human foibles. Indeed, we are here to *serve* them,
beginning with the food we place upon the altar. The Torah adapted this
earlier view, describing each sacrificial offering as "a sweet-smelling savor
for Y-H-W-H." When we replaced animal carcasses with pious words as
our offering, these too were said to ascend to heaven, forming a crown for
our Creator, just like the rings of smoke had formerly risen from off the
altar. Only much later were the hasidic masters to admit that it was not
the words themselves, but the love and awe they arouse in us, that rise to
heaven and awaken joy in the One above who receives them.

But what of us? Is "giving pleasure to God" still a phrase that means
anything to us? Our God is no longer seen as a loving Jewish parent or
grandparent who wants nothing more than *nakhas* from His children!
"The mysterious oneness of being" or "the bodiless Self of the universe"
can hardly be described as a pleasure seeker. Perhaps the Chernobyler is
right after all. *We* are the ones who take pleasure in God's service. Devotion lies in the great pleasure we find in the ultimate act of giving.

What, then, are we doing in the act of prayer? It cannot be that we
are just acting to pleasure ourselves! "No," he would answer. Prayer is
what the great mystics always told us it was: bringing together the cosmic
forces, uniting the blessed Holy One and *shekhinah*, the indwelling presence, restoring the wholeness of a broken cosmos. We do so, however, not
by the complex mental gymnastics prescribed by the kabbalists, but by the
simple devotion of our own hearts. This becomes possible when we truly
realize that we too are a vital part of *shekhinah*, along with everything else.
Our souls are the energy channels through which all the world is uplifted
to become one with its Creator. The division between God and world is
only superficial. The great gift of mind or awareness that makes us human
is a vehicle we can train to see through to the underlying oneness of all
that is. That insight, carried forth by our devotion and our deeds, actually
makes the unity real. But that act of unification is also the fulfillment of a
deep soul-longing, a desire implanted within us, hence the source of our
pleasure as well.

Levi Yizḥak continued to hesitate. Even though he understood that
his companion wanted the energies of prayer to reach the heavens, not just
give pleasure to humans, he still found himself thinking differently. The
real job, he thought, was not for us to reach up and unify the heavens, but
to bring God down to earth. When we offer our prayers as a gift to God,
we create the desire in God to turn toward earth, to give blessing to the

world, especially to those most in need of God's blessing. *That* should be the focus of our prayers.

Now another player enters the stage where our debate has been taking place. An oriental sage, wandering off from the ancient trade routes linking East and West, has wound up a guest in our Ukrainian *shtetl*. He is one trained in spiritual traditions that are not so bothered by the West's rigid insistence on the distinction between self and other. He recognizes that he is in the presence of powerful spiritual teachers, and admires their devotion to doing good. He wants to understand what it is they are saying, because he intuits that they are grappling with the essential "Why?" of living the good life. But once the debate is translated from the Yiddish/ Hebrew into a language he understands (this itself was no small feat!), he bursts into peals of laughter.

"You want to know whose the pleasure is? Whether it belongs to God or to the worshipper? Who is giver here, and who receiver? The answer, my friends, is 'Yes!'" And he laughs again.

The mind opens. The great fullness is seen. The world fills up with cosmic bliss. Was that bliss there before it was seen? Of course! That is the paradox with which we opened; God's blissful presence is always there. Did the moment of insight increase that bliss? Surely! It is now present also in the mind of the beholder. (Does that mean the bliss was *changed* by that insight? Don't be silly.) The bliss radiates from the One to the one, from the one to the One, ping-ponging back and forth as many times as you like. There is only one bliss. There is only One.

The next day they told their master about their debate, about the strange visitor and what he had said, and about his laughter. The Maggid responded in silence, as he often did, but gave them a knowing smile. "That oriental costume," he thought to himself, "worked pretty well. I'll have to use it again, every now and then."

Barukh Atah

REFLECTIONS ON THE PRAYER BOOK

A Dedication

D EFINING MYSELF, EVEN AFTER all these years, as a Jewish seeker, I feel a bond of heart with a whole array of such seekers, including some who have found their way into Judaism, coming from a great distance, and others whom I met on their way out, who needed to find another spiritual path. I never condemn such people, knowing as I do the complexity of inner journeys, and the various needs, both spiritual and psychological, that have to be fulfilled along the path.

I want to tell you the story of one such seeker, and dedicate this little piece to him, knowing that he is one of many.

In 1972, five years after I was ordained as a rabbi, I was invited to partake of "A Day of Spiritual Teaching" at Fordham University in New York. The topic was "Spirituality and the Seasons of the Year." There were four speakers: Benedictine brother and poet David Steindl-Rast; Swami Satchidananda, leader of Integral Yoga and a very popular teacher at the time; the head of the New York–based Zen Studies Society; and myself. A majority of those who attended were the swami's disciples, glad for the opportunity to hear him speak in New York.

In my turn, I spoke of Judaism's two sacred seasons, fall and spring. Since it was spring, following Pesaḥ, I spoke especially of Shavu'ot and of what it means to journey back to Sinai with an open heart, hoping to receive Torah anew. Following my talk—which I thought had gone quite well—a young man dressed in the uniform of the swami's group raised his hand and said: "That's very nice, Rabbi. But is that *really* what Judaism is about? Isn't it about a God who is sitting up in the heavens, watching and keeping account of every deed you do, writing it in His book, and getting ready to punish you for your sins?"

I looked at the young man with much sympathy, thinking to myself: "Another Jew ruined by some Long Island Hebrew school!" In my most pastoral young-rabbi tone, I explained to him that this was a child's way of understanding the tradition, that which he was probably left with on ending his Jewish education at Bar Mitzvah. I suggested that the folks who had taught him might themselves not have had a very deep understanding of Judaism, and that he should go back and begin studying as an adult. He smiled and sat down. Afterward he came up to me quietly and said: "I just want you to know that I left [and here he named a famous New York ultra-Orthodox *yeshiva*] a year before *semikhah* [ordination]."

I have had that young man on my heart for nearly fifty years now, because he represents so many. He also reminds me how much work there is to do, even among those are supposedly getting a "higher Jewish education."

There are many reasons why young Jews turn away from Judaism and do their seeking elsewhere. Some are best understood sociologically—the awkwardness of maintaining positive minority-group identity in an open society, for example—and others psychologically—the need to strike out on one's own and leave one's parents' ways behind, even to declare them wrongheaded or superficial, in order to make that break. All these are well known and frequently documented, especially in literary treatments, increasingly also in film. But I am most interested in the *theological* or *spiritual* reasons why Jews leave Judaism, and it is here that I think I have something to say.

Sophisticated theological reflection has existed for a long time in Judaism. Both philosophers and mystics have dwelt in realms far beyond the naïve religious conceptions about God that we all imbibe in childhood. But biblical images of the deity are hard to escape. When Judaism was watered down for presentation to modern, Westernized Jews, it was the God of the traditional prayer book (pre-philosophical and largely nonmystical in its editing) that seemed to survive. Both the philosophers' "Causes of Causes" and the kabbalists' "Endless" were left behind, and "Our Father, our King" reigned supreme. When Jewish seekers walk into the synagogue, what they hear are sounds like the heaping of praises on the head of that seemingly insatiably needy Parent/Ruler, all presented without any reservation or sense of humor. No wonder they turn away.

Opening to the "You"

Of all the many words in the traditional prayer book, the hardest one for the contemporary seeker—or the word that was hardest for *this* one, along the path—is *atah*, "You." It is to that word, or the use of the second person in prayer, that I wish to turn our attention. What does it mean to say "You" to Y-H-W-H in prayer? We have already suggested that Y-H-W-H is best translated as "Is-Was-Will Be" or "BEING." How do I say "You" to the totality of existence, that which includes me along with everyone and everything else?

Let me first respond in midrash, a Jewish way of speaking, and then translate what I mean. The word *atah* comprises three letters: אתה. Its first two letters, *aleph* and *tav*, are the first and last letters of the Hebrew alphabet. Since we have an ancient belief that the world was created by the letters (see discussion below), *aleph* and *tav* constitute all that has been created. "Everything from A to Z," you might say.[1] But those same two letters also form the word *et*, an untranslatable particle that indicates the definite direct object. (In Hebrew you have to say: "I see *et* the house" or "I ate *et* the biscuit.") When you refer those two letters to the whole of existence, you are treating it as an object. *Tat tvam asi.* "It is what it is."

But then you add the letter *heh* to it, the *heh* that stands for Y-H-W-H, the mysterious name of Being. In doing so, you convert *et* to *atah*, moving it from third to second person, transforming object into fellow subject. This means that you are speaking *to* Being, not only speaking *of* it. In that act of speaking to, you announce your preparedness to be in dialogue. If I can speak to Being, I am also ready to be spoken to, to be addressed by Being.[2] I am prepared for a two-way conversation, though one that will quickly reach beyond words. A *relationship*, you might say.

Note that I am choosing to avoid using the word *God* or *the Creator* here. Philosophically, I am a monist; I believe that there is only One. I therefore do not make a sharp distinction between Creator and Creation. I rather understand that oneness flows into multiplicity, or takes on its garb, in a constantly self-renewing process that we experience as biological, cultural, and spiritual evolution. Or, viewed from the other end, our mind can penetrate the multiplicity and its coat of many colors, seeing through to the oneness that lies beneath.

Is there, then, a certain amount of *pretending* when I say *barukh atah*, "Blessed are You," in prayer? Am I acting *as though* there were a God "out there" somewhere, when I really don't believe it? Am I playacting at depicting the One as an "other," so that I can talk to it?

Yes, this needed transformation of existence from "It" to "Thou" necessarily bears within it an element of distortion. The Thou is of necessity the Other. When I address you as a person, I am both presenting myself as person to you and recognizing your distinctness or otherness from me. Our communication seeks to overcome that gulf between us. But when the "other" to whom I speak is Y-H-W-H, something different has crept into the picture. That One is surely "in here," in my innermost me, as well as "out there," as Your outermost You. Y-H-W-H is necessarily the drawing together of all opposites, surely including this most basic of separations, that between "self" and "other." This is the *atah* of prayer: the Thou who is in truth no other.

The answer to this challenge, you're probably not surprised to hear, is both yes and no. The monist in me cannot be completely happy with the positing of the second person. If there is only One, why do I seek dialogue? But reality tells me that the One of which I speak is indeed very different than my ego self, the individual human being present in this body, with all my needs, loves, and inadequacies. Yes, the Self of the universe dwells within me as well as outside me, if that distinction is in any sense real. But to say that Being is present within me is not at all to say that it is identical with my individual self or identity, precisely that which I need to transcend if I am to touch upon this deeper reality.

Why do I bother? Why do I undergo the contortions required to enter into this dialogue? The answer is clear and unambiguous. It is because I want to be *addressed* by Being. I have always been deeply moved by the Hebrew word *hineni*, "Here I am," as it is spoken in the Bible, by Abraham at Moriah, by Moses at the burning bush, by Isaiah in his vision of the angels, but most especially by young Samuel in the tent at Shiloh.[3] I want a God who can call me, call upon me to transcend myself, demand of me a deeper reach, a higher purpose.

If Judaism teaches anything distinctive, it is that a religion is not serious until it can make demands. Those are articulated by the word *mitsvah*, which the *hasidim* read as "being joined together," but in its primary sense

does mean "command." The commanding voice is the one that pulls me
beyond myself, but it is also the voice that gives meaning.

No, that does not mean that I hear a heavenly voice calling out to me,
saying: "Stop! Don't eat that cheeseburger!" Or "Tie those straps around
your arm!" But I do seek—and occasionally hear—a voice that says: "Remember Me! Be aware!" All the particulars of how to do so are human creations, evolving over time. I choose to engage with the ancient reminder
system of my people. "So that you remember and do all My commandments" (Num. 15:40; last section of the *shema*ʿ) is what it's all about. The
forms are there to induct us into the possibility of holy living.

This desire for "a second-person" relationship with the One has everything to do with the underscoring of my own humanity. To say *atah* to
God is to stand face-to-face. To claim that God has a face, as in "May His
face shine upon you" (Num. 6:26), is to say that our own faces are important, that our faces can be receptors of divine light. It is also saying that
being face-to-face with another is a worthy position. Because I too have
a face, which is capable of receiving light from "above," perhaps I too can
pass on some bit of that mysterious divine light.

The choice to say *atah* in prayer is also directly related to the most basic claim of Jewish ethics, that every human being is created in the image
of God (Gen. 1:27–28). This notion of *tselem Elohim* means that humanity
itself reflects the presence of divinity.[4] As I open myself to fully meet another person, both of us are opened to the presence of eternity within and
between us. My choice of Judaism as a religious language is very much
about that. I recognize that the act of personifying God is an affirmation
of the person and the personal, *a claim that the holy and the personal belong
together.* Transcending *ego* in the spiritual journey need not mean going
beyond one's *personhood.* Perhaps just the opposite is true.

Still, the dangers of idolatry and ossification accompany this sort of
dialogic theology, as they do any other. Especially because the powers of
both scriptural imagery and childhood fantasy remain so strong in our
religious imagination, there is always a danger that we become too depen-
dent on the God we picture in our mind's eye as we open ourselves to this
conversation. We need to keep in mind that such an imaginary (I do not
fear that word) figure, God as *atah*, continues to serve as our bridge to the
ineffable mystery that lies within and beyond it. A personified deity who is
the absolute, as the Zohar has taught us, is too likely to become a Golden
Calf. This is the essential radicalism of a Jewish mystical theology, and it
should not be passed over lightly.

Such a mystical theology, one that seeks to invoke the second person while at the same time pointing toward a unitary reality beyond it, puts me at odds with the followers of Emmanuel Levinas, a very important and highly respected voice in Jewish theology today.[5] Levinas's insistence on the absolute character of the other is the result of impressive ethical considerations. We do need to know other persons in the fullness of their difference from us, in order to respect them on their own terms. For the mystic, however, that can never be the final step. We are told, "Love your neighbor as yourself" (Lev. 19:18), not "as another." Love ultimately derives from an inner sense of oneness, a realization that the ones I love and I belong to the same greater Self that is present in each of us. Love is a stage in the lifting of that veil, of seeing the One within each other and hence transcending multiplicity.[6]

Commentary: A First Look at My *Be'er*

For many years now, I have been composing a commentary on the Hebrew prayer book. That document, which now "lives" only in my computer, is titled *Sefer Be'er Le-Ḥai Ro'i*, an almost untranslatable phrase that originally may have meant (see Gen. 24:62) "the well where God sees me," but in my hasidic-style punning means something like "the interpretation through which I catch a glimpse of the Divine." Hopefully, someday it will be published in its entirety. In it, the reader will indeed catch a very different glimpse of me. After a lifetime of immersion in the hasidic homilies, ever playing with the texts before them for the sake of spiritual insight, I find that I too am best able to come across as my more devotional (as distinct from both the academic and the theological) self when engaged with the texts of Torah or prayer.

To truly share with you who I am as a religious person will therefore require that I offer you a dip into my *Be'er*. I am offering here two sections from it. The first may seem quite obscure to some. It is a commentary on the *korbanot*, the sacrificial passages included in the early-morning service in the prayer book—now skipped by most praying Jews, or mumbled through with little attention. I recite these four passages (following the Sephardic/hasidic rite) faithfully each morning. They have, in fact, become a very important part of my daily prayers. You might say, in good sacramental language, that they "set the table" for the prayers—and the day—that are to follow. They should be read alongside the Torah passages on which they comment, as indicated.

1. Parashat ha-Kiyyor (Ex. 30:17–21): On Purification before Prayer

וַיְדַבֵּר יְהֹוָה אֶל מֹשֶׁה לֵּאמֹר: וְעָשִׂיתָ כִּיּוֹר נְחֹשֶׁת וְכַנּוֹ נְחֹשֶׁת לְרָחְצָה וְנָתַתָּ אֹתוֹ בֵּין
אֹהֶל מוֹעֵד וּבֵין הַמִּזְבֵּחַ, וְנָתַתָּ שָׁמָּה מָיִם. וְרָחֲצוּ אַהֲרֹן וּבָנָיו מִמֶּנּוּ אֶת יְדֵיהֶם וְאֶת
רַגְלֵיהֶם בְּבֹאָם אֶל אֹהֶל מוֹעֵד יִרְחֲצוּ מַיִם וְלֹא יָמֻתוּ. אוֹ בְגִשְׁתָּם אֶל הַמִּזְבֵּחַ לְשָׁרֵת
לְהַקְטִיר אִשֶּׁה לַיהֹוָה וְרָחֲצוּ יְדֵיהֶם וְרַגְלֵיהֶם וְלֹא יָמֻתוּ. וְהָיְתָה לָהֶם חָק עוֹלָם לוֹ
וּלְזַרְעוֹ לְדֹרֹתָם.

Y-H-W-H spoke to Moses, saying: Make a basin of copper and a stand of copper for it, for washing; and place it between the Tent of Meeting and the altar. Put water in it, and let Aaron and his sons wash their hands and feet [in water drawn] from it. When they enter the Tent of Meeting they shall wash with water, that they may not die; or when they approach the altar to serve, to turn into smoke an offering by fire to Y-H-W-H, they shall wash their hands and feet, that they may not die. It shall be a law for all time for them—for him and his offspring— throughout the ages.

Kiyyor. "A basin." Washing one's hands before approaching the altar. The priests had to wash in a basin of water as they entered the Tent. Purify yourself—heart as well as hands—before entering the "tent" of prayer. To come into prayer demands of us that we examine ourselves and enter in a state of purity, as best we are able.

Purity in these texts is a ritual category; we mean it primarily as a moral one. But the act of ritual purification called forth here gives us a chance to reflect on the moral purity of our prayer as well. Do I come into my prayer feeling clean enough to speak its words?

To me that means mostly: "Am I sure I'm not doing this to impress someone (either God or persons) with my piety?" Is there nothing in me that is "showing off" during prayer?

How do we go about this act of purifying ourselves? It helps to recall that the basin and its stand were designated as to be made out of the old copper mirrors that the women of Israel had brought out of Egypt, then donated to the *mishkan.* They were not even melted down, the rabbis say, but just fastened together to form the basin. *We purify ourselves in a basin made of mirrors.* That means looking at yourself from every angle, from every position in which a mirror might catch you.

Some days I read *ve-natata shamah mayim* ("and place water there") as in *eyn mayim ela Torah:* "water" always refers to Torah. Since we are told that "words of Torah do not become impure," it is the act of Torah study before prayer that best cleanses our hearts and prepares us to pray.

Note especially where the basin is located, *midway between the altar and the Tent of Meeting.* The priest (and I assume all readers of this commentary to be spiritual *kohanim,* seeking to serve others and bring them to holiness) has to wash hands, whether turning to serve God at the altar or toward the people in the Tent, to interact with them. Both of these are forms of *'avodah,* devotion, and both require being pure of hands and heart.

Ve-raḥatsu yedeyhem ve-ragleyhem. "They will wash their hands and feet." I regret that we, unlike the Muslims, have given up the practice of washing feet as well as hands before prayer. Hands represent our actions, the things we will accomplish in the course of the coming day; these need to be kept pure. But so too do our footsteps, the directions in which those actions lead us. The text reminds us that as we wash our hands, we should keep our eyes on our feet as well, and look where we are going.

Yirḥatsu mayim ve-lo yamutu. "They will wash in water and will not die." To our ears, the notion that death is the punishment for approaching the altar with unclean hands seems horrifying. But suppose we are speaking not of divine punishment, but of a person being psychologically crushed, "deadened," by the burden of guilt. The verse offers the possibility of purification, of sin being "washed away." This can be a message of great liberation. Whatever you have done, you may wash your hands and be welcomed into the community of prayer. The custom of having a place to wash upon entering a synagogue is one worthy of renewal.

But there is another reading of this passage, one that has nothing to do with purification, which is not mentioned here. Suppose this dipping of the hands and feet in water is anticipatory of the two passages that come after it, both of which call for offerings of fire. Perhaps the water comes first in order to cool things down, to keep those inner fires from burning too hot and getting out of control. The specter of Nadav and Avihu, Aaron's two young sons who approached the altar with too much enthusiasm, is never entirely absent from the Jewish imagination.

2. Parashat Terumat ha-Deshen (Lev. 6:1–6): Clean Out the Ashes, Keep the Fire Burning

וַיְדַבֵּר יְהֹוָה אֶל-מֹשֶׁה לֵּאמֹר: צַו אֶת אַהֲרֹן וְאֶת בָּנָיו לֵאמֹר זֹאת תּוֹרַת הָעֹלָה הִוא
הָעֹלָה עַל מוֹקְדָה עַל הַמִּזְבֵּחַ כָּל הַלַּיְלָה עַד הַבֹּקֶר, וְאֵשׁ הַמִּזְבֵּחַ תּוּקַד בּוֹ. וְלָבַשׁ
הַכֹּהֵן מִדּוֹ בַד וּמִכְנְסֵי בַד יִלְבַּשׁ עַל בְּשָׂרוֹ, וְהֵרִים אֶת הַדֶּשֶׁן אֲשֶׁר תֹּאכַל הָאֵשׁ
אֶת הָעֹלָה עַל הַמִּזְבֵּחַ וְשָׂמוֹ אֵצֶל הַמִּזְבֵּחַ וּפָשַׁט אֶת בְּגָדָיו וְלָבַשׁ בְּגָדִים אֲחֵרִים,
וְהוֹצִיא אֶת הַדֶּשֶׁן אֶל מִחוּץ לַמַּחֲנֶה אֶל מָקוֹם טָהוֹר. וְהָאֵשׁ עַל הַמִּזְבֵּחַ תּוּקַד בּוֹ לֹא
תִכְבֶּה. וּבִעֵר עָלֶיהָ הַכֹּהֵן עֵצִים בַּבֹּקֶר בַּבֹּקֶר וְעָרַךְ עָלֶיהָ הָעֹלָה וְהִקְטִיר עָלֶיהָ חֶלְבֵי
הַשְּׁלָמִים. אֵשׁ תָּמִיד תּוּקַד עַל הַמִּזְבֵּחַ, לֹא תִכְבֶּה.

Y-H-W-H spoke to Moses, saying: Command Aaron and his sons thus: This is the ritual of the burnt offering: The burnt offering itself shall remain where it is burned upon the altar all night until morning, while the fire on the altar is kept going on it. The priest shall dress in a linen vestment, with linen breaches next to his body; and he shall take up the ashes to which the fire has reduced the burnt offering on the altar and place them beside the altar. He shall then take off his vestments and put on other vestments, and carry the ashes outside the camp to a clean place. The fire on the altar shall be kept burning, not to go out: every morning the priest shall feed wood to it, lay out the burnt offering on it, and turn into smoke the fat parts of the offerings of well-being. A perpetual fire shall be kept burning on the altar, not to go out.

Zot torat ha-'olah can be read literally as: "This is the teaching of the ascent," the offering wholly consumed on the altar, rising up to God. But it can also mean "The teaching concerns the one who rises up." This calls us to ascend in *hitlahavut*, becoming enflamed in the ecstatic moment that lies at the heart of prayer. A large part of "prayer in place of sacrifice" is that of the ascending fire. In letting ourselves rise up, we agree to being consumed on the altar of prayer. But also remember to keep the fires fresh. Clean out the ashes, the remains of all past fires, every morning. Otherwise they will snuff out the new flame you need to light in this moment.

Zot ha-'olah hi ha-'olah. Read it as: "This is the ascending offering; it is *she* who goes up." The repeated "she" in this verse is an answer to the Song of Song's *mi zot 'olah*, "Who is she that rises up?" The answer, of course, is the soul. It is not the words of prayer that "ascend" but *she*.

Esh tamid tukad. "May fire burn on the altar always, and not go out." *Tamid* here has the sense of constancy; the fire within our heart should be there always, in every moment. This is the essential teaching of Hasidism. No matter what we are doing, even in the most mundane activities of our lives, we must always keep that fire burning. Every thought, word, and deed that we encounter should be added to it, turned into fuel to nurture our devotional flame.

3. Parashat ha-Tamid, "The Daily Offering" (Num. 28:1–8): Regularity of Prayer

וַיְדַבֵּר יְהוָה אֶל מֹשֶׁה לֵּאמֹר: צַו אֶת בְּנֵי יִשְׂרָאֵל וְאָמַרְתָּ אֲלֵהֶם אֶת קָרְבָּנִי לַחְמִי לְאִשַּׁי רֵיחַ נִיחֹחִי תִּשְׁמְרוּ לְהַקְרִיב לִי בְּמוֹעֲדוֹ. וְאָמַרְתָּ לָהֶם זֶה הָאִשֶּׁה אֲשֶׁר תַּקְרִיבוּ לַיהוָה: כְּבָשִׂים בְּנֵי שָׁנָה תְמִימִם שְׁנַיִם לַיּוֹם, עֹלָה תָמִיד. אֶת הַכֶּבֶשׂ אֶחָד תַּעֲשֶׂה בַבֹּקֶר וְאֵת הַכֶּבֶשׂ הַשֵּׁנִי תַּעֲשֶׂה בֵּין הָעַרְבָּיִם וַעֲשִׂירִית הָאֵיפָה סֹלֶת לְמִנְחָה בְּלוּלָה בְּשֶׁמֶן כָּתִית רְבִיעִת הַהִין. עֹלַת תָּמִיד הָעֲשֻׂיָה בְּהַר סִינַי לְרֵיחַ נִיחֹחַ, אִשֶּׁה לַיהוָה. וְנִסְכּוֹ רְבִיעִת הַהִין לַכֶּבֶשׂ הָאֶחָד בַּקֹּדֶשׁ הַסֵּךְ נֶסֶךְ שֵׁכָר לַיהוָה. וְאֵת הַכֶּבֶשׂ הַשֵּׁנִי תַּעֲשֶׂה בֵּין הָעַרְבָּיִם, כְּמִנְחַת הַבֹּקֶר וּכְנִסְכּוֹ תַּעֲשֶׂה, אִשֵּׁה רֵיחַ נִיחֹחַ לַיהוָה.

Y-H-W-H spoke to Moses, saying: Command the Israelite people and say to them: Take care to offer to Me the sweet-smelling fire-offerings of food due to Me, at their stated times. Say to them: These are the fire-offerings that you are to present to Y-H-W-H: As a regular offering every day, two yearling lambs without blemish. You shall offer one yearling lamb in the morning, and the other at twilight. As a meal-offering, a tenth of an ephah of fine flour, with a quarter of a hin of fine oil mixed with it—the regular burnt offering instituted at Mount Sinai, an offering of fire of pleasing aroma to Y-H-W-H. The libation with it is a quarter of a hin for each lamb, an offering of fermented drink poured out to Y-H-W-H. The second lamb you shall offer at twilight, preparing the same meal-offering and libation as in the morning—a sweet-smelling fire-offering unto Y-H-W-H.

Shnayim le-yom 'olat tamid. "A regular burnt offering every day, two . . ." The daily offering, morning and evening, reminds us of the regularity of prayer. Each day the same offering, at dawn and dusk. Celebrate those sacred moments of the change of light. Listen to the birds, who know in instinctive faith when those sacred times are drawing near each day. Let our prayer join into the chorus of their song. The simple insight that these two daily moments are sacred and need to be noted with prayer is among the most understated yet profound teachings our tradition has to offer.

But note the different meaning of the word *tamid* here. Rather than *constancy*, it means *regularity*. This is the side of us that knows we could never live up to the demand for constant *hitlahavut*, passionate religious intensity in each moment. We therefore accept the obligation of regularly scheduled worship, *'avodah*. We submit to a discipline that designates certain moments (those chosen by God and the birds, of course) to be the special times of devotion. This will suffice for us mere humans, though we surely continue to strive for the higher goal as well.

The point is that all of us are both the *kohen* ("priest") and *beney yisra'el* ("Children of Israel") here. Aspirationally, each of us worshippers longs to be the *kohen*, keeping the fire burning constantly, never turning away from the altar. But we know ourselves well enough to realize that a simple "two each day, a regular offering" is hard enough for ordinary people like us to achieve.

Ve-amarta 'aleyhem . . . ve-amarta 'aleyhem. "Say to them . . . say to them." The repetition is strange here, especially after we already have "Speak" and "Command." It feels as though the verse is looking forward into our day, when this daily sacrifice will become a verbal act, rather than a physical one. It seeks to reassure the worshipper that this too is a form of *'avodah*, a *real* offering to Y-H-W-H, offered on the altar within the heart and expressed in speech, rather than placed upon the altar in the Temple.

'Olat tamid ha-'asuyah be-har Sinai. "The regular burnt offering instituted at Mount Sinai." This statement corresponds to nothing that is described in the Torah's Sinai narrative. There was no daily offering at Sinai! But the point is that our daily offering recalls that which happened at the base of the great mountain. Our regular daily worship is intended to take us back to Sinai, the moment of our covenant, including the "Sinai" moments in each of our spiritual lives, those times when the heavens opened and truth became clear to us. It is in the regularity of daily prayer that they become realized in our lives.

This is the way R. Barukh of Miedzybozh reads it: *'Olat tamid*—Our constant ability to rise upward—that was made at Mount Sinai!"

4. Parashat ha-Ketoret (Ex. 30:34–36; 30:7–8): The Lasting Effect of Prayer

וַיֹּאמֶר יְהוָה אֶל מֹשֶׁה קַח לְךָ סַמִּים נָטָף וּשְׁחֵלֶת וְחֶלְבְּנָה סַמִּים וּלְבֹנָה זַכָּה בַּד בְּבַד יִהְיֶה. וְעָשִׂיתָ אֹתָהּ קְטֹרֶת רֹקַח מַעֲשֵׂה רוֹקֵחַ מְמֻלָּח טָהוֹר קֹדֶשׁ. וְשָׁחַקְתָּ מִמֶּנָּה הָדֵק וְנָתַתָּה מִמֶּנָּה לִפְנֵי הָעֵדֻת בְּאֹהֶל מוֹעֵד אֲשֶׁר אִוָּעֵד לְךָ שָׁמָּה, קֹדֶשׁ קָדָשִׁים תִּהְיֶה לָכֶם.

And Y-H-W-H said to Moses: Take to yourself the herbs stacte, onycha, and galbanum—these herbs together with pure frankincense; let there be an equal part of each. Make them into incense, a compound expertly blended, refined, pure, sacred. Beat some of it into powder, and put some before the Pact in the Tent of Meeting, where I will meet with you; it shall be Holy of Holies for you.

On it Aaron shall burn aromatic incense; he shall burn it every morning when he tends the lamps, and Aaron shall burn it at twilight when he lights the lamps—a regular incense offering before Y-H-W-H throughout the ages.

The incense offering. What happens *after* prayer is the most important question to address in your life as a praying person. Here the aroma of the offering lasts long after the sacrifice is offered, remaining with you as an incense that accompanies the rest of your life throughout the day. Your day, and your deeds, should be *geshmak funem davnen;* they should smell and taste of the aroma and flavor of your daily prayer.

Kah lekha samim. "Take to yourself." The construction here is the same as *lekh lekha,* God's original call to Abraham. The meaning too is the same. "Go into yourself"; "Take them into yourself"; *interiorize* the fine aroma of your prayer.

Kodesh kodashim tihyeh la-khem. "It shall be a Holy of Holies for you." Yes, this fine aroma of prayer that remains with us through the day can become a Holy of Holies in our lives, an inner sanctum into which we may retreat, a sacred place where no "stranger" or distraction may enter. My intent in this prayer I am about to begin is to open the doorway to that inner Holy of Holies. It is from there that my prayer is to come.

Ba-boker ba-boker . . . beyn ha-'arbayyim. "Every morning" and "at twilight." The incense with which our lives are perfumed is renewed each day, morning and evening, in the act of prayer.

Uve-ha'alot Aharon et ha-nerot. "When he lights [literally 'raises up'] the lamps." Levi Yizhak of Berdichev reads it to say:

The worshipper who lifts the sparks out of chaos binds them [to their Source], so that they are "before Y-H-W-H throughout the ages."

Listening to the *Shema'*

The second offering from my *Be'er* is my commentary on the *shema'*, beginning with an introduction. You may choose to read it side by side with the text of the *shema'*, found in any traditional prayer book.

Shema' Yisrael. "Listen, Israel" (Deut. 6:4–9). The core of our worship is not a prayer at all, but a cry to our fellow Jews and fellow humans. In it we declare that God is one—which is also to say that humanity is one, that life is one, that joys and sufferings are all one—for Y-H-W-H is the force that binds them all together. There is nothing obvious about this truth, for life as we experience it seems infinitely fragmented. Human beings seem isolated from one another, divided by all the fears and hatreds that make up human history. Even within a single life, one moment feels cut off from the next, memories of joy and fullness offering us little consolation when we are depressed or lonely. To assert that all is one in Y-H-W-H is our supreme act of faith. No wonder that the *shema'*, the first holy words we learn in childhood, is also the last thing we are to say before we die. The memory of these words on the lips of martyrs deepens our faith as we call them out each day.

"Listen, strugglers!" we call out twice each day. No more idols! No more gods bound in space or in time! No more gods depicted and enframed! Y-H-W-H runs away from such frames, the eternal free-flow of Being, ever beyond our grasp. Y-H-W-H *Eloheihu* Y-H-W-H Echad—"Is-Was-Will Be our only God, Is-Was-Will Be One!"

Unknowable Secret, unspeakable Word, hidden in our loving submission, our all-too-human calling out of *Adonai.* "Master!" "Lord!" "O Y-H-W-H, let me make You human, let me fashion You in our image! Let me do to You what You ever seek to do to me: let me remake You as my own! For this I will do anything; I will even give my life. I stand before You and call You My Lord." Yes, as we struggle together, You and I, we reshape one another.

Both of these together: the ever-elusive Y-H-W-H of the desert and the all-loving, all-knowing *Adonai* of my soul. These two revealed to be one and the same. *Eleh ḥamdah libi,* "These"—and their union—"are my heart's desire."

Shema' Yisrael. "Listen, Israel, Y-H-W-H our God, Y-H-W-H is one!" by definition cannot be a prayer. Prayer as we usually know it exists within the framework of dialogue, and dialogue requires duality, "I" speaking to God as "You." But in the *shema'* there is no "You" because there is no other. There is only one. We are capable of that deep insight into reality only for a moment, only in the intense flash of crying out the *shema'.* In saying the *shema'* we peer for a moment into a different reality, that of the total oneness of being. "Yes, I know—there is none other!" But until that moment, as well as in all those that follow, we live in the realm of self-and-other, I and Thou. The rest of the *siddur* is all written in the language of *barukh atah,* existing in a world where I am me and You are You. How do we make the transition from one world to another? That is why the *shema'* is surrounded on both sides by outcries of love, God's love for Israel and our love for God. Love is the apex of intimacy within the dualistic world, the moment in which duality has the possibility of transcending itself. In love the relationship of self and other gives us a glimpse into something beyond, into the possibility that we are one, indeed that all is one. We are carried into the *shema'* on the wings of love, *ahavah rabbah,* and we are carried forth from it, back into the world where we must live and act, on those same wings: *ve-ahavta.*

Ve-ahavta. "You shall love." But is it "you shall" or "you will"? Is this an imperative or a declarative statement? The commentators classically struggle with the impossibility of commanding love, leading to the need for another reading. The latter would go like this: The realization that all is one, that there is nothing that is not filled with the presence of Y-H-W-H, will cause you to be overwhelmed with love. Love is the only possible reaction to this great discovery, one that transforms your perception of all that is. The *vav* at the beginning of the word in this case really is an "and," as though to say: "Proceeding from *shema' yisra'el* is a love that will grasp you in all of your heart and soul, in all that you undertake." "You *will* love Y-H-W-H your God, with all your heart, soul, and means."

The rest of the paragraph does not move on from this assertion, but unpacks it. It tells you what will happen when you fill
up with this love. "These words will be on your heart! You will
find yourself talking about them all the time—at home and on the
road, lying down and getting up. You will talk to your kids about
them, over and over again! You'll bind them on your hands and
between your eyes, so you'll never forget them! You'll be so in
love that you'll find yourself scribbling them on your doorposts
and your gates!"

Ve-hayah 'im Shamo'a. "If you truly hear." The second paragraph of the *shema'* (Deut. 11:13–21) begins with *Le-AHAVAH et
Y-H-W-H eloheykhem.* It appears as though a noun has replaced the
verb here: it is not *le-ehov*, "to love" in the usual verbal form, but
le-ahavah, to be in the state that can only be described as "love."
There is a hidden warning here not to take this second paragraph
of the *shema'* too simplistically. The simple or childlike reading of
this passage tells us that if we really love God, lots of goodies will
come our way. If we don't, "better watch out." That is the faith
of childhood; it doesn't work for adults, who have seen that the
world isn't constructed that way.

But we adults have something else; we have an understanding
of *le-ahavah*, of the state of being in love, as something that has the
potential to transform our vision. If we learn to look through the
eyes of love, *le-ahavah*, we may see our world—the same world,
with the same pain, the same losses, the same arbitrariness—in a
different way. We will *accept* life, and the world in which we live it,
with all its faults, as only longtime lovers can. How much we learn
to accept in the one we love! So too the "One" we love. When we
do that, we can receive the real reward this passage promises, at its
very end (as our teacher R. Zalman translated it): "heavenly days,
right here on earth."

This paragraph describes a journey, one that lasts through the
course of an entire human life. "Yes, let yourself dare to love! Be in
that state of loving Y-H-W-H, which means loving All that is! Be
ready to serve, with all your heart and all your soul." You will *love*
doing it; you will fill up on the rewards of all that love: inner versions of wine, corn, and oil. But watch out; these things don't last
forever. Constant joy is no joy at all, as the Ba'al Shem Tov taught.
One day, when your heart just isn't paying attention, you will find

yourself distracted, "turned aside," and worshipping something else. The heart is always worshipping something. When we turn aside from Y-H-W-H, there are countless other preoccupations lined up to take that place, to become our "gods" for the moment. False gods, of course.

But then you look around and "the heavens will shut up and there will be no rain." How quickly you will feel that you've lost your moorings upon the land! All of a sudden you will feel that faith has abandoned you, that all is lost, that there is nothing left. Yes, these moments happen in the life of every religious person.

What is the life raft you hold onto in such a moment? It is then that those once spontaneous responses to the discovery of oneness, of Y-H-W-H filling all and being expressed everywhere, need to be turned into ritual. "Tie them on your hands! Bind them between your eyes!" "Write them on your doorposts!" Then you will be more than thankful that you have the wherewithal to do that. It is in these moments of feeling totally lost and without moorings when we most need the reassurance of ritual, of familiar religious forms. Those simple and down-to-earth things will bring you back to life, helping to hold your faith in those moments of doubt and despair that happen in every religious life. Trust in them and they will carry you over to the place where you and your offspring will indeed enjoy those "heavenly days right here on earth." Trust me. I know.

Ve-limmadetem otam et beneykhem. Here the verb *lammed* takes the place of *shanen* that we had in the first paragraph of the *shema'*. *Lammed* really means "teach"; *shanen* means to repeat. The first level of teaching is one that just repeats the message over and over again, hoping it will penetrate. But real teaching calls for understanding, seeking the right channels toward opening the child's mind. The difference between them is made remarkably clear in the lines that follow. In the first paragraph it went, following *ve-shinantam*, "You will speak of them." But here, where the children truly learn, it says: "You will teach them *to your children to speak of them.*" Here *they* become the speakers. Only *limmud*, true learning, as opposed to *sheninah*, repetition or indoctrination, will empower them to make the tradition their own, so that *they* can speak it, passing it on to the generations that will follow.

The final paragraph of the *shema'* (Num. 15:37–41) is called *parashat tsitsit*, "the passage on the fringes." It takes a single *mitsvah* as paradigmatic for the entire life of religious doing.

Ve-hayah la-khem le-tsitsit u-re'item oto. "It shall be a fringe for you and you shall see it." "What do you see?" ask the hasidic authors, picking up on an ambiguity in the Hebrew text. They answer: "You see God." They read the word *tsitsit* ("fringe") as derived from a verb stem meaning "to peer," *le-hatsits.* They then connect it to Song of Songs 2:9—"Here He stands behind our wall, looking through the windows, peering through the cracks." God our Lover peers at us through the cracks in our "wall" of defenses, our self-made *kelipot*, shells. But the *tsitsit* allow us to peer back at our Beloved. *U-re'item oto* is then translated "You shall see *Him*," rather than "it." Read the verse this way: "Let the *tsitsit* be a peek-hole for you, through which you gaze at Y-H-W-H." The first word of the verse, *ve-hayah*, is, after all, nothing but God's own name in hidden form.

Le-ma'an tizkeru. "So that you remember." The *tsitsit*, like all the forms of religion, are there as reminders for us as we go about our daily lives. All of us have had moments when we most became ourselves, liberated from our "Egypts," the inner narrow straits that hold us back from seeing our truth. We can all think of moments when we discovered those great inner truths that lend meaning to our lives. Those moments are vital and precious to us, forming the "Sinai" of our individual lives. But then the fast pace of life as well as the petty angers and frustrations of daily living cause us to form a hard shell about us, to protect those most precious feelings. Somehow the memories themselves get lost behind that very shell, which comes to dominate our personality. Now we take a moment to remember who we are, to peek through the cracks in our self-made wall.

Ve-'asitem et kol mitsvotai. "You will do all My commandments." Remembering who we truly are brings us to a transformative realization. I want to live all my life in faithfulness to the memory of those moments. Read "all My commandments" with a hasidic eye: Make *all* become *My commandments.* Your task is to make everything you do into a *mitsvah*, paying attention to the deep well of divinity that is present within it, offering it as a form of service. The specific *mitsvot* of the traditions are paradigms to show you how to do that.

Ani Y-H-W-H eloheykhem . . . li-heyot la-khem le-Elohim. "I am Y-H-W-H your God who has brought you out of the land of Egypt to become your God." Whatever inner "Egypt" you have come out of, whatever was tying you in knots and keeping you from being free—understand that it was Y-H-W-H who brought you forth. And it all happened for a clear and single purpose: *li-heyot la-khem le-Elohim*, so that you might be free enough to enter into this relationship with Y-H-W-H, embracing all that is. That is what it means to live in faith.

Ani Y-H-W-H eloheykhem. "I am Y-H-W-H your God." This dramatic conclusion to the *shema'* of course says all that needs to be said. *This is what we have been listening for, ever since saying* shema', *"Listen!"* This is the divine "I am," the *anokhi* that opens the revelation at Sinai. It is all the One needs to say. It is said in the mysterious breath-word Y-H-W-H, as it is in the silent *aleph* or in the divine act of breathing existence into all that is.

But there is something else said here as well. It is not only an "I am" with which the *shema'* concludes, but an "I am *yours*." I take this to be the divine voice that assures me *dodi li*, "My Beloved is mine," before I am called upon to say, in the coming *'amidah*, *va-ani lo*, "and I am His." The *'amidah* is our act of *'avodah*, worship, in the most proper and total sense; it is that which comes to replace the daily offering. In it we submit, place ourselves on the verbal altar, give ourselves to Y-H-W-H. *Va-ani tefilati*, "I *am* my prayer"; all I have to give You is myself. But how can I be called upon to do it, to take this risky act of loving You and offering myself, unless I know that I am loved by the One to whom I open up my heart?

None of this deeply personal and emotional prayer is diminished by careful thinking about what we mean by "God." The One who calls out to me calls out in eternally resounding silence. That silence is far from being an empty or meaningless silence. Just the opposite: it is so filled that words cannot express it. Only I, as a mere verbal and mortal being, need to (and permit myself to) respond in language, that ever-inadequate human tool. The One that undergoes and is present throughout our long astrophysical and evolutionary journey is present within every life-form, including the one that for this instant I am allowed to call "me." That presence is an act of love, a statement that the One spreads its being, its Y-H-W-H, into this particular form for this split second of eternal time. I behold that as an act of love for this self, in this moment, along with all the others. I bow down in gratitude. I am filled with the renewing energy that says: "Yes! I understand why I am here! Now I can give myself to You."

The Seeker Returns

THE KABBALISTS, WHEN TRYING to articulate some of their most profound secrets, spoke of a hidden realm of divine mystery. This transcendent and unfathomable reality lay far beyond the God of biblical or rabbinic tradition: the blessed Holy One, Ruler on the heavenly throne, Creator, Sustainer, and Judge of the lower world. One set of symbols referred to this hidden aspect of divinity as the mind of God, the realm out of which the divine Person was first conceived. Others saw it as the womb out of which God was born. For some parts of the kabbalistic imagination, even these images seemed too concrete. They turned instead to speaking of the primal Nothing, or of the Endless, a One that had no name, and yet could be present within all names, all words.[1]

That transcendent, ungraspable One then turns out to be identical with the immanent God, the One a person of faith encounters in each moment, flooding the universe with light, filling the world with perceptible and tangible glory. "You surround all worlds and fill all worlds"; the mystical moment is the discovery that these two aspects of divinity are one.[2]

The journey from that abstract, mysterious divinity to the personal God of tradition was a long and arduous one. Perhaps the distance between them is itself infinite, never to be fully traversed. But the kabbalists tried; they employed an array of metaphors and symbols by which to convey it. Among them: the flow of light out of supreme darkness, the rush of water from a hidden source, the flow of divine seed into the mysterious birth chamber of the cosmic Mother, the journey from silence to sound, underlying the birth of the primal word.

This is a new Judaism that the mystics created. While constructed out of ancient mythic fragments preserved in the rabbinic mindset, the product was one very unlike anything in the prior tradition. There the personal God and ultimate reality were always one and the same. Even after the very anthropomorphic God-language of biblical and rabbinic Judaism was linked to Greco-Arabic ways of philosophical inquiry, no space was allowed to exist between the One and the divine Person. But now, by joining that philosophical tradition to the powerful channels of symbol and myth, Kabbalah was able to open up new dimensions of religious language and experience. That created a multidimensional inner divine reality, revealed through a series of graded steps. These steps could be traversed in both directions, a "downward" flow of divine self-manifestation into the world, and a return journey in the human spiritual quest to restore unity, to discovering the One within the many. "Behold, a ladder, angels of God going up and down on it" (Gen. 28:12). In trying to investigate these stages in the journey, and to ask how they might best be translated into categories that could be useful to the contemporary Jewish seeker, we find ourselves turning to the language of depth psychology.

To do this, we need to turn mystical speculation sideways, as it were. The kabbalists are deeply wedded to the vertical metaphor, something they had inherited from the ancients. From earliest times, Western civilization had seen God (or the gods) as dwelling in high places, far above the earth. The sacred journey was depicted as a vertical one, an ascent to heaven. This was true in the ancient Near East as it was in Greece. God was to be reached by climbing the great mountain, by steps on that ladder reaching to heaven. The older Jewish esoteric tradition even exaggerated this. The divine throne was in the highest of seven heavens; the journey to it was an ascent through multiple worlds, for which one needed to be prepared by both moral fitness and esoteric knowledge.

While mostly accepting this hierarchical view of the cosmos, and hence a vertical map of spiritual journey, the mystics also made it clear that the direction of that quest could be conceived as inward as well as upward. The *sefirot*, or stages of emanation, were then depicted as a series of concentric circles, beginning from deepest within, rather than as steps of a ladder.[3] We, as seekers in a more psychological and less hierarchical era, may find it easier to relate to that sort of understanding. The voyager is contemplatively penetrating into ever-deeper realms of mind, rather than ascending the seven heavens. The stages beyond all our images of "God" are those inward rungs where one transcends consciousness of individual identity or personhood, inner "places" where the ego-self has vanished into the recesses of the cosmic Self, and that Self, in turn, into a realm of inner Nothingness.[4]

While the kabbalists may formally claim that the deepest levels of reality are by definition beyond the grasp of human experience (since there is no "self" left to enter them), they are not entirely to be believed on this score. The thick mythic description of those metaphysical realms is surely an attempt at giving an account of something the voyager has indeed "seen" or felt. The tools of phenomenology are often useful here, pulling forth from the kabbalistic texts a matrix of inner experience that the authors were too shy to make explicit.

We are dwelling here in a psychic realm where the borderline between "experience" and "imagination" is extremely fuzzy, sometimes nonexistent. The Zohar and other mystical writings speak with great boldness about the inner birth process of divinity, the personal God of the biblical-rabbinic tradition ("the blessed Holy One") being born out of the womb of *binah*, the Great Mother of divinity, but also the inner mind of God. But viewed psychologically, this theogonic (or "birth of God") myth that is such a striking feature of Kabbalah is strikingly parallel to the mystic's own experience of reentry into human reality. The return from a state of contemplative trance demands the reconstitution of personality, including various aspects and complexities of gender. This rebirth of human self, a repeated experience in the life of the mystic, is referred to a cosmic paradigm, the constant rebirthing process of the personal self of God.

But which is primary? The Godself, like the self of the mystic voyager, is ever reemerging out of *eyn sof*, an inner place beyond all oppositions, including those between light and darkness, good and evil, self and other, male and female. Might we say that in returning to the world, the kabbalist needs to make a great effort to reestablish these, lest the journey into oneness turn out to be a maddening one, following which the mystic can no longer function in our world of distinction and multiplicity. Hence God was seen as engaged in the same process as that of the mystic: struggling to cast out the roots of evil, emerging into properly balanced personhood, separating male and female aspects of the self in order that they might reunite as two recovering a lost oneness, and hence propagate new generations as well.

Or are we to view this from within the kabbalist's perspective, where all that human experience comes about not because we project it onto the cosmos, but because we are in the divine image, merely repeating the inner divine process of birth, growth, maturation, and coupling within our own individual lives, both physically and spiritually?

Without resolving this question unequivocally—something I have no desire to do—I want to suggest that many of us, in recent generations, have been involved in another version of this same great journey. For some—myself included, in a certain way—that is what our return to Judaism has been all about. Our journey back has been from the nameless to the named, from mystery to God, from the blank slate of Nothingness to a willingness to paint the universe with a human face.

Our religious lives did not begin with a personal God. We are not involved in Jewish life because a heavenly voice called or commanded us to do so. Perhaps later in our journey we came to feel addressed by such a voice, but that is not where we began. Like so very many in our era, Judaism had been lost to us, and needed to be re-created. Whether it was due to the rationalist secularism of twentieth-century living, or the Holocaust's ultimate challenge to traditional faith—or, most likely, both—the old identification of ultimate reality with a willful and ruling God was gone, beyond retrieval. For those coming of age in the twenty-first century, the challenges are different—the utter flexibility of identities, the overly suspicious critical voice that reduces all to meaninglessness—but no less disturbing. In the postmodern world, "meaning" itself becomes a word without meaning. The seeming demise of our old religious language means that most Jews are left with nothing. Simply nothing, with no capital N.

But for the seeker, that was the beginning, rather than the end, of the quest. Many such Jewish seekers turned eastward, spending years in meditation and chant, absorbing alien teachings that always hovered between the abstract and the devotional. The desire to open the heart, while still worshipping the abstract oneness of being, seemed to work better in some simplified form of Eastern religions than it did with the overwhelmingly personified traditions of the West. Others went the philosophical route, perhaps through Wittgenstein or Heidegger, only to discover that they were really religious contemplatives at heart. Not a few of us took the psychedelic path, undergoing would-be transformative inner experiences that seemed to lead nowhere, until they were combined with the tools needed to implant their lessons in our everyday lives, those in which traditional Judaism so abounds.

We come back to Judaism as a special sort of *ba'aley teshuvah*, returnees. We are drawn to "return" to the One via the mystical tradition, an

aspect of Judaism that most Jews today have never known. We were impressed by the wisdom of prior generations and the profundity of their
teachings. Precisely because of what we have brought with us from our
own spiritual journeys, we understand that great truth and inner experience underlie them, and that these are accessible to us if we make the
effort to learn them well and to open our hearts to them. To do so is an
act of faith, both in the value of the teachings themselves and in our own
ability to respond to them.

But in turning toward that mystical Holy of Holies, some of us relative newcomers also have the audacity to want to reshape it. We want
to say openly that we choose it as our own particular path of devotion,
without denigrating other faiths or claiming a monopoly on the truth. We
want to take on observance at our own pace and in ways that seem authentic, without feeling less than whole in our love of God or our embrace of
Torah. We want to feel welcome within our own Jewish selves, whatever
our gender or choice of whom to love.

But this opening also requires faith, and that means a certain submission and letting go of our own willfulness.[5] Here I have to pause and say
something of what I mean—and don't mean—by invoking the familiar
yet powerful word *faith*. I begin with an assertion that there is something
irreducibly real about religious experience, in all its many "varieties." It
is upon that essential phenomenal datum that all theologies should be
erected. It cannot be dismissed as merely an effect of measurable brain-
wave patterns or as a projection of societal norms. Yes, the tools of both
physical and social science may help us understand the inner life, but they
do not exhaust its truth. Therefore, we must listen to the testimony of the
faithful, both those of the past and those who continue to live as communities of faithful religious Jews. The claims that their experiences, and the
religions built upon them, make upon the heart that opens to them are
worthy of respect. They call for our attention, teaching us profound lessons about our lives and the ways we are to live them. When the language
or music of those accounts confirm what we ourselves have begun to feel
in moments of openheartedness, we know that we are walking in the right
direction.

Having made the switch from the vertical to the internal as the matrix
of the spiritual journey, I do not need to claim external or "objective" ver-
ification for the truth of faith. My faith community, in our case religious
Jewry, is a communion of hearts open to the same language for invoking
religious truth. We love and tremble together at the foot of Sinai; we stand

together with the high priest as he enters the Holy of Holies on the ho-
liest day of the year. These events are real insofar as they live within us,
serving as paradigms for our own spiritual journeys. None of this is literal,
but all of it is real. The Torah narrative is not simply a collection of tales
about our ancestors, but a series of gateways—made up of words, letters,
images, even white spaces in the text—through which we may enter into
an interior universe. These are real for us in a way untouched by questions
of historicity or other external criteria. Their truth dwells not in the past,
but in the eternal present, not because they once happened, but because
they can still happen within us.

"Faith" does not require assurance that things will turn out the way
we want. We are spiritual adults, meaning that we have seen too much to
expect that. It is not in search for such a God that we have come back to
Judaism. *Part of our faith is in the power of faith itself.* That which we have
known to be true in our deepest moments of openheartedness does not
abandon us. It remains with us, both in the hardest and the most ordinary
of times, enabling us to get through, even to rejoice. The God in whom we
trust can give us only God, the presence of Y-H-W-H in our lives. "One
thing I ask of Y-H-W-H; it is that which I seek: to dwell in the house of
Y-H-W-H all the days of my life, gazing upon divine beauty, visiting His
palace" (Ps. 27:4). That is all we seek and, ultimately, all we need. *Raza
di-mehemenuta*, "the secret of faith" in the Zohar's Aramaic, is the ability
to hold together the synergy of various planes of truth, gazing upon the
multiplicity of the world while still holding fast to the singular vitality that
underpins it all, coursing through it like a font of ceaseless energy.

But who or what is it that I am talking about here? I began with experience and with faith, but as soon as I turn to the biblical sources, they
seem to be talking not about abstract principles, but about a deity, *elohim*,
which I have inadequately rendered as "God." So let us spend a few moments with that Hebrew word *elohim*, the third word in the Torah (as in
"In the beginning God created . . .") and explore its meaning. *Elohim* is the
Torah's generic name for "god" or "deity," in contrast to Y-H-W-H, the
proper name belonging only to the One.

The first thing any beginning Hebrew student will notice is that the
word's form is plural, with the classical "*im*" ending. But how is that possible? Why should the religious language of the first great monotheistic
tradition have a plural name for God? The answer is that monotheism did
not come out of nowhere. The prior existing religions, over against which
the Bible was asserting itself, all had a multiplicity of deities. There were

gods assigned to specific functions, such as war, love, healing, or fruitful crops. And there were gods who belonged to particular places, such as the gods of Canaan or the gods of Egypt. *Elohim* is in fact a *collective* noun, asserting that all of them are now subsumed within the one.[6] In addressing *Elohim*, you are turning to all the forces in the cosmos, now held together in hopefully stable balance. (Alas, that is not always the case!) In saying *eloheynu, our* God, we are saying that all those forces, with that same need for balance, are arrayed within the human self as well. We are created *be-tselem Elohim*, in the image of that same multiple/unitive divine Being.

But the kabbalists attach a deeper secret to the word *elohim*, written like this in Hebrew: אלהים. In the opening pages of the Zohar, the greatest work of Kabbalah, it is said that Elohim, אלהים, is a combining of two other words: *mi*, מי, and *eleh*, אלה, meaning "who?" and "these." They are reading a biblical verse (Is. 40:26) that says: "Lift up your eyes and see *who* created *these*." In the biblical context, "these" refers to the stars of heaven. But the kabbalist has something very different, and even more sublime, in mind. "These" are for him the seven *sefirot*, or inner divine realms, which are the framework on which all descriptions of God, both personal and impersonal, are structured. Anything about which we can say: "God is . . ." is part of "these." But beyond them all lies a realm so mysterious that it can be designated only by a question, not an answer. That realm is referred to by an unanswerable "Who?"

For a word to truly contain God, says the mystic, it must at once embrace both "these" and "who?," both *endless answers and eternal questions*. But then the Zohar adds a devastating aside. Those who worshipped the Golden Calf, it reminds us, called out, "*These* are your gods, O Israel" (Ex. 32:4). Idolatry is a form of worship that thinks it has answers, but has lost sight of the unanswerable question.

In fact, the relationship between "God" and "Mystery" is a key theme for the kabbalists. Ever lovers of language and its subtleties, they use the first-, second-, and third-person pronouns (*ani, atah*, and *hu* in the masculine Hebrew) to refer to three distinct levels within divinity. While they often depict these in vertical and hierarchical terms, I prefer to view them as referring to successive depths of *inward* perception. *Ani*, "I," the God of "I am Y-H-W-H your God," is *shekhinah*, the indwelling presence of divinity through all of Creation. It is called *ani* because of its immediate accessibility; when we first open ourselves to the sacred realm, this is the God we encounter. This is the God we discover, or that reveals itself, saying, "I am." This is the God to be found within natural beauty, the God who naturally floods the soul. It is the God of the natural mystic, of "the whole earth is filled with God's glory!"

Beyond that *ani* there lies a level of divinity encountered as *atah*, "You." This is the God we meet as divine "Other." It seems to stand as though outside us, thus enabling it to be a commanding presence. (A God who is only an *ani* and not an *atah* is too easily squashed into the personal self and its endless neediness.) Here transcendence is uncompromised, although our encounter with it, to be sure, is another rung of inward experience. That *atah* deity is the one most identified with the God-figure of scripture and Jewish tradition. But that divine *atah* is also that which enables us to enter into relationship with human others. Every human *atah* contains something of the divine *atah* within it, as Martin Buber taught us. To say *atah* is to place a limitation upon one's own expansive self, to make room for the other to be real, and to allow that other, both divine and human, to make demands on us.

But then there is a third divine level, referred to only in the third person as *hu*. This is the God of mystery, the One, indeed, designated as "Who?" Here we are seemingly beyond imagery, beyond myth, staring directly into the unknowable Truth. It is the One out of which we emerge, into which we shall all return.

But the kabbalistic imagination is endlessly inventive and complex. The most mysterious of these three realms, sometimes called "the hidden world," turns out to be the cosmic Mother, the One out of whose womb both the *atah* and the *ani* figures (also called "blessed Holy One" and *shekhinah* or "Presence") are born. Intimacy, even of the most passionate maternal love, reaches into the unknown. All harshness and forces of judgment in this world need to be uplifted and restored to *binah;* only there can they be "sweetened," transformed.

This whole set of images is surely one of the most daring innovations of the mystics' reinvention of Judaism: the God of Hebrew scripture is in fact *born* out of a higher or deeper mystery, one that nurtures Him and remains the source of His ongoing power. The image of this blessed Holy One, whether the King seated on His throne or the cosmic Elder called Israel, is still just one of "these," a metaphor that offers one window among many into a reality that by definition transcends them all.

The figure of a Great Mother, the womb of all being, of course calls forth the possibility of a Great Father as well, the force that impregnates her and sets the cosmic wheels in motion. That figure is called by the ancient name *hokhmah* or "Wisdom," perhaps equivalent to "the mind of God."[7] *Hokhmah* is seen as the primal point of existence, the first step in the great chain of emanation. This tells us that the yin and yang of the kabbalists, described in terms of "male" and "female," reaches all the way back into the most recondite levels of mind and existence. The twin forces of giving (*mashpi'a* is literally "flowing into" or "*influencing*") and receiving, "male" and "female," exist throughout the universe, and the same being may take on both functions. Giving and receiving are deeply intertwined, as any good lover knows.

If *ḥokhmah* is the beginning point of reality, one would hardly expect to look beyond it. But here, too, the kabbalist pushes the far edges of our speculative imagination. The primal point of *ḥokhmah* is symbolized by the letter *yod*, itself no larger than a dot, in the manuscript tradition. But that dot has a thin pointed line at its top, taken to mean that it points beyond itself, toward that which cannot be spoken. Here we are indeed in the realm of cosmic, or deep internal, silence, the undisturbed bastion of the Endless One.

In the course of this movement toward the inner One, however, we are inevitably brought back to the personal. How could this not be the case? We humans have spent most of our lives learning how, when, and how much to trust other people. Where does our need for intimacy seek fulfillment, if not in interpersonal relations? Where does our pain live in the face of either loss or rejection? Our emotional lives are all about the interpersonal. When we open our hearts to the universal One, how could these personal feelings not be evoked? (How sad we feel for those we meet who can do it with trees or dogs, but not with people!) We want to put our trust in someone who *cares* about us, one to whom we make a difference. That does not need to be a parent God who can "make it all better" by giving us the lollipop we had so fervently sought. But it does have to be One who can hold us, wipe our tears, say, "I hear you," and respond with love. That is the God of *ani* and *atah*, the One who is ever present within us and the One to whom we call.

I believe that this projection of a personal image onto the face of mystery is our greatest act of humanization, in more senses than the seemingly tautological. It underscores our own humanity, valuing our own ability to care for others. It serves as a beacon to help us seek out the divine mystery within the human soul, both in others and in ourselves. In Western history, at least, it makes for what we call the *humanities*, a cluster of studies, values, and ideals now so much under threat. *Of course* they are under threat, in an era when we have been taught to tear that human mask off the face of reality, to view our existence in mechanistic and random terms, rejecting the whole effort of *humane* meaning-making called religion.

We have no choice. Our soul will only respond to Being with a human face—or, if the Zohar has its way—with multiple human faces. That face shines its light into ours and makes us feel blessed. "But is it *true?*" you want to ask. "Does it correspond to external reality?" But that is no longer our question. Since both the journey and its goal lie within, so too does the test of its truth.

You may be helped, however, as I have been, by one line from our ancient sages, and by one teaching of a hasidic master. In a Midrash, Rabbi Yudan says: "Great is the power of the prophets, who liken the form to its Maker."[8] This version of the statement is actually backwards, perhaps for euphemistic reasons. The prophets, its author wants to say, dare to liken man to God, describing the divine as having a human face. But in fact the verse quoted here refers to the appearance of God as "an image like that of a human" (Ezek. 1:26), likening the Maker to the (human) form! In this reversal, they are staring directly into the question of "Who is the projection of whom?"

The hasidic master Rabbi Avraham Yehoshua Heschel of Apt commented on the verse "What does Y-H-W-H your God want of you?" (Deut. 10:12). The Hebrew word *mah*, "What?" is numerically forty-five, he notes. That is also the value of *adam*, human being. For a more general audience, he might have been saying: "God wants you to be a *mensch.*" But then he adds, in just a brief note intended for the closer reader, that he is really referring to the vision of Ezekiel, the same verse, 1:26: "And upon the image of the throne was the image of a man upon it, from above."[9] What God wants of you, O man, is that you place a human upon that heavenly throne.

In ways we cannot fully understand, we sense that we are created in the image of God. And that God calls upon us to return the favor. In doing so, of course, we are engaged in a dual process. We both humanize God and glorify humanity. Once that human image is placed upon the divine throne, every human face will have to be seen as containing something of the divine within it, and will need to be treated with ultimate respect.[10] Such a theology is necessarily pluralistic. If each face refracts the divine light in a unique manner, surely the multiple spiritual languages of humanity offer a wealth of lenses through which that refraction may take place. We are ever participating in—or at least becoming fully cognizant of—"And God created humans in His image; in the image of God did He create them, male and female" (Gen. 1:28). But it is by gazing into the human face, in all its endless varieties, that we also come to glimpse the face of God.

All about Being Human

W E HAVE SEEN THROUGHOUT these essays that the faith of Judaism has been characterized over the course of its history by commitment to a *personal* religious language. The biblical legacy that describes God as a super-person, one with both emotional and something like physical characteristics, has never been fully overcome, despite many attempts to discover some deeper truth within or behind it. Jewish philosophers were embarrassed by this language and sought to explain it away. The mystics chose rather to absorb these personal images in a great sea of symbol and metaphor, one in which *all* of language was a way of speaking about God.[1] But Jews everywhere continued to use the personal address form of prayer, speaking both to and of God as though God were a person.

The origin and nature of being, seemingly the most abstract of all questions, is addressed in personal terms. "Lift up your eyes," says the prophet (Isa. 40:26), "and see *who* created these." The exclusive hold of this religious language in the Western tradition is being seriously challenged in our day. The new encounter with Eastern religions has taught many seekers that it is possible to have a deep spiritual (even religious, in the devotional sense) life outside this personalist language. Yet Judaism, even that of the most sophisticated Jewish thinkers, insists on holding on to it.

Some of that may simply be a sense of tradition and history. New understandings of God were piled atop one another over the course of three thousand years of history, but no new insight was ever permitted to quite displace those that had come before. Each offered another layer of truth, an appeal, perhaps, to a different rung of mind. As such, each was seen as deepening one's perception of the reality encompassed by the term Y-H-W-H. But that name also retained a reference to its earliest uses, when still a tribal deity of ancient Canaan, leading His people in battle against the foe.

But there is another, more important reason why abstract Jewish theologies have never let go of the personalist image. The humanlike view of God is the basis for Judaism's most central moral teaching, the claim that each person is created in God's image. This statement in the opening tale of Genesis is the basis for all of Jewish ethics. It is, according to some of the ancient rabbis, the most basic rule of Torah.[2]

The Genesis account begins with two words for what we call "the image of God." *Tselem* is "image" in an almost physical sense, the way in which the child is "the spittin' image" of the parent. The old Targum or Aramaic translation sometimes renders the word by the Greek "icon"; every human being is God's icon.[3] No wonder we have no icons in the synagogue; the synagogue is filled with icons as soon as we walk in! The word *tselem*, by the way, is the basis for the modern Hebrew *matslemah*, the word for "camera," a device that can capture this sort of image in a single click. The second Genesis term, *demut*, is somewhat more subtle. "Likeness" is probably the right word for it. To be "like" something is to be comparable to it. But here later Judaism has a great problem, if one is looking for inner biblical consistency. The prophet says quite clearly, in an early move toward a more abstract theology: "To whom will you compare Me, that I be likened?" and "To whom will you compare God? What likeness can you offer to Him?" (Isa. 40:18, 25). Can we indeed be "like" God?

Tselem refers to our hard wiring. We have within us a soul or a spark of inner divinity that is absolutely real and uncompromised. The entire macrocosm, the Self of the universe, is there within each human self, along with the ability, each in our own way, to discover that truth. But *demut* is all about potential. To continue the computer imagery, it is the program we create on the basis of that great hardware, the life we fashion out of the tools we've been given. We *are* the *tselem* of God; we can choose to *become* God's *demut* as we work to live and fashion our lives in God's image.

Memory is one aspect of what it means to be in God's image. Memory begins as soon as there is humanity; our humanity itself is rooted in the soil of memory. To be human is to remember. To lose memory is to lose a piece of ourselves. To lose all of memory is one of the great human tragedies; some part (though surely not all) of the divine light in us goes out with it. We remember our own lives as individuals; each person's uniqueness develops over time out of the memories that he or she carries. But we also remember as families, tribes, nations, and societies. Civilization is built on the passing down, celebration, and interpretation of memory. Rabbi Naḥman of Bratslav, in one of his famous *Tales*, asks: "Who remembers the oldest thing?"[4] One of the speakers in the story remembers infancy, another recalls being in the womb, still another remembers the moment of his own (or the world's) conception, all expressed in symbolic terms. But the youngest of the company, who was paradoxically the greatest rememberer of all, says: "I remember nothing." This, of course, is the great Nothing that precedes creation. "And all agreed," Rabbi Naḥman concludes, "that this memory was indeed the greatest."

We Jews are *commanded* to remember. We believe that all humans share the imperative to remember Creation and the covenant with Noah, of which we are all a part. The covenant is God's promise not to destroy the world. The memory of Creation has to become our promise to do the same. Today it is we humans, not the blind forces of nature, who are the more likely enemies of the world's survival. To remember Creation is to remember that we are here for a purpose: to become aware, and to act on that awareness. We are here to know, articulate, celebrate, and share with all others the truth that being is one, that H-W-Y-H, "being," is Y-H-W-H, that there is none other.

Here we need to turn from the old Creation story to a new one, creating a sacred retelling of the narrative of evolution, an effort just beginning to emerge in our day. After a long and wearying battle against the science of evolution, today's spiritual teachers, so concerned with earth's survival and fitness for human habitation, see the need to move in a different direction. Evolution itself is being recast as a sacred narrative. The evolutionary process is depicted as the ongoing effort of the divine One to express itself in each life-form that exists, and in their great diversity. The journey from the simplest, most elemental life-forms toward the emergence of more complex and intelligent beings (and not only humans) is a process that has been taking place across the arc of planetary history. Today the old twentieth-century battle between science and religion is replaced by a religious acceptance of evolution, but one that insists on seeing the world through eyes of wonder and a sense of daily miracle. The narrative of evolution thus becomes the greatest of all sacred stories. It is the tale of God's long evolutionary journey toward "the sixth day," the emergence of intelligent beings that could become aware of the entire process, continuing evolution as self-aware embodiments of the divine image that underlies all existence.

We humans now control the fate of this planet, including the future of every other species that inhabits it alongside us. Where are we leading it? How will we awaken enough to overcome the stupidity and shortsightedness of our political leadership, so ready to sacrifice future existence for the sake of short-term economic gain? We will do so only by seeing where we stand in this long evolutionary and historic journey. *Memory* and *awareness* are the only tools that can save us.

In contemplating our existence in this way, we also come to ask the purpose of our own individual lives. Each of us is present on this planet for an instant of evolutionary time, here and gone with the flick of a cosmic eye. Why do I exist? Why has the single animating force of being clothed itself in this person I call myself for the instant I am here alive on earth? What is it that the One within wants from each of us? Why are we here, we creatures who have begun to have some inkling of the process that brought us here, and of the One within it? One answer is that we are here to *re-member*, or to rejoin the links of a creation that has been rent asunder. The One seeks that we become more fully conscious, that we cultivate *da'at*, or spiritual awareness, as fully as we are able, and spread that awareness forward among others. In this way, we become active participants in the evolutionary process, involved in bringing forth still more fully aware beings as the process inches ahead. The job of each human being is to teach every other human being that we are all part of that same One, and to find ways in our behavior, as well as our thought, to include all other creatures within that vision of oneness as well. Such awareness will call upon us to act for the protection of the planet and its ongoing evolution.

This is the basis of all religion. Judaism teaches us that there are two kinds of commandments: those "between person and God," referring to spiritual and ritual praxis, and those "between person and person," encompassing the moral/ethical life. Both of these categories, I believe, may be universalized in the religion of natural mysticism I am suggesting here. *We exist in order to become aware, to lend our particular kind of self-articulation to the One.* That, if you will, is the first commandment of a natural mysticism. But it is also the first commandment of Sinai, or at least of its opening words: "I am Y-H-W-H your God." With that awareness, we are commanded to bring the transcendent mystery of divinity into our human minds, to give it articulation within our human language. All the rest of religion, insofar as it applies to the realm "between person and God," is just a spelling out of this, an ongoing creation of forms through which we remember the single truth. The forms themselves vary from one religion to another; ultimately they are all arbitrary. We change or restrict our behavior in a certain way, we say certain words or undertake certain actions, in order to remind ourselves, on a regular basis, of the truth of Y-H-W-H and the oneness of all being. In this sense, we admit that all the forms of expression, including all the words that command them, are of human origin; it is people and societies that create or evolve religions. But all of these forms are created as a way of *responding* to an inner, almost instinctual, drive to recall that deeper truth. In this sense, we may say that they are also of divine origin, and in this very abstract way we may say that a divine imperative stands behind them. This is an imperative—or perhaps a plea—that we remember who we really are, and of what we are a part—"the soul is a part of God above"—and that we thus create forms to help us do so.

Our second job as religious people is to share this realization of oneness with others. We do so most successfully not by preaching, but by actions. We let others know that we and they are part of the same One when we treat them like sisters and brothers, or like fellow limbs of our same single universal body. "Love your neighbor as yourself," interpreted to include *all* our neighbors, is also a good "basic principle of Torah." Here all the commandments "between person and person" have their natural root. And here too the sharing is based on human experience and forms of social interaction that are wholly ours, yet the imperative that lies behind them comes from a deeper place. We are called upon to proclaim the oneness of being throughout the world, to treat others as fellow parts of that same One, and to enable all those with whom we come in contact to feel themselves as part of that oneness as well.

But we Jews have some other things we have to remember. In fact, there is a traditional list of six remembrances, based on six biblical verses that call us to particular memories. In old-fashioned prayer books you sometimes find them listed following the daily morning service, as six things you are enjoined to recall each day. Here I would like to expound briefly on each of these, with some significant updating.[5] All of them, we should say at the outset, follow upon the primal "memory" of creation/ evolution and the origin of life, which we now know that we carry in us in the form of our DNA.

First comes the memory of slavery and liberation. The first commandment itself, we will recall, goes on to say " . . . who brought you forth from the Land of Egypt, the House of Bondage." "Remember the day you came out of Egypt, all the days of your life" (Deut. 16:3), we are told. Both the fact that we were once slaves and the fact that we are now free need to be remembered. These are an essential part of our Jewish vision of being human. Why? The memory of our enslavement is our way of identifying with human suffering, especially that of the oppressed. The Torah repeatedly tells us to remember slavery when it instructs us on how to treat the stranger who lives in our midst. To recall that we were slaves has to make it impossible for us to enslave or oppress others; to do so is a betrayal of our own worst nightmares. To remember the liberation from Egypt is to recall the struggle to become free.

That struggle is never a simple one. The move from slave to free person is not an overnight transition. Our own story of the Israelites across forty years of wandering in the desert, rebellious and ungrateful at every turn, is ample testimony to that. We should remember it well when we interact with our African American neighbors, who are still struggling mightily with issues of dignity and self-worth, after a prolonged aftermath of slavery that never allowed them to become fully free. We should recall it as we behold societies in Africa, Latin America, and elsewhere, still struggling to emerge from the aftermath of imperialism and colonialism. The memory of our own slavery and liberation is a call to empathy and participation in the liberation of others. Even as we confront the ongoing and complex nightmare of the Israeli/Palestinian conflict, it does not depart from us. Is it possible that we liberated slaves could have allowed ourselves to become oppressors?

Second, we are to remember Sinai. "But take utmost care and watch yourself scrupulously, so that you do not forget the things that you saw with your own eyes and so that they do not fade from your mind as long as you live. . . . The day you stood before Y-H-W-H your God at Horeb" (Deut. 4:9–10). I take this as an imperative both for the individual and for the Community of Israel. Each of us has moments of "Sinai" in our lives, moments when we stand on the mountaintop of our existence. In such moments, our hearts fill up with gratitude and wonder. We understand that our lives are a gift, and we respond in a spontaneous combination of love and awe before whatever Source has given us so much. In retrospect, it is hard to believe how quickly we forget those moments, even run away from them, and from the level of living they might demand.

To remember Sinai is to keep faith with the greatest moments within our own lives.

But the Community of Israel is also called upon to remember Mount Sinai. It was there that we committed ourselves to becoming a holy people, a nation that exists in order to bear its message for humanity, to serve and to teach. Our very difficult history is intertwined with that message, but sometimes the legacy of suffering and the real threats to our existence make us forget who it is that we are supposed to be. The call of "Come, let us be like the nations" (Deut. 17:10 and 1 Sam. 8:20) has a long history in the Jewish people, and is especially loudly heard in our day. Being survivors of genocide is something not quickly overcome. But Israel's worst enemies score a victory each day that their din and threats cause us to forget who we are and why we are here. We are not just a tribe of the descendants of Abraham. We are "a kingdom of priests, a holy nation" (Ex. 19:6), forged at the base of that mountain. "Israel stand under oath since Mount Sinai."[6]

Following this most positive of all memories is the third, a negative one. "Remember what Amalek did to you on your journey, after you left Egypt—how, undeterred by fear of Y-H-W-H, he surprised you on the march, when you were famished and weary, and cut down all the stragglers in your rear" (Deut. 25:17–18). Yes, there is real evil in the world, and you may have real enemies. Have the courage to admit that, and the discernment to know when to press for peace and when to stand up and fight.

The designation of "evil" deserves at least a brief comment. I confine its usage to vicious and malicious human behavior, inflicting pain and death upon others, including passive indifference to suffering brought about by such conduct. Unfortunately, such behavior does exist in our world, and we are called upon to denounce it and fight against it, to confine and sometimes even to kill such evildoers, when there is no other alternative. I do not consider the Torah to command pacifism. But I draw this definition of evil carefully and narrowly. I cannot consider all my own enemies, or those of my country or my people, to be evildoers. They have different memories than I do, different narratives of the same events that have taken place between us. In such cases, I am called upon to meet the other, to listen, and to compromise. The demonization of the other, simply proclaiming him or her as "evil," is liable to do me more moral harm than it is to hurt that other.

The designation of Amalek—but only Amalek—in this way (and not Midian or Edom, for example) is to tell us both that such absolute evil does exist in the world, and to warn us that it is too easy to put all those we dislike into that camp. This is an appropriate warning for our day, one in which we have indeed seen the face of absolute evil. We should know enough not to toss about that designation too lightly.

While on the negative side of the ledger, we are also called to a fourth memory, that of the sin of the Golden Calf. "Remember, never forget, how you provoked Y-H-W-H your God to anger in the wilderness. . . . You had made yourselves a molten calf; you had been quick to stray from the path that Y-H-W-H had enjoined upon you" (Deut. 9:7, 16). Yes, it is important to remember how easy it was to slip into idolatry. Israel had just had the great privilege of receiving the word of Y-H-W-H, yet within forty days we were up and dancing before the Calf. This memory is probably the closest thing our tradition has to a notion of "original sin,"[7] meaning that each of us can always fall into its trap, and constant vigilance about it is required.

But what do we mean by "idolatry"? Calves (at least those of the bovine sort) are not venerated in our society. Here we need to look first to the Ba'al Shem Tov's reading of a line in the *shema*: "You will turn aside and worship other gods" (Deut 11:16). "As soon as you turn aside from Y-H-W-H," he says, "you are worshipping other gods."[8] A person is always worshipping something. If not Y-H-W-H, the eternal wholeness of being, it is undoubtedly an idol.

There are plenty of easy targets for designation as idolatry in our day. The worship of money and material wealth quickly come to mind. We live with a level of creature comfort that prior generations could barely have imagined, and still we long for more. The cults of eternal youth and physical beauty also leap up before us when we think of idolatry in our day. Just think of all those overdressed folks attending various award shows they broadcast on television, all of them hoping to get something that in fact does look like a little bronze idol. The deification of sports figures in our world is not far behind the idolatries of Hollywood. They too all seem to be chasing one idol or another—and lots more cash than they know how to spend—at the same time.

Among the idols of greatest concern to me is that of "success," seemingly the drug of choice in our own highly educated Jewish community. The way we punish and reward our children, keeping them in line to climb that ladder, can be frightening as an idolatrous preoccupation. This is as true, incidentally, in the observant community as it is among other Jews, reflecting a cultural insecurity that seems to cross denominational lines.

But I also think we cannot avoid talking about a degree of subtle idolatry that can exist within our own religious lives. The hasidic masters felt that it was possible to fashion an idol out of Talmudic study, if it kept one away from fully opening mind and heart to the presence of Y-H-W-H throughout the world.[9] I worry that in some Jewish circles there is a worship of the State of Israel and loyalty to its policies that becomes the supreme test, one to which God and the spiritual life are to become second. Even within our spiritual lives, we should recall the sharp critique the Zohar offers in saying that those who worshipped the Golden Calf called out, "These are your gods, O Israel," revering "these," meaning their own images of God, without leaving space for the divine mystery that soars beyond them.[10] "God," too, can become an idol.

The fifth required daily memory is "Remember what Y-H-W-H your God did to Miriam on the journey after you left Egypt" (Deut. 24:9). Moses's sister is punished with an affliction of the skin after she speaks ill of her brother's wife, possibly in an incident of racism. I take this visible sickly whitening of her skin to be a divine recompense for her wicked tongue, and a good reminder to us that "words can kill."[11] We should all take heed. As one who was privileged to share my life with a loved one who, toward the end of her days, lost most of the ability to speak, I have a heightened sense of what a precious gift language is. Coarseness of language, vulgarity, hostile speech, and verbal dishonesty all work to debase this most defining of human abilities, a gift given to us, say the hasidic masters, for the purpose of *sacred* speech, that of Torah and prayer—but also containing a hint that *all* speech, if treated well, may become a dwelling-place for God.

But this is also a good occasion to remember daily what *we* did to Miriam—and all her sisters through the ages. Moses's sister was there with him, singing and dancing to celebrate liberation at the Reed Sea—yet our liturgy recalls only "Moses and the Children of Israel" doing so. We survived forty years of wandering only because of Miriam's miraculous well of water following us wherever we went. But all we can recall her for is that moment of nastiness toward her sister-in-law. That speaks volumes about how a male-dominated tradition has stereotyped and looked down upon women. Enough! That too needs to be remembered every day, as a call to action.

The last of the six remembrances is that of the Sabbath. We are not only to celebrate it weekly, but are to remember it throughout the week—referring both to the Shabbat past and the one coming. That admonition also takes us back to Creation and forward to the great Shabbat of the redeemed future, completing a circle. But since Shabbat is the subject of a separate chapter in this collection, I will not expound upon it here.

We do need to say a word, however, about the *dangers* of memory as well. There is a degree of submission to memory that can imprison us, or impede our perception of reality. Victims of trauma, whether as children or adults, are sometimes crippled by memories that give them no rest. Even worse, these memories color other aspects of perception, sometimes causing them to see threats where they do not exist, to treat others who enter their lives as potential perpetrators of the terrible things that were done to them or that they once beheld. Recovery from such trauma can be a long and painful process, and healing is often less than complete.

There is no easy criterion for determining what is or is not a traumatic memory. Many people hold onto inner wounds that others think they might—or "should"—have gotten over long ago. Fellow survivors of the same incident or upbringing may react in entirely different ways, one leaving it by the wayside, another still acting as though traumatized by it many years later. None of us is in a position to judge how deep are the wounds felt by another. The same thing is true of groups, including both small communities and historical peoples.

For that reason, memory is a precious gift that needs to be treated with great care and judgment. When to hold on and when to let go are vital questions in our allowing ourselves to become who we want to be, people who stand in the presence of Y-H-W-H. Memory makes us human, helping to form our identity and keep us faithful to it. But it also brings us as close as we can to being divine, or realizing our oneness with the Source. God is the great Rememberer of our tradition, as we proclaim each Rosh Hashanah: "You remember the most ancient deed. . . . You recall all that is forgotten." In the eternal mind that is Y-H-W-H, past, present, and future are all one, eternally present and in harmony. We seek to partake of that eternity, in whatever small way we can. Both our memory of the past, making us live beyond the present moment, and our dreams of a yet unborn future are part of that effort. Our own act of memory, stretching our mind, pushing to reach beyond its limits, rather than narrowing and closing it, is among our greatest acts of *imitatio dei*, learning to be like God.

Judaism as a Path of Love

לזכר אשתי האהובה מרת קריינדל בת שמעון ולאה, שהלכה
לעולמה ביום ט׳ אלול תשע״ז. תנצב״ה
In memory of my beloved Kathy, departed on August 31, 2017

A MIDRASHIC SOURCE DATING FROM the early Middle Ages quotes the famous second-century sage Akiva as saying: "Had the Torah not been given, the world could have been conducted by the Song of Songs alone."[1]

What a world that might have been! Instead of the quaking, fiery mountain and the earth trembling at God's voice, we would have only "I will go into the mountain of myrrh, the hill of frankincense" (Cant. 4:2). Instead of forty years in the wilderness, we would have only "Who is she who ascends from the wilderness, leaning on her beloved?" (8:5). Instead of all the sacrifices, the food and sexual taboos of Leviticus, there would be only "Eat, O companions! Drink and become intoxicated, O lovers!" (5:1). Quite a world indeed. But from these verses we would have been able to reconstruct the entire Torah, such as would have allowed us to sustain the world. This is the full-throated message of Rabbi Akiva: there is no separation between the most precise detailing of the commandments, both ritual and moral, and the inward face of mutual divine-human love.[2] God gave us the Torah as an act of love, and we return that love by studying and fulfilling it.

Ordinarily we do not pay too much attention to attributions to famous sages appearing many centuries after their time. This would be especially true of an invocation of Rabbi Akiva, who is quoted so very frequently by these later sources. But this statement fits strikingly well with much that the earlier sources tell us of Akiva. It was he, after all, who got the Song of Songs included in the canon. In the second century, the sanctity of three books was still being debated. When it came to the Song of Songs, Akiva declared: "There can never have been any doubt about this one. All of scripture is holy, but the Song of Songs is the Holy of Holies!"[3]

Just what did he mean by that claim? Love is at the heart of the religious life. "The merciful One wants the heart."[4] In Akiva's eyes, the Torah narrative is really all about the powerful love between God and His beloved, the Community of Israel. The tales of the patriarchs, the Exodus, Sinai and the wilderness, the laws and statutes, were all a spelling out of that love. The Song of Songs was in fact first spoken at Sinai itself, the day of their mystical marriage.[5] While the public voice of God may have been heard as declaring dos and don'ts, at the very same moment He was whispering sweet nothings into His beloved's ear. Those "nothings," of course, came with a capital N.

A major avenue of Jewish spiritual reflection views the very pinnacle of the religious life as a constant repetition of the heady mixture of emotional states we felt while standing at the base of that mountain: love and awe joined together as one. As so frequently, the traditional prayer book says it best: "Unify our hearts to love and fear Your name."[6] The burning fire of that mountain is also the fire within the beloved's heart, her desire for her Lover who descends from the highest heavens to dwell in her midst. Following each utterance that came forth from the mouth of the blessed Holy One (and these utterances are nothing other than "the kisses of His mouth"), we are told that "Israel's soul passed out of them," following the Canticles verse that says, "My soul came forth as He spoke."[7] "The mountain burned into the very heart of heaven" (Deut. 4:11)—this is the fire within the human heart. The mountain quakes, but at that very moment the heart fills up with love.

To stand in God's presence is to live a life shaped by love. It requires an open heart, one that is able to receive the love of God that pours into us in each moment of our existence, and one that knows how to take in that blessing, that gift of love, and reshape it into a love for those around us, both within the human community and extending to the full fellowship of God's creatures, amid whom His presence dwells. There is no response to the love of God other than that of sharing it, acting with love toward God's creation.

Lest the reader think that these sentiments are those of a naïve religious romantic, I need to say a few words about the theological context within which they are being spoken. As a student of my revered teacher Abraham Joshua Heschel, I am a Jew whose thoughts are much inspired by the words of the early hasidic masters. Behind them stand many generations of kabbalists, especially the holy Zohar. But, like Heschel, I also live in the wake of Maimonides, and my thoughts inevitably are shaped by him as well. His apophatic or negative approach to the question of divine personhood is life saving (or faith saving) for me, permitting me to dare to think of myself still as a believer. Throughout his long discussion of divine attributes in the *Guide to the Perplexed*, Maimonides remains silent on the question of divine love. Is it possible to claim that God loves this world He has created, or the creatures within it? Yes, the act of creation attests to God's *ḥesed*, defined as "practicing beneficence toward one who has no right to claim it."[8] Y-H-W-H, the source of all existence, does good for those creatures in every moment. But is this the same as saying that He[9] *loves* them? Regarding anthropomorphism, the uncompromising views of the RaMBaM are well known. He attempts to be equally strict when it comes to anthropopathism, denying the attribution of human emotions to God. To illustrate this, however, he conveniently chooses to list some emotions that we would be happy to remove from the divine sphere: sadness, anger, jealousy, and the like.[10] These might be considered imperfections even in the human character, after all. But on the simple questions—so well known to those of us who live surrounded by a Christian culture—"Do you believe that God loves you?" and "How do you understand that love?" he remains remarkably silent.

Any reader of my book *Radical Judaism* is aware that I too operate out of a highly abstract theology, quite unlike that of Heschel, indeed more directly, in this sense, derivative from the Maimonidean approach to God. I understand God as the oneness of existence, the unitive Source that underlies and is manifest in each of the varied forms of existence that appear before us. This God is indeed "the One to whom there is no second," as the old philosophical hymn *Adon 'Olam* tells us so clearly. But I need to understand this claim against the background of twenty-first-century science, including both astrophysics and evolutionary biology, not that of the Middle Ages. Of that Maimonides would surely approve. My theology (differing here from that of Maimonides quite sharply) leans in a panentheistic direction, seeing the One as reflected within the many. Regarding that infinite which lies beyond the creatures, I prefer to keep silent, following the Tiqquney Zohar's rather Maimonidean formulation "There is none who knows You at all."[11] I am speaking of this One that was there "before" the Big Bang, if one may use temporal language here at all. It was present in every bit of gas, in every fleck of rock-in-making that spewed forth from that event, and is the underlying stuff of every star in the skies and every form of being on our own beloved and much-threatened planet. This force of existence (the One named Y-H-W-H) became the stuff of existence (energy manifest as matter), and then coalesced into the pond of chemicals that came to constitute life. It (the One, Y-H-W-H) has then existed in every life-form that has come to be in our long step-by-natural-selection-step evolutionary journey, including ourselves. The very fact that we have begun to understand some bit of this process is testimony to our being a part of this great single mind of being, slowly revealing itself to us in the process that we often prefer to call scientific discovery.[12] But it also attests to the greatness of the mystery.

That One has been present in each life-form that has existed on this planet in the last 14.5 billion years, as it has been revolving around our sun. Because it has made the journey from the very simplest forms of life, one-celled creatures beneath the sea, to the great complexity of the still-mysterious human mind, we may assume that it has an appreciation for and seems to seek out both *complexity* and *diversity*. Or, to quote an earlier version of this story, we may say: "God saw all that He had made, and behold it was very good." This sacred process, in which the One is both hidden and revealed, is driven by that inner quest, one I suggest we humans might translate into a word based on our own emotional experience as "love."

I tend to respond to the question "Do you believe that God loves you?" with a liturgical reference, based on the order of our daily prayers. Each morning and evening, our service opens with two blessings, recited in order. One is a blessing to God for the wonders of Creation: the great lights, the drama of day and night. Its central line is "God renews constantly, each day, the work of Creation." The second blessing is that of love: "With great love have You loved us, the house of Israel, giving us Your teachings." I do not believe that God does anything different in the transition between those two blessings. Y-H-W-H shines light upon the earth; the trees in the forest stretch upward to receive that sunlight, absorbing its rays into the chlorophyll they produce in order to exist. The sun stands as a metaphor for the divine light, toward which all nature stretches. That is the first blessing. In the second blessing, we acknowledge that we too stretch forth to receive that same light. We convert it into *our* chlorophyll; we call it "love." That is our stuff of life, the inner juice that allows us to be as fully human as the tree is fully tree. We then verbalize that love, share it, reflect on it, and turn it into teachings that help us to live, to pass the love on, and to become ever more human, ever more the divine image. Those teachings indeed come from God—as does the chlorophyll.

That is who we are, little engines of humanization, humming away at the translation of *ḥiyyut*, the divine stream of energy or life force, into our beloved and life-giving force of love. In gratitude for the gift of life, we give to the One that underlies all existence the only thing we really have to offer: the gift of our own humanity. We fashion God in our image, making the cosmic One into a "Thou," a loving partner. But we do this in response to a deep, innate sense of the mystery that dwells both within and around us. To say it in a way that may sound playful but is meant with complete seriousness: *We sense that God creates us in the divine image, and we are obliged to return the favor.*

I have chosen to live my spiritual life within the Jewish tradition partly because I rejoice in our tradition's ability to speak of this underlying oneness of being in *personal* terms. Theologically, that is what I mean when I thank God each morning for having made me a Jew. To see the ultimate as having a human face, a face radiant with blessing, calls me to ever-greater humanity. Yes, I fully understand that this personification is a result of projection, our human attempt to understand the mysteries of the universe in the language of human experience. But I am also open to the possibility— and this is an essential point—that the need to project a God-figure onto the cosmos is itself the result of a deep inner truth implanted within us, an instinct for meaning-making that is aware that we stand in the face of great mystery. That inner quest for meaning, existing in the space between love and mortality, is also what makes us most fully human. This humbling awareness ("Know whence you have come and where you are going"), itself a gift of God, gives birth to mythical creativity, to the poetic muse, inspiring us to create religions.[13] It also lies behind the drive for scientific investigation. The human is born to be a seeker.

Religion has insisted since most ancient times that our relationship with that One is expressed not only by intellectual quest, but by emotion. In hasidic language, *da'at*, the faculty given us in order that we might attain intimate knowledge of the One, is composed of *ahavah ve-yir'ah*, love and awe. The stretching of the mind toward the One is ever to be accompanied by the opening of the heart.

This attempt to understand what we might mean today when we speak of the Jewish language for divine love and its mutuality will require some historical background. How and when did Jews learn to speak about the love of God? We will begin with scripture, proceed with the rabbis, and then turn to the mystical tradition, where it is given its richest expression.[14] The description of our relationship with God as a loving one first occurs in Deuteronomy, the source of most of our vocabulary to describe religious emotion: *ahavah, yir'ah, devequt, ḥesheq:* love, awe, attachment to Y-H-W-H, and passion. This concluding book of the Torah is cast as a series of Moses's parting admonitions to Israel before his death. There he speaks both of God's love for His people and of our obligation to love God "with all your heart, all your soul, and all your might." This love is mostly to be expressed in acts of loyalty, following His commandments and not rebelling, as did that generation of the wilderness. But where is R. Akiva's love in the first four books of the Torah? Why are we never explicitly told that God loves Abraham, that He redeems us from Egypt because He loves us, or that He is giving us the Torah out of Love? One hasidic author suggests that the daily face-to-face contact with God known by that generation obviated the need for the articulation of love as such.[15] Only when there is a possibility of separation, after the child is weaned, we might say, does the parent need to say "I love you" and begin to ask the child: "Do you love me?"

The love that emerges from the passages in *Devarim* is that of God as loving Ruler, whose protecting love and authority over us are one and the same, just as is ideally the case in either feudal fealty relationships (the knight defends his peasants; they reward him with the work of their hands) or in the more passionate but no less loyalty-demanding relationship of parent and young child. Show your love of God by following the rules; act well and you will be rewarded with a great and genuine outpouring of God's love. The Eden of childhood offers a sheltered existence so long as you obey the rules.

The relationship, we may say, is a mutually obligating one, but hardly a love between equals. "Our Father, our King" is the great refrain of liturgy we still intone in our holy season of repentance. That element of submission has not disappeared from Judaism, and it is indeed an essential part of the religious life. Even when the prophets began to use the metaphor of spousal love, equal partnership was hardly what they had in mind. When Hosea hears God tell him to go marry a prostitute, in order to feel what God feels in His covenant with Israel, we are hardly in the realm of egalitarian marriage. Only when He tells him to take that wife back, having forgiven her sins, as God has done for us, do we begin to feel that Y-H-W-H too has become vulnerable in this relationship. His love for us is so deep as to make Him unable to let go of us, despite all our inadequacies. Allowing Himself to love us, as Heschel would have said it, means that God allows Himself to *need* us.[16]

All this inequality is transcended, however, in the moment when Akiva proclaims the Song of Songs to be the Holy of Holies. Of course he means that the Canticle is to be seen as a love poem sung between God and Israel, with the angels standing as the chorus of "maidens of Jerusalem" in the background. But the Canticle, if you read it carefully, is all about seduction and pursuit. The two of them, shepherd and shepherdess or king and maiden, run through the gardens and across the hills, filled with longing for one another. It is a remarkably egalitarian tale of love and desire, peril and delight. The love is never routinized; it is more about courtship than it is about marriage, although we do get a wedding day. But certainly there is no sense of an impending marriage contract, where the husband will "acquire" a wife. Yes, she pines for him—"On my bed at night I seek the one my soul loves; I seek him but I find him not" (3:1). But he too longs for her, so that he feels great fulfillment and rejoices when he finds her—"I have come into my garden, my sister, my bride" (5:1).[17]

While this love affair was mostly depicted as a collective one, carried on between the blessed Holy One and the Community of Israel, occasionally a verse from this scripture would be applied to an individual moment or a single life. This was the case with Rabbi Akiva himself, subject of the best-known account of a mystical journey in the rabbinic tradition. "Four entered the orchard," we are told, Akiva and three of his friends. One died, one went mad, one became a heretic. Only Akiva, the text goes on to say, "entered in peace and came out in peace. Of him the Canticle says: 'Draw me after You; let us run. The King has brought me into His chambers'" (1:4).[18]

The sense that the passion of *Shir ha-Shirim* is to be applied to the individual's relationship to God, as it is to that of the people, grew over the generations (Christian interpretation of the song had it already in third-century Origen),[19] perhaps with this image of Rabbi Akiva playing a role in it. Listen to the RaMBaM, despite his refusal to depict God as loving humans, speak of the worshipper's love of God: "What is the proper love? One should love Y-H-W-H greatly and most powerfully. One's soul should be bound up in the love of Y-H-W-H, constantly engaged (obsessed?) with it. It should be as though one is lovesick, the mind never free from the love of that particular woman . . . and the entire Song of Songs is a parable of this."[20]

Maimonides thus understands quite well what is at stake in the project of *Midrash Shir ha-Shirim*. It is the passionate love of the throbbing heart, with all its vulnerability, that he is talking about, when it comes to human love of God. But the love in the Song of Songs is *mutual* in that regard, surely more than that "acting with beneficence" that he finally allows for at the *Guide's* conclusion. Perhaps in self-conscious defiance of the RaMBaM, in the kabbalistic tradition the sense that Creation is an act of divine love is portrayed quite graphically. "Everything depends on love," to express it in the language of the Zohar. Listen to the Zohar reflect upon the divine name as a description of the inner life of God:

> All is called love and all exists because of love, as Scripture says: "Mighty waters cannot quench love" (Cant. 8:5). Everything stands upon love, because such is the holy name. We have established that the upper tip of the *yod* is never separated from it because it dwells upon it in love. . . . Regarding *heh*, we know that *yod* is never separated from it; they are in constant love and are inseparable. Thus *Yod Heh*. Of this we have learned: "A river *flows* from Eden" (Gen. 2:10) [in the present tense]. It is constantly flowing; they cleave to one another in love. *Vav* is always the bridegroom of the bride. *Yod* with *heh*, *heh* with *vav*, *vav* with *heh*. That is why all is called love. And one who loves the King becomes bound up into that love. Hence: "You shall love *with* Y-H-W-H your God" (Deut. 6:5).[21]

The divine realm is depicted as containing both male and female elements, and it is out of their union, an act of love, that the lower worlds are born and constantly sustained. While the Zohar is most interested in the birth of human souls, and especially the souls of Israel, as resulting from the *zivvuga qadisha*, it is quite clear that the same applies to all that exists in the kabbalistic version of the "sub-lunar" world, everything beneath the *shekhinah*.

But the presence of gender, love, and union does not begin with *shekhinah*. The Zohar's boldest mythic assertion is that the blessed Holy One

Himself is the product of an act of love. That aspect of God is conceived in the womb of *binah*, the cosmic Mother within divinity, and is born—and constantly reborn—of the union of *ḥokhmah* and *binah*, "two inseparable companions." They are the *yod* and *heh* of this passage, with the tip of the *yod* pointing to an ineffable mystery that transcends even them. The God who is the object of our worship (= *vav*, "the blessed Holy One") is one who is Himself born of love, a love that transcends even Him. He is forever radiating the blessing of that parental love, however abstract, into His beloved Bride, *shekhinah*, and thence into all the worlds below.[22] A notion of love that is at once highly abstract and boldly concrete and erotic lies at the very heart of Kabbalah. Even the mysterious forces that lie within the deepest inner mind of the universe are linked by something that can be called "love."

God's love for the world, and specifically for humanity, for Israel, and for the righteous, is depicted through metaphors of both of the great and passionate loves known to most humans, the parent/child and the erotic/spousal relationships. The image of God as loving parent of His creatures and the calling out to God in the language of "Father!," while found only occasionally in the TaNaKh, is a mainstay of rabbinic teaching, where God is regularly *Avinu Malkenu*, "our Father, our King," or *Avinu sheba-Shamayim*, "our heavenly Father." The exile of Israel is frequently depicted as the tragedy of a father who has, in a moment of justified anger, cast his beloved children out of his palace and longs for their return as passionately as they do, ever seeking their redemption. Repentance is then depicted as the duty of a loving son (or daughter, as in the famous tale by Rabbi Naḥman) to return, bringing about his own redemption, but also bringing consolation to the devastated and weeping Father.

In the Zohar, where Israel has a mother, the *shekhinah*, as well as a father, the picture becomes more complicated.[23] Among the most touching of the varied pictures of parental love to be found there derives from the midrashic reading of "Due to your sins, your mother was exiled" (Is. 50:1). The Zohar depicts Israel as the child of a mother whose husband has divorced her because of her children's waywardness.[24] "It is our fault," as the children of a divorced couple so often and so sadly feel. This strand of Zohar teaching says that we perform the *mitsvot* in order to effect their reconciliation. We so adorn Her with beauty that Father will no longer be able to resist, and will bring both Her and us back into His bosom. We study the secret Torah of their love and devotedly perform the *mitsvot* that serve as Her adornments, ever hoping to rekindle the flame of their marriage. We endlessly declare and praise Her beauty. How could Father

possibly resist taking her back? "Renew our days as of old!" (Lam. 5:21)—
when we were all a happy family.[25]

It is a form of this parental love that takes the place of primacy in
hasidic discussions of love, found widely throughout the sources but nowhere more than in the teachings of R. Dov Baer, the Maggid of Mezritch.[26] It may be shyness about discussing the erotic that turns the love
attention of these pietists toward the parental. But it may also be a certain
lack of experience in the erotic love of man and woman. In a society like
that of premodern east European Jewry, where arranged marriages took
place in the years immediately following puberty, child bearing then beginning immediately afterward, there was little time to develop feelings of
such passion, and little if any legitimacy is given to them. In fact, they are
seen mostly as the workings of the "evil urge." But love between parent
and child suffers no such societal strictures, and much of the force of *eros*
comes to be channeled in that direction. Thus the familiar parables of the
father teaching his child to walk, always stepping backward so that the
child will increase his skill, *tsimtsum* described as the father simplifying
his profound thoughts so that the child will be able to access them, and
many more.

The spousal love of God and Israel, such a major theme in the Midrash (developed especially in *Shemot* and *Shir ha-Shirim Rabbah*), is largely
replaced in the kabbalistic sources by the love of male and female elements
within God. The blessed Holy One and *shekhinah*, called *kenesset yisra'el* in
the Zohar, are not God and the Jewish people, but "male" and "female" or
"giver" and "receiver" sides of the same divine self. It is this bold change
in the meaning of *kenesset yisra'el* that allows the kabbalists to claim the
ancient midrashic love-language as their own. But this surely does not
mean that God loves Israel, or the created world as a whole, any less. I
have suggested elsewhere that the interposing of a feminine hypostasis between God and the male community of kabbalistic devotees allowed for a
fuller and less awkward expression of erotic passion, avoiding the obvious
homoerotic implication of such intense love.[27] Both God and the earthly
Community of Israel are passionate lovers of the same bride, a feeling that
achieves its highest expression in the refrain to Alkabetz's famous poem
Lekha Dodi li-qr'at kallah, where we call upon God by the rarely used term
dod, or Lover, evoking the Song of Songs, inviting Him to join us as we
together go forth to meet our shared bride.[28]

This sharing of love for the bride is quite explicit in the Zohar, long
before *Lekha Dodi* was composed:

"From each person (kol ish) you shall take my offering." Who is *kol ish?* This refers to *tsaddiq,* who is called *kol.*[29] . . . Master of the house, whose passion is toward the Mistress, like a husband who loves his wife always. And even though they are never separated in this love . . . from Him are you to *take My offering.* In the way of the world, if someone seeks to take a man's wife from him, the husband is severe and does not let her go. But the blessed Holy One is not that way. This One (*zot*) is the offering. She is *shekhinah.* Even though all Her love is toward Him and His toward Her, from Him are you to take Her, causing Her to dwell among you, from that high place where there dwells the love of Man and Wife, from there *shall you take My offering.* Blessed is the lot of Israel![30]

This mutuality of divine-human love is also carried forth in yet another metaphor that is neither parental nor spousal, and therefore more surprising in the Jewish context. I refer to a striking midrashic reading of "Love your neighbor as yourself" (Lev. 19:17), in which God is seen as the *re'a,* the neighbor, friend, or lover (depending on the context) who loves you and therefore seeks your love in return. This reading begins with a midrashic interpretation of Proverbs 27:10: "Do not abandon your friend (*re'a*) or the friend of your father."[31] Israel are then described as the "friends and brothers" of God, as in "for the sake of my brothers and friends" (Ps. 122:8), making God our *re'a* as well, the one to whom we owe our love.

One does not usually expect to find God as a brother in Jewish sources. If anything, this sounds more like the language of evangelical Christianity than that of mystical Judaism. God becomes human in Christianity; it is obvious to depict Jesus as an elder brother. As the new Adam, he is the first among humans. In Judaism, where God's embodiment is chiefly in Torah, the "brother" or "friend" metaphor does not come as easily. That is why it is particularly exciting to find it among the kabbalists, including both the Zohar and in the remarkable treatise on love by Elijah De Vidas, the disciple of Rabbi Moses Cordovero, a part of his *Reshit Hokhmah,* one of the great treasures of kabbalistic *mussar* literature.

It is well known that two brothers ordinarily love one another. In times of trouble, each of them will make every effort to save the other, even risking his life for him. The blessed Holy One is in that sense a Brother to us . . . just as brothers love one another

. . . as Scripture says: "Two are better than one" (Eccles. 4:9). And between two friends, when one feels that the other loves him with heart and soul, he will love him in the same way, revealing to him the secrets of his heart.[32] Any good that he can do for him, he will . . . and all these categories exist in the blessed Holy One, who is Partner to a person from his mother's womb until the day of his death, helping him.[33]

And in another place:

> A person's love for a friend is through the soul, because the soul's desire is for love. Even though in body we are distinct and separate from one another, the souls of this one and that one are of the spirit. In spirit there is no such separation; they are joined in absolute oneness. As one person's soul awakens its desire to love his companion, the soul of the companion will be aroused to love him as well. Those two souls are then one, as the verse says of David and Jonathan: "The soul of Jonathan was bound to that of David; Jonathan loved him as his own self." David's love for Jonathan conceived his love for him, as it says "They kissed one another and wept . . . until David wept exceedingly" (1 Sam. 20:41).[34]

He brings the same scripture again when describing "Love that does not depend upon any [extraneous] matter": "Kisses come only from love, tears from attachment [*devequt*]. 'Until David was overcome' refers to the exile of *shekhinah*. David and Jonathan point to the secret of the lovers above. The enlightened will understand."[35]

De Vidas is being circumspect in this final comment, but such "enlightenment" should not be too difficult for us to attain. "David" is a perhaps surprising but regular cipher for the (usually feminine) *shekhinah*. It is clear that here Jonathan is *tsaddik* or *yesod*, Her divine Lover. Their shared maleness seems unimportant here, as they are translated into the symbolic realm amid this utterly unconditional love. They could be Boaz and Ruth or Jacob and Rachel, as they are elsewhere. Here they happen to be Jonathan and David. Still, the claim that this pair refers to "the secret of the lovers above" is most striking, and we cannot avoid its complete acceptance of love (asexual, of course) between two men. Perhaps what we see here is a reflection of the intense brotherly love that existed in the Safed fraternity of kabbalists, as it had in the Zohar's literary circle (imaginary or real) as well.[36]

The word *love* in everyday human speech bears a wide range of meanings. We sign letters—or today emails (if we bother signing them)—with "love," whether the correspondence is between spouses or lovers, parents and children, siblings, or dear friends. The same word, but not exactly the same love. But when we say the phrase "I love you"—in any of these contexts—we are getting more serious about the matter. Those words imply real openheartedness, one that carries with it a certain degree of need and vulnerability. We take a risk when we say "I love you" to another human being, because in doing so we are signaling that we hope for, even admit that we need, their love in return. God's *ahavti etkhem* ("I love you"— Mal. 1:2) also implies such a risk. When God places his love, borne by the creating breath of his own mouth[37] into humanity, He seeks our love in return. When He chooses Israel as His own, blessing them with a unique covenant of His love, He expects us to love Him as well. His need for that love is witnessed by His deep hurt when Israel's love is not forthcoming. Rabbinic sources hint by their language in a few places that God's need for humans reflects His own need for salvation.[38] The kabbalists erected huge mountains upon these words. As God's love for us allows us to love, saving us from a life of emptiness,[39] so does our love for God save Him from destroying His world in acts of rage and futility.

What are the means for expression of this divine-human love? How do we both give and receive this love? Through verbal expression, the sacred words of both *Torah u-tefillah*, one might say: study and prayer, as well as through deeds, both the ritual and interpersonal *mitsvot*. The mutual divine-human self-expression in language is central to the distinctively verbal Jewish character of this relationship. If we permit ourselves to jump for a moment from Kabbalah to Hasidism, we see this in the very powerful way in which the *Sefat Emet* (based on medieval sources) reads Deuteronomy 26:17–18 as saying that both God and Israel are *verbalized*, in the literal sense of *transformed into speech* in their encounter with one another.[40]

Indeed, we might venture a guess that the RaMBaM avoids mention of God's love because he was in something of a bind on this question. To say that "love" was another homonym when applied to God would give him nothing more than a pure Neoplatonic love, a divine love that is unlike anything we humans might mean by that term when applied to us bodily creatures. This would offer only a rather weak and unspecific love when compared to the passionate deity of the biblical and rabbinic tradition. As we have seen, the love he wanted to call forth in the other direction, human love for God, was indeed quite passionate. But he also understands that to allow God to truly love, in the fullness demanded by the human analogy, would involve him in what he considered a far more dangerous theological enterprise: admitting the possibility of divine vulnerability or need. If love means taking the risk of admitting that "I need you," that was something the RaMBaM could not permit his God to do.[41]

There is indeed a danger in admitting divine need, which is the basis for the theurgical approach that characterizes the religion of Kabbalah. Theurgy shares a border with magic. If God is in need of our love, might we withhold that love from Him in order to gain what we will? Then we are no longer giving unconditional love, nor can we expect the same. This is particularly true when theurgy becomes automatic or technical, depending upon the correct pronunciation or writing of the proper divine names, and is cut off from its devotional roots, of worship for God's sake alone. But the admission of divine need also has a great advantage: it makes for a more equal divine-human relationship. To admit that God needs us, as Heschel did, is to say that our lives and deeds are ultimately important.[42] We become real partners in the work of redemption, a task that involves the redeeming of God as well as that of humanity and the world. Living as we do today, in a world that so desperately needs human action to save it from destruction, I believe that we should take the risk of accepting God's need for us as a challenge to act.

The Ba'al Shem Tov, following the pietistic teachings of prior ages, takes an additional step regarding the love of God. He taught that there exists only one single love in the world—that is, the love of God for all His creatures. That love flows through all existence and penetrates every creature. It is manifest in the *ḥiyyut* within each of us, the power that both animates us, driving us forward, and plants within us the desire to return to God. Ultimately this means that God's love for us and ours for God cannot fully be distinguished. But that force enters into the physical world in a fallen or broken state. We necessarily become alienated from our single Source in the course of our individuation, in becoming ego-selves.[43] The love that energizes us thus may come forth in broken, hidden, sometimes even painfully distorted ways. Many of us spend our lives in flight from God's love, because we fear it will bring up too much pain. That love is also the source of desire, even lust, that which causes both animals and humans to mate and propagate their species. Even forbidden desires, he insisted, are part of that same stream of divine blessing.[44] They are not to be acted upon, he taught (this was, after all, the eighteenth century!), but their energies should be recognized for what they are, transformed and turned back into an engine to charge our love of God.

The Ba'al Shem Tov had much in common with another great Jewish teacher, only a century and a half later, and in a place not far removed from his. I refer to Sigmund Freud, who also believed that all of *eros* is a single continuum, originating in libidinal energy and then shaped by the civilizing forces of repression and sublimation into love's various expressions as we know them. The ultimate in sublimation, he would have said, might be the love of God, that love that seems most distant from its libidinal origins. For Freud, of course, *eros* here has been refined into the ultimate absurdity, the love of an illusion. Both Freud and the Ba'al Shem Tov, in other words, are looking at love as the same single spectrum; one is viewing it from below, the other from above.

Having given you some idea of what I mean by the love of God in Jewish sources, I now have to turn to our own era and ask how this approach to religious life might work in our time. How can a person with a theology as abstract as my own speak of the love of God? Attracted as I am by the kabbalists' passion, what do I do with my inner RaMBaM? This question stands alongside two others that cannot be ignored. How do we dare to speak of the love of God as Jews living after the Holocaust, the greatest test of faith that has befallen us since the destruction of the Temple, a test from which the body politic of world Jewry (the two-thirds of us who were not among the slaughtered) is just beginning to recover? And how do we live in that love in an age after the great foundations of our faith have been shaken to their root, both by scientific approaches to the origin of existence and by critical approaches to the origin of religion, including the history of our own texts and tradition?

Please notice the way I formulate these questions. "How?" is the question. "How do we dare to speak . . . ?" and "How do we live in that love . . . ?" "Dare" and "live" we must! I do not doubt for a minute that God's love exists, any more than I doubt that the world exists. So too do I not doubt that our proper response to that love is to love God in return, expressing that love in a love for all of God's creatures. But nevertheless, something has indeed changed.

The hasidic teachings to which I am so attracted are filled with the ideal of serving God only for the sake of *shekhinah*, only to restore unity. There are constant warnings in this literature not to seek reward, either in this world or the next. But at the tail end of such teachings, they almost always offer a postscript. If you do this with full *kavvanah*, not thinking of yourself at all, you too will be blessed, by the way. That blessing may even take classical material forms, including offspring, health and longevity, and prosperity, let alone the untold blessings of the afterlife. While quite aware which is the higher value, they cannot hold back from offering an additional prize. The same is true on the negative side. Although the kabbalists refer to true "fear of heaven" as the awe of standing before Mount Sinai and openness to infinity, the child's fear of God as a judging and potentially punishing parent lurks in the background as a spur toward observance of the *mitsvot*. Particularly because the hasidic masters were seeking to create a popular movement, they felt that they had to buttress their spiritualized offerings with these promises, and occasionally even threats, as well.

For me, as a Jew of the post-Holocaust era, all that is ended. The assurance of reward undercuts the teaching rather than reinforcing it. The meaninglessness of such promises has been thrown in our faces 6 million times. I expect no reward for loving God or for observing the *mitsvot* other than a purely spiritual one. I live in the face of a historical reality that tells me to accept fully that "there is no reward for *mitsvot* in this world."[45] And of another world I simply know nothing.[46] This means, in effect, that all we religious faithful have left is love, our love of God, of our religious traditions, and hopefully of one another. All the other motivations for religious behavior—mainly fear of divine wrath or hope of reward—have simply melted away.

This possibility of understanding the *sho'ah* as a moment that leads to the purification of faith, rather than to its destruction, is essential to my own religious life. We Jews, descendants of both Abraham and Isaac, are those strong vessels that the potter chooses to test in the heat of fire, in that well-known midrash on the *'akedah*.[47] We are left with no reason to love God and Torah beyond the inner drive of love itself. As a Holocaust survivor from Frankfurt, a onetime student in Franz Rosenzweig's *Lehrhaus*, once said to me: "We are called upon to be God's witnesses in the world. How strong would our witness be if we had received only good from His hands?" No, we do not believe *because* it is absurd, as the church father Tertullian claimed, and as reenters Western religious thought via Kierkegaard. We value reason and would prefer a faith without absurdity. But that choice has not been given to us. Our ongoing life of faith is a *defiance* of absurdity. It allows, even forces, us to say, "One thing I ask of Y-H-W-H . . . to behold the face of Y-H-W-H and to dwell in His house" (Ps. 27:4), and not to be secretly counting on the postscript. Of course, the spiritual reward remains very great, and to call myself in that sense a person who serves without thought of reward would be outrageous *hutzpah*; I am deeply rewarded every day.

When Heschel was asked, as he was frequently when lecturing in the Jewish community in the early postwar years, "Where was God during the Holocaust?" his standard reply was: "That is the wrong question. 'Where was man?' is what we have to ask." Human deeds are human responsibility. This is an important answer, but a partial one. Because I am a Jew living after the Holocaust, I am no longer able to say that I believe that historical events, whether collective or individual, happen because of divine will and intent. I have no answers. Mystery, *tsimtsum*, and the hiding of God's face are all active parts of my religious vocabulary.

But to say that events are not brought about by the willful action of a controlling God does not release me from seeking the face of God in those same events. If I believe that *shekhinah* is everywhere, then all that takes place in the world takes place within God, within that trans-temporal One that embraces all. "There is no place devoid of Him" is my most essential theological claim. Yes, the face of God may be a tortured one, that of "I am with him in distress" (Ps. 91:15). It may be in the surviving islands of true humanity, the divine image, and the bits of kindness people did for one another in the most unimaginably awful of circumstances, or in faith itself, in the face of absurdity and utter debasement of the *tselem Elohim*, that God dwells. That is enough for me. Or it may simply be the silently weeping face of God that one may find there. But divinity is never completely absent. God's love can be found, in the words of poet Aaron Zeitlin, the son of our teacher Hillel:

Afile nokh ale tfiles,
Afile nokh ale afiles.

Even after all the prayers;
even after all the "evens."

The Zoharic image of the love between God and the human soul as that of brothers and friends, especially as illustrated by David and Jonathan, presses me toward understanding our love of God as a brotherhood with all of God's creations. God loves us as God loves every one of them, both people and trees, as I have said. We return that love with an all-embracing openheartedness that demands utter vulnerability. This is a Jewish version of the sort of love of God embodied throughout Creation that is found in Saint Francis, in Rumi, in Tagore, Whitman, and other great spokesmen of the divine-human spirit. Hear it in the words of Rabbi Menahem

Mendel of Vitebsk, disciple of the Maggid and founder of the hasidic community in *erets yisra'el*, speaking of the love of God:

> In this love you are bound, as a matter of course, to all who come into this world, to all other humans, who are just like you. Since such love is a blessing that flows from above, you are absolutely aware that you have not achieved it on your own. You could not have done this at all. Rather the blessed Holy One has given it to you freely. Had God given this gift to another, your fellow person, she or he would be just as enflamed [with love] for His great name as you are. That being the case, in what way are you better than your fellow?
>
> . . . So *of course* you will love all of Israel, even the wicked among them, because you truly understand and are aware of how close they are to you. You belong to them. You are just another person; you have nothing over them, other than that which has taken you by storm from the heavens.
>
> Therefore, when you rise up in your love of God, they, by the thousands, all rise up with you. . . . You and they constitute a single soul. By whatever rod you can measure, you are tied to those thousands, even tens of thousands, of people. When you rise up, they rise with you.[48]

If the Creator of all is also the Friend who is there at my side at all times, I can only do the same for all those others that He has created in the same single ongoing act of love.

This mystical unitive faith lives in a complicated tension with the notion of love. Love is required to open our heart to the reality that we call God. Along with its partner *yir'ah*, it is the basis of our spiritual life as Jews. Unlike some Buddhists, and perhaps certain old-school HaBaDniks as well, I do not seek to transcend emotion in order to seek the one in an act of detached contemplation, but rather to open myself through the gateway of religious emotion. But love, in our human experience, requires a subject, an other whom we love. This is surely the whole focus in religious existentialism, indeed, in much of Western mysticism, as well as in the various forms of bhakti yoga. But how do we love if God is not an "other"? In a world where there is only one, and where we seek to enter that one, is there a place for love? Note again the words of De Vidas: "Even though in body we are distinct and separate from one another, the souls of this one and that one are of the spirit. In spirit there is no such separation; they are joined in absolute oneness." This is the deeper love of which I speak when I talk about the love of God, one that recognizes contiguity rather than separation. It is a love that carries us back into the embrace of those "two inseparable companions" who are nothing other than the inner mind of God.

Once again, R. Menaḥem Mendel of Vitebsk, in a passage immediately preceding the one just quoted:

> The most essential root of all is [to understand that] you as a person on your own could not perform a single *mitsvah* or good deed, those things that attach you to the ways of Y-H-W-H. It is the Creator who lights the fires of love and awe in His presence. . . .
>
> You do not have the power within your mouth to speak. You do so only by the word of Y-H-W-H, as in "O Lord, open my lips, that my mouth might flow with Your praise" (Ps. 51:17). Both your love and your awe come from God! Who is the one who loves, if not the living God, flowing through your soul? And whom does He love, if not God? And what is that love? It is hewn out of the flowing essence of divinity. It joins itself and becomes one with the lower world, reducing itself into that microcosm called the human being. Wherever you stand, you are standing within blessed Y-H-W-H, since He is the locus of the world, surrounding and filling all the worlds at once.
>
> When that quality of love attacks you, you don't know what is happening. "If you gave all your worldly goods for it, they would shame you" (Cant. 8:7). All is naught in the face of it, because "It comes from Y-H-W-H" (Ps. 118:24). The more you become enraptured, [the more] you will grasp in your heart the truth that this is not your own doing. What have you done? What could you possibly do, given the great coarseness of both your body and mind? This is the spirit of Y-H-W-H speaking within you, His word upon your tongue. This love is a brand plucked from the divine fire. [As you realize this], you will become ever more enflamed, the voice growing louder, without ceasing. The written page could not contain, nor could oceans of ink express, the great openness of heart in that true love.[49]

Let me again transfer this powerful description of love back into the language of commentary on our liturgy, the spiritual setting within which much of my religious life takes place. The Zohar, and the hasidic Tanya in its wake,[50] designates the opening verse of the *shema'* as depicting "the upper unity," the absolute oneness of all being in Y-H-W-H, existing ever since "Creation" exactly as it had before. Nothing has changed. That which we call "Creation" is the donning of an outer garb, a world of appearances that does not affect the single core of Being. The whispered second line, "Blessed is His glorious kingdom forever," added to the biblical text, represents the "lower unity," the ongoing oneness of Y-H-W-H as it is manifest within the endless procession of created forms, the one immanent within the many.

There is only One. That is the ultimate truth of all the mystics. But how do we mere mortals, living in this broken world in which each of us so struggles to assert his or her own unique identity, grab hold of that truth? If there is only one, how much am I called upon to let go of that ego-self I have so assiduously cultivated? Will my very mental stability not be called into question if I do? Do I not risk the fate of R. Akiva's friend Ben Zoma, who "looked and suffered damage"?

But here is why the *shema'* is preceded by this blessing on love. Love is the great gift given to us by our Creator (or by human nature, if you insist) allowing us to reach beyond ourselves. Love allows us to feel a sense of oneness with the other, to go beyond our ego's limits, to stretch toward unity with another, hence potentially with all others, and with the great "Other." Through the mirror of love, we are given a glimpse into the oneness of being, should we choose to open our hearts to it. It is through the pathways of "Great Love" and "Love Eternal," in the language of our daily prayer book, that we come to open our hearts to the oneness of Being.

Immediately following the cry of "Hear O Israel!" we proceed with the next line in the biblical text: "You shall love Y-H-W-H your God with all your heart, all your soul, and all your might." Just as love has led us to the possibility of seeing and calling out God's oneness, so does that moment of being in the one call forth a response within us. We return from oneness with a commandment to respond in love, to turn the mystical insight back into the this-worldly language of loving the other. Our love of God is to be demonstrated by the love we share for His creatures, both within and beyond the human sphere. The great proclamation of God's oneness, the line for which martyrs ever since Akiva himself gave their lives, is thus sandwiched between two declarations of love.[51] It is our realization of God's love that allows us to reach that moment, and it is with our love for God and for God's creatures that we are to come forth from it. It is our ability to live with that love, allowing it to sustain us even in moments of doubt and unfaithfulness (that is the subject of the second passage of the *shema'*, as I understand it), that leads us to the grand conclusion of the *shema'*, where we hear the divine voice call out to us in the first person, "I am Y-H-W-H your God." That is what we have been listening for, since the first word.

Of course, much of the discussion of love in our sources is built around the love of the blessed Holy One and the Community of Israel, whether earthly or divinized. We cannot conclude a discussion of God's love in Judaism without confronting that question of exclusiveness. It is true that few Jewish sources say that God loves *only* the Jews. The sense of God's love for all His creatures, including non-Jewish humans, remains strong through most of our tradition, and not only for apologetic reasons. Nevertheless, we have to notice that all the great expressions of intimacy and openheartedness, from God toward humans as well as in reverse, are offered in an exclusively Judeocentric context. Even the beautifully universal passage I have just quoted from the Vitebsker bounces back and forth between "person" and "Jew."

The fact that other traditions also make exclusive claims does not suffice to justify ours, especially because our way of loving God is linked to belonging to an ethnic community. When Paul and the church broke this link, we remained loyal to Jewish peoplehood in its original covenantal sense. Whereas classical Christianity came to be marred by the sense that God loves only *the Christian faithful*, we are stuck with a God who seems to love only *our people*, something potentially veering even closer to a sort of spiritual tribalism. I fear we have to admit that there are members of our tribe for whom that leans over into a real racism, or at least an inability to fully appreciate the image of God in the non-Jewish other.

I understand the vital role that this unique claim on God's love had in the preservation of Jewry throughout long ages of oppression, especially since that oppression took place at the hands of members of two faiths that saw themselves as superior and superseding religions to Judaism. Our claim that God continues to choose us and love us, despite what must have seemed like mountains of historical "evidence" to the contrary, embodied a stubborn courage that needs to be understood and respected. Even in the modern world, where oppression gave way to assimilationist pressures for Jews living in mostly Christian surroundings, the need for such assertion is understandable, even as it became harder to defend.

Jewish thinkers of the early twentieth century already tried to deal with this problem. Rosenzweig insisted on widening the triangle of God,

Torah, and Israel to include all of humanity. Buber was also a universalist in expanding the message of Hasidism, sometimes calling forth objections that he had overly denatured it. Their contemporary, Hillel Zeitlin, even though writing in Hebrew and Yiddish, read by Jews only, also called for a new and more universalized Hasidism as early as the 1920s. Abraham Joshua Heschel offered a universalist spirituality in distinctively Jewish garb. The uniqueness of Judaism, for all these thinkers, lay in the beauty and moral richness of the inner life it contained, not in a sense that God had chosen this people above all others as an object of His love.

But all these thinkers lived and wrote in an era when the Jewish people still had the moral luxury of relentless victimhood. Today we live in an era when the world is rife with religiously inspired violence on a horrific scale. We also live in a time when Jews have reentered the realm of political history, having responsibility for the legal and moral climate of a real state, one that has a non-Jewish minority of some 20 percent and also stands in great need of achieving positive and respectful relations with its (mostly Muslim) neighbors. In the minds of not a few observers, Jews are seen as victimizers of others, rather than victims of circumstance, as we prefer to see ourselves. The need to follow these thinkers' lead and universalize our message about God's love and care for every human life—indeed, for every creature on our much-threatened planet—takes on a new urgency. Jewish statehood and the role taken by diaspora Jews as free citizens in multiethnic democracies have brought the issue of exclusivism back to the fore. To see God's love as focused on us alone is too dangerous. And it is wrong, both morally and theologically.

It helps me to take a long-range view of this question, understanding it as an internal Jewish debate that has been going on throughout our history, at least since Second Temple times. I place before you two psalms, both composed in that period. I see their authors sitting across from one another, somewhere in that Temple courtyard. One psalmist is the author of our Psalm 136, called *hallel ha-gadol* in our tradition. It is an antiphonal poem, the congregation calling out, "For His compassion endures forever!" after each strophe. Following several lines around Creation, the author turns to the history of Israel as the locus of divine compassion. Here (notice, by the way, no mention of either Sinai or Torah) he depicts quite a merciless deity when it comes to the fate of others. He drowns Pharaoh and his hosts in the Reed Sea, strikes down the kings who rule east of the Jordan, giving their land to Israel, His servant. There is no indication that God gives a whit for the poor draftee in the Egyptian army or the frightened subjects of Og and Sihon before the conquering Israelite forces. This God is strictly "on our side." Perhaps an editor felt this and added "He gives food to all flesh" at the very end, in an attempt to soften the harshness.

Across the table from this psalmist sits another, the author of Psalm 145, which we know as *Ashrei* (without the two introductory lines, added later from elsewhere in the psalter). Notice first that there is no specific Israelite reference in the entire psalm: no Zion or Jerusalem, no patriarchs or Exodus, and so on. But notice also, beginning with the ninth verse, how frequently the word *kol* appears in the text. "Y-H-W-H is good to *all*; His compassion is over *all* His works"; "*All* Your works praise you"; "Your kingdom is one of *all* eternity"; "Y-H-W-H sustains *all* the falling, uplifting *all* who are bent over." I hear in him an outrage at the fellow across the table. "How dare you limit God's compassion to Jews alone! God loves *all* His creatures!" His outcry reaches a crescendo as he thunders on: "You open Your hand and satisfy *all the living* with desire": "Y-H-W-H is near to *all* who call upon Him, to *all* who call to Him in truth," ending with "And may *all flesh* bless His holy name." The emphasis couldn't be clearer.

The Psalm 136 forces came to dominate in Jerusalem at the very end. Perhaps this offers another understanding of the *sin'at ḥinam*, baseless hatred, that led to the destruction. Under their leadership, the Second Temple did not end very well for us. Not only was Jerusalem destroyed, but the universalist strain within our tradition—the voice of Psalm 145— was carried off to Rome and became Christianity. We were left with the narrower vision, which then came to serve as our protective shell for the next two millennia.

It might make sense for us this time to try our hand at *ahavat ḥinam*, love even toward those who seem not to have earned or "deserve" it. There are no guarantees in history, but at least we'll be on God's side, doing for others what God has done for us—all of us—recipients of divine love, far beyond what we could even begin to merit.

Year

ON THE JEWISH CALENDAR

Seasons

A REFLECTION ON THE JEWISH YEAR

T WAS ONLY AFTER many years of living by the rhythms of the Jewish
calendar that I began to think about its essential structure. This came
about partly because I was teaching the calendar to would-be rabbis
who were themselves relative newcomers to it, something that had
never been the case for me. Although I was raised in a secular and assimilationist home, my maternal grandparents' old-world *yiddishkeyt* was very
much alive for me. On the Sunday before Pesaḥ, all the grandchildren
would gather to carry *peysekhdike* dishes down from the attic. Sometime
in June, Grandma would be making *teyglekh*, twists of dough in honey,
so they would be tooth-cracking hard by Rosh Hashanah. On Hoshana
Rabbah, she would announce, "I know I'm supposed to make *kreplekh* today, just like on Erev Yom Kippur," even though she never did. Above all,
yizkor days were always noted, and one was careful to get to *shul* early, not
like all those who "just flew in and out" for the memorial prayers. These
household and *shul* memories were reinforced by early Jewish education,
adding such things as Purim carnivals and Ḥanukkah candles to the mix.
So my sense of the Jewish calendar was all quite natural and unreflective.

But when I began teaching it, I came to notice that the year was
marked by two parallel sacred seasons, one in fall and the other in spring.
The spring season is famously fifty-one days long; the fall cycle, counting
from the first of Elul, the day we start blowing the *shofar*, is fifty-three. To

say it briefly, one celebrates the national liberation from Egypt; the other, the personal liberation from sin. Each is marked by a great event, in one case opening the season (Pesaḥ), and in the other occurring in the middle (Yom Kippur). These are each followed by a period of wandering in the wilderness, and then conclude with a great celebration of Torah, one for receiving it and the other for the renewal of its cycle. It did not escape my notice that the Christian calendar, with its two sacred seasons of Lent and Advent, each anticipating the great event, is very much in the same mold, and the two traditions probably influenced one another in this regard.

At first glance, as presented above, the spring season is focused on the Jewish people and its sacred history. Israel, as a people, was liberated from Egypt, crossed the Reed Sea, wandered in the wilderness, and received the Torah at Mount Sinai. The fall season is mostly not historical. Although Rosh Hashanah celebrates Creation (actually commemorating the creation of humans on the sixth day), it is mostly about personal rebirth and renewal. Yom Kippur, as we shall see, is given historical context by the rabbis, but that is hardly its primary meaning. Sukkot, though partially historicized in a single biblical verse (Lev. 23:43), remains mostly a harvest festival, turned into a time of simple rejoicing after the wiping away of sin.

But neither of these characterizations remains entirely true, especially if one reads the calendar through a hasidic lens. "Egypt" is a state of mind. It is awareness of God (*da'at*) or the possibility of sacred speech (*dibbur*) that is essentially in exile.[1] Each person has his or her own *mitsrayim*, "Egypt" reread as "narrowness" or "constraints," from the grip of which we seek liberation. It is each individual, dwelling amid the people, who stands again at Sinai on Shavuʻot, studying Torah through the night in preparation for receiving it anew at dawn. So too are the people present on the Days of Awe, which is the great communal gathering time for Jews everywhere. On Yom Kippur, we famously recite our sins in the plural, confessing as a community, not just as individuals. The ancestral guests who visit on Sukkot also represent the collective memory of Israel, binding together the array of families, each in its own *sukkah*.

Each of these two sacred seasons is intended to serve as a font of energy, a semiannual opportunity to recharge one's spiritual batteries, as it were, in order to withstand the several months of profane time to come. Of course, those months are still dotted with weekly *shabbatot* and monthly *rosh ḥodesh* celebrations, including festive *hallel*, so the tyranny of the mundane never entirely takes over. In the winter season, suggests R. Levi Yizḥak of Berdychiv, Ḥanukkah and Purim are so placed to prepare us for the great spring awakening of Pesaḥ.² The hidden miracle that takes place within seemingly natural events, he says, opens us to the possibility of greeting the great and transformative miracle of our liberation when its proper time has arrived. The miraculous component was least obvious in Ḥanukkah, because the Hasmonean army actually fought the Greek overlords, and the victory may have been partly a natural result of their own military prowess, a triumph of guerilla warfare. In the Purim story, the victory was won without a fight (he ignores the somewhat embarrassing account of the book's concluding chapters). Even though God's name remains absent from the Esther story, the divine hand may be seen lying behind the coincidences in the plot, as it is in the plot of all our lives. Once we perceive that, he says, we are ready to be taken out of our "Egypt" by God's outstretched arm.

But let us turn back to the fall season itself. It opens with *Rosh Ḥodesh Elul*, a month of preparation for the Awesome Days to come. Elul is traditionally read as an acronym for the words *Ani Le-dodi Ve-dodi Li*, "I am my beloved's and my beloved is mine" (Cant. 6:3). The *Sefat Emet* asks why that verse should be hinted at here, since the same scripture earlier says *Dodi Li Va-ani Lo*, "My beloved is mine and I am his" (Cant. 2:16), which would make for Dalul rather than Elul. The point is, he says, that the process of *teshuvah*, or return, has to begin with us.³ We have a scripture that says, "Restore us to You, O Y-H-W-H, and we shall return" (Lam. 5:21), and another that says, "Return to Me and I shall return to you" (Zech. 1:3). The point, he says, is that we have to make the first move. The Midrash says, speaking of the *teshuvah* process, "Open for Me to the width of a needle's eye, and I will open for you an entry-way that wagons and coaches could ride through."⁴

The spring season begins with what the kabbalists call *it'aruta dile-'eyla*, "awakening from above." God makes the first move, announcing to Moses at the burning bush that He has heard the cries of Israel and is about to bring them forth. Yes, there is talk in the sources both for and against the merits of Israel in Egypt, debating whether they had "earned" or deserved their redemption.⁵ But the actual process of their liberation is initiated by God, for His own purposes. God wants to give Torah to the world, and Israel have to be free to receive it. This process is relived annually: Israel are called upon to respond at the end of the spring cycle, having prepared ourselves in seven weeks of wandering and anticipation. Only then do we again say, *na'aseh ve-nishma'*, "We shall do and listen," reaccepting the gift of Torah.

But *teshuvah* is something that no one else—not even God—can do for you. The Sephardic custom of reciting *selihot*, penitential hymns, along with sounding the shofar, early each morning for the full month of Elul, truly prepares us for what is to come. The Sephardic manner of chanting these hymns, while filled with contrition, is considerably more cheerful and less oppressively guilt-ridden than the tearful Ashkenazic style of penitence.

The kabbalists find a striking parallel between the two seasons in the role of *binah*, the figure of God as cosmic Mother, within the symbol structure of the ten *sefirot*. It is *binah* who brings Israel out of Egypt, the compassionate Mother who can no longer stand by and behold Her children's suffering. *Binah* is referred to in the kabbalists' reading of the Haggadah as *ve-hi she-'amdah*, "She who stood up for our ancestors and ourselves." *Binah* is connected in various ways with the number fifty. "Fifty measures of *binah*, 'Understanding,' of wisdom exist in the world, and all were given to Moses, except for one."[6] That fiftieth measure or "gate" is *binah* Herself, the ultimate knowledge of God. She is the third *sefirah*; all the lower seven are born of Her ever-fruitful womb. Since they all contain one another, they total forty-nine.[7] *Binah* thus also represents Shavu'ot, the fiftieth day, the moment when Torah can be revealed from that highest (or "deepest"!) place. The spring sacred season thus both begins and ends with *binah*. She redeems Israel by an act of "awakening from above," but we then need to come toward Her, step by step, until we reach the place where we are fully ready, through our own preparation, to receive Her teaching.[8]

But Yom Kippur is also a day devoted to *binah*. Rosh Hashanah, the Day of Judgment, is something like an exalted Coronation Day. God is seated on the throne, surrounded by all the royal finery of heaven. Indeed, the effort of our prayer on that day is to move the Holy One from the throne of judgment to that of mercy, following the vision of Daniel, who beheld a God linking two thrones. But Yom Kippur is the day of a higher power than that of God as King. "The Mother comes and cleans up after Her child" may be taken as a way of describing what takes place on Yom Kippur.[9] *Kippur* literally means "covering over." The Mother is willing to cover up the sins of Her children, even those who have been found guilty by the Rosh Hashanah Judge. According to a well-known hasidic quip, the Torah refers to Yom Kippur in the plural as Yom ha-Kippurim, which the Hasidim read as Yom Ki-Purim, "a day like Purim." On Purim, we are told to be so inebriated that we cannot tell the difference between wicked Haman and righteous Mordecai.[10] On Yom Kippur, God gets so "high" on the prayers of Israel as to also transcend any distinction between the righteous and the wicked, thus atoning for them all. But this is also a folkloric way of saying that *binah* is an inner "place" within the Godhead that is higher than all such distinctions, hence a font of unflagging compassion.[11]

Another teaching of R. Levi Yizhak offers an interesting link-up of the spring and fall cycles.[12] Sukkot, the great fall full-moon festival, lasts eight days, while its spring parallel is only seven. "Why is that?" he asks. The seven festival days represent the seven *sefirot*, the seven cosmic stages through which blessing flows forth from its endless Source. The eighth day stands for the recipient of that blessing, Israel or the world. Indeed, the blessing is symbolized by rainfall, which we call forth on that day, named Shemini, "the eighth," 'Atseret. He reads *'atseret* to mean "stopping," or the place where the flow ceases and the blessing is taken in. We are prepared to receive that blessing, he says, because we have gone through the entire process of penitence and atonement, beginning way back on Rosh Hodesh Elul. In the spring season, however, the order is reversed. The great festival comes at the beginning of the sacred season, not at its end. We have not had time to be purified enough to receive the blessing. Hence the festival is only seven days,[13] time enough for the blessing to flow forth toward us, but not yet to be received. We then go through seven times seven days of anticipation, climaxing in Shavu'ot, the great festival of receiving, also referred to as *'atseret* by the rabbis. Then we are ready to receive the blessing, which comes to us in the form of Torah.

The parallel between the two seasons also helps us understand the origins of a medieval folk custom that rather quickly became normative and entered the highly conservative canon of *halakhah*. I refer to the festival of Simhat Torah, something with no biblical or Talmudic basis and unknown before twelfth-century Europe. I would suggest that Simhat Torah developed as a parallel to Shavu'ot. The spring cycle ended with a great dramatic flourish: the Jew stands before Sinai and receives the Torah once again. The power of this moment was to be great enough to carry one through the dry months ahead. The fall season, on the other hand, ended with Shemini 'Atseret, the most bland of all the festive days. "Stay with Me just one more day" was the midrashic way of describing it.[14] Simhat Torah allowed the fall season to end with a great bang of its own, another celebration of Torah, one that similarly could help one last through the succeeding season. The dramatic conclusion of one season was copied into the other, where it was needed. It was a custom that almost *had to* be created, shoring up the fall season to climax as powerfully as did the spring—and so it was.

Reflecting on the two seasons this way also causes one to think in terms of two essential religious motifs. The fall season is centered on creation, even through its reflection on the re-creation of both the natural cycle and the individual. We prepare through Elul to be born anew with the birth of the new year. This is headlined by the Torah reading for the first day of Rosh Hashanah, the story of the birth of Isaac, the birth that defines the newly dedicated family. The Ten Days of Awe, beginning with the tale of that birth, conclude with Jonah, who is reborn by being spit out of the whale's mouth, now ready to fulfill his life mission. We are born of our anxious parents, symbolized by Abraham and Sarah, on Rosh Hashanah. As each of us is born, so are the world and humanity born again in us. But we are "born again" at the conclusion of Yom Kippur. The true penitent, like the convert, is a newborn babe.

Sukkot, so filled with agricultural and outdoor symbols, is on some level all preparation for *Geshem*, the prayer for rain that will allow for the birth (or germination) of new seeds beneath the earth. We dwell in our *sukkah*, vulnerable to the rains, yet hoping they will hold off during the festival and bring us blessing in its proper time.

The spring season is essentially about revelation. God is revealed to Israel by the outstretched arm of the plagues in Egypt, at the Reed Sea, and, most significantly, at Sinai, the climax toward which the whole season has been building.[15] As we shall see when we turn to Pesaḥ in more detail, liberation—both national and personal—is viewed as a moment in which God's presence is revealed.

This two-moment reading of the tradition's rhythms stands in pointed contrast to the three-pronged reading of Judaism most associated with the writings of the great early twentieth-century Jewish philosopher Franz Rosenzweig: religion defined around the three poles of Creation, Revelation, and Redemption. Rosenzweig read the three pilgrimage festivals this way: Pesaḥ as the birth of the people, a national Creation story; Shavu'ot as revelation of God's purpose in choosing them; and Sukkot, dwelling intimately in the divine shade, as a foretaste of messianic Redemption. The three Shabbat services were depicted in the same way: the Shabbat eve *'amidah* as quoting God's rest in Creation, the Shabbat morning *'amidah* referring to the Shabbat commandment of Sinai, and the *minḥah* text referring to the future Shabbat to come.[16] But close examination of the sources leads me to question whether this is really the intent.

The "redemption" link is somewhat weak in both cases. Sukkot is *zeman simḥatenu*, "the season of our joy," not *zeman ge'ulatenu*, "the time of our redemption." It is more about the sheer joy of dwelling in God's presence here and now than it is about dreaming of a future redemption. The same is true of the Shabbat *minḥah* text.

In both of these cases, "redemption" seems to dwell in the sacred present, anticipating the elusive future. The messianic dream remains, of course. Shabbat is still *me-'eyn 'olam ha-ba*, a foretaste of that future world, one in which humans, human communities, and even the forces of nature will dwell in peace and harmony. *'Olam ha-ba*, as understood by the Zohar, is an elusive reality that somehow ever remains just a step ahead of us, reflected in our experience of Shabbat.[17] But that Shabbat, like the two seasons, is a celebration of Y-H-W-H as Creator of life and Revealer of Torah, the teaching that guides us in seeking life's meaning. Only by protecting that Creation and by living the way of life revealed to us at Sinai do we become the harbingers of Redemption, a process we continue to bring about, throughout the year, day by day.

Shabbat

A NEW INTRODUCTION

OUR TORAH OPENS WITH its account of Creation. "God said: 'Let there be . . .' and there was." But the dramatic focus of this story is not centered around anything that God created, not even the creation of humans in God's own image. That took place on the sixth day, and is still part of the lead-up to the tale's climax. The whole focus of the story is on the seventh. The tale of Creation is really there to tell us about God's rest from creating on that seventh day, and hence to teach us about Shabbat.

Why should the Torah begin with Shabbat? Why should the universal opening of the Torah's narrative deal with the question of Sabbath rest? Isn't this a ritual form, better left to the legal sections of the Torah, where it is in fact repeated? The point of the story is a very sharp one: it proclaims that as soon as there were human beings, there had to be Shabbat. Human life is just *inconceivable* without Shabbat. That is one of the great truths of Judaism, something we still need to stand for, and to teach the world.

What does this mean? The privilege of rest, of ceasing your labor, of getting off the constant treadmill of pursuing your livelihood and all the other things that keep you trapped, is essential to being human. The notion that the entire people, not just the king and the nobles, were given the divine gift of rest, sharing it with God, was one of the great innovations of biblical religion. In the ancient Near Eastern world, only the gods rested; people were created in order to serve them, to allow them to rest. But the Torah gives us the right, even the obligation, to partake of divine rest. "A day of rest and holiness have You given to Your people," we say in the Shabbat afternoon service. Notice that *menuḥah*, rest, comes first here, before *qedushah*, holiness. The same is true in the Genesis narrative. "God rested on the seventh day" comes before "and proclaimed it holy." There is no *qedushah* without *menuḥah*, no holiness without rest. We need the spaciousness of rest in order to even conceive of holiness. *As soon as there is humanity*, the Torah is teaching, *there must be Shabbat*. Without it, the creation of humans is incomplete. We are rendered human by our ability to rest.

How did we Israelites come up with such an idea? The answer is completely obvious: ours is a religion conceived by a nation of liberated slaves! The bitter memory of slavery never left us; it shaped our Torah in more ways than we can count: the way we treat strangers, the poor, and the land itself, the way we take responsibility for one another and build community. But when we former slaves first began articulating our values, the human need and desire for rest, including the sense that rest was holy, rose right to the surface. Rest belongs to God; it has been given to us as God's most precious gift.

The Mishnah (*Avot* 5:8) contains a fanciful list of things that were created on that first Friday afternoon, just as the sun was setting. Most of the list is made up of miraculous objects, scattered through the Torah narrative: the rainbow of Noah, the ram of Isaac's near sacrifice, Moses's staff, the two tablets, Miriam's well (that followed Israel everywhere in the wilderness), the mouth of the earth that swallowed Korah, and the mouth of Balaam's talking ass. Why were all these things created just as the sun was setting before the first Shabbat? And why are there no such miracles to save us in our own day?

Here's my own *midrash* on this story. The sixth day was intended as that of creating the animals. God did that and saw that it was good, as with all the other things created. In God's original intent, that was all that was going to be created on that day. But then, toward midafternoon, God looked around and felt that there was still something missing; Creation was not complete. God then said (we don't know to whom, though there are plenty of conjectures): "Let us make humans!" As soon as God said it, it happened. But then something unexpected happened to God. As soon as there were people, there was *history* as well. As long as the world was populated just by animals, there was no history. They ate, propagated, and died, generation after generation. No memory was conveyed that could make for history, for later accounting and interpretation of the past. But all that changed as soon as there were humans. They had adventures, took risks, made history. They were able to learn from their mistakes, yet often they failed to do so. "Oy!" said the Master of the Universe. "They're going to get into trouble! What can I do to help them?" And immediately God began to fashion miracles: a rainbow for Noah, a ram for Abraham, a well for Miriam, a mouth for Baalam's ass, and all the rest.

So why are there no miracles in our day? Why didn't God provide help to get us out of all our troubles as well? Because the sun set! He had only started this process late on Friday afternoon, and miracles take time! By the time God had finished with that talking donkey, the sun was setting and work had to stop. Of course, God can do anything—He could have gone on creating enough miracles to last forever, but then He would have desecrated the first Shabbat. If God had done that, no one would ever have taken it seriously. So the Creator faced a choice: He could give us miracles as we needed them, or He could give us *one big miracle:* the ability to rest from our work every week, to renew our humanity and to discover God's presence in the world.

Surely He made the right choice. God is God, after all.

But we do not have to go to this fanciful reading of a Mishnah to learn the essential truth of Shabbat and its relationship to the legacy of slavery. Look back at the Torah text itself. Along with being the focus of our creation story, Shabbat is the only religious practice that is included in the ten commandments (really "words") of Sinai, the innermost core of our revealed truth. Those ten commandments come to us in two versions, one in Exodus and the other in Deuteronomy. The Exodus command begins with "Remember the Sabbath day"; the Deuteronomy version with "Keep the Sabbath day." Tradition has it that these two were spoken at once, in a miraculous way that transcends our understanding.[1] But that claim refers not only to the two words, but to the entire command that follows. Listen to the explanation for Shabbat given in these two sources:

Exodus 20:11: For in six days did Y-H-W-H make the heavens and the earth, the sea and all that is within them, and He rested on the seventh. That is why Y-H-W-H blessed the seventh day and made it holy.

Deuteronomy 5:15: Remember that you were a slave in the Land of Egypt. Y-H-W-H your God brought you forth from there with

a mighty hand and an outstretched arm. Therefore Y-H-W-H
your God commanded you to make this Sabbath day.

The divine Shabbat, reaching back to creation, and the human Shabbat,
the need of poor, overworked slaves to get a day of rest, are miraculously
one and the same.

What is the message of this story for our own day? We are living through
an age of traumatic change in the history of the human race. Due to the innovations of the electronic era, the pace of our lives is increasing at a dizzy-
ing rate. We are called upon to produce and to respond at a pace prior generations could not have imagined. Our inner mental engines are constantly
being revved up to our top racing speed. This is an age when Shabbat, the
right to cease from labor, is more important than ever. *Shabbat may be the
greatest piece of Jewish wisdom that we have to share with the contemporary world.*

But how do we do it? Most Jews today are not going to accept the
rules of Shabbat as they were classically defined by *halakhah* or Jewish law.
Even many centuries ago, the Mishnah understood that they had grown
wildly beyond the Torah text itself, calling them "mountains hanging by a
hair."[2] Since then they have become much more extreme. But Shabbat is
not owned only by the strictly observant minority of Jews; it belongs to all
of the Jewish people. If we are going to offer it to the world, as I believe we
should, we first need to find a way to observe it ourselves. Below I offer a
list of ten counsels on how to observe Shabbat in our day, how to achieve
a contemporary day of rest. There are five positive suggestions ("Dos")
and five "Don'ts." I urge you to try them out. If you are a traditional Shabbat observer, you already do most of these, but there are some additional
things here to think about. If you are not, these are a good place to start.

Remember that the Torah does not define what sorts of labor are forbidden on Shabbat. Only two activities are explicitly forbidden: gathering
sticks and lighting a fire (Num. 15:32; Ex. 35:3). That tells you something
about the era in which the Torah was written. In a Stone Age world, lighting a fire and gathering wood to feed it constitute the very essence of
constructive labor. Think about how you might transpose those categories
of labor to create a Shabbat for our contemporary era. I suggest that we
would have to begin somewhere else, perhaps with spending money and
turning on the electronic devices.

Here are my ten counsels. No, they are not "commandments." Rather
than absolute rules or ends in themselves, they are ways to help create
something that reaches far beyond them. Give them a try.

Shabbat shalom!

Ten Pathways toward a New Shabbat

Do:

1. *Stay* at home. Spend quality time with family and real friends.
2. *Celebrate* with others: at the table, in the synagogue, or wherever you choose to gather.
3. *Study* or read something that will edify, challenge, or help you to grow.
4. *Be* alone. Take some time for yourself. Review your week. Ask yourself, "Where am I in my life?"
5. *Mark* the beginning and end of this sacred time, your own version of candles and *kiddush* on Friday night and *havdalah* as Shabbat ends.

Don't:

1. *Do anything* you are required to do for your work life. This includes obligatory reading, homework for kids, unwanted social obligations, and preparing for work as well as doing your job itself.
2. *Spend money.* Separate completely from the commercial culture that so wholly surrounds us during the week. You do not exist to be a customer or a client. This should include refraining from business of all sorts. No calls to the broker, no following up on ads, no paying of bills. It can all wait.
3. *Use devices.* Turn off the laptop, the iPhone, the smartphone, or whatever has replaced them by the time you read this. Live and breathe for a day without checking messages. Declare your independence from the new electronic masters over our minds and time.
4. *Travel.* Avoid especially commercial travel and places like airports, hotel check-ins, and similarly depersonalizing encounters. Stay free of situations in which people are likely to tell you to "have a nice day." (Shabbat already *is* a nice day, thank you.)
5. *Be entertained.* Do without the TV as well as the computer screen. Avoid especially canned or commercial entertainment. Discover what life has to offer when you are *not* being entertained.

Rosh Hashanah

A SEASON OF REBIRTH

Blow the *shofar* on the New Moon, concealed within our festive day.

—PSALM 81:4

OUR SAGES APPLIED THIS verse to Rosh Hashanah, the Jewish New Year festival, occurring on the new moon of the month Tishrey. They described it as a festival that has a new moon hidden within it.[1]

Rosh Hashanah itself was a hidden festival in most ancient memory. The Torah twice refers (Lev. 23:24; Num. 29:1) to a holiday on the first day of the seventh month (following the old pre-exilic calendar that began in spring), without ever mentioning what the occasion for that festival is. Unlike all the other festivals, it is not even given a name. This creates a suspicion that there must have been some controversy around this occasion. The biblical authors could not avoid listing it—meaning that it probably had a popular following among the people—but they did not want to dignify it, certainly not by calling it a celebration of the New Year.[2]

This ambivalence of religious authorities toward a festival calls to mind various parallels in other cultural contexts. Persians and related ethnic groups have since ancient times celebrated Nowruz, the new year of the vernal equinox. The ayatollahs who rule Iran since the Islamic revolution were at first rather cool toward this pre-Islamic celebration, rooted in the old Zoroastrian culture. But they found that they could not uproot it, and have in recent years abandoned the struggle and joined into the festivities, seeking (based on some older sources) even to give them Islamic meaning. Catholic authorities were once hostile to the old Mexican Day of the Dead, an Aztec festival honoring the ancestors. Finally, they assimilated it into All Saints' Day, a European Catholic festival on November 1, and it became legitimate.

Something similar must have taken place in ancient Israel, I am suggesting, around the festival we now call Rosh Hashanah. It may have had to do with ill feeling about the shift of calendars, from the old Israelite spring-based count to the Babylonian tradition of beginning in the fall. The early Talmudic sages were still debating whether the world had been created in Nisan or in Tishrey. But it is likely that something deeper than a calendrical dispute, or a struggle between the Land of Israel nativists and Jews influenced by Babylonian culture, is hidden here.[3] The Babylonian New Year festival was a coronation rite, one in which both gods and their earthly representative, the king, were invested with power for another year. Both the notion of the king as god-man and some of the rites involved in that celebration were anathema to a rather puritan streak to be found in the Hebrew prophets.

The one feature of this holiday that could not be done away with, however, was the custom of *teru'ah*, making a great noise, probably originally intended to scare the evil spirits away at a moment of great (and therefore somewhat risky) transition. Both mentions of this obscure festival in the Torah refer to that practice. In our Western celebrations of the secular New Year we also hear noisemakers, probably stemming from the same ancient roots.

What is most interesting to see here, especially for the Jewish worshipper who also has an eye open toward the history of religion, is how the rabbis preserved and transformed an already ancient set of traditions, adapting them to their own moral purpose. The coronation motif of this day was preserved, even enhanced, in the Jewish poetic imagination. But it became a paean to the singular kingship of God, without any connection to an earthly ruler. If anything, it underscored the vanity of all this-worldly polities, insisting that true rule belongs to God alone. That was appropriate to the liturgy of a Jewish community after its own worldly sovereignty had ended, when they began to see the entire political order as transient and unsanctified. In the old Babylonian tradition, the gods were known to possess "tablets of destiny," on which the names and fates of all the living were inscribed.[4] Lots were thrown on the New Year to determine how the die would be cast for each. The Jews transformed the metaphor. For them, it was no longer a tale, perhaps ironic, of divine caprice or the arbitrariness of fate. Rather, it bespoke the combination of stern moral responsibility and personal care and compassion that underlay their own ethos. God came to be described as a loving parent-ruler, one who knows and loves each of His subjects and seeks their good.

Avinu Malkenu, "Our Father, our King," became the (fully gendered) theme song of the Ashkenazic liturgy for the Days of Awe, reflecting the themes of suffering and martyrdom so central to the lives of Jews in northern Europe in the Middle Ages. "See how much we have suffered for You! Help us in our helplessness! Forgive our sins! Give us life! Help us to prosper!" The combining of these two titles, the parental, with all its loving intimacy, and the royal, filled with awesome pomp, tells us a great deal about the sort of piety Judaism seeks to create, especially apparent in the Rosh Hashanah service.

We think of kingship as a metaphor of distance and submission to authority. This is not the Coronation Day of a constitutional monarchy, where the ruler is just there to be adorned in finery and trotted out one day a year, while real power lies elsewhere. This is a King who has absolute power, especially that of life and death, over His subjects. Yet who among us has ever really seen the King, as a questioning character in one of Rabbi Naḥman of Bratslav's tales asks of a believer.[5] One is reminded of Franz Kafka's parable of the emperor's message, sent to you from a monarch so unapproachable that it has no true chance of ever getting through to you, other than in your dreams.[6]

That is why it is crucial that the King in this story is also Father. The Talmud says, speaking in an entirely different context, that "all Israel are royal children."[7] You are not to see yourself merely as the subject of the King, but as His beloved child. Just as we are to approach God with a balancing of love and awe, so do we see God relating to humanity as powerful Ruler, Author of life and death, while at the same time as a loving and caring parent. This gives birth to a wonderful series of tales and parables, including this one by Rabbi Dov Baer, the Maggid ("preacher") of Mezritch, told as an introduction to the sounding of the *shofar* on Rosh Hashanah, but recorded by his disciples in two distinct versions:

I

There was a king who sent his only son away to a distant land, for some reason known only to him. As time passed, the son became accustomed to the ways of the villagers among whom he lived. He became a wayward fellow, forgetting the niceties of life with the king. Even his mind and his most intimate nature grew coarse. In his mind, he came to think ill of the kingdom.

One day the son heard that the king was going to visit the province where he lived. When the king arrived, the son entered the palace where he was staying and began to shout out in a strange voice. His shout was in wordless sound, since he had forgotten the king's language. When the king heard his son's voice and realized that he had even forgotten how to speak, his heart was filled with compassion. This is the meaning of sounding the *shofar*.[8]

II

A king sent his beloved children to a far-off country. They spent long years there, exiled from their father's table. But they were constantly concerned with how to get back, how to come to dwell again in the restful home of their father's innermost royal court. How happy they had been when sharing in their father's joy! How much better things were then than now!

They began to send affectionate messages to their father, hoping he would take pity on them and bring them back. But once they got close enough to the royal court, they saw that their father's countenance was not the same as it had once been. They kept calling out and begging for his mercy, but they were met with silence.

After a long period of receiving no reply, the king's children began to wonder what they might yet do to reawaken their father's former love. "Why is it that we call out and receive no answer? Surely our father has no lack of mercy! There must be some reason for this."

They decided that maybe over the course of their years in that distant land they had forgotten the king's language. "We became so mixed up with other nations that we took on their ways and started speaking their language. We have no way to communicate with the king. That's why our words are not heard in his palace!"

So they decided to stop calling out in words or language. They would just let out a simple cry to arouse his mercy, since a cry without words can be understood by anyone.[9]

The Jewish people has long viewed itself as a community in exile. But the interpretation of this exile as one mutually painful to parent and child also has an ancient history.[10] "This hurts me more than it hurts you!" says the punishing parent to the child. In these hasidic parables, there is no reason offered for the child's exile. The old sense of exile as punishment for our sins, so prominent in the prophets and the early liturgy, seems to be long forgotten. Exile is the human condition, one to which we are all subject, ever since our expulsion from Eden. So, too, in a version of this tale by Rabbi Naḥman of Bratslav, where it is the king's daughter (probably a stand-in for the soul) who is condemned to exile, simply by a curse that escaped her father's lips in a moment of anger.[11] The task of Israel, standing in here for all of humanity, is thus a return homeward to the only vaguely recalled "palace" of our origin, even if we had actually grown up in a hovel in one of the little townlets that dotted the Ukrainian countryside. "The greatest temptation," says Rabbi Shlomo of Karlin, "is that the King's child forget who she or he is."[12]

It is in this way that the two motifs of Rosh Hashanah, those of divine kingship and human repentance, are joined to one another. The *shofar* blast awakens us, as Maimonides says, from our moral slumber, calling us to "return from evil and do good."[13] But that same decision also leads us to rediscover our truest selves and to reset ourselves on course for our life's journey. That trek is one of return to the royal household, from which we have been exiled, or just wandered away.

But just what is that "palace"? Is it knowable only in the afterlife, meaning that there is a death-wish fantasy hidden somewhere within this dream? Is it the soul's otherworldly abode for which we long? Or is it perhaps the warmth of infancy, the precious moment before the process of individuation began, and with it the inevitable separation from unceasing parental embrace? Is "the father's table" but a cipher for the mother's womb? Or the nonexistence that lies on the far side of that most ancient of memories?[14]

The Rosh Hashanah liturgy does not allow us to remain with such an interpretation. The call homeward is indeed a powerful one, but it is not the sirens' call into a self-destructive solipsism of divine embrace. The warmth of that return is a crucial step in our inner process, but we are not allowed to remain within the palace, at least not in this lifetime. We go back to our root in order to be reborn into this world, only so that we can go forth again, but in a new direction. The author of the *shofar* parables also taught the following, here employing a nonpersonal metaphor to talk about the process of human growth and transformation:

> Everything must have a root above, as the sages said . . . : "There is not a single blade of grass that does not have a star in the sky that strikes it and says to it: 'Grow!'"[15]

It is known that everything in the world, once it is brought to its root, can be changed into something different than that which it was previously. Take wheat, for example. When you want to change it, to bring forth multiple [new] stalks of wheat, you have to take it back to its root, which is the power of underground growth. That is why it can only grow beneath the soil, nowhere else. Even there, it cannot grow until rain comes and moistens the soil. Then it [breaks down], losing its prior form, and reaches the category of Nothingness. That is the state of prime matter, identical to [divine] wisdom. This is the root of all, of which scripture says: "You have made them all in wisdom" (Ps. 104:24). Then the power of growth can enter it, and multiple new stalks of wheat can grow out of it.

So it is with a person. When you bring yourself into your root, the state of Nothingness, you make yourself small, just as wisdom itself does. Then your personal qualities can be transformed.[16]

You are to go home to your Father's palace, the "soil" in which you first grew, because it is from there—nourished by the "rain" of an unquestioning sense that you are loved—that you can find the strength to begin again, setting forth on a new—and hopefully better—course on your journey through life. That is why the Torah and prophetic readings of this season are so much about birth and rebirth. Both Isaac and Samuel, long-awaited and much-loved sons of seemingly barren mothers, are born and dedicated to a life of covenant and God's service. The *'akedah* (binding of Isaac), read on the second day of Rosh Hashanah, was also seen by the ancients as a tale of his rebirth, rising from near—or possibly even real—death on the altar.[17] The season concludes with the tale of Jonah, the prophet who has fled his mission in life, born again as he is spewed forth from the mouth of the whale, and set on course to fulfill the task from which he had previously run away.

The message could not be clearer. The *shofar* calls us to come back to ourselves, to turn to that place where the priest will enter on Yom Kippur—our inward Holy of Holies, the place of the soul. That coming homeward, an act of checking in with our truest selves, will give us the strength to reset our course. In the act of *teshuvah*, or return, we will ask ourselves all the tough questions. Where have I been in the course of this year? What are the things I've done that I'm really proud of? Not by the measures of professional or financial success, of course. We Jews are much too driven by that endless push to "succeed." But on the personal level: In the way I've related to those I love, to the causes and values I care most about, how am I doing? We also ask ourselves the harder side of that same question: What are the things I have to be ashamed of this year? How can I get out of their grip, as I strive to live better?

Those two questions—my pride and my shame—are reified in the Jewish mythic imagination as the defending and accusing angels in the courtroom of our annual self-judgment. The tradition that we create our own angels by our merits and misdeeds is an ancient one; their transposition here to the realm of inner fantasy is not meant to render them any less powerful. In facing them, we undergo a *trial*, a translation of the Hebrew *nisayon*, not just a courtroom verdict, but something of an ordeal of self-confrontation.

Emerging from that ordeal, we ask to be inscribed again in the Book of Life, another motif borrowed from the ancient Babylonians. But note how the best of Jewish thinkers transformed it. The *Sefat Emet*, a hasidic master of late nineteenth-century Poland, says that every living person (he would have said "every Jew") has the word *life* inscribed on his or her heart. "Inscribe them on the tablet of your heart," in scripture's words (Prov. 3:3, 7:3). Over the course of a year, that word gets covered with grime, the result of both sin and neglect, caused by our fast-paced living. Rosh Hashanah is a time to scrub the dirt off those tablets, to let the word *life*—and the fact of our being truly alive—shine forth once again.[18]

Yom Kippur

LEARNING TO RESPOND

THE SECTION OF THE Talmud that deals with Sabbath and festival observances is called Mo'ed, meaning "festival" or "occasion." This is formed around one of the six "orders" or major subdivisions of the Mishnah. Its individual tractates are each named for the occasion they discuss, in fairly obvious ways: Shabbat, Pesaḥim, Sukkah, Megillah, Mo'ed Katan, or "Minor Festivals," and so forth. But the tractate on Yom Kippur is simply called Yoma, "The Day," making it clear that Yom Kippur is *the* day within the Jewish year, needing no further designation.

While the Torah contains several calendars within it, listing all its festivals, there are only two sacred occasions in the year that it describes in great detail: Pesaḥ, combined with the Festival of Matsot (Ex. 12), and Yom ha-Kippurim (Lev. 17). Pesaḥ is a national festival par excellence. Every Israelite family is to prepare its Paschal lamb; all are to eat of the unleavened bread and bitter herbs that accompany it, and the seven-day abstention from leaven is incumbent upon the entire people, with the severest consequences if violated. Partaking of this festival defines one as an Israelite; strangers are forbidden to share in it. Concern is shown even for the smallest or poorest families, who are allowed to share a lamb with neighbors, so that they too may participate in the rite.

The description of Yom Kippur, by contrast, is priestly. It happens entirely within the desert sanctuary. Its high point takes place inside the

Holy of Holies, which the high priest alone may enter, and on just this occasion. The people were mere observers of this great but hidden event. The Mishnah recalls the Second Temple version of it, in which those standing in the courtyard fell on their faces when they heard the priest utter the holy name, crying out, "Blessed be the name of His glorious kingdom for ever and ever!"[1]

The Israelites' portion in carrying out this observance is limited to a somewhat obscure phrase found twice in the book of Leviticus (17:27, 23:29), *Ve-'initem et nafshoteykhem*, usually rendered as "You shall afflict yourselves." This is the basis for the practice of fasting on this day, along with four other forms of "affliction": abstinence from sexual relations, bathing, perfuming, and wearing shoes, all of which were considered essential creature comforts. Eating *matsah* on Passover and fasting on Yom Kippur are probably still the two most widely followed rites on the Jewish calendar, although (God bless America!) Hanukkah candles are surely catching up to them.

This word *ve-'initem*, "You shall afflict," is an intensified form of the verb stem *'-n-h*, which in its ordinary form means "answer" or "respond." I like to think of the "affliction" as a means of pushing forward the response, making us *responsive* or *responsible*, even in the face of our reluctance. We fast on Yom Kippur not because God needs us to (Isaiah 58, the Yom Kippur Haftarah, already makes that quite clear), but as a sign that we are working hard at opening our hardened hearts, making us something like "first responders" to the many needs all around us, ready to enlist ourselves in all that God needs us to do. The fasting and other deprivations of the day are intended to awaken that responsiveness.

This sensibility has everything to do with the event that the rabbis designated as the origin of Yom Kippur. It was the day of the giving of the second tablets at Mount Sinai. The revelation at Sinai (as you will recall, of course, because you were there!) first took place on the sixth day of Sivan, later linked to the holiday of Shavu'ot. It was then that we Israelites heard the first two of the ten commandments spoken directly, the living Word of God, and the other eight as related to us by Moses.[2] Moses then went up the mountain and disappeared into the cloud covering it. He emerged forty days later, carrying the tablets in his hands. By then, however, Israel had grown impatient and anxious over his delay, and had begun to worship the Golden Calf. Moses smashed the tablets on that day, later designated as the fast of the 17th of Tammuz. Moses went up the mountain again on the first of Elul, the beginning of our penitential season. It was over the course of those ensuing forty days that he had his great confrontation with God. "Let Me go!" God said, "and I will destroy them and make of you a great nation!" (Ex. 32:10). But Moses responded: "If you abandon this people, wipe me too out of Your book" (Ex. 32:32). Then God instructed Moses to make the second set of tablets.[3]

The first tablets had been fashioned and inscribed by God alone. But now Moses is told, "Carve on your own two tablets like the former ones, and I will write upon them" (Ex. 34:1). The new tablets are to be a collaborative effort, created jointly by God and Moses, representing Israel.

I like to think of this event as a renegotiated marriage. The first time around, the more powerful party to the match was dominant, dictating all the terms. That sort of marriage brought them to disaster, the other partner's infidelity being an acting out on her inability to accept those terms. Properly outraged, the powerful partner wants to walk away, end the marriage, and seek a new relationship. Moses here plays the role of God's rabbi, a skillful marriage counselor. "But you still love each other," he tells the wounded Spouse, "and I can help you make it work."

So now Moses, representing Israel—since he is, of course, human—carves, and God writes. But how are these second tablets different from the first? Aren't they the same "ten statements"?[4] We do not have a reading of the second tablets in Exodus 34, where all this takes place. We do, however, have a repeat of the ten in Deuteronomy 4, differing slightly from the inscription in the first account of Sinai in Exodus 19. This is often taken to be the text of the second tablets, those given on Yom Kippur. The changes, though subtle, immediately set up the need for negotiation between the two versions. Why should one text say "*Remember* the Sabbath" and the other say "*Keep*" it? Why are the last five commandments joined by "ands" on the second tablets, but not on the first? Is there a link between murder and adultery that needs to be explored? Or between theft and coveting?

All this sets up the need for an interpretive process, that which is called "Oral Torah." The second tablets carry with them the origin of a need for interpretation, negotiating between differing versions of the divine word. This process can take place only on earth, amid the community of the faithful.[5] This makes for a tremendous equalization of power between the partners in this marriage. This is what Moses has negotiated in his confrontation with God on that Yom Kippur! God remains God, Giver of the Law. But Israel becomes the interpreter, eternally empowered to ask: "But why did You say it *this* way? What did You *mean* by that?" That "soft power" has made all the difference, allowing Judaism to exist through history as an evolving and dynamic faith. "She," the Community of Israel, has say over how the divine law is to be interpreted and carried out.[6]

It is in the final moments of this encounter, just before Moses again descends the mountain, that the Torah offers its fullest description of God, spoken by a mysterious and unidentified voice. As the power dynamic shifts and a new balance emerges, the once-dominant Partner allows for a moment of self-revelation (and that always means vulnerability), calling out: "Y-H-W-H Y-H-W-H, a God merciful and gracious, long-suffering and of abundant compassion and truth! Preserving compassion for the thousands, bearing iniquity, sin, and transgression, though surely not cleansing it, visiting the sin of the fathers upon children and grandchildren, to the third and fourth generation" (Ex. 34:6–7). One might call this "the good news and the bad news" of divine self-revelation. Yes, there is great compassion and the possibility of forgiveness. But ill deeds have consequences, not only for oneself, but for the future.

Later generations, however, boldly executed their authority as interpreters, even of this direct revelation of divine personhood. They used the first portion of it as the refrain for all penitential liturgies in the emerging tradition, while simply ignoring its second half. Yom Kippur in the synagogue, ever since the early Middle Ages, has been characterized by multiple calling out of these "thirteen attributes of mercy." They found their way also into both festival and fast-day worship throughout the year. (The Sephardic and hasidic liturgy in fact recites them every day.) But we do so only in their edited version, as they appear in all our prayer books: "Y-H-W-H Y-H-W-H, a God merciful and gracious, long-suffering and of abundant compassion and truth! Preserving compassion for the thousands, bearing iniquity, sin, and transgression, and cleansing!" The sages took that form of the verb *naqeh* (called an infinitive absolute by grammarians) and completely reversed its meaning. Instead of underscoring the negative ("*surely* He will not cleanse"), they transformed it into an emphatic positive ("He cleanses!"). Such is the power of interpretive boldness.

A well-known feature of the Yom Kippur service is a list of sins, repeated in doubled alphabetic form. They are recited standing, while beating one's chest, as though to chastise the heart within it. They are recited in the plural, to emphasize the collective responsibility that Jews all have for one another. At the very end of this list comes a sin referred to as *timhon levav*, usually rendered as "timidity of heart." I would like to suggest that we are indeed collectively guilty of that sin in fulfilling our duty as the reinterpreting partner in this annually renewed marriage. We have become too timid, too cautious, in carrying our tradition forward and allowing it to breathe. That is a very interesting and significant note on which to end our list of sins. Our final sin is that we have become too timid in the presence of God. Rabbis, take notice![7]

To what, then, are we to become responsive on Yom Kippur? What is the real call of our self-imposed "affliction"? It is the God of compassion who calls out to us on this day, the God of the emended list of thirteen attributes. The message seems completely obvious, though it is often ignored. We are to respond by living out those same attributes in the course of our human interactions. Yom Kippur calls upon us to be more compassionate, forgiving, patient, gracious, and truthful. It calls us to let go of hurts and insults, not to "stand our ground" for every harm we have suffered, but to share some of their burden, extending a hand even to those who have harmed us.

If this ethos sounds too "Christian" to you, maybe you've been reading the wrong Jewish sources. Start with my very favorite among the classic works of Hasidism, *The Light of the Eyes,* by Rabbi Menahem Nahum of Chernobyl. He quotes the Talmudic source (b. Rosh Hashanah 17b) that forms the basis of using the thirteen attributes in worship, noting that the text reads this way: *Im ya'asu le-fanay ka-seder ha-zeh,* "If you act before Me according to this order, I will surely forgive you." It does not say: "If you call them out before Me" or "If you repeat them enough times and pronounce them correctly," but "if you *act*" according to them.[8] The message is clear. *Become more forgiving, and you will be forgiven; act with more compassion, and you will receive compassion from its divine Source.* That's the way compassion is: the more you give, the more you get.

How do we manage to observe Yom Kippur, to "get through" the fast until the stars come out, and yet fail to absorb its simple and obvious message? We seem to be so caught up in seeking our own forgiveness that we forget what we are there to learn. The only way to worship a God who forgives is by forgiving others. All the God of compassion seeks of you is that you live with the gift of compassion that you have been given. You only need to find it within you.

Yom Kippur is the day on which God forgave Israel for its gravest sin, the worship of the Golden Calf. That act represented unfaithfulness, a violation of the covenant almost as soon as it had been made. We, too, have been unfaithful. We have turned aside from the covenant by which Jews, both individually and collectively, are supposed to live. The Talmud describes Israel as merciful, modest (or "capable of shame"), and acting with compassion.[9] Yom Kippur comes to remind us that this is who we truly are. We only need to act that way. "The Day" is a call from beyond, or from deep within. We only need its *'innuy*, "affliction," to learn to respond.

Sukkot

DWELLING IN GOD'S SHADE

THE TWO GREAT PILGRIMAGE festivals of the Hebrew Bible, Pesaḥ and Sukkot, begin on the days of the spring and fall full moon. Biblical scholars have long understood the origins of these festivals in ancient seasonal rites, tied to the agricultural cycle of spring planting and fall harvest. As presented in the Torah, they are at midpoint in the course of transformation from agricultural season festivals into celebrations of the national saga of redemption, the rituals of a sacred people tied to its collective history, rather than to the land itself. Pesaḥ, combined with the festival of Matsot, has completed that transition as presented in the text; the old festival of slaughtering spring lambs is completely subsumed within the Exodus narrative. Sukkot is just beginning that transition, as presented in the Torah. Amid much talk of the harvest, a single verse says, "For I caused your ancestors to dwell in booths as I took them forth from the land of Egypt" (Lev. 23:43).

I have long had a suspicion—for which I can marshal no evidence— that there may be a still more ancient layer of memory behind these agricultural festivals. The transition from the hunter-gatherer period of human history, continuing into the wandering herdsman's way of life, to that of agriculture and settlement, marked one of the first great changes in human history. Because it took place before written documents, and maybe even before the full development of language itself, we have no clear record of it. But it is reflected in the tale of Cain and Abel, as well as in earlier Near Eastern parallel texts. (The theme of herdsman—or "rancher"—versus farmer is familiar to all of us who grew up watching western movies.) I suspect that the trauma of this change brought about a nostalgia for prior times that somehow needed to be ritually commemorated. Thus were created two great ritual occasions. Beginning on the spring full moon, for a week one ate only the food that was consumed before there were ovens, before humans had learned how to bake bread, a defining feature of settled existence in the West. *Matsah*, laid out in the sun to bake as best it could, took the place of risen bread. On the fall full moon, one went out and dwelt in huts for a week, just as we had "in the olden days," when we still wandered with the flock. The *sukkah*, or "temporary" home, a kind of Bedouin tent, took the place of the real and solidly built farmhouse.

Sukkot is surely a festival that puts us in touch with some of the most ancient of human memories. The *hosh'anot*, or "Save us!" processions around the synagogue, carrying the fruits of the trees, culminating in the "stripping of the willows" rite on the seventh day, Hosh'ana Rabbah, a day of awesome judgment evoking echoes of Yom Kippur, place us back in the vulnerable mindset of early farmers in an arid climate, living on the edge of a desert, calling out for rain. Our waving of the *lulav*, or palm branch, in all directions on each day of the festival is also surely a vestigial form of rain dance, urging the blessed water-filled clouds to appear from one direction or another.

Just as Yom Kippur is simply called *yoma*, "the Day" in Talmudic sources, Sukkot is named *ḥagga*, or "the festival." But the root of that word (the same as *ḥaj* in Arabic, by the way) really means "circle." In Temple times, Sukkot was the great annual pilgrimage festival, the time when Jews from throughout the land, and even from abroad, would gather in Jerusalem. The main feature of that celebration was circumambulations around the altar, still copied in the synagogue in the ritual of *hosh'anot*. The palm, willow, and myrtle branches we carry, along with the bright yellow *etrog*, also carry an awful lot of history within them.

All of these things have, of course, long been spiritualized, transformed into rites in which we seek both collective and personal meaning. The early rabbis saw the four species as representing four types of Jews or four vital organs that constituted the moral self.[1] The hasidic masters speak beautifully of waving the branches in each direction, then coming back to the heart, as an exchange of blessing between the inner self and all the farthest corners of one's daily life.[2] In their spirit, we, too, seeking out a more universalist Jewish spirituality, see the innermost self reaching forth in all directions, extending our love and concern to the four corners of the earth, reaching also up toward the sky and down into the soil, but then bringing that love and concern back into our hearts. Judaism thrives on its unique way of preserving ancient religious forms and remaining open to their constant reinterpretation. But in this case, I also find something attractive about pausing in our rush to reinterpret, just to enjoy living in the presence of these most ancient of ancestral memories. This historical perspective on our sacred calendar does not diminish the power of the festivals for me, as it does for some refugees from a fundamentalist Judaism ("If God didn't really command that we do these things, why do we have to do them?"). On the contrary, it deepens and enriches their power, and makes me *more* want to immerse myself into their full praxis. This is what I mean by a post-critical or postmodern return to Judaism. The historical dimensions of Jewish religious life, including our many borrowings from various cultural settings amid which we have lived, make the ritual forms all the more interesting and attractive. Certainly, my *kavvanah* or inner intent in doing them will focus on the spiritual, but the historical and anthropological "baggage" that comes along with that becomes part of the inspiration. The fact that my Sukkot celebrations draw me nearer to the Plains Indian, dressed up for his Rain Dance, or the Masai shepherd in Kenya who is still undergoing the transition from nomadic to settled existence, enhances my sense of partaking in our Jewish version of the great human drama called religion.

There is certainly a profound demonstration of human frailty and vulnerability in the command to "go forth from one's permanent home to this temporary dwelling."[3] Although the authorities were lenient in allowing one to leave the *sukkah* if being there causes suffering, the very fact that you have to leave your true "home" and seek shelter elsewhere is itself a significant statement. With all the great systems of protection we have—be they residential, medical, economic, or whatever—the truth is that we are utterly frail, vulnerable human creatures. We do not know whether a plague, a sudden fall, a heart attack, or an aneurysm might cause us to disappear from this world tomorrow. The hastily thrown together shelter in which we are told to dwell for this week serves as a reminder that our vast network of creature comforts and security devices creates nothing more than an illusory bulwark against mortality.

Sukkot comes at the moment of seasonal transition. In the Land of Israel, the endlessly sunny summer is over, and the much-needed rains are about to begin. At the conclusion of Sukkot, we will pray for rain, and will begin to ask for it daily in our winter *'amidah*. But in our four-season climate, too, this is the week when we end our summer of outdoor living, knowing that we will need shelter from the rain, snow, and frost to come. That we first enter into this frailest of all structures is a way of recognizing the frailty of all our efforts to protect ourselves. It is only by entering the true inner *sukkah* that the kabbalists call "the shade of faith" that we will really find ourselves protected.

It is almost ironic that this demonstration of vulnerability is given to us in the context of the single festival that is liturgically designated as *zeman simḥatenu*—"the season of our rejoicing." The joy is in celebration of the fact that we are still here, even in the face of all that vulnerability. The psalms of Hallel, chanted throughout the festive week, are very much in that spirit. They are not proclamations of simple joy, but of the special gratitude for having been saved from the seemingly arbitrary clutches of death. "I shall not die, but live, and recount the deeds of God." "For you have saved my soul from death, my eye from tears, my foot from stumble." "The dead praise not Y-H-W-H, nor those who go down into silence. But we"—the living—"shall praise YaH from now and forever!" (Ps. 118:17, 116:8, 115:17–18). There is a sense here of proclaiming immortality, not by defeating the inevitable, but by our continued existence in the ongoing community of the faithful, who will forever continue forward in their songs of praise. That defeat of death represents a special quality of joy.

This sort of celebration is, of course, entirely appropriate to the season. The harvest is in; the fields are empty. Soon they are to be devastated by winds and rain—in our case, covered with snow. Some of us, as individuals, will also be harvested or culled from the flock in the course of this harsh season, and will no longer be here when the spring comes. But there will be a spring, and there will be a community singing Hallel once again. The passing of the fall full moon means that the spring full moon is now less than half a year away.

As we engage in this demonstration of vulnerability, it is not surprising that our remotest ancestors, desert wanderers that they were, show up for a visit. The original *ushpizin*, spiritual "guests" we welcome into the *sukkah*, are Abraham, Isaac, Jacob, Moses, Aaron, Joseph, and David. Greeting those ghostly guests (and hopefully their favorite companions; my choices are Sarah, Rebecca, Rachel, Zipporah, Miriam, Esther, and Jonathan!), along with all the real flesh-and-blood guests who show up with them, is an essential part of this celebration, where bounty and vulnerability are tied together. Harvest time—there is suddenly more than we could possibly eat (think of the price of zucchini in September!), and it won't keep very well. So let's invite our poorer neighbors in. They have been having a hard year, but we know full well that it could be we who will be struggling next year. There is a sense here that we are all bound together; all of us in our farming community, studded with these little huts—but also all of Israel, all of humanity, all of nature—face the same threat of mortality, and are thus called upon to share. The patriarchs—and now the matriarchs and other heroines of Jewish history who have decided to join them in these visits—are here to remind us of all that.

As the produce is gathered in from the fields, so are we gathered, and sometimes crowded, into our tightly packed *sukkah*. We can make room for yet another guest only by loving each other a little more, as a hasidic saying would have it. That too is why the *sukkah* is called by the Zohar *tsila di-mehemenuta*, "the shade of faith."[4] It is our faith—in Y-H-W-H and in the human community—that shades and protects us from the hot sun beating down on us, here perhaps a stand-in for the pressure of mortality. We will wither under it if we stand out there alone. Here, being together under these frail branches, we find a bit of shade. Dwelling in the *sukkah*, together with guests both real and imagined, is a statement of our collective survival in the shade we share.

That consolation, however, is not enough to shield us anymore. Sukkot, with its combined celebration of the harvest's plenty and awareness of life's frailty, is a festival that calls out to be transformed once again. As we made the move from the fall full-moon festival to the memory of our ancestors' wanderings, then on to commemorating the Temple rites long after they were gone, the inner voice demands yet another step in this celebration's long history. Sukkot is a time to acknowledge that today our planet, including all its future harvests and all our ensuing generations, is under dire threat, much of it caused by the intentional and irresponsible blindness of the society in which we live, especially by our so-called leaders. In the face of what is to come, the fine homes we have built for ourselves will protect us even less than the flimsy *sukkot* in our backyards. As lovers of God's created world, we cannot be guilty bystanders to its rampant destruction by forces of human greed. In times like these, our gathering around the *sukkah* table should contain an element of strategic planning alongside the celebration. What can we do, in this longer winter season ahead, to thwart the plans of those who consistently put short-term profiteering above protection of our shared natural legacy?

What can we do this year to bring their wicked plans to naught? Think of Rabbi Akiva and his friends sitting all night at the *seder* table on Pesaḥ. Were they indeed, as some have claimed, planning the Bar Kokhba rebellion? How can we, following God's call to our generation, become *sukkah* revolutionaries?

Simḥat Torah

THE WORD AS TREE OF LIFE

לכבוד תלמידי היקר אבן לידר, שחידש לנו את החג הזה

IMḤAT TORAH IS AN invented holiday, first appearing among Ashkenazic Jews in the Middle Ages. I have had occasion above, in the chapter called "Seasons," to offer you my theory of why it came to be. In our day, it is often celebrated in a noisy and raucous way, turned into something like a fall-season version of Purim.

But its real meaning is quite different from that. Simḥat Torah is a celebration of completing the cycle. We have now read through the entire Torah, and we are about to begin it again. We have also completed the cycle of fall holidays, having fulfilled all our sacred obligations of the season. Now a new "real" year is about to begin, as we transition from sacred to ordinary or profane time. So there are two major transitions taking place on this day. Such a moment of liminality, of stepping through the threshold into the as yet unknown, can be threatening. Perhaps that is why the common practice has turned it into such a moment of raucous joy.

It was the early Muslims who first referred to Jews as the "people of the book."[1] Unlike many other names our non-Jewish neighbors called us, we liked this one and made it our own. Judaism—indeed, like Islam—is a religion defined by our relationship to our holy book, and the performative public reading of it lies at the heart of our weekly Shabbat service. Learning how to chant the Torah text aloud, following the ancient musical tropes, is something that many Jews (now including women as well as men) aspire to achieve, a skill in which they take great pride.

Torah actually means "teaching." It is derived from the root Y-R-H, originally meaning "to shoot an arrow." A good teaching goes right to the heart, you might say, except that it brings life rather than death. The term *Torah* can be used in the widest sense, applied to any teaching, or in the more specific sense of referring to the body of Jewish sacred teachings. But within those as well, it can be used so widely as to embrace the entire tradition, including the ongoing oral process of interpretation along with the text or, more narrowly, to refer to the written text, the five books of Moses, which are inscribed on parchment in the Torah scroll. Occasionally, in the old rabbinic sources, the term *Torah* was even used to refer specifically to the ten commandments, the teaching Moses brought down from Mount Sinai.[2]

But to really understand Jews as "people of the book," one also has to understand that we are, in addition, the people of interpretation. The process of creative reinterpretation is the lifeblood of Judaism. We remain ever attached to the text of Torah, we parade it around the synagogue and read it with due pomp, we fuss about dressing up the sacred scroll—but we are also that text's loving, and sometimes fearless, reinterpreters.

Two Torahs were given to Moses, we are told, the written and the oral. The written text is fixed, laid out even to the smallest details by the Masoretes, who worked around the eighth century. Since then, no letter, vowel, or musical trope has been changed. But Oral Torah is a constantly moving process. Contrary to what many Jews have been taught, it does not consist of sets of books sitting on the shelves of the *bet midrash* or house of study. Those indeed contain summaries of what earlier generations did in carrying forth this process. But Oral Torah dwells not on the *shelves*, we might say, but in the *selves* of those who engage with it. A well-known hasidic master, the *Sefat Emet*, taught that "the eternal life You have implanted within us," mentioned in the blessing recited after reading from the Torah, refers to that oral teaching, ever to be used as a tool of reinterpretation.[3] Every Jew contains that Oral Torah. The Written Torah ever stands ready, waiting to meet the particular version of Oral Torah that only you, as a unique Jewish soul, can bring forth. Only when they meet together does God again "give the Torah." An earlier hasidic master insisted that the written text alone is only half the Torah, and that anyone who denies the right of each generation to reinterpret it in its own way is denying the Torah itself.[4]

The only true sin, in a religion like this, is that of disengagement. To think that you have nothing to offer, or that there is nothing of value in this ongoing tradition of rereading the text, is to cut yourself out of the picture. Radical inversions of the text, cries of protest against some of its surface meanings, impatience with the slowness of change are all part of the process.[5] The tradition is tough and enduring; whatever objections you can throw at it, it has seen and taken tougher blows before. Disinterest and indifference are its only enemies.

To show up on Simḥat Torah is to place yourself inside the picture. "Here I am, O Torah, to be with you in this great moment of looping and renewal, when we tie together the end of the narrative, the death of Moses, back to its beginning, the creation of the world. 'In the eyes of all Israel, God began to create the heavens and the earth!'"

But showing up to dance, and even to recite the blessing, is not enough. These are a promise, one that needs to be fulfilled throughout the year. Simḥat Torah should be taken as a challenge as well as a celebration. How am I going to both study and reinterpret Torah during the coming year? Where and how will I find a sufficiently engaging text, study partner, teacher, and approach to make this a crucial part of my daily life? The sacred season is now over. I will not be around the synagogue and the Jewish community as much as I have been this month. I face a long half year of mostly *ḥol*, ordinary time. How will I fill it with Torah?

Remember: Judaism offers two essential ways of relating to God: Torah and *mitsvot*, study and deeds. *Mitsvot* are half the picture, and they embrace the whole ritual realm, including prayer, as well as the domain of interpersonal ethics and behavior. To shake a *lulav* and to act for justice are both *mitsvot*. But Torah is the other half. That means learning, challenge, and growth. Ideally, it should be transformative learning, a process through which you are ever becoming a different person, shaped and refined by your ongoing encounter with Torah. *But it should also be one in which Torah itself is transformed*—in which Torah becomes better, broader, deeper—because it has met the likes of you.

Since Christianity diverged from an early stage in the emergence of rabbinic Judaism, I sometimes find structures within it helpful to use as an explanatory tool. I did this above in the "Seasons" section, where I suggested that the two annual seasons of Lent and Advent are a transposition of the two sacred seasons of the Jewish calendar. But in a broader sense as well, I believe that *torah u-mitsvot* stand in an interesting and sugges-tive parallel to "faith and good works" in the salvific theology of classical Christianity. Just as *mitsvot* include both ritual and ethical obligations, so do "good works" include both the sacraments and commitment to a moral code. But, in a crucial difference, "Torah" stands in the place of "faith" as the other pillar of relationship with God. The Jew partakes of God's pres-ence within Torah by means of *engagement* in Talmud Torah,[6] the ongoing process of learning, growth, and interpretation. Judaism is less demanding of faith than it is of this engagement. Yes, there is a certain faith that un-derlies the commitment to study, but it is more a faith in the *worthwhileness of engagement* than it is in a particular version of theological truth.

"She is a Tree of Life to those who take hold of her," says a verse that we recite after each public Torah reading (Prov. 3:18). The relationship between Torah and her interpreters—one that develops over the course of a lifetime, as well as across the centuries—is hardly a one-way affair. We are ever learning and discovering Torah; "she" is ever revealing herself to us. The text is not a passive object upon which we work the cold magic of interpretation, bringing forth meanings that are nothing but our own conjure. We fully believe in the mutuality of this relationship. To "take hold of" Torah, *le-haḥaziq bah*, is to hold "her" strongly, but also means "to gain strength from her."[7] She, Torah, divine wisdom—described by the Zohar as a beautiful maiden hidden away in a palace—reveals her face (indeed, her many faces) only to the one who loves her.[8] We do not impose interpretation upon the text; we *seduce* the text to reveal something of her endless meanings to us, allowing ourselves to be seduced by her as well.

Do not be uncomfortable with this personification of the Torah. How could she *not* be "person" to us? If God is Father in much of Jewish im-agery, Torah is both Mother and Bride.[9] She charms us with the beauty of her subtle language and endless meanings; we respond to her charms and seek always to unlock her secrets. "Open to me, my sister, my love, my dear and perfect one, for my head is filled with dew, my locks glisten with the night" (Cant. 5:2). Interpretation and teaching of Torah assure that both the *giving* and *receiving* of Torah go on "through the night." That "night," say the sages, is the night of exile, the profane world of ordinary time in which we live.[10]

The ten commandments begin with the word *anokhi* (consonantally A-N-K-Y), "I am." This is the opening of revelation, however literally or metaphorically we understand that event. It all goes back to the divine "I am." But the Talmud says that this word can be read as an acronym for the

Aramaic phrase *Ana Nafshai Katvit Yahavit*, "I Myself wrote it and gave it."[11] Later interpreters read the phrase to mean something different: "I wrote and gave Myself."[12] What God gives in Torah is nothing other than God's own Self, but now in verbal form, so that we mortals may "read" God in the garb of language. This is what all sacred teaching needs to be: the divine presence parlayed into words. Since we understand that language is a human institution, we are the ones who can and must effect that transformation. The hasidic author understands this well when he reads Deuteronomy 26:17, *et ha-shem he'emarta*, as "You have brought God into speech." But he is also wise enough to understand that when we engage in this work of articulating divinity, we mere humans are also transformed and uplifted, so much so that we humans become the voice—indeed, the only verbal voice—of God in the world. The verse goes on to say (26:18): *ve-ha-shem he'emirekha*—"God [or the silent divine presence within you] has caused you to speak, has transformed you into language." In speaking Torah, we become God's living word. Make us Your Word, Lord, and speak us in truth.[13]

Ḥanukkah

H ANUKKAH IS A time of miracles. The phrase *nes Ḥanukkah*, "the Ḥanukkah miracle," is widely used in the sources and is even reflected on the dreidel. But just what was—or is—the miracle of Ḥanukkah? This leads us into an interesting bit of Jewish history.

At first, it would seem, the obvious miracle was the victory of the Maccabees. A dedicated little band of guerilla warriors, fighting on their home turf, achieved a surprise victory over the much larger and better equipped Seleucid army, successors to Alexander the Great's vast empire. The occupiers clearly were the stronger power, but the ragtag band led by Mattathias and his sons drove them out. For those of us living after Vietnam and Afghanistan, the success of such warriors over a greater power may not seem so miraculous. But in its day, it surely seemed as though it was the hand of God. Who knows? Who can determine what is or is not a miracle?

But by the time the tale of Ḥanukkah reached the rabbis, the kingdom of the Maccabees' descendants had fallen into disrepute. The grandchildren of those who had fought so valiantly had themselves become small-time autocrats and purveyors of the same Hellenistic values their ancestors had risen against. Eventually, the Hasmonean kingdom became a Roman vassal-state, then just was absorbed into the empire. The rabbis did not want to celebrate the victory of a Jewish kingdom that ultimately had sold out to the Romans.

But the festival of Ḥanukkah, so it seems, already had a popular following, and could not so easily be ignored. What did the rabbis do? They
chose another miracle. The story of the small bit of oil that burned for
eight nights, lasting until more could be obtained, became the miracle of
Ḥanukkah, the reason for celebration, reenacted by Jews the world over.
Ever since then, Ḥanukkah has been the festival of light. Coming at the
beginning of winter, just as days are getting shorter and light seems to be
disappearing from the world, Hillel's custom of adding another light each
night (as opposed to Shammai's, who wanted one candle fewer each night,
representing the diminishing oil) is a sign of hope that the brightness will
grow again.

But lighting the candles each of eight nights, reciting the blessing to
thank the One who "performed miracles for our ancestors" in this season,
gives us a chance to think about miracles. What are the things we consider
miraculous in our lives? Is it the big achievements? The milestones or top-
hit successes? Wow, I made it through graduate school! I got that great
job! I climbed the mountain! I got to see the Great Wall of China! Or
is it, hopefully, more intimate things? I met, fell in love, and mated with
the person I still love, all these years later. Or your kids: their birth, their
growing up, every step along the way. Or is it just the fact of life itself?
That you're still here, after all these years?

Once you start down this path, thinking about it with an open and
grateful heart, you soon get to the question: "What *isn't* a miracle?" Is it
all a matter of perspective?

One of the great sages of medieval Iberian Jewry, Rabbi Moses ben
Naḥman, spoke of two types of miracles, the hidden and the revealed.
Revealed miracles are the obvious ones, those around which sacred narratives and great sagas are written: the plagues of Egypt, the splitting of the
Reed Sea, Miriam's moveable well in the wilderness, the sun standing still
amid Joshua's battle. Hidden miracles are those cases where you have to
look hard to see the divine hand in events that seem like they might just
be following the course of nature.[1]

It is not completely clear what Naḥmanides means by the latter category. Is he talking about something like the Maccabean revolt, where
"You placed the many in the hands of the few, the wicked in the hands of
the righteous," and so on, as the prayer says?[2] Some Jews like to view the
Israeli victories of 1948 and 1967 in that light. "God was on our side,"
or "was watching our back," as it were. The problem with that theology,
of course, is that the Jewish skeptic within us immediately jumps up to
say, "So where was God in 1944?" That makes us go back and look again

at naturalistic—in this case military—reasons for those victories. Alternatively, Naḥmanides might, in speaking of hidden miracles, have been talking about the sunrise, the birth of a child, or falling in love. Surely we experience these as hidden miracles, even though they are also entirely natural occurrences.

Yes, the miracle is in the eye of the beholder. No one can perform a hidden miracle for you. Only in retrospect, as you see an event unfolding, can you declare it such a miracle. That has everything to do with an awakening of a sense of wonder within you, a moment when you feel in the event the presence of a greatness that transcends the ordinary. What is happening may be entirely natural, yet completely extraordinary.

How do you respond to such a moment, other than with prayer? "We thank You . . . for Your miracles that are with us every day, evening, morning, and afternoon."[3] The Hebrew word for "miracle" in that prayer is *nes*, the same word as in *nes Ḥanukkah*, "the Ḥanukkah miracle." But the word *nes* really means "banner." The miracle is a "banner moment," one that sticks out, rising above the rest, and calls out: "*Here* I see the divine presence! Let me wave its banner!"

Some hidden miracles just happen to us; their power is so overwhelming that we cannot deny them. In many cases, however, we choose our miracles. I drive up to the mountaintop early in the morning in order to see the sunrise from there. I feel a shudder of divine presence in the way that child looks at me because she means so very much to me. I open my heart and allow a glimmer of mystery and eternity to enter me, putting aside my fears, banishing my inner skeptic in order to allow for such a sacred moment.

In choosing to make the lasting of the oil the true miracle of Ḥanukkah, the rabbis made Ḥanukkah into a festival of light. A festival of light in the midst of winter of course has echoes that reach far beyond the borders of Jewish history and the Maccabean story. Yes, it is likely that the theme of light was picked from broader cultural influences, just as the Christian festival in the same season came to be celebrated by lighting up the dark. Our tradition is filled with such universal influences, and there is no reason to deny or flee from them.

Light has been associated with divinity since ancient times. Many biblical verses, especially in the Psalms and Proverbs, use light in a semi-metaphorical way when seeking for a language to describe the ineffable or to reach in to the core of religious experience.[4] "Y-H-W-H is my light and my salvation" (Ps. 27:1). "In Your light we see light" (Ps. 36:10). "For You light my candle" (or "kindle my lamp"); "Y-H-W-H brightens my darkness" (2 Sam. 22:29). "Happy is the people who know the joyful shout; O Y-H-W-H, they walk in the light of Your countenance" (Ps. 89:16). "Y-H-W-H is God, and has given us light" (Ps. 118:27). "The soul of a human being is the lamp of Y-H-W-H, revealing all the inmost parts" (Prov. 20:27). "For Y-H-W-H shall be a light to you forever" (Isa. 60:20). Philo and the Neoplatonic philosophers described God as light as well, and distance from God as increasing darkness. We turn toward the ethereal to try to grab hold of the abstract. Reaching for God is a reaching toward the inner light. Light, along with air, seems to be the most insubstantial reality we know, yet its presence is essential to our well-being. The heart fills up with joy as we step out of darkness and come into a place of light. Light is the first of God's creations. Torah is associated with light: "The commandment is a candle and Torah is light" (Prov. 6:23). Hence our English word *enlightenment* for education. Shabbat also is described as a time of light; it begins and concludes with the lighting of candles.

When mystic seekers try to describe their experience, they often first turn to the language of light. Quite a few treatises in the Jewish mystical tradition bear titles like *The Light of the Eyes* or *The Shining Light*. The greatest of all Jewish mystical writing is the Zohar, meaning "Shining" or "Brilliance"; it is a work filled with images of sublime inner light. So too in other mystical traditions.

Or ha-ganuz, "the hidden light," is one of the most ancient and beloved of Jewish legends. The light with which God first created the world was so bright that with it "a person could see from one end of the world to the other" (yes, the world must have still been flat when the tale was first told!). God saw that it was too bright for us to handle; it was a light that would allow for no hiding, no secrets. So God hid it away for the righteous, living in a future time when they could be trusted to handle it well.[5] That is why our light is only that of sun and moon, created on the fourth day, not the first. But where is that light hidden, waiting for those righteous to discover it? Can we catch a glimpse of it, enough to sustain us through the dark of winter, or the darkness of daily life? Some of it is in the Torah, which itself is called "light."[6] Those who truly delve into it become "enlightened," in the true sense of the word. But that light is also to be seen in the faces of children, in spring mornings, and in moments of generosity and love.

Some of that divine light is found also in our modest little Ḥanukkah candles or oil lamps. This is a time to contemplate them, to be grateful for that light, and to feel the miracle of what it does to our hearts as we look at them. Maybe *that* is the real miracle.

Purim

LIVING IN AN UPSIDE-DOWN WORLD

O N THE FACE OF things, Purim is the simplest and most obvious of Jewish festivals. For a people who lived as an oppressed minority for most of our history, often victims of severe persecution, to have a day of raucous celebration over defeat of our enemies seems healthy and natural. Purim is the ultimate holiday of that line often used to describe a whole series of Jewish celebrations: "They persecuted us. We survived. Now let's eat!" Except on Purim the conclusion is more like "Now let's drink!"

We have no historical evidence for the biblical tale of Mordecai and Esther saving the Jews from slaughter in the Persian capital of Shushan. There is much about the story that suggests it is an early work of fiction, perhaps even parody (the similarity of "Esther" and "Mordecai" to the old Babylonian gods Ishtar and Marduk is hard to ignore). But Jews have taken it quite seriously, tying its villain Haman back to Israel's first enemy in its desert trek, Amalek, and then making him into the prototype of all Jew haters through history. "So many Hamans," goes an old Yiddish proverb, "but only one Purim!"

The story told in the scroll of Esther also appears to be an entirely secular one. The events come forth on their own, with no mention of divine interference. Esther is a skillful player at the game of court politics, using her "female wiles" to her best advantage. For this reason, there was considerable debate about including it within the biblical canon, and it was among the last books (along with the Song of Songs and Ecclesiastes) to be declared holy, early in the second century CE. By then, it would seem, the festival was widely observed. It is likely that the canonization of the text was in response to popular demand.

For many Jews today, however, Purim raises questions of conscience. The latter chapters of Esther tell us how the Jews, once they were vindicated, went about merrily, so it seems, slaughtering their enemies throughout the empire. Haman's ten sons were hanged along with him, and the audience (both the literary "audience" of Shushan Jews and the real one of later readers) seems to rejoice at that part of the tale as well. There is a famous story about a well-known Israeli educator, Professor Ernst Simon, who refused to celebrate Purim, even though he was otherwise an entirely observant Jew. Purim is celebrated on the fourteenth of the month of Adar in most places, but in Jerusalem, as well as other ancient walled cities, on the fifteenth, as it was in ancient Shushan, according to the biblical text.[1] Simon, who lived in Jerusalem, would each year travel to Tel Aviv toward the end of the fourteenth, and stay there through the next day. Thus he was never in a place where the obligation to observe Purim would be binding upon him.

Professor Simon (1900–1988), a disciple of Martin Buber, was one of the key figures in Brit Shalom, a group of Jerusalem intellectuals who worked hard to try to find a way for Jews and Palestinians to live together in peace and mutual respect. He no doubt understood that the Purim story, while perhaps having served as a healthy outlet for oppressed Jews in the worst times of our history, looks rather different in an era when Jews are in power, and when others are subject to us. Years after Ernst Simon's passing, most Jews were horrified to hear that a fanatical Jewish settler used Purim as an occasion to slaughter a large group of Muslim worshippers during their prayers at the grave of our common ancestors Abraham and Sarah in the ancient city of Hebron. *Most* Jews were horrified—but not all. There is still a hard core of followers who see that murderer as a martyr, an exact mirror image of the way Palestinians have granted martyrdom to people who have committed the most horrendous acts of terror against innocent civilians in Israel.

Yet we refuse to abandon Purim. Partly that is because of some of the nicer practices associated with it: a festive meal, lots of laughing and joking, the exchange of little gifts of food between friends, and special attention to the needs of the poor. Drinking is especially recommended on Purim, including inebriation to the point where one can't tell the difference between "Blessed be Mordecai" and "Cursed be Haman!"[2] Needless to say, there are Jews who are careless about lots of other practices that occur in the course of the Jewish year, but are quite strict about observing this one.

But there are also some more profound thoughts associated with Purim, and the hasidic teachers made the most of these. First, they noted that Yom Kippur in the biblical text is always referred to in the plural form, *Yom Kippurim*. But this makes it sound just like *Yom ki-Purim*, "a day like Purim."[3] On Purim, as we said, we are to get so drunk that we cannot tell Mordecai from Haman; on Yom Kippur, God gets so inebriated from rejoicing at all the prayers of Israel that He, blessed be His name, also cannot tell the righteous from the wicked—so He has to forgive everyone.

The notion that God gets drunk on all those prayers may seem a little strange. It based on the Hebrew root *b-s-m* and the verb derived from it, *le-hitbassem*. More strongly than in English, it contains the full range of "to be intoxicated." *Bosem*, from the same root, is "perfume," with its intoxicating aroma. The lovers' garden in the Song of Songs is full of *reaḥ besamim*, "intoxicating aromas."[4] The prayers of Israel are so sweet to God that they turn the divine away from judgment, awakening love and compassion. We should do the same on Purim, say some hasidic voices that turn away from the excesses of the day.

At the crucial turnaround moment in the Esther story, the narrator used the phrase *nahafokh hu*, "just the opposite happened" (Esth. 9:1). That becomes a theme in Purim celebrations, allowing for plays and skits at the meal where leaders and teachers may be gently mocked. Headstands are also used as expressions of *nahafokh hu*. But the verb *hafokh* can also mean "to be transformed," and there are various Purim teachings about how a person may be transformed by new insight, even while living in what seems to be an entirely natural world. Others talk about the transformative power of limitless joy, the hilarity of Purim serving as a breakthrough moment for one whose skies are overly clouded with depression or too much seriousness about life.

Pressing deeper, hasidic authors look for hints in the story that the divine hand is present after all. Is this the sort of "hidden miracle" we discussed in our Ḥanukkah chapter? Where might the hidden hand of heaven be discovered in the Purim story? Was it the grace that "Esther found in the eyes of all who beheld her" (Esth. 2:15)? Might that have been something other than mere physical beauty? Might the secret lie in Mordecai's courage in not bowing down before Haman? Was the surprising gesture of the king in raising his scepter to Esther perhaps guided from beyond? Might it have been just a subtle touch of divine intervention that kept the king awake one night, when the plot against him was revealed, setting up all the rest of the story? All these and many other suggestions are to be found in the vast corpus of teachings around Purim.

Toward the end of the Purim story, the text says that the Jews "fulfilled and received" all that Esther had instructed them. Because this verse can appear to be repetitious (Esth. 9:23, 27), the Talmud refers it to a different meaning: the Jews then "fulfilled what they had already received."[5] This represented a second acceptance of the Torah. The Talmud narrates a legend that God held the mountain over Israel's heads at Sinai and said: "If you accept My Torah, it will be good. But if you do not, you will be buried here." But this creates a moral problem. If Israel did not accept the Torah freely, is it really binding upon them? Doesn't the covenant have to be entered into out of free will? It resolves that difficulty by saying, "They accepted it again in the days of Ahasuerus."[6]

The hasidic master Rabbi Levi Yizḥak of Berdychiv refuses to take that legend literally.[7] The "mountain held over their heads," he says, was the obvious presence of miracles. There were so many miracles displayed in that generation: the plagues of Egypt, the splitting of the sea, the great smoking mountain itself. How could the Jews possibly *not* have accepted and agreed to fulfill the Torah? But that, he suggests, is a kind of forced acceptance, a case of "holding a mountain over their heads." At the time of Esther, they accepted it again. That was precisely a time of no visible miracles, he noted, a time just like ours. Only a Torah accepted in those times, when we expect nothing out of the ordinary to happen—yet struggle to see everything as being "out of the ordinary"—is a Torah by which we can live, and that will obligate us, in our day as well.

The Zohar particularly loves the book of Esther. Because it is scripture, its verses may be quoted along with any others to give us a glimpse of the upper realms into which the mystical text seeks to draw its readers. Verses describing the luxury of the king's palace in Shushan are thus employed, sometimes together with verses from the Song of Songs, to tell us about the lush chambers and gardens that exist in the heavenly palaces. Even descriptions of "the king"—foolish, wicked old Ahasuerus—are applied to *the* King, the blessed Holy One Himself.[8] Later kabbalists wrote whole commentaries on Esther, interpreting it just this way. "The heavenly kingdom is like the earthly kingdom," the Talmud says.[9] If we're going to use royal imagery to speak of God, why not go all the way? Still, to compare the divine kingship to this particular monarchy is itself a real example of *nahafokh hu*, turning the world upside down.

Indeed, perhaps we live in an upside-down world. Fiction has become reality and reality is fiction. Even if there was no historical Haman, our history is filled with Hamans. The Purim story gives reality a run for its money. Elie Wiesel, in the frontispiece to one of his books, tells the story of his encounter with his grandfather's *rebbe* after the war (and I paraphrase): "What do you do?" the *rebbe* asked. "I write stories," Weisel replied. "What kind of stories? Are they true?" "What does 'true' mean?" asked the writer. "Well, you know, did they really happen?" Then Weisel looked up at the *rebbe* and said: "If what we've just been through in the Holocaust teaches us anything, it's that there can be truth in things that never happened, and that some things that indeed happened cannot possibly be true."[10]

He could have said that about all of Jewish history. And Purim is the "true" story that goes along with it. Somehow that makes it worth acting out the drama, even with all the risks involved.

Purim is also a great reminder that the tradition comes wrapped up in a good sense of humor—something too easily forgotten. Part of being Jewish is knowing how to laugh at ourselves. Without that, religion *really* gets dangerous.

Pesaḥ

SOME QUESTIONS OF MY OWN

WE BEGIN WITH THE wicked child, the one who seems to get such a "bum rap" in the Passover Haggadah. He asks, "What does this service mean *to you?*," a question remarkably close to that posed by his brother, the young sage.[1] But "because he took himself out of the group," we are told, he is to get his teeth whacked. "Had he been there," back in Egypt, "he would not have been redeemed."

Ouch! What an awful punishment for a kid who frames his question the wrong way! Can we imagine either God or Moses being so vindictive as to leave him behind, alone in Egypt, after "all the hosts of Y-H-W-H went forth" (Ex. 12:41)? The only way to understand "would not have been redeemed" is to turn the responsibility back toward him. This "wicked son" would have refused to leave Egypt when he had the chance.

Sadly, this is a figure all too familiar from Jewish history: the Jew who did not leave in time. Jews who willingly stayed in Germany or Austria until it was too late, Jews who didn't flee Poland after the Hitler-Stalin pact, Jews who stayed in Syria in the 1980s—and the list goes on. They weren't necessarily "wicked," of course, just foolish, perhaps too rooted in the old soil, or too attached, either to material goods or to a way of life, to imagine leaving when they should have.

But what about us? If *mitsrayim* (literally "the straits") or "Egypt" refers to *anything* that enslaves you or constricts your spirit, as the hasidic masters tell us over and over again, are we too in that group of "Jews who refused to leave"?[2] What is it that enslaves us, and why do we fear to break the chains? Are we ready to leave our particular forms of "Egypt," or are we among those who will choose to stay behind? These are the tough questions that a true celebration of Passover forces us to confront. It's not just matzoh balls!

Let us remember what a fortunate Jewish generation we are. We live in a very rare moment of history when nowhere in the world are Jews being oppressed by the state for the "crime" of being Jews or living out their Judaism. We have the great luxury, in our day, of not having to see this story through the eyes of a still-oppressed people. Yes, there are still anti-Semites in the world, and vigilance remains appropriate. In recent years, with encouragement from a certain prominent person, they seem to be crawling out of their post-Holocaust holes. But nowhere do they govern over Jews or tell them what they may or may not do. Indeed, we Jews are undeniably a force in the power establishment that rules over others, both by our relatively high status (economically, educationally, and so on) in Western countries, especially the United States, and in the State of Israel. This forces us to ask whether we may have switched roles in the Passover story. Could one part of our enslavement be that of being stuck in the role of oppressor?

Jews are surely among the most successful immigrant groups of the many that have sought refuge on U.S. shores. Although most of our ancestors were not here to participate directly in the oppression of either Native Americans or African Americans, we live off the fat of the land that was made wealthy, in significant part, through their loss and suffering. Where does that put us, as we read the tale of liberation from Egypt, knowing how deeply others have drawn on that story and found in it the strength to struggle toward their own liberation? What do we need to do about it? Pesaḥ reminds us of a bondage to our comfortable upper-middle-class complacency—just as Sukkot does, in its own way—that we dare not ignore.

Our personal and individual "Egypts" are too numerous and varied to be listed, but they too are at the very heart of our neo-hasidic Pesaḥ. They may consist of patterns of behavior, addictions, unhealthy relationships, and lots more. The call to liberation forces us to look them in the eye. The hasidic sources also speak of enslavement to the patterns of *hergel*, habitual behaviors, or just resignation to the seeming ordinariness of life. This can include unthinking or unfeeling religion, a matter with which the hasidic masters were very much concerned. The sense of miracle is an essential part of liberation from Egypt. It was God's "outstretched arm" by which we went forth, the revealed and obvious presence of something beyond the ordinary, a reality that defies description in language, but fills us with awe. That means an awareness of divine presence that uplifts us from our daily lives, calls us to wonder, and gives us a new sense of being truly alive.

Here we are. It's Pesaḥ, and we are celebrating our liberation. The narrative of the Haggadah begins that way: "We were slaves to Pharaoh in Egypt, then Y-H-W-H our God brought us forth." All well and good, except that before we begin to tell the tale, there is a formula by which we invite the hungry to join us at our table. There we said: "This year we are slaves; *next year* may we be free."

So which is it? Are we celebrating our freedom or acknowledging our bondage? The answer, of course, is yes. Both are true at one and the same time. It may even be that they are deeply connected to one another. In the hasidic reading, the most essential form of exile and bondage is that of the mind. *Da'at*, best translated as "spiritual awareness," is what is in exile, both in the Egypt narrative and in our own lives. That awareness is the natural state of humanity; children have it in greater measure than most adults. It gets covered over, in the course of our lives, by a series of *kelipot*, "shells," that we build around ourselves, or *meytsarim* (= *mitsrayim*, "Egypt"), narrow straits that limit our view of who we are and where we live.

The first step in liberation from such blinders is the recognition that they exist. "This year we are slaves" is that admission. At the same time, however, we also celebrate our liberation. The celebration itself calls upon us to make that freedom ever more real, for ourselves and for those around us.

The way we choose to engage in that celebration is also intriguing. We celebrate our liberation *by telling its tale*. The key *mitsvah* here is that of narration, called *haggadah* (only later does that become the name of the book through which we do it). "You shall tell it to your child" (Ex. 13:8) is the operative verse here. Compare it for a moment to other festivals. Most of them have a central symbolic form that defines them. On Ḥanukkah we light the candles; on Rosh Hashanah we blow the *shofar*; on Sukkot we dwell in the *sukkah*. Of course, we also explain the meaning of the day and tell its story. But only on Pesaḥ is that act of narration, alongside the eating of *matsah* and the bitter herb, an essential fulfillment of the holiday obligation.

Why? I would suggest that it is because we are supposed to *talk our way into freedom*. If liberation is to begin with the freeing of our minds, removing the blinders that limit our awareness, we need to engage in convincing ourselves that we can indeed be free. "Yes, we used to be slaves," unaware of our own souls, of our potential for knowing Y-H-W-H and living in the light of God's presence. We tell the story in order to make it real. Now that we have reached this freedom—and the narrative assures us that this is the case—our task is one of carrying its torch forward, passing its vision on to our children and extending its reach to others.

The word *haggadah*, understood as "narration" but originally meaning "flowing forth," has a parallel in the Hebrew word *sippur*, "story." This *mitsvah* we fulfill at the *seder* is often called *sippur yetsi'at mitsrayim*, "the story of the Exodus from Egypt." We are commanded to be storytellers. But that root s-p-r in Hebrew has three meanings, linked to one another as early as the ancient *Sefer Yetsirah*, to which we have referred several times here. S-p-r can mean "to tell a story," as in *sippur*, but also to count, as in *mispar*, "number." (You might think of "counting" and "recounting" in English.) The third meaning, "to shine," is originally from a different source. The Torah (Ex. 24:10) refers to a precious stone called *sappir*, "sapphire" in English. The Jewish esoteric tradition sees them all as one. To tell the tale is to polish up the events as they happened, to make them shine, to turn them into a beacon.

Our liberation from Egypt is paradigmatic. Freedom movements all over the world have responded to that beacon, taking up the Exodus narrative and making it their own. Surely that is part of the blessing that the scripture of ancient Israel has given to the world. But what does that reality call upon us Jews to do? Yes, it means affirming the cause of our own liberation. Ours is not merely an ancient memory, now taken over by others. In a generation when a third of the Jewish people had just been slaughtered, the ingathering of exiles and the proclamation of independent Jewish statehood was surely one of the great liberation moments of modern history. It is almost impossible for us, as Jews living after both 1945 and 1948, to tell the tale of leaving Egypt without hearing echoes of our people's exodus from Europe in those years. The continuing redemption of oppressed Jewish communities that came in its wake is also on our minds; the exodus from Iraq, from Yemen, from North Africa, from Ethiopia, and from the former Soviet Union all come to mind. To see the wondrous in the ancient tale and deny its echoes that have resounded in our own memory would be folly.

At the same time, we must remember that the gift of liberation was not given us only that we might sit back and enjoy its blessings. "I am Y-H-W-H your God who brought you forth from Egypt *to become your God*" (Num. 15:41). It was for the sake of engagement and commitment that we were redeemed from slavery. That has to mean active concern for the liberation of others. We cannot make an exception when there is a conflict between their liberation and the self-interest of the Jewish people. Whatever the right solution to the Israel-Palestine conflict is—and here is not the place to adjudicate that—the reality of suffering and oppression on the other side is something we cannot fail to notice. And once we notice, we are called upon to act out of care.

The narrative section of the Haggadah ends as we raise our second cup of wine (we have been careful to recite the tale over a full cup of wine, indicating great festivity) and we recite the blessing *ga'al yisra'el*, blessing God who "has redeemed Israel." The hasidic master R. Levi Yizhak of Berdychiv asked: "How can we say this blessing in the past tense, when Israel is still in exile?" He responded by telling the tale of a young child, sitting at the table a long time (as we have during the course of the *seder!*) where there is a plate of cookies in front of him. He knows he is not supposed to eat them, but finally cannot restrain himself. What does he do? He calls out the words "Blessed are you Y-H-W-H our God, eternal sovereign, who creates various types of food," the blessing recited over a cookie. What can the father do? He cannot let it hang there as a mean-ingless blessing! He has no choice but to give the child a cookie. We, says Levi Yizhak, are like that child. Perhaps calling out, "Who has redeemed Israel" will force the divine hand.

Of course, R. Levi Yizhak said that at a time when the people Israel was living in the czarist empire, very clearly unredeemed. But what is our situation now? Yes, we are out of Egypt—but we are still in it. "Next year may we be free people!" our Haggadah has proclaimed. We still live in an unredeemed world, even those of us who live in a Jewish state. Sadly, evidence of that unredeemed condition is before us every day.

Our liberation brought us to the foot of Mount Sinai, where we were declared "a kingdom of priests and a holy people." Priesthood only makes sense if there is a broader community that is to be served by those priests. Here that refers to the entire human community. We are to serve others by sharing with them the account of our liberation, reminding both them and ourselves that once "we were slaves to Pharaoh in Egypt." All that we have created, ranging from the moral insights and institutions of Torah and rabbinic tradition all the way to the free Jewish society reestablished in the Land of Israel, has come about in response to our ongoing liberation. The commandment to celebrate freedom is one we are meant to share, inspiring others to seek freedom as well.

Immediately following the *seder* and its account of our liberation, we begin a period called *sefirat ha-omer*, when we publicly count off each day for the next fifty, concluding with the holiday of Shavuot. (Hence the Greek term *Pentecost*, for the fiftieth day.) While originally a practice used for calculating the agricultural season, the rabbinic tradition used it to establish a deep connection between these two festivals.[3] Passover celebrates the redemption of the Hebrew slaves from Egypt; Shavuot commemorates the receiving of the Torah, which took place "in the third month" (Ex. 19:1) following the Exodus. We needed to be free in order to receive God's word, to accept responsibility as free people about to constitute "a kingdom of priests, a holy nation" (Ex. 19:6).

This noble sentiment, key to the rabbinic understanding of our sacred history, stands in contrast to an earlier tradition that saw the Exodus itself as an event in which the hand of God was seen (Ex. 14:31) and God's love for Israel fully revealed. In that view, the liberation from bondage was a sacred moment standing on its own, not seen as a preparation for the great revelation to come. Talmudic tradition says that "a handmaiden at the splitting of the sea saw more than Isaiah or Ezekiel," the greatest visionaries among the prophets.[4] At the Reed Sea, another tradition tells us, we saw God so clearly that we pointed with our fingers and cried out: "*This* is my God, and I will glorify Him!" (Ex. 15:2).[5]

Liberation itself is sacred. To come out of bondage is to discover God, even if you don't call it by that name. To exult in freedom is to reclaim the divine image that had been robbed from you by your oppressor. *When the Torah says (in Deuteronomy 26:8) that God brought us forth from Egypt "with great awe," the Passover Haggadah comments: "This was God's presence revealed!"* This truth is confirmed by accounts of liberation throughout the world, and on every scale. Ask a Jew who came out of the displaced persons (DP) camps after the war, a black South African who survived apartheid, or your gay kid who came out of the closet this year.

The crossing of the sea is celebrated on the seventh day of Pesaḥ, following the order of the biblical tale. The Torah reading for that day includes the Song at the Sea (Ex. 15), the first of what the sages called the ten great songs that echo through history.[6] But this is also the day on the yearly calendar when the Song of Songs is read in the synagogue.[7]

This ode to love, read throughout the tradition as witnessing the courtship between God and Israel, is linked to the Song at the Sea by the
second-century sage Rabbi Eliezer, who claims that "the Song of Songs
was spoken at the Sea."[8] The "handmaiden" at the sea, who saw more than
the prophets, turns out to be Israel herself, the slave girl whom God has
redeemed and taken as His bride.

We then have two messages that seem to emerge from the celebration of our freedom. One tells those who struggle to seek freedom (which
means most of us, of course): "Your liberation is just the first step along
the path. Now you must take responsibility, discipline yourself, and create a new life." That is the message of counting the days. Coming out of
Egypt was only preparation for the covenant of Sinai. The real goal is
that of accepting Torah, commitment and dedication to our holy task. But
there may be an older and simpler truth hidden behind this one. "Rejoice!
Celebrate your freedom! Find God in this very moment!" Your liberation
means that you are loved.

The answer, of course, is that both of these are true; each has its place
in our ongoing lives, as individuals and as communities. The struggle to be
free and our gratitude for whatever measure of freedom we have attained
are not to be taken lightly. They deserve our full celebration. But the call
to move beyond, to ask the quintessentially Jewish question "What does
this freedom *demand* of me?" is never far behind.

Shavu‘ot

FOR MANY JEWS IN North America, Shavu‘ot is surely one of the least known and least observed Jewish holidays. Another irony of Jewish history: the holiday of the book, forgotten by the people of the book.

Shavu‘ot, which commemorates the giving of the Torah at Mount Sinai, should by rights be the apex of the Jewish festival cycle. Passover, the time of liberation, leads up to it. We count the days from Exodus to Sinai as though liberation itself were just a prelude. In order to be wedded to our God at the Mountain, we have to be free from bondage to all our inner and outer pharaohs. Sukkot, the third partner in the pilgrimage cycle, basks in the afterglow of Sinai. In it we celebrate our wandering through the wilderness and eternal preparation to enter the Promised Land, there to fulfill the Torah we have received. Neither of these makes sense without the main event, the revelation of God at the Holy Mountain. This is the way the ancient rabbis construed the Jewish calendar, and that structure carries through in the world of hasidic teachings as well.[1]

Sinai takes us to the heart of the Jewish faith: it claims that God communicates to humans; that such communication took place between Y-H-W-H, Moses, and Israel at the mountain in the wilderness; and that this revelation makes known the divine will. In one form or another, this set of claims stands as the basis of all of classical Judaism. Objections to it, both theological and literary/historical, and defenses against those

169

objections, have served as a break-point between Orthodox and liberal Judaism over the course of more than a century. Recent developments within the intellectual leadership of modern Orthodoxy have shown some remarkable openness toward movement on these questions, and new creative formulations have begun to emerge.[2]

What I seek to articulate here is a mature and believable Jewish faith based on an ultimate commitment to a *nondualistic* vision of the universe, one that seeks to look beyond the radical separation of "God," "world," and "self."[3] Such a worldview was broadly hinted at in the teachings of kabbalists and hasidic authors centuries ago, but was buried by the proclamation of a nonmystical "mainstream" in the emergence of modern Judaism. Essentially, this mystical theology understands that what God reveals at Sinai is God's own Self, the Self of the universe.[4] The entire Torah is naught but this, equivalent to God's own "name." All the rest is commentary. Put differently, the divine Self manifest throughout all of Creation is now revealed; the Torah is a series of symbolic keys through which one may unlock the secrets found within the created world, hidden behind the mask of "nature." But those to whom that Self within Torah is revealed are themselves also part of that Self, microcosmic reflections of the oneness that is Y-H-W-H. Revelation is the realization of that truth.[5]

If revelation and commandment at Sinai are the heart of Jewish faith, they are also the most difficult and "scandalous" claims made by the religious traditions of Israel. Taken at face value, they form the very essence of Jewish "supernaturalism" and seeming theological arbitrariness: Y-H-W-H, the Creator of the universe, chooses at a particular moment to reveal *Him*self uniquely to the Jewish people, addressing them in words and pledging eternal loyalty in covenant with them if they will accept His specific will as manifest in the practice of Judaism. Both mind and conscience reel at such a thought! What does it mean to say that God speaks? Does God speak to Israel in a language that Israel understands, commanding a Torah made up of laws, ethics, rites, and traditions that seem remarkably parallel to, or enacted in response to, forms of worship extant among the pagan nations in whose midst Israel then lived? Can we imagine a God so arbitrary as to choose one nation, one place, and one moment in human history in which the eternal divine will was to be manifest for all time? Is there no revelation of Y-H-W-H, the unifier of all Being, to any culture or in any language but our own? Does "uniquely" have to mean "exclusively"? How can we attribute to Y-H-W-H, who becomes "person" only through our encounter, this sort of arbitrary willfulness? How outrageous is it for us to insist that we alone stood there at the mountain, and thus continue to stand at the center of human history for all time? For these reasons and others, thinking Jews in our time, including many who seek a serious approach to questions of the spirit, balk at accepting the "yoke" of Sinai. The insistence on belief in its literal truth has helped to drive many away.

But hear another voice from deep within the tradition. "Moses spoke and God responded in a voice" (Ex. 19:19). The rabbis comment: God responded "in the voice of Moses."[6] This seems to say that the *only* voice heard at Sinai was that of Moses, sometimes speaking on his own and sometimes possessed by the divine spirit, God responding from *within* Moses's own voice. Rather than a "voice from heaven," there was the voice of a prophet transformed by an inner encounter that can only be characterized as "heaven." Jews over the centuries have debated how to refine the naïve biblical depiction of Sinai and the experience of revelation. The phrase "Shekhinah [divine presence] speaks from within his throat" was often applied to prophets.[7]

The fact is that any sophisticated theory of revelation recognizes a moment in which the divine and human minds flow together. Indeed, we speak of the "mind" of the Divine only by analogy with the human mind. If Y-H-W-H is the incorporeal essence of the universe, and mind or soul is the incorporeal essence of the person, we *call* God the mind or soul of the universe.[8] But in God as Y-H-W-H, embracing all of being as one, there is no ultimate distinction between "mind" and "body," or spirit and matter—as is the case with us humans as well, of course. In seeking to comprehend revelation we may, however, speak of Y-H-W-H as cosmic mind, present in the depths of each human mind, and impressing itself in a unique way upon consciousness. The universal One seeks to be known by the human, this manifestation of its own self that is also, paradoxically, its "other." But its "seeking" or "calling out" to its "other" (the human) is not of language. It is only humans who can make the divine articulate in words, since words themselves are a human innovation. In fact, the most likely correct translation of Exodus 19:19 would render it "Moses spoke and God responded in *thunder*."[9] *Y-H-W-H speaks in thunderclaps; it takes a Moses to translate God's thunder into words.*

If the Jewish mythic imagination regards the divine and human as separate, God dwelling in "heaven" and humans on earth, revelation is the act that comes closest to bridging this division. Moses goes up to the top of Sinai, according to the Torah, and God comes down upon the mountain

(Ex. 19:3, 20). But at that moment the entire top of Sinai is covered by thick cloud—as though to say that the border between the "upper" and "lower" realms is lost. Later accounts of the revelation are more fanciful; they actually depict Moses as riding on the clouds, entering the heavenly realms, and holding on to God's Throne of Glory, thus protected from the angels who seek to burn him with their fiery breath.[10] Moses returns from the revelation still human, but his face glows with the light of that encounter, one in which the upper limits on human spiritual attainment had been momentarily cast aside. He returns to the "world of separation" from an experience of transcendent unity, the Torah now "translated" within him. God's thunder and Moses's words are now one. Moses's face radiates with divine glory; his mouth gives verbal expression to divinity itself.

But the God who speaks in thunder is still the sky god, still the one who dwells in heaven and atop the highest peak. We are seeking a more fully *internalized* version of that foot-of-the-mountain experience, one in which *Sinai is a vertical metaphor for an inner event.* The journey "up the mountain" is in fact a journey to a "higher" rung of consciousness. That "higher," in our contemporary parlance, needs to be rendered as a *deeper* truth than that of ordinary perception or reason. The "heaven" that is its goal exists within the human soul. That was clear to both Maimonides and the kabbalists, long before the challenge of modern biblical criticism.[11]

But suppose we were to search for a different metaphor, one that more fully reflects the inward turning of that quest?[12] Remembering that our earliest ancestors were diggers of wells in the desert, suppose we allow ourselves to turn the high mountain into a deep well. Abraham observed Torah, say the rabbis, before it was given at the mountain. He knew it from seeking within. Let us try to imagine Torah as it was seen by that digger of wells, turning inward to discover the truth.[13] Remember also that the miraculously portable well from which Israel drank for forty years in the wilderness was there by the merit of Miriam, Moses's sister. How might a Torah drawn from a woman's well of wisdom differ from that descending from the top of a man's mountain? Instead of being brought "down" from the mountain, this wisdom or Torah would flow forth like water from deep within the earth. In this spirit, we try to understand revelation as the most profound of *inner* experiences. Seen this way, the prophet's experience has something in common with the creative act, one that reaches into the innermost recesses of the mind, a "place" that necessarily contains an element of mystery. This is an experience known to the artist, the musical composer, the mathematician, and others, along with the religious figure.

We are talking here about an inner straining of the human mind to the breaking point—but rather than a break*down* that leads to madness or confusion, this becomes a break*through* to new achievements of understanding or creativity. These may come in the form of a novel insight or a flash of intuition. Usually, these are instantaneously translated into the medium in which the creator works: into music, into mathematical formulae, into words. The creative spark, like the divine light, is undifferentiated. Only the tools and mindset that lead one to that flash of intuition, and back from it into articulation of its message, draw on the rich stores of inner reserve that person has gathered, thus directing each creative impulse to be embodied in a specific way. (The rabbis say that at Sinai the very senses were confused, and Israel "saw the audible and heard the visible."[14] We can only imagine a state of creative elation from which Einstein would return with a symphony and Beethoven with a mathematical formula!) *At this level of inner experience, lines between "creativity," "discovery," "inspiration," and "revelation" are impossible to draw.* Those lines may have as much to do with the attitude and mindset of the recipient of that insight as they do with the process itself. I come away from the reverie of such an experience bearing a truth, an insight, or a creation that I did not have before. Where did it come from? Is it "mine," or did it come from something or someone "beyond" my own self? Is that "beyond" somehow present within me, a force other than that of my ego-self? How do I answer such a question? The language we have for drawing such fine distinctions belongs to a level of consciousness other than that at which these inner events occur. It takes place as a part of after-the-fact reflection on such moments, not within them. The free flow of inner energies that characterize such moments does not admit clear borders between "I" and "Thou" or between "mine" and "Thine."

When the soul (the human capacity to love and tremble in awe) as well as the mind (the human capacity to understand) participate in the creative, inspirational, or revelatory event, that event takes on a religious character. The human striving for revelation involves joining the emotional and the intellectual life fully.[15] We Jews assert that *Moshe Rabbenu*—Moses our Teacher—had such an experience. The religion of ancient Israel, as embodied symbolically in that moment at Sinai, continues to represent for us the result of one of the great human encounters with Divinity. For us as Jews, it is, in existential terms, the greatest such encounter of all time. We are *covenanted* to this moment of Sinai. We recognize that other such moments may exist—perhaps in the life of Jesus or Mohammad or the

Buddha, for example—but they are not existentially open to us; they are not *ours*. True participation in a spiritual language requires the whole of the human heart. Each heart can speak only one such language. Our heart is given wholly to this one. While we recognize that there may be others, we cannot *know* them, in the biblical sense, cannot "set them upon our heart."

The Jewish people throughout our history has accepted the task of forming a communal religious existence and creating a civilization that stands in response to the event at Sinai. This is what I mean by "accepting the Torah." What we accept is the reality that Divinity is present in humans, and is manifest in our ancient traditions, garbed in human language and human institutions, as it is throughout the natural world. We accept the challenge to create a society, with all its institutional trappings, that embodies this presence. We are no less charged with that task today than we were thousands of years ago. Part of our charge is to maintain and keep trust with the traditions of the past. We are here to be faithful bearers of our heritage. But every generation will have to create some new forms and reinterpret many old ones in order to keep the fire of Sinai alive, to keep it from becoming mere ash.[16] Maintaining a sense of balance between these two, and not losing our awareness of Y-H-W-H while we are engaged in that balancing act, is no small task.

Generations of believers have invested boundless emotional and spiritual energy (*kavvanah*) in the forms of Jewish devotional life, including the words of prayer, the cycle of the calendar, its sacred music, and tales and commentaries. I believe that the power of this *kavvanah* is never lost. The intensity with which a form is used as a vessel of spiritual life grows and builds through each generation of devotion to it. The spiritual depth borne by the words of prayer or the form of offering increases in richness over time. A latter-day seeker, especially one coming from outside the tradition, who opens him- or herself to that form may discover the tremendous riches of *kavvanah* that lie waiting within it. The Jewish people have both created and accepted these forms in love. That love is never lost or diminished, but is only hidden until we discover it again. The forms may not have been *given* by God from Sinai. But they are *what we bring to the mountain*; we invest them and forever associate them with the holiness we encounter there.

The relationship between the memory of Sinai and our ever-evolving religious lives as Jews is not a simple one. There *is* divinity to be discovered within the *mitsvot* (commandments), but this is not the divinity of a commanding God who insists on their proper performance. Judaism *is* a way of reaching inward and outward toward the One, a way sanctified not by power of divine fiat but by the testimony of generations who have walked along the path. *The light that lies hidden within our Torah, made up of the countless points of love and devotion placed there by our ancestors, is also the hidden light of Y-H-W-H.*

Is it then *imperative* that Jews seek out this light? Does the God who has dwelt within the hearts of so many generations, and who has been given expression through these forms, become an immanent *metsaveh*, a "commander," who will stand behind the *mitsvot* as the indwelling embodiment of religious authority? I find myself to be rather close to this position, but I am not ready to assert it in any but the most personal and subjective ways.

In my own religious life, I have come to recognize the need for *submission* to Y-H-W-H (remember to say "Is-Was-Will Be" and not just "God"!) as part of religious devotion. I fought long and hard against this aspect of religious life, but I now, perhaps with long-delayed maturity, have come to accept it. I believe there is no room for God—however defined—in our lives until we can overcome our own willfulness. To thus submit, to "negate your will before the divine will," is essential to accepting our covenant as I understand it, to be ready to serve as a channel for divine presence in the world.

In Judaism, this submission, usually described as *kabbalat 'ol malkhut shamayim*, "accepting the yoke of divine rule," is joined to *kabbalat 'ol mitsvot*, "accepting the yoke of commandments." For myself, I recognize the necessity of this link, and sense that religious awareness becomes constant in life only through the regularity of religious discipline. But I remain constantly aware also of the pitfalls of submission as a religious value. It can lead to the cultivation of an overly passive or submissive personality. Some expressions of submission, in our tradition as well as elsewhere, border on self-rejection. Most seriously, from a devotional point of view, the emphasis on submission may be at the expense of the true joy and exultation that are the heart of religious awareness. I turn to religious language to express the fullness of my heart. Let me be wary that religion itself not serve to diminish that fullness and joy.

The ritual forms or *mitsvot* in such a Judaism are a means, and an often arbitrary one, to a greater end. They are opportunities or loci to encounter and celebrate the presence of the One.[17] Out of my love for our ancestors and the divine voice that has addressed me through these traditions, asking that Jews not abandon them, I choose to be faithful to the religious discipline they represent. I will do so wherever this discipline does not bring me into conflict with religious principles I hold even more deeply: recognizing all humans as embodying the divine image and following the seven Noahide commandments as I have chosen to understand them.[18]

I seek to affirm this commitment anew each day, to keep it an act of faith ever chosen in freedom. I need to cross the Sea each day, a reminder of my freedom, before I can renew the covenant. I am helped in this struggle with authority in religion by the very *helplessness* of God. The One who is present in these *mitsvot* is really no longer the frightening commander on the mountaintop. I thank the ever self-revealing Y-H-W-H for the gifts of biblical scholarship and historical study of religion, which have helped to break the excessive yoke of religious authority, making our generation a post- rather than a premodern one. The Presence that remains within the forms is the still, small voice of our people's deepest inner self. The God I know is a divinity that cannot act or be realized in the human world at all except through human actions. Knowing full well that I live in an age of choice and freedom, one in which I can opt to leave the domain of this religion at any moment, I choose to remain "at home" with the life rhythms of the Jewish people. In doing so, I let myself hear that pleading voice of the One who has so long inhabited these traditions, and who asks not to be abandoned by yet another one of Israel's children.

Such an "imperative" is, of course, an entirely personal one. I share it with the reader without advocacy. I have seen too much of the dark and dangerous side of religion to dare prescribe submission for anyone but myself. Though I take delight in others who join us on this path, I will not permit myself to become anyone else's surrogate "commander." You who seek to stand before that mountain, to hear the voice, to be commanded— you must get there by your own path. There is no better time to start than the night of Shavu'ot, a special moment when the heavens of your heart can open, and Torah can be given all over again.

Tish'ah be-Av

STRUGGLES WITH SACRED SPACE

TISH'AH BE-AV IS UPON us again.
Oy! What a complicated day! We try to sort out memories of the distant past, feelings about the present, and fears for the future—but they all seem to fall back in on each other, no matter which way we turn. The First Temple was destroyed because prophetic warnings were ignored; Jeremiah laughed at self-assured Jerusalemites who were sure that God would never allow His Temple to fall. *Heikhal Y-H-W-H*, "God's own Temple!" (Jer. 7:4), he hears them say, over and over again. But down it went; there was no mercy, either from heaven or from the Babylonian armies. The Second Temple went down as a result of baseless hatred, Jews turning against one another.[1] Rebels to the end must have viewed someone like Rabbi Yoḥanan ben Zakkai as a spineless compromiser. These end-time visionaries were struggling against realists of all sorts, whom they must surely have disdained. In both cases, we were a small power that ultimately fell victim to greater powers' interests. "Trust not in princes," as the psalmist (146:3) said. Where does all that leave us today, when we dare to contemplate the present and the future? How is it possible not to notice elements of all of these ancient scenarios playing themselves out again?

Like so many American Jews, I first learned the power of Tish'ah be-Av in the context of a Zionist/Hebraist summer camp—in my case Ramah of the mid-1950s. In those heady days of Zionist enthusiasm, there was much talk of the *yishuv*, the resettlement of Jews in the Land of Israel, as a *bayit shlishi*, a third Jewish "home," but using a word that also meant "Temple." Perhaps, some argued, we should fast just half a day on Tish'ah be-Av, turning the latter half into a time of celebration. The notion of weeping over a destroyed Jerusalem made no sense at that point, as we saw the city and the country living through an era of intense rebuilding. Our exuberance at Jerusalem's renewal seemed like a proclamation that the forced exile of Israel was at an end. True, the city was still divided by barbed wire and the rifle nozzles of opposing armies. We did not have the Old City or the Temple Mount. I recall one of my teachers in those days saying that this fact itself was an act of God, because possession of those holy sites would so deeply divide the Jewish people. A rather prescient remark! "He prophesied without knowing what he was prophesying," the rabbis say.[2] But it still felt as though at least half of Tish'ah be-Av should be turned toward celebrating the miracle of the return to Zion and the building of the Land. We were innocent, then, of the memory that Shabbatai Zvi had already tried the trick of transforming this day into celebration, an act that was a key symbol of his soon-to-fail messianic movement. So too had we not yet heard Gershom Scholem's warnings—issued after a lifetime of studying Shabbatai—against Zionism playing the messianic card, one that can be terribly painful to retrieve. We therefore muddled along, most of the adult role models still doing the full-day fast, but not quite able to explain successfully why they had chosen to do so.

Then came 1967—a week of elation and relief, followed by fifty years of muddle, obfuscation, and intentional moral blindness. On the one hand, we now possessed all of Jerusalem. *Har ha-bayit be-yadeynu*—"The Temple Mount is in our hands!" became the great rallying cry of that victory. But what, exactly, were we supposed to do in the wake of that conquest? Pushing Arab residents out of their homes and neighborhoods hardly seemed to be the noble act for which we had all been waiting for two thousand years. Nor did parades and proclamations of a "unified" Jerusalem, when you couldn't fail to notice that there was hardly any sense of such unity among the holy city's diverse population.

To understand the magnitude of the Six-Day War's effect on the Jewish psyche, we have to turn to *'olam* and *shanah*, two of the ground concepts around which this book is structured: sacred space and sacred time. The spatial and temporal realms are two key dimensions (along with *nefesh*, sacred person) in which religions seek to concretize their notions of holiness, or particular divine presence. In his book *The Sabbath*, my teacher Abraham Joshua Heschel famously described Judaism as a religion that gave primacy to sacred time over sacred space.[3] Shabbat was his main focus there, but the implications of this prioritization extend far beyond it. It touched on the relative absence of Jewish contributions to creativity in the plastic arts, especially architecture, in contrast to the two dominant religious cultures amid which Jews had lived. It explained why the synagogue was not built to have quite the same awesome aura of sacred space as the cathedral or the grand mosque. On the side of time, it exposed its readers to the hasidic notion of the festivals as *mikre'ey kodesh*, moments that "call forth holiness" in the lives of Jews.[4] Surely part of this notion of holiness in time is derived from one of our tradition's most profound and simple insights: that the two daily changes of light, dawn and dusk, are sacred moments, calling out to be celebrated, once by sacrifice, and now in prayer.

Many years ago, I published an essay suggesting that this choice of time over space arose in response to the destruction of the Second Temple and the sense of exile that so marked Jewish existence.[5] The "palace in time" could be erected wherever Jews found themselves, while sacred space was connected to a place far away, a distant memory. The real Jerusalem, a city that existed on earth, was a place almost no Jews got to visit. It became quite fully joined in the Jewish imagination to an "upper" Jerusalem, a heavenly city dwelling somewhere beyond the clouds, in the realm of myth. The places where Jews lived, scattered about the globe, were profane spaces in their eyes. The locating of divine presence in particular moments, rather than in spaces, simply accorded to the situation of Jews in history, as well as to our self-definition as a community living in exile. That perception did not seem to change very much with the advent of modernity and the decline of oppression as the Jew's daily lot.

All that did change, almost overnight, on June 6, 1967, with the Israeli Army's conquest of Jerusalem's old city, including the Western (no longer to be called "Wailing") Wall. In 1967, the Jewish people reasserted their faith in sacred space, intimately connected to their claim of permanent ownership of this particular sacred spot. Travel to Israel, with the encouragement of both the Israeli Tourist Office and local religious groups, is now often cast as *pilgrimage* to the Holy Land, with special emphasis on visits to the Wall. The "Birthright" claim is that every Jew has a right, perhaps even an obligation, to visit and stand in relationship to the Land of Israel, as well as the Jewish state that exists there. The high point of such journeys is a visit to the Wall. The Wall has, on one hand, become semi-secularized, the site of swearing-in ceremonies for the Israeli Army, and lots more. In that context, it is said to belong to the entire Jewish people—except, so it seems, to non-Orthodox Jews who want to pray there. Only the iconoclastic philosopher Yeshayahu Leibowitz dared call the veneration of the Wall "idolatry," something contradicting the essential truth of Judaism.[6] Most Jews dismissed his view. But I believe that our new situation calls for some rethinking on this subject of time and space.

Secular Zionist thinkers, in the decades leading up to the establishment of the State of Israel, were not focused on the holiness of the Land, except perhaps in a very general and romanticized sense. Their concern was rather with the Jewish people, and the ways in which return to the land (not capitalized here) might be redemptive for them. They indeed spoke of "redeeming" the Land as well, which meant Jewish ownership and cultivation of it. But the true goal was the redemption of the Jewish people from their downtrodden and "unnatural" exilic state. In its earliest formulations, *the land was to redeem the people!* This had to do with rerooting Jewry in the soil itself, an agriculturally based attachment to earthbound reality, saving them from their prior status as *luftsmenschen* (detached, rootless, or "airy" people). Later it was the creation of an independent Jewish society, one that included manual laborers and police officers, as well as academics and merchants. Neither of these visions was concerned with holiness, and certainly not with Jerusalem and its Wall. The dream of the former was centered around the fruitful Jezreel valley and the newly drained Huleh swamp. The latter cared most about growing Tel Aviv, the first all-Jewish city, and the urban versions of the "new Jew" that would emerge there.

Religious Zionism, represented by the Mizrachi Party, a minority within the Zionist movement almost since its inception, did, of course, have a somewhat different vision. Its most inspiring figure, mystic visionary Rabbi Avraham Yizhak Kook, saw the return to Zion in proto-messianic terms. Before 1967, however, not too much attention was paid to that element within his thought. Opposed by the ultra-Orthodox rabbinate that dominated in Jerusalem, Kook was known mainly for his years as "rabbi of the settlements," a religious leader who validated the efforts of nonobservant Zionists as being an unwitting part of the divine plan of redemption. The proudest achievement of the religious Zionists was a series of religious *kibbutzim* established before and after the founding of the state, places where hard work and sacrifice combined with the articulation of Judaism's highest moral and spiritual values. Politically, the Mizrachi movement devoted itself mainly to defending the sectoral interests of observant Jews, an often-struggling minority in a secular-dominated society.[7]

Even though Jerusalem became the capital of the newly founded state in 1948, these visions largely held sway. Jerusalem was seen as a city of university professors (in the days when Hebrew University was *the* university of Israel) and religious fanatics, a place most Israelis wanted to visit only occasionally, as tourists, if at all. It was a city of the past, not the future, which clearly belonged to Tel Aviv, to the *kibbutz*, and to the efforts at building new communities around Israel's borders, including the reclamation of the Negev. As transportation improved, many secular politicians and government officials chose to live in greater Tel Aviv and commuted to work in the capital.

All that changed after 1967, as the Jewish people—both within the Land and beyond it—strongly reclaimed the dimension of sacred space. Foremost among holy places was the Wall, but Jerusalem as a whole was increasingly referred to in religious terms (Naomi Shemer's "Jerusalem of Gold" was a semi-secular expression of this). Now Jerusalem became the city of a different past—not that of Me'ah She'arim and the ultra-Orthodox way of life, but of ancient Israel, the City of David, and dreams of the Temple Mount. So, too, were Hebron, Safed, Tiberias, and various other traditional sites, some of them only recently rediscovered as sites linked to earlier epochs of Jewish history. The political and religious narratives here are deeply intertwined. The defenders of a Judaism of sacred spaces tend toward the right in their views of Israel/Palestine and are willing to mostly disregard the claims of Arab populations; a Judaism of sacred time has become more Western and liberal in its orientation, interestingly linking Heschel's theology and his politics. But it would be too simplistic to simply accept that lineup and take up the case for the temporal over the spatial, thus denying the collective voice of the contemporary Jewish people in defining themselves, but also ceding some key elements of our ancient legacy.

It is true that sacred time is given primacy in the biblical order. The story of Creation climaxes with God's rest, declaring Shabbat as the first entity to bear holiness. Places are declared holy only later, beginning with Jacob's dream in Genesis 28. These include Jerusalem, "chosen place" of Deuteronomy and "My holy city" of the prophets, but also Mount Horeb of Exodus 3:5 ("Take your shoes off your feet, for the ground upon which you stand is holy"), a holy place clearly outside the Land. There is hardly any biblical notion of the entire Land of Israel as sacred space. It is, of course, the land flowing with milk and honey promised to our ancestors. But the notion of "Holy Land" is mostly a post-biblical construct.[8]

Nevertheless, the intensified presence of Y-H-W-H in particular places is certainly an important part of the biblical worldview. Solomon's humble introduction to his great speech in dedicating the First Temple stands out as a key statement of the tension in the developing religion of ancient Israel regarding the location of divinity. "Behold the heavens and the heaven of heaven do not contain You. How much less so this house which I have built!" (1 Kings 8:27). Nevertheless, "You will hear in Your dwelling-place in heaven" (8:30) as people pray in this earthly abode that You have chosen. The unique holiness of that spot, and therefore the terrible sin of its defilement, remains central to the message of the prophets, especially resounding in the voice of Jeremiah. The promise of its future restoration plays a major role in the prophecies of Second Isaiah and Ezekiel, as through the mostly Second Temple–period psalms.

Because the rabbinic tradition saw itself as tied primarily to the Torah text, where the narrative takes place prior to the entry of Israel into the Land, much of the post-biblical discussion of sacred space, both in halakhic ("legal") and aggadic ("narrative") sources, in fact deals with verses describing the *mishkan*, the wilderness tabernacle, rather than the Jerusalem Temple. This *mishkan* was a tented structure that could be disassembled and moved each time the camp of Israel did so, rather than a grand building set into a specifically designated locale. This made for a rather looser notion of sacred space than one might expect. Moses's encounter with the burning bush at Mount Horeb (later identified with Sinai) best described the *experience* of standing on holy ground, even though the rabbis made it clear that its holiness, in contrast to that of the future Jerusalem, evaporated once the particular theophany had passed.[9]

But the verses ascribing holiness to the tabernacle provided ripe homiletical fruit for Jewish preachers as early as Philo and as late as the hasidic masters to internalize or spiritualize the amorphous "place" to which they were referring. Exodus 25:8's introductory "Let them make Me a sanctuary and I will dwell *be-tokham*" came to be translated "within them," rather than the probably intended "in their midst."[10] The priest who entered the Holy of Holies became the worshipper turning toward his inmost heart. The same did not happen with regard to sacred time. Shabbat was real, and needed to be observed in proper form. The Jew "entered into" Sabbath, rather than becoming it.[11] *Mishkan* ("tabernacle") was the distant object of fantasy, hence easily transformed into symbol. But Judaism was greatly deepened by the opening of that symbolic well. Mystics and poets, both medieval and modern, have been nourished by that notion of an inward journey into God's house, of the human heart as God's true dwelling. Think of the wide usage, and now the singing, of verses in the penitential Psalm 27: "One thing I ask of Y-H-W-H; that is what I seek. May I dwell in the house of Y-H-W-H all the days of my life."[12] The intent of the verse is quite entirely spiritualized when read in that context. Indeed, the psalmist himself, one cannot help but think, might have been thinking of something more abstract than just a never-ending visit to the Jerusalem Temple.

Where does all this leave us, now that a full half century has passed since 1967? It is clear that in our great eagerness to celebrate the historic victory of 1967, including the great relief from the worst of our Holocaust-inspired fears, we refused to take notice of the fact that old Jerusalem, while a Jewish dream, is also a mostly Arab city. Efforts, both by governmental and private agencies, to change that reality have been ugly, underhanded, and sometimes brutal. Jerusalem, at least Jewish Jerusalem, is indeed being built every day. But it is hardly the psalmist's dream of "a city joined together" (Ps. 122:3). That dream can be fulfilled only when the *people* of Jerusalem's two (or more) sides are "joined together" in peace.

What is and should be the nature of our contemporary Tish'ah be-Av in the face of all this? Having reembraced sacred space, it feels like we must pay the price. Spiritualization of the notion of "holy place" becomes harder when one has to defend one's people's attachment to a real geographical sacred center. And that center is at the core of more than one conflict that tears at the Jewish soul. Jews possessed of any sense of human decency and memory of Jewish suffering have to be horrified at not-so-subtle efforts to push the Arab population out of the city. And even if we did, the city's past would remain to haunt us. That which we love about the Old City has much to do with Mamluk and Ottoman architecture, not created by Jews. At the same time, Jerusalem has been increasingly claimed by parts of the Jewish people from whom I feel deep alienation, the exclusivist ultra-Orthodox at the Wall, treating women whom I know and care about in simply disgusting ways, and the ultra-nationalists, creating a noisy presence on the Mount, dreaming aloud about destroying the mosque and building a third Temple. Such a rebuilding would be a suicidal act for the Jewish state, for more than one reason. We have seen much of the Israeli public overtaken by a flammable combination of land hunger, triumphalism, and ongoing insecurity, with more than a little bit of racism thrown in. We shudder to think how this all this lines up with those things tradition tells us brought about the destruction of the first two Temples. Idolatry? Baseless hatred? It all sounds entirely too familiar.

A couple of decades ago, I recall hearing the phrase "Friends don't let their friends drive drunk" applied to American Jews and Israelis. But by then we realized that the car keys were not in our hands, and we could not reach the emergency brake. We have watched the country we love, the Zionist experiment we still treasure, engage in what I believe to be indeed suicidal policies, especially that of unrestricted settlement in occupied territories, bringing about inhumane disruption of the lives of local Arabs, then resorting to language and actions that devalue those lives altogether, in order to defend such policies. *Oy, meh hayah lanu:* "Woe, what has become of us!"

We who love Israel, despite it all, still have much to celebrate: the rebirth of Jewish life, the ingathering of Jewish tribes, the renewal of Hebrew and its culture, and lots more. I, for one, also confess to having been swayed by the rebirth of sacred space consciousness in the collective Jewish soul. I do feel a deep attachment to the Wall, the focus of Jewish dreams and prayers for so many centuries, even though I seldom go there anymore. I still have not gone up to the Temple Mount, feeling myself not yet fit to enter those sacred precincts. I do have a special sense of *kedushat ha-arets*, the sanctity of the Holy Land itself. But that is one that leads to obligation, not to privilege. The claim that *erets yisra'el* is *holy* should not be read as a statement of *ownership*.[13] Holiness means a belonging to God, not to us, since we are not God's exclusive earthly representatives. Holiness of the land is rather a declaration that such rules as the sabbatical and jubilee apply there, symbolizing a concern for protecting that land, no matter who owns or governs it. They, in turn, should serve to sensitize us to respect for all earthly soil, wherever we may live. I support recent efforts to apply such "holy land" thinking regarding the treatment of crops and soil outside the land as well. But that should not diminish our special sense of responsibility for *erets yisra'el* itself as a holy place. My recent discovery of holy places outside the Land (see the essay "Pilgrimage 2019" in this volume) also does not diminish my sense of *kedushat erets yisra'el*.

One of the later hasidic masters suggests a reading of the three realms of sacrality (space, time, and person) that is quite redemptive of the whole insistence on particularism that so characterizes Jewish religious language. The *Sefat Emet*, who deeply influenced Heschel,[14] refers in several places to a source that was originally purely a device for legal scholars to justify derivations of praxis from scripture. "Any unit that was part of a larger category," it says, "and became an exception to that category, did so in order to teach something not only about itself, but regarding the entire category."[15] He then applies this notion with surprising breadth to a whole series of specifics and general rules. The Land of Israel was within the category of lands. If it became an exception to that category—in becoming a Holy Land—it did so not only to make a statement about itself, but to teach that all land, the earth itself, is holy.[16] Shabbat was in the category of days. Its becoming an exception, a holy day, comes to teach us about the holiness of the day itself, showing that every day is holy.[17] He says it also about priests or Levites and the rest of Jewry, as also, in what may have been the most daring application in his time and place, about Israel and the rest of humanity.[18]

To express it more abstractly: ritual, or the ritually sacralized space or time, is paradigmatic. The way we relate to it is intended to teach us how to relate to all moments, all places. Here the panentheistic teaching of Hasidism is brought back to the fore: God is to be found everywhere—or everywhere that we let God in. Specific to the author's place in hasidic history is also a certain democratizing within Jewry: the way we seek holiness in the priest, to be read as the *tsaddik*, is a paradigm of the way we are to treat all, encountering each as bearing the divine presence.[19]

Reasserting this attitude toward the specifically holy in Judaism is a crucial item on the contemporary theological agenda. The holiness of the Land is not to be denied. The Torah's special concern for its protection, through the laws of sabbatical and jubilee, reflects the great love our ancient ancestors felt God to shower on that unique and special place. It is a sign of health that the Jewish people have rediscovered that particular love—as long as it is used paradigmatically, as a reminder and a "demonstration project" indicating that all places in God's created world deserve to be cherished, loved, protected. Sacred space no longer exists in a mythic and inaccessible realm, somewhere between heaven and earth, as it did for so many centuries. Most Jews who care about their religious legacy either live in the Land of Israel or visit it quite regularly. But if we understand the holiness that adheres to that land and soil only in an exclusive—and even politicized—way, we will be missing the point.

Tish'ah be-Av is a time to think about responsibility. We diaspora Jews for fifty years have been watching in horror as messianic politics transformed so much of the Jewish moral landscape, beginning in Israel but eventually overcoming much of our own community as well. We were cowed into silence, and accepted it. *'Al ḥet she-ḥatanu bi-shetikah ke-hoda'ah.* We mourn today for our own sinfulness in acquiescence by silence. Yes, we mourn for the past and for the present; we will not permit ourselves to mourn for the future. But this is indeed a day to cry out loudly our fear for that future, and to express in full voice our distress at several of the paths that Israel—both state and society—are taking.

We know why the first two Temples were destroyed. Let us make sure the third one does not totter due to the great sin of our era, that committed by silent bystanders.

World

LIVING IN GOD'S CREATION

Creation

AWAKENING TO GOD'S WORLD

Celebrating and Believing

EACH FRIDAY NIGHT I raise my cup of wine and proclaim: "On the seventh day God completed the work that He had made, resting on that seventh day from all the work that He had done. God blessed the seventh day and made it holy, for on it He had rested from all the work that God had created to be done" (Gen. 2:2–3).

That moment is the highlight of my week. It is the most personally significant ritual act in which I regularly engage as a Jew. But what is my relationship to that text I so fervently call out? It is one of love and commitment, a feeling that the text is as filled to the brim with meaning as my cup is with wine. It is a statement of my faith in divine Creation, of my gratitude for the gift of perceiving a sacred presence that underlies all that is. But surely it could not be called "belief" in the Torah's creation story in any literal sense. I understand that this planet is something like 13 billion years old, that it came to be as a result of a great stellar explosion that took place several billion years earlier. I also understand that the seas and dry land, the trees, grasses, and plants, the birds, fish, animals, and creeping things all described as created on one or another of the six days preceding that first Sabbath of Genesis 1 actually evolved over the course of a long and complex bioevolutionary process, running across thousands of centuries, rather than being "declared" into existence all within a week, however that "week" is conceived.

Yet the story of Creation, and the weekly repetition of it, is vital to my religious life. Nothing is more important to me than my nonliteralist faith that we live in a created world. Both my personal quest for meaning—indeed, the very idea that such a quest is possible—and my sense of responsibility to act in protection of this beautiful and fragile planet are tied in to that faith in Creation. I therefore need to unpack for you what I mean by a theology of Creation, and to do so on more than one level. I will begin in the world of myth, retelling ancient Jewish stories about how this world came to be. I do so because I sense a profound kernel of truth in these tales. Hence the need for myth, the only verbal garment that can contain and reveal such truth. Slowly, we will inch our way toward "reality," telling the new Creation story, the one that is being created every day by astrophysicists, geologists, evolutionary biologists, and lots of others. The goal is somehow to bring these tales together, to lend to the new story some of the mystery and depth of the old. For surely behind both of them lie the eternal human questions: *Where did we come from? Where are we going?*[1] *What is this journey all about?*

Stories of Creation I

When God set out to create the universe, says an old rabbinic story, all the letters of the alphabet crowded in before the Holy Throne.[2] Each of them cried out, "Create the world with me!" In the best-known version of this tale, the letters begin their appeal from the rear of the alphabet, working their way up to *bet* which, like the Latin *b*, is the second letter from the top. *Tav*, the last letter, is rejected because it is associated with death, and God's creation is to be the home of life. *Shin, kof,* and *resh* are all rejected because they together comprise the Hebrew word *sheker,* meaning "lie," while God's creation is to be a realm of truth. And so the tale goes on, upward through the letters of the alphabet, until it comes to *bet. Bet* is the letter of *berakha* (fortuitously translatable with a *b* as "blessing" in English).

As the story unfolds, the letters compete for the position of first letter in the Torah. Tradition says that "God looked into Torah and created the world"; the first letter of Holy Scripture would then also be God's first tool in the creation of the universe. The *bet* of *bereshit* (or the *b* of "In the beginning"), victor in this contest, becomes the primal surge of divine energy through which the project of the world's existence was launched.

The midrash of the letters reveals an interesting dimension of the ancient Jewish love affair with words and language. The universally known creation narrative of ancient Israel is the opening chapter of Genesis. There God (*Elohim*) simply spoke the world into being: "God said: 'Let there be light.' And there was light." As simple as that. God calls each aspect of existence into being by stating its name. This means that ultimate power, that by which all things come to be, resides in language. This verbal myth was so very powerful, we should recall, that it displaced the much more richly pictorial—and indeed far bloodier—Babylonian and Canaanite myth that saw creation as the culmination of a great battle among the gods, or as the triumph of Y-H-W-H over the watery forces of pre-mundane chaos. The old tale receded to the edges of the Genesis narrative in the face of this new and all-powerful myth of the word: the true creative power of divinity (and of God's human image, of course) lies in language. How very primally Jewish this is, setting an agenda for a people who would, in both the sacred and secular realms, achieve their place in history largely through the power of words and books.

But the authors of our midrash of the letters are not satisfied with this assertion that speech is the ultimate root of God's power. They seek to enter into or get behind this primary speech-act. They want to break down the first divine word into its component parts; they say that letters (here they seem to be thinking of written letters, not just the aural sounds they represent), rather than words, brim with divine energy. Each of the letters seeks to put its stamp on God's great project. God the primal speaker has been replaced by God the cosmic kabbalist, arranging the creative powers by juggling the letters of the sacred Hebrew alphabet.

Why does *bet* win the contest? The version we have seen argues that since God wanted to bless the world, or since the divine wisdom foresaw creation as a source of blessing, the letter of blessing was the natural victor. Another version pays attention to the graphic form of the *bet*, written ב. *Bet* is "closed" (meaning it is written with unbroken lines) above, below, and from behind. It is open only looking forward (looking from right to left, of course, in Hebrew order). Similarly, readers of God's Torah or inhabitants of God's universe had best not turn their eyes to what is above, below, or behind the world, but should look only forward, into history, in order to know God's ways.[3] The gift of blessing and the lesson of humility are both given to us when *bet* is selected to begin the Torah.

But what of *aleph*? Why should Creation not take place through the first of the letters? How can the contest be called off before the primary contender has a chance to show its stuff? Here interpreters have made a variety of apologies and explanations. *Aleph* begins the word *arur,* or cursed. God feared creating life under the sign of a curse.[4] Others note that *aleph* had already been given the gift of standing for "one" and thus beginning the number sequence (for the Hebrew consonants also serve as numbers); it could not claim the mantle of beginning the Torah as well as being the first of the letters and numbers. And some point to the fact that the slighted *aleph* would one day be given its due: when God spoke the ten commandments at Sinai, they began with an *aleph,* that of *anokhi* ("I am"). What more could the first letter want?[5]

Here, I think, our reading of the midrash needs to be pushed a step farther, in a direction that seems obvious, yet is not found in any of the textual traditions that I have seen. *Aleph,* as we said, stands also for the number one; *bet* is two, and so forth. The creation of this world is the creation of a universe of *bet,* or the emergence of duality. It marks the passage of the all-embracing One into the realm of self and other, or the transformation of the One as cosmic *aleph* into *Elohim,* a God whose very name indicates plurality, even when used with a singular verb. *Elohim*—the name used for God throughout the creation story in Genesis 1—is author of the world of *bet,* a divinity that has to coexist in a universe shared with others. Creation begins with *bet* because that is precisely what creation is: the origin of multiplicity out of the realm of the undivided One.[6]

As though to dramatize this point, the Genesis story is told as a tale of pairs: light and darkness, earth and heaven, upper and lower waters, sea and land, sun and moon, male and female, weekday work and Sabbath rest. These are the primal pairs through which creation becomes manifest. The most basic of dualities, to which all these others point, is that of God and world, testament to the crucial change that the One has undergone by becoming Creator. Creation, so we would imagine, means that the limitless One is forced to become the One-in-relation. Its endless and ever-renewing energy is now to be manifest in the cacophony of infinite growth and diversity, rather than in the austere silence of changeless eternity. In doing so, God too becomes *Elohim,* a God of diversity and multiplicity.

Yet the midrash of the letters insists that the *aleph* is still there, waiting patiently behind the *bet.* The unity that precedes and underlies all of being has not been essentially changed by creation. What has been added is only another perspective, that of the creatures. From our point of view, God is indeed *Elohim,* a seemingly plural Self who shares the stage of existence with countless other selves, including our own. But from the divine point of view, all is as it was before. One remains one. This unitive truth will be shared with humanity at Sinai, when the *aleph* will manifest itself as the starting point of God's "I am." There the *aleph* will open "I am (*anokhi*) Y-H-W-H your God."[7] Y-H-W-H, containing all that ever was, is, and will be, is identical with *Elohim*, which is revealed as an all-embracing collective, not a plural. Sinai's revelation contains all of Being as a single whole. It will show us the path that leads toward repair of the primal breach that is the inevitable concomitant of Creation, the breaking of the one into the many. The process of individuation requires each being to fend for itself, to insist on its right to self-perpetuation and gratification. The inevitable by-product of that assertion is the sense of each creature's aloneness in the world, the exile of the spirit, and alienation from the One. The revelation at Sinai will begin to show humans the path that will bring us back from there, allowing us to live as distinct beings while still recognizing and serving the One. It will do so once again through words and language, confirming forever the centrality of these to the Jewish mind.

It is no accident that this healing speech begins in silence. *Aleph* on its own is an entirely silent letter; only an accompanying vowel sound can make it speak. The whole Torah, a hasidic master once noted, is contained in that silent *aleph*, waiting to be spoken.[8] But how long does it take to move from *aleph*'s silence to the sound of that "Ah," the sound of the vowel that voices that *aleph*, and the place where all words begin? What is the process that moves the cosmos from silence to speech? On this point even the Torah itself remains silent.

Here our contemplation of the mystery of *aleph-bet* leads us to the question of all questions, the essential conundrum that has teased mystics and would-be mystics since the beginning. If all is one, how do we get to the many? If there is only *aleph*, where does *bet* come from in the first place? In the tale of the creation, the question forms around the origins of the world's existence, seemingly separate from its Source. If divinity is a perfect One, all of reality contained within a single *aleph*, how does our world, called '*alma de-peruda*, the "world of separation" or multiplicity, come to be? When we speak of revelation, the question is reformulated in terms of word and silence, but it is not essentially altered. If all is one in divine silence, how could we ever imagine that silence being broken by the fragmented—and therefore potentially profane—character of speech? Only when we turn to redemption, the third eternal moment of the cosmic schema, is the question reversed: How do we go from speech to silence, from the many to the One, from our world that began with *bet* back to the realm of the silent *aleph?*

The kabbalists tried to deal with this problem by shading the stages of the transition from One to many in almost indiscernible gradations. They described the primal stages of emergence from the One as occurring with the utmost subtlety, and refined them still further, over and over again. First, the One was surrounded by an ether, an air so fine that it could not be grasped. Then there appeared a line so thin that it could not be drawn, then a paradoxical "lamp of darkness," and a primal point.[9] Step by step, stage by stage, with a step backward for each glance forward, the changeless infinite began to approach definition. Each stage in the defining process necessarily brought about an exclusion; if it is this, it is not that. Hence the origin of multiplicity and opposition.

The kabbalists describe the fully manifest divine realm as a network of ten potencies, or *sefirot*, which together constitute the divine Self. This means that the unity of God is dynamic, ten-within-one, rather than static. These *sefirot*, called by a great variety of symbolic names, serve both as stages in the unfolding self-manifestation of the hidden entity out of which they emerge and as rungs the mystic has to traverse in order to restore divine wholeness. But the kabbalists' discussions of these ten powers are also replete with hints that this ten does not represent a multiplicity at all. Ten is, after all, merely one carried to the next power; one need add nothing but a zero in order to create it. So too one hundred and all the rest, they like to remind us, hinting that even the greatest multiplicity can come to be without betraying the One.

But gradation does not adequately solve the problem. I look around at the world of multiplicity, knowing (from both tradition and experience) of the One that lies behind it. When I ask, "Whence the many?" I find the kabbalist prepared to induct me into his realm of complex and subtle myth. I sense the delicacy of his mind and find something more than delicious in its elevation and refinement. In his tale of the origins of the many, I cannot but sense that he *knows* something. He hints to me (without ever needing to say it directly) that he too has been joined to the One, that he knows what it is to emerge from a state of utter absorption and to have to create again, on the far shores of mystical unity, the mind of the many.

But I want more. To the question "How did the many emerge from the One?" the answer "Very gradually" ultimately will not do. So I turn to the next stage of Kabbalah, one that seems to have a different answer to the great question, maybe due to sensing that inadequacy. Here the mystics of the Lurianic School add the notion of *tsimtsum*, or divine self-contraction, to their theory, opting for a quasi-spatial metaphor in order to explain reality.[10] The One is all that exists, they say, and it fills all of primal space. The One indeed leaves no room for the many; any multiplicity emerging within it would instantly be reabsorbed into endless oneness. In order for the many to exist, therefore, the One first has to create the naught. It does this by an act of self-constriction, by removing itself from a certain realm, from which it is then quite totally absent. The first creation is that of the naught, or of the primal space that is the non-God. It is within this vacuum that the domain of the many comes to exist, created by new and specifically directed rays of divine energy beamed in from without—for as soon as we posit the existence of such a kabbalistic "black hole," we have a distinction between "within" and "without." The many represents a strange combination of the absence and presence of the One. It can exist only because of the One's absence, because the divine all-in-all has chosen to become transcendent (read: "absent," "distant") in order to allow for the existence of an "other." But the life source of that other is nothing but the One, for no being could be imagined that does not have its root in Being.

Here, too, the kabbalist's rendering both attracts me and leaves me disquieted. I feel close to the kabbalist in his struggle to be other, to distance the ever-present One from his own inner space so that his separate identity as a created self might emerge and find itself real. But the tension wrought by this void is more than I can bear. To say that I exist thanks only to God's absence is to make me a being who thrives on alienation, who needs to be far from the One at least as much as I need to be near. Will I then seek darkness as much as light? Evil as much as good? How then do I dare to speak of union? If I need divine absence in order to thrive, how do I keep religious passion—the desire for intimacy—from being at least half a lie?[11]

So I turn to the early hasidic masters, my favorite guides and teachers in these inner realms. The first hasidic masters were heirs to kabbalistic cosmology in its most baroque form. Kabbalists since the sixteenth century had elaborated an almost infinitely complex map of worlds, potencies, and restored "countenances" of the divine, interwoven with the mysteries of divine names, letters, and numbers, all in every imaginable combination. One needed vast knowledge of these symbols and their carefully ruled inner dynamics in order to play on the chessboard of Kabbalah, where each move was seen as effecting potential salvific bounty for the universe and each misstep was sure to bring about defilement and divine wrath. The cosmic harmony originally intended in Creation had been shattered by a cataclysm that preceded it, and the purpose of human existence was nothing less than that of restoring wholeness to God. This could be effected only by means of kabbalistic gnosis, a recondite religious intellectuality that supported acts of extraordinary ascetic devotion.

In a move that may be considered one of the great acts of cosmic housecleaning in the history of religion, the first hasidic masters set aside all of these domains. The "heavens" of the mystic's mind were emptied of all their way stations, potencies, and symbolic configurations. These were henceforth to be considered only of psychological importance, and were to be drawn on mostly for metaphoric use. Were we dealing with a polytheistic system, we would say that all the deities and demigods were set aside. Here their rubrics are perforce those of realms and symbols, sometimes personified as angelic and demonic forces, rather than "gods," but the psychological force of their elimination is not much different. The upper realms are redeemed of their clutter and the mystic mind is redeemed of the burden of gnosis, of the need to identify with and unite with each of these arcane principalities in the course of its journey.[12]

The cosmos is now empty. No more ten rungs, five "faces," four worlds, 231 gates, 310 universes, or any of the rest. Now all has been reduced to two. These are the primal pair: nothingness and being, emptiness and fullness, transcendence and presence. The first and the last of the kabbalist's rungs, or *sefirot*, have been retrieved from the ruins of his system. At one end of the empty cosmos stands *ḥokhmah* (divine wisdom), the first point on the map of the One's journey into being. Here all of existence is present in the state of not-yet; *ḥokhmah* is the One out of which all being is to be. At the other end of the cosmos is *malkhut* (divine kingship), the world in all its fullness, the One dressed in the garb of the many, all that potential realized in concrete but ever-changing existence.[13]

Now the task of the mystic is utterly simple. The two have to be revealed as one. Emptiness and fullness, the one and the many, God and the world, need to be unmasked as two modes of the same reality, two perceptions of the same truth. The unchanging One that underlies reality, that existed "before" it and out of which the many emerged, stands over against the One that exists within the many, partaking fully of all the variety of life, evolving, growing, changing in each moment, borne within each being. The quest for truth is the attempt to reveal their oneness.

One of the hasidic masters offers a particularly intriguing reading of the verse in which God says to Moses: "Come to Pharaoh" (Ex. 10:1).

"Come" in Hebrew is *bo*, spelled *bet aleph*. In order to overcome Pharaoh, to triumph in the victory against evil, you have to discover the *aleph* hiding behind the *bet*, to understand that there is always a one behind the faces of duality.[14]

The ultimate symbol for discovery of the one behind the many is to be found within the *aleph* itself. An ancient reading of the forms of letters shows that *aleph* as classically written (think here also of Chinese calligraphers contemplating their brushstrokes) is composed of three letters: two letters *yod* joined by a diagonal *vav*. The two *yod*s represent these two faces of reality, the changeless and the ever new, the two modes of Being. The *vav* (this letter is used for "and" in Hebrew) is thus the *principium conjuntionis*, the force that joins the two together. All is contained within the single *aleph*, a One to which there indeed is no other.[15] The many exist only on the plane of our ordinary reality. We live, we love, we bring forth new generations. We bring this world to the edge of destruction; we stop and seek to heal it. In the midst of all this drama it is good to remember, once in a while, that all of it takes place only within a single pen stroke within the endless and unchanging cosmic *aleph*.

Stories of Creation II

Here's another version of the myth. "By ten utterances was the world created," says the tractate *Avot*.[16] *Ma'amarot*, "utterances," is a nominal form of the root *'amar*, "to say," referring to the ten times the Torah mentions "God said" in the Genesis 1 account of the Creation. (There are actually only nine such verses, but we'll get to that later.)

Faith that the world was created by the divine word, taken quite literally, played a significant role in Judaism through the ages. The notion that God "looked into the Torah and created the world" is another version of this idea, as though primordial wisdom had already garbed itself in verbal form.[17] The biblical "Forever, O Y-H-W-H, your word stands in the heavens" (Ps. 119:89) is read by Rabbi Shne'ur Zalman of Liadi, the founder of Chabad Hasidism, to mean that "the actual words God spoke in saying 'Let there be X' stand forever," and form the essence of all existence, the physical forms of things created merely serving as their outer garb.[18] Here we have returned from the breakup of speech into letters and we are talking about actual words, divine "speech" taken quite literally. "By the word of Y-H-W-H were the heavens made; all their hosts by the breath of His mouth" (Ps. 33:6).

While this view is given particularly strong expression by the kabba-lists, faith in it was universal among premodern Jews, receding only in the face of Spinoza and his followers' awareness of the origins of language itself—including the holy tongue—in the prehistory of humanity.

But in a deeper sense, it may be said that this notion that language stands at the core of all reality is an important building block not only of Judaism, but of what emerged as Western civilization altogether. The three religions that emerge from the Fertile Crescent are all based on faith in the creative role of language, beginning with the divine speech that took place "in the beginning," but then extending into revelation in verbal form and verbal prayer as an appropriate response to this God, the One who by speaking lends potential holiness to the spoken word.

Translated functionally, it comes to mean that verbal conceptualiza-tion is the gateway to comprehension of, and hence mastery over, the natural world, and ultimately all one's surroundings. The power to frame our experience of reality in language-based thought and expression is that which makes meaning out of raw sensory data, saving us from chaos and giving us the possibility of some sense (or illusion?) of control. This is true in the history of societies as it is in the life of the individual.

A somewhat more elaborate version of this teaching opens the brief text called *Sefer Yetsirah*, a most puzzling little document that stands as the earliest speculative text in the Hebrew language.[19] "By thirty-two won-drous pathways of wisdom did YaH Y-H-W-H of Hosts, God of Israel, living God, Eternal Ruler El Shaddai, merciful and compassionate, high and exalted, dwelling in the heights, uplifted and of holy name, inscribe and create His world."

The thirty-two are soon revealed to be the twenty-two letters of the Hebrew alphabet and ten *sefirot*, here meaning the numbers from one to ten.[20] Here the mathematical is added to the linguistic as a tool of mastery and understanding. Language and number are the twin keys to existence; the verbal and the numerical together comprise the wisdom of Creation, and mastery over their secrets allows the creative genius of divinity to pass into human speech.[21] They provide the keys for governing the three primal realms of space, time, and the inner self (*'olam, shanah, nefesh*) and exploring the interconnections among them. *Sefer Yetsirah* winds up being a brief guidebook toward which philosophers, kabbalists, and magicians all looked for inspiration over many centuries.

The message here is that divine Creation and human creativity are to be seen as a continuum, rather than as two separate matters. This is manna for us religious evolutionists. The creative mind and hands of every person, each a unique image of God, are participants in carrying forward the singular creative project of Being itself, a process that has never ceased, as God "renews each day the work of Creation," or as the evolutionary process continues.[22]

The discrepancy between "ten utterances" and the fact that "God said" appears only nine times in the chapter was already noted by the Talmud.[23] Its resolution of the conflict was to say that "'In the beginning' is also an utterance." This strange-sounding assertion makes sense only against the background of an assumed link between *reshit*, "beginning," and a primordial divine wisdom or teaching, the "Torah" God looked into to create the world.[24] This inevitably takes the seeker across a line that some thought to be taboo, speculation on what existed before the Creation of the world, that which lies behind the arched back of that first letter *bet*. For the contemporary reader, this is like seeking to peer behind the curtain of the Big Bang.

"Beginning" as the first utterance sounds like a divine Ruler presiding at an event, perhaps the royal games or royal theater. He has to call out "Begin!" before the play can start. But for God to do so at the outset of Creation, language must already exist. If the first act of Creation is one of divine speech, the capacity to utter words has to be taken for granted. This is something of what *Sefer Yetsirah* means in proposing the twenty-two letters of the alphabet as building blocks of Creation. Language stands in the background of God's speech in Creation. The word is there, but has not yet been spoken. God as the proto-kabbalistic wizard reappears here, forming things by permutations of letters, prior to speaking them as words. The text's authors already have a clear sense that language has a structure of sounds or "letters" underlying it, and that structure must precede its first use.[25]

An old midrash says of the architect who designed Moses's portable tabernacle in the wilderness that "Bezalel knew how to combine the letters by which heaven and earth had been formed."[26] This means that the secrets of Creation can be called forth by other forms of creativity, in this case architectural, not just by the verbal. This greatly expands the link between divine and human creation. Surely the ten primal numbers of Creation might also have been useful to Bezalel in setting out to measure proportions and spatial relations. Those same numbers, one might imagine, could also find expression in musical notations, translated into tone and tempo to create a symphony. Whatever the form of creativity, something of that divine *reshit* ever remains present within it.[27]

The kabbalists added another dimension that spread the creative net even wider, making it the possession of the entire human (and animal) family. They revealed that Creation and *procreation* partake of the same energy. They asserted that even in the most recondite realms of divine mind, there exist forces that operate somehow like sperm and egg. Ḥokhmah and *binah*, two stages within the process of divine intellection, they claimed, are joined together in eternal coital embrace "like two lovers who are never separated."[28] This is a mythic way of saying that *eros* is the force that underlies all creation, both divine and human. It is out of the intimacy within our craving to unite with the other that our creative energies are aroused and ultimately are pulled forward. Every human procreative act partakes of divine creativity, reaching back into the source of energy with which the world began.[29]

Another look at *Sefer Yetsirah* tells us that the ancients were aware of the connection between verbal and progenerative creativity. The two organs that lie front and center in the human form, that work tells us, are mouth and sex organ. Each of them is the locus of a covenant (they were thinking of the male, of course) between the divine and human realms, a covenant that must be fulfilled if the creative output of that organ is to emerge in purity. The covenant of the mouth is that of sacred speech, meaning a commitment to keep the tongue from being defiled, either by speaking untruth or by verbal filth, including gossip and slander. The covenant of the flesh demands sexual purity, the terms of which were once clear, but now demand redefinition in accord with contemporary norms.[30]

What might the contemporary seeker do with the notion of divine speech and its role in Creation? Cultural anthropology has taught us that language itself is not much more than fifty thousand years old in the multibillion-year history of our planet and solar system. Any notion of divine speech can be rescued only by transference to the realm of metaphor, but this is especially true when applied to the primal stages out of which our universe came to exist. To say that God created the world by speaking it into existence is our mythic way of saying that language, including the sort of thought that underlies and is expressed in verbal concepts, is a worthy path through which to seek ultimate religious meaning as we contemplate existence. Turning around the subject and object of that sentence, we might say that existence, or Being, or Y-H-W-H, "speaks" to us, addresses us.[31] We employ the language of divine verbal activity, but we can base such claims only on that which we "hear." But this myth of primal divine speech also permits us to assert that we do not have to retreat into utter silence in our quest after the One. "'In the beginning' is also an utterance" means that language extends into the highest/deepest realms.

"Take words with you," says the prophet, when you "return to Y-H-W-H" (Hos. 14:3).[32]

The text with which we opened, "By ten utterances was the world created," is followed by a (probably later) response: "Why ten? Could God not have created by a single word? But the tenfold Creation is there to increase [tenfold] the calamity coming upon those who destroy the world and to increase [tenfold] the reward of those who act to preserve it." This is a much-needed moral rejoinder, as though made for our era of environmental crisis and multiple threats to planetary existence. But it also opens the door to an understanding that the difference between "one" and "ten" is other than essential, as we have said above. Here we link another rabbinic source to the *Sefer Yetsirah* tradition. The kabbalists seized upon the text in *Avot* as a reference to their doctrine of the ten *sefirot* within an accepted, and already ancient, text. Indeed, it is likely that the tale of the ten utterances linked up with *Sefer Yetsirah*'s ten primal numbers in forming the cosmology that the kabbalistic imagination was to create. Divine speech-acts in Creation came to be identified with what were seen as the inner stages of self-revelation in the emerging divine Self. God "speaks" Godself into being, as it were. The process of the unfolding of one into ten is also the emergence of the divine word out of the recesses of cosmic silence, according to a very well-known trope within the Zohar.[33] The birthing of "God" out of mystery is also the birth of speech out of silence.

That takes us back to the first of the ten utterances, the one that doesn't have a "God said" to account for it. "'In the beginning' is also an utterance" now comes to refer to the highest (or deepest!) of the ten *sefirot*, called *keter*, or the Crown of God.[34] In the cosmic process that leads toward Creation, this represents the first stirring of desire within infinity to become manifest in the vast array of forms or "garments" that it was to take on in the course of moving from static oneness into the endless variety within existence as we know it. In the person (remember that we are in the divine image, and therefore this applies to each of us as well), this is the preconscious mind (*qadmut ha-sekhel* is the Hebrew term), the place where the individual unconscious is still fully plugged into the collective unconscious, to borrow the Jungian term, prior to the first point where individuation begins to take place. All of us have that "place" hidden deep within us. Indeed, the purpose of all mystic teachings, one might say, is to raise our awareness of that inner place and to put us in contact with it.

But the perceptive reader is anticipating yet another set of ten. These are the ten words of Sinai, rendered in English as "the ten commandments," but in Hebrew called simply *dibrot*, "words," quite similar to *ma'amarot*, utterances. These ten stand at the heart of the Sinai revelation, both as described in the biblical accounts and as amplified in later Judaism. There was a certain tendency to downplay the role of the ten commandments in some rabbinic sources, possibly in response to the Christian claim that only these, rather than the full 613 commandments, remained binding. But this effort did not succeed in dislodging the ten from their place of primacy.[35]

The parallel between the ten speech-acts of Creation and the ten of Sinai is a well-known trope of classical Jewish homiletics, especially among the mystics.[36] Their juxtaposition reinforces the claim that Creation is a moment of divine self-revelation, the undefined breath-energy of Y-H-W-H revealing itself through its presence in created forms. Creation (and evolution, I would add) allows for the revelation of the One precisely by means of its masking behind and within the infinite variety of created life. The Sinai revelation repeats that act; now the divine Self is present, hidden, and revealed through the infinite forms of language, present also in all the infinite interpretations and constructions that can be built around the written Word of Torah.

But there is another difference made by Sinai as well. Now the utterances of Creation are repeated in *imperative* form. The message is clear. The divine hand is indeed to be found throughout Creation, referred to as "the power of the Maker within the made." One can come to know Y-H-W-H and to stand in awe of God's presence without the help of religion. But the Torah of Sinai provides a path by which to *respond* to that discovery, creating a system of obligation that sets forth a life of sacred service. As we Jews number the ten commandments, the first serves as something of a preamble: "I am Y-H-W-H your God, who brought you forth from the Land of Egypt, the house of bondage." This is no commandment at all, but rather a declaration, offering a reason to heed those that follow. This first commandment, in other words, is like "In the beginning," a primal statement that was not yet in words, or like *keter* at the head of the *sefirot*, a first arousal of divine energy that has not yet begun to flow. It is what the Zohar calls *reysh hurmanuta de-malka*, "the headpoint of divine manifestation."[37] Nothing has yet happened in the moment of its existence, yet everything is transformed by it. No wonder that the very first word of Sinai, *anokhi*, "I am," has aroused such intense quest for understanding among Jewish seekers, both early and late.[38] Even its first—and silent—letter is said to contain all that needs to be spoken.[39]

The entire Torah, with all of its 613 commandments, is contained within the ten, and the ten within the one.[40] The fullness of Creation, all that is ever to exist, is called forth by the ten utterances, and all of them are contained within the first. The whole of emanating reality, all the worlds, are present in the ten *sefirot*, and all of them are fully present within *keter*, the divine *ayin*, or Naught, as it stands on the edge of existence. There is only One.

Our Story of Creation

To be a religious person is to perceive that we exist in a world infused with divinity and to live in response to that awareness. To be a religious person in the twenty-first century is to accept the account of planetary origins provided by the astrophysicist, of life's origins by the biochemist, and of the emergence of species by the evolutionary biologist, but to see them all as reflecting a sacred process, in our language describable as the self-manifestation of Y-H-W-H in every form of existence.[41] This linking of the old and new accounts of origins is an essential task of a contemporary Jewish theology. How do we embrace the scientific narrative without losing the essential value—and great spiritual power—of "God said: Let there be . . . "?

The question of Creation was to a large extent ignored or circumvented in Jewish theological writing in the late twentieth century. Religious existentialism, coming in the wake of Martin Buber and Franz Rosenzweig, saw the individual's personal relationship with God as the center of its concern, leading back to Sinai and hence to the challenge of accepting the *mitsvot*. Creation was not much on the theological agenda.[42] The writings of Abraham Joshua Heschel, which dominated much of the theological landscape, were deeply imbued with a sense of wonder and mystery in facing the natural world, replete with many quotations to that effect from the psalms and prophets, but also did not engage the question of our living in a post-Darwinian era. The theologies that came in the wake of the Holocaust and the establishment of the Jewish state were mostly concerned with vital issues of collective Jewish identity and of reconstituting the Jewish people following the terrible destruction. Questions of providence and authority dominated much of the conversation, but with rather little reference to God as Creator or what we might mean by that term in a contemporary religious context.

But the question of Creation cannot be ignored. I believe it must be placed front and center in any theology of Judaism in the twenty-first century. This indeed has much to do with the ecological agenda and the key role that religion needs to play in changing our attitudes toward the world within which we humans live. There is no more vital and urgent item on the human agenda in our lifetimes. Without such a change, we will wantonly destroy ourselves, as becomes more evident in the headlines from day to day. It is also clear that the world's religions, as source and pre-server of the myths by which most people live, need to be deeply involved in this process of change. But the need also emerges from our society's growing acceptance of scientific explanations as the source of truth about such matters. The finality of this acceptance seemingly means the end of a long struggle between so-called scientific and religious views regarding the world in which we live. This leaves those of us who insist on speaking the language of faith in a peculiar situation. Is there then no connection between the God we know and encounter daily within all existence and the emergence and history of our universe? Does the presence of eternity we feel (whether we call ourselves "believers" or not) when we stand atop great mountains or at the ocean water's edge exist only within our minds? Is our faith nothing more than one of those big mollusk shells we used to put up against our ears, convinced we could hear in them the ocean's roar? Is our certainty of divine presence, so palpable to the religious soul, *merely* a poetic affirmation, corresponding to nothing in the reality described by science? We accept the scientific account of how we got here, or at least understand that the conversation about that process and its stages lies within the domain of science. Yet we cannot absent God from it entirely. Even if we have left behind the parent God of childhood, the presence of divinity within nature remains essential to our perception of reality. A God who has no place in the process of "how we got here" is a God who begins in the human mind, a mere *idea* of God, a post-Kantian construct created to guarantee morality, to assure us of the potential for human goodness, or for some other noble purpose. But that is not Y-H-W-H, the One that underlies and unifies all of being.

The One of which I speak here indeed goes back to origins and stands prior to them, though perhaps that priority cannot be depicted in a purely temporal sense. I speak here of a God who underlies all being, who *is* and dwells within (rather than "who controls" or "oversees" from beyond) the evolutionary process. This is the One about which—or about "Whom"— we tell the great sacred tale, the story of existence. I thus insist on the centrality of "Creation," but I do so from the position of one who is not quite a theist, as understood in the classical Western sense. I do not affirm a Being or a Mind that exists separate from the universe, who "then" created it and acts upon it intelligently and willfully, as humans understand those terms. This puts me quite far from the contemporary "creationists" or from what is usually understood as "intelligent design." My theological position is that of a *mystical panentheist*, one who believes that God is present throughout all of existence, that Being or Y-H-W-H underlies and unifies all that is. At the same time (and this is panentheism as distinct from pantheism), this whole is mysteriously and infinitely greater than the sum of its parts, and cannot be fully known or reduced to its constituent beings.[43]

"Transcendence" in the context of such a faith does not refer to a God "out there" or "over there" somewhere beyond the universe, since I do not know the existence of such a "there." Transcendence means rather that Y-H-W-H—or Being—is so fully present in the here and now of each moment that we could not possibly grasp the profundity of that presence. Transcendence thus dwells *within* immanence. There is no ultimate duality here, no "God and world," no "God, world, and self," but only one Being and its many faces. Those who seek consciousness of it come to know that it is indeed *eyn sof*, without end. There is no end to its unimaginable depth, but so too there is no border, no limit, separating that unfathomable One from anything that is. Infinite Being in every instant flows through all finite beings. "Know this day and set it upon your heart that Y-H-W-H is *elohim*" (Deut. 4:39)—that God within you *is* the transcendent. And the verse concludes: "There is nothing else."[44]

By *mystical* panentheism I mean that this underlying oneness of being is accessible to human experience and reveals itself to humans—indeed, it reveals itself everywhere, always—as the deeper levels of the human mind become open to it. Access to it requires a lifting of veils, a shifting of attention to those inner realms of human consciousness where mystics, and not a few poets and artists, have always chosen to abide. The "radical otherness" of God, so insisted upon by Western theology, is not ontological but epistemological, an otherness of perspective. To open one's eyes to God is to see Being—the only Being there is—in a radically different way. Such a unitive view of reality is *entirely other* (*ganz andere*, in theological German) from the way we usually see things, yet it is the same reality that is being viewed. I am also one who knows that religious truth belongs to the language of poetry, not discursive prose. I recognize fully and without regret that theology is an art, not a science. We people of faith have nothing we can prove; attempts to do so only diminish what we have to offer. *We can only testify, never prove.* Our strength lies in grandeur of vision, in an ability to transport the conversation about existence and origins to a deeper plane of thinking. My faith, but also my human experience, tells me that this shift profoundly enhances our understanding of our own lives and of the world in which we live. Opening our minds, and ultimately the mind of our society, to the truth accessible from that inner "place" constitutes our best hope for inspiring change in the way we live on this earth. There is nothing *mere* about poetic vision.

The task of theology, then, is one of *reframing* the accepted accounts of origins and natural history offered by the scientific consensus, helping us to view them in a different way, one that may guide us toward a more profound appreciation of that same reality, and indeed inspire us to help to preserve it. The tale of life's origins and development, including its essential building block of natural selection, is well known to us as moderns. But what would it mean to recount that tale with our eyes truly open?

We would come to see the entire course of evolution, from the simplest life-forms millions of years ago, to the great complexity of the human brain (still now only barely understood), and proceeding onward into the unknown future, as a *meaningful* process. That is how I understand "God said . . . and there was" or "God looked into Torah and created the world." The process by which the world came to be is ultimately a decipherable and meaningful one. It can be translated from the realm of transcendent mystery into the linguistic symbols we need in order to wrap our minds around it. That translation is as close as we can come to "divine speech." Moses (shall we think of him as symbolically embodying the human quest for wisdom?) at Sinai serves as the *meturgeman*, the translator, for a God who dwells in a realm beyond language, who speaks only through thunderclaps, and perhaps all the other sounds of nature as well.[45] The Torah of Moses is our guide in making meaning out of that cacophony. Kabbalists and scientists might agree that there will always be a part of it that eludes us. Remember that the kabbalists taught that there were lights behind the letters. Those "lights" were a way of referring to a greater abstraction, leading toward something still more elusive.

Translation: There is a One that is ever revealing itself to us within and behind the great diversity of life. That One is Being itself, the constant in the endlessly changing evolutionary parade. Viewed from our end of the process, the search that leads to discovery of that One is our human quest for knowledge and meaning, embracing both scientific advance and religious interpretation. But turned around, seen from the perspective of the constantly evolving life energy, evolution can be seen as an ongoing process of revelation or self-manifestation. We discover; it reveals. It reveals; we discover. As the human mind advances (from our point of view), understanding more of the structure, process, and history of the ever-evolving One, we are being given (from its point of view) ever-greater insight into who we are, how we got here, and where we are going.

I do not view this ongoing self-revelation through the process of evolution as a conscious, willful process, the way we humans understand those terms. But since the One is Y-H-W-H, Is-Was-Will Be all at once, every bird, flower, ant, and human soul ever to exist is eternally present within it. So too are every disease, earthquake, and tsunami, every love and every hate. As Kohelet (Eccles. 3:1–8) knew so well, there is a time for each of them to step forward. When that One is translated into the narrative of our Torah, the story needs a beginning, middle, and end. Hence "In the beginning . . ." When it is translated into the realm of *mitsvot*, or religious praxis, another "language" through which it speaks, it needs specific defined forms in which to exist, infinity thus pouring itself into (humanly created, culturally evolved) vessels of specific dimensions and limits. These are the endless jugs that Elisha's widow keeps bringing, to contain the ever-flowing oil. In these cases the ongoing Community of Israel translates in the name of Moses, one "whose presence spreads forth in each generation."[46]

The One has entered into this dance that we call "evolution" in order to make itself manifest, *be-gin le-ishtemode'a*, in the Zohar's language. It extends itself into endless varieties of being, moving (though not consistently) from the simple toward forms of great complexity, all resulting from this self-manifesting energy. If human language were adequate to this, we would say that "it wants to become known." Here on this smallish planet in the middle of an otherwise undistinguished galaxy, something so astonishing has taken place that it demands to be called by the biblical term *miracle* rather than by the Greco-Latin *nature*, even though the two are pointing to the exact same set of facts. The descendants of one-celled creatures grew and developed, emerged onto dry land, learned survival skills, developed language and thought, until a subset of them could reflect on the nature of this entire process and seek to derive meaning from it.

Does that make us humans the be-all and end-all of Creation? I hardly think so. If our generations don't destroy this planet as a fit habitation for higher species (and there are lots of reasons to fear we will), I imagine a

being existing here some thousands of generations from now in the ongoing evolutionary process who will be about as comfortable with having us
on its family tree as we are with the rhesus monkey. Meanwhile, however,
the present is as far as I can see. When I read the old midrashic and hasidic
texts that say, "The world was created through Torah" or "The world was
created for the sake of Israel," I have to universalize them in the course of
my affirmation. Yes, it is all here to reveal wisdom to us, a wisdom that is
not separable from the single divine Self. That is "Torah." And yes, it is all
there for the sake of those—from any nation and through any symbolic
language—who wrestle with it, taking *yisra'el* in its original sense.

What will it mean to retell the current story of "Creation"? It will not
mean, of course, continuing the old battle of the deniers of science to try
to find some "hole" in the argument, a chance to be able to say that evolution is "just a theory." Not at all. It may mean, however, picking away at
some of the philosophical substratum often taken for granted in the modern world. Yes, natural selection is real, and so is much of the randomness
of the survival or nonsurvival of various species. But does that fully prove
the lack of teleology in the process, even a sense that in its broadest out-
lines evolution is moving, however imperfectly, in the direction of greater
variety and complexity? Or does the fact that evolution wrought such a
wicked species as we are, potential destroyers on such a massive scale, itself
render any such positive judgment ridiculous?

The true religious reading of our new narrative of origins is simply to
look at the same story that science tells us, growing richer in detail with
discoveries (or "revelations") from day to day, but to do so with our eyes
wide open. It is the sense of wonder, our readiness to stand in awe of it all,
that turns the scientific account into a holy drama.[47]

The incredibly complex interplay of forces and the thick web of mutual dependency among beings are no less amazing than the distance traversed in this long evolutionary journey. The interrelationships between
soil, plants, and insects, or those between climate, foliage, and animal life,
all leave us breathless as we begin to contemplate them. The emergence
of both bees and blossoms, and the relationship between them, took place
over millions of years, step by evolutionary step. How could that have
happened? There is an endless ingenuity to this self-manifesting Being,
an endless stream of creativity of which we are only the tiniest part. There
is indeed something "supernatural" about existence, something entirely
out of the ordinary, beyond any easy explanation. But I understand the
"supernatural" to reside wholly within the "natural." The process may be

an entirely natural one, yet by no means is something to be taken for granted, passed over as though it were not filled with mystery. The difference between the "natural" and the "supernatural" is one of perception, the degree to which our "inner eye" is open, to which we are fully paying attention.[48]

Telling the Story: The Old as the New

Several years ago, the students and faculty of Hebrew College Rabbinical School, at my urging, issued the following declaration. Following it has become the regular practice of our daily prayer community, and many have taken it on, along with me, as personal practice as well. I urge my readers—Jewish and non-Jewish—to consider joining us in this community of prayer for our world. This also means, of course, acting in ways that conform to it, including both personal habits and political action:

> A renewed faith in this world as divine Creation is the most important task of religion in our world today. We call upon all Jews to join in universal human efforts to protect our environment, including the purity of air, land, and water. All of us must learn to change the way we view the natural world and act toward it. Otherwise humanity will not survive, nor will the many other forms of life entrusted to our care.
>
> Faith in Creation does not demand a biblical literalism, but does mean that we see the presence of God underlying all existence, each creature a testament to the Torah's "God saw that it was good." Viewed through the eyes of awe and wonder, heaven and earth continue, in our scientific age, to declare God's glory. Evolution itself is a sacred story.
>
> Our faith in Creation is celebrated in an ancient Jewish rite that we seek to renew. The Mishnah (Ta'anit 4:1) tells us that when the Second Temple stood, those Israelites whose priestly neighbors were called up to their annual week of Temple service would support them by reciting the seven days of Creation throughout that week. This recitation was seen as their way of participating in the very sustenance of the created world. This custom of *ma'amadot* became a part of Jewish worship, but in recent years it has been almost completely forgotten.

Ours is the time to bring this practice back to life. We too believe that the world's very existence depends on us. We call upon
all our fellow Jews, both those who already pray daily and those
who do not, to join us in this daily proclamation of the world as
God's Creation and to hear it as a daily call to awareness and to
action.

On Sunday, at the conclusion of morning prayers, say:

בְּרֵאשִׁית בָּרָא אֱלֹהִים אֵת הַשָּׁמַיִם וְאֵת הָאָרֶץ. וְהָאָרֶץ הָיְתָה תֹהוּ וָבֹהוּ, וְחֹשֶׁךְ
עַל-פְּנֵי תְהוֹם, וְרוּחַ אֱלֹהִים מְרַחֶפֶת עַל פְּנֵי הַמָּיִם. וַיֹּאמֶר אֱלֹהִים יְהִי אוֹר, וַיְהִי אוֹר.
וַיַּרְא אֱלֹהִים אֶת הָאוֹר כִּי טוֹב, וַיַּבְדֵּל אֱלֹהִים בֵּין הָאוֹר וּבֵין הַחֹשֶׁךְ. וַיִּקְרָא אֱלֹהִים
לָאוֹר יוֹם, וְלַחֹשֶׁךְ קָרָא לָיְלָה, וַיְהִי עֶרֶב וַיְהִי בֹקֶר, יוֹם אֶחָד.

When God began to create heaven and earth—the earth being unformed and void, with darkness over the surface of the deep
and a wind from God sweeping over the water—God said, "Let
there be light"; and there was light. God saw that the light was
good, and God separated the light from the darkness. God called
the light Day, and the darkness He called Night. And there was
evening and there was morning, a first day.[49]

On Monday:

וַיֹּאמֶר אֱלֹהִים יְהִי רָקִיעַ בְּתוֹךְ הַמָּיִם, וִיהִי מַבְדִּיל בֵּין מַיִם לָמָיִם. וַיַּעַשׂ אֱלֹהִים אֶת
הָרָקִיעַ, וַיַּבְדֵּל בֵּין הַמַּיִם אֲשֶׁר מִתַּחַת לָרָקִיעַ וּבֵין הַמַּיִם אֲשֶׁר מֵעַל לָרָקִיעַ, וַיְהִי כֵן.
וַיִּקְרָא אֱלֹהִים לָרָקִיעַ שָׁמָיִם, וַיְהִי עֶרֶב וַיְהִי בֹקֶר, יוֹם שֵׁנִי.

God said, "Let there be an expanse in the midst of the water,
that it may separate water from water." God made the expanse,
and it separated the water which was below the expanse from the
water which was above the expanse. And it was so. God called
the expanse Sky. And there was evening and there was morning,
a second day.

On Tuesday:

וַיֹּאמֶר אֱלֹהִים יִקָּווּ הַמַּיִם מִתַּחַת הַשָּׁמַיִם אֶל מָקוֹם אֶחָד, וְתֵרָאֶה הַיַּבָּשָׁה, וַיְהִי כֵן.
וַיִּקְרָא אֱלֹהִים לַיַּבָּשָׁה אֶרֶץ, וּלְמִקְוֵה הַמַּיִם קָרָא יַמִּים. וַיַּרְא אֱלֹהִים כִּי טוֹב. וַיֹּאמֶר
אֱלֹהִים תַּדְשֵׁא הָאָרֶץ דֶּשֶׁא עֵשֶׂב מַזְרִיעַ זֶרַע עֵץ פְּרִי עֹשֶׂה פְּרִי לְמִינוֹ אֲשֶׁר זַרְעוֹ
בוֹ עַל הָאָרֶץ, וַיְהִי-כֵן. וַתּוֹצֵא הָאָרֶץ דֶּשֶׁא עֵשֶׂב מַזְרִיעַ זֶרַע לְמִינֵהוּ, וְעֵץ עֹשֶׂה פְּרִי
אֲשֶׁר זַרְעוֹ בוֹ לְמִינֵהוּ, וַיַּרְא אֱלֹהִים כִּי טוֹב. וַיְהִי עֶרֶב וַיְהִי בֹקֶר, יוֹם שְׁלִישִׁי.

God said, "Let the water below the sky be gathered into one
area, that the dry land may appear." And it was so. God called

the dry land Earth, and the gathering of waters He called Seas. And God saw that this was good. And God said, "Let the earth sprout vegetation: seed-bearing plants, fruit trees of every kind on earth that bear fruit with the seed in it." And it was so. The earth brought forth vegetation: seed-bearing plants of every kind, and trees of every kind bearing fruit with the seed in it. And God saw that this was good. And there was evening and there was morning, a third day.

On Wednesday:

וַיֹּאמֶר אֱלֹהִים יְהִי מְאֹרֹת בִּרְקִיעַ הַשָּׁמַיִם לְהַבְדִּיל בֵּין הַיּוֹם וּבֵין הַלָּיְלָה; וְהָיוּ לְאֹתֹת וּלְמוֹעֲדִים וּלְיָמִים וְשָׁנִים; וְהָיוּ לִמְאוֹרֹת בִּרְקִיעַ הַשָּׁמַיִם לְהָאִיר עַל-הָאָרֶץ, וַיְהִי כֵן. וַיַּעַשׂ אֱלֹהִים אֶת שְׁנֵי הַמְּאֹרֹת הַגְּדֹלִים, אֶת הַמָּאוֹר הַגָּדֹל לְמֶמְשֶׁלֶת הַיּוֹם וְאֶת הַמָּאוֹר הַקָּטֹן לְמֶמְשֶׁלֶת הַלַּיְלָה, וְאֵת הַכּוֹכָבִים. וַיִּתֵּן אֹתָם אֱלֹהִים בִּרְקִיעַ הַשָּׁמַיִם לְהָאִיר עַל הָאָרֶץ. וְלִמְשֹׁל בַּיּוֹם וּבַלַּיְלָה, וּלְהַבְדִּיל בֵּין הָאוֹר וּבֵין הַחֹשֶׁךְ. וַיַּרְא אֱלֹהִים כִּי טוֹב. וַיְהִי עֶרֶב וַיְהִי בֹקֶר, יוֹם רְבִיעִי.

God said, "Let there be lights in the expanse of the sky to separate day from night; they shall serve as signs for the set times—the days and the years; and they shall serve as lights in the expanse of the sky to shine upon the earth." And it was so. God made the two great lights, the greater light to dominate the day and the lesser light to dominate the night, and the stars. And God set them in the expanse of the sky to shine upon the earth, to dominate the day and the night, and to separate light from darkness. And God saw that this was good. And there was evening and there was morning, a fourth day.

On Thursday:

וַיֹּאמֶר אֱלֹהִים יִשְׁרְצוּ הַמַּיִם שֶׁרֶץ נֶפֶשׁ חַיָּה וְעוֹף יְעוֹפֵף עַל הָאָרֶץ עַל פְּנֵי רְקִיעַ הַשָּׁמָיִם. וַיִּבְרָא אֱלֹהִים אֶת הַתַּנִּינִם הַגְּדֹלִים וְאֵת כָּל נֶפֶשׁ הַחַיָּה הָרֹמֶשֶׂת אֲשֶׁר שָׁרְצוּ הַמַּיִם לְמִינֵהֶם, וְאֵת כָּל עוֹף כָּנָף לְמִינֵהוּ, וַיַּרְא אֱלֹהִים, כִּי טוֹב. וַיְבָרֶךְ אֹתָם אֱלֹהִים לֵאמֹר פְּרוּ וּרְבוּ, וּמִלְאוּ אֶת הַמַּיִם בַּיַּמִּים וְהָעוֹף יִרֶב בָּאָרֶץ. וַיְהִי עֶרֶב וַיְהִי בֹקֶר, יוֹם חֲמִישִׁי.

God said, "Let the waters bring forth swarms of living creatures, and birds that fly above the earth across the expanse of the sky." God created the great sea monsters, and all the living creatures of every kind that creep, which the waters brought forth in swarms, and all the winged birds of every kind. And God saw that this was good. God blessed them, saying, "Be fertile and increase,

fill the waters in the seas, and let the birds increase on the earth."
And there was evening and there was morning, a fifth day.

On Friday:

וַיֹּאמֶר אֱלֹהִים תּוֹצֵא הָאָרֶץ נֶפֶשׁ חַיָּה לְמִינָהּ בְּהֵמָה וָרֶמֶשׂ וְחַיְתוֹ אֶרֶץ לְמִינָהּ, וַיְהִי
כֵן. וַיַּעַשׂ אֱלֹהִים אֶת חַיַּת הָאָרֶץ לְמִינָהּ וְאֶת הַבְּהֵמָה לְמִינָהּ וְאֵת כָּל רֶמֶשׂ הָאֲדָמָה
לְמִינֵהוּ, וַיַּרְא אֱלֹהִים כִּי טוֹב. וַיֹּאמֶר אֱלֹהִים נַעֲשֶׂה אָדָם בְּצַלְמֵנוּ כִּדְמוּתֵנוּ, וְיִרְדּוּ
בִדְגַת הַיָּם וּבְעוֹף הַשָּׁמַיִם וּבַבְּהֵמָה וּבְכָל הָאָרֶץ וּבְכָל הָרֶמֶשׂ הָרֹמֵשׂ עַל הָאָרֶץ.
וַיִּבְרָא אֱלֹהִים אֶת הָאָדָם בְּצַלְמוֹ, בְּצֶלֶם אֱלֹהִים בָּרָא אֹתוֹ, זָכָר וּנְקֵבָה בָּרָא אֹתָם.
וַיְבָרֶךְ אֹתָם אֱלֹהִים וַיֹּאמֶר לָהֶם אֱלֹהִים פְּרוּ וּרְבוּ וּמִלְאוּ אֶת הָאָרֶץ וְכִבְשֻׁהָ, וּרְדוּ
בִדְגַת הַיָּם וּבְעוֹף הַשָּׁמַיִם וּבְכָל חַיָּה הָרֹמֶשֶׂת עַל הָאָרֶץ. וַיֹּאמֶר אֱלֹהִים הִנֵּה נָתַתִּי
לָכֶם אֶת כָּל עֵשֶׂב זֹרֵעַ זֶרַע אֲשֶׁר עַל פְּנֵי כָל הָאָרֶץ וְאֶת כָּל הָעֵץ אֲשֶׁר בּוֹ פְרִי עֵץ
זֹרֵעַ זָרַע, לָכֶם יִהְיֶה לְאָכְלָה. וּלְכָל חַיַּת הָאָרֶץ וּלְכָל עוֹף הַשָּׁמַיִם וּלְכֹל רוֹמֵשׂ עַל
הָאָרֶץ אֲשֶׁר בּוֹ נֶפֶשׁ חַיָּה אֶת כָּל יֶרֶק עֵשֶׂב לְאָכְלָה, וַיְהִי כֵן. וַיַּרְא אֱלֹהִים אֶת כָּל
אֲשֶׁר עָשָׂה וְהִנֵּה טוֹב מְאֹד. וַיְהִי עֶרֶב וַיְהִי בֹקֶר, יוֹם הַשִּׁשִּׁי.

God said, "Let the earth bring forth every kind of living creature: cattle, creeping things, and wild beasts of every kind." And
it was so. God made wild beasts of every kind and cattle of every
kind, and all kinds of creeping things of the earth. And God saw
that this was good. And God said, "Let us make man in our image,
after our likeness. They shall rule the fish of the sea, the birds of
the sky, the cattle, the whole earth, and all the creeping things that
creep on earth." And God created man in His image, in the image
of God He created him; male and female He created them. God
blessed them and God said to them, "Be fertile and increase, fill
the earth and master it; and rule the fish of the sea, the birds of the
sky, and all the living things that creep on earth."

God said, "See, I give you every seed-bearing plant that is upon
all the earth, and every tree that has seed-bearing fruit; they shall
be yours for food. And to all the animals on land, to all the birds
of the sky, and to everything that creeps on earth, in which there
is the breath of life, [I give] all the green plants for food." And it
was so. And God saw all that He had made, and found it very good.
And there was evening and there was morning, the sixth day.

Shabbat Kiddush on Friday evening completes the recital,
celebrating God's presence throughout the created world.

וַיְכֻלּוּ הַשָּׁמַיִם וְהָאָרֶץ וְכָל צְבָאָם. וַיְכַל אֱלֹהִים בַּיּוֹם הַשְּׁבִיעִי מְלַאכְתּוֹ אֲשֶׁר עָשָׂה,
וַיִּשְׁבֹּת בַּיּוֹם הַשְּׁבִיעִי מִכָּל מְלַאכְתּוֹ אֲשֶׁר עָשָׂה. וַיְבָרֶךְ אֱלֹהִים אֶת יוֹם הַשְּׁבִיעִי
וַיְקַדֵּשׁ אֹתוֹ, כִּי בוֹ שָׁבַת מִכָּל מְלַאכְתּוֹ אֲשֶׁר בָּרָא אֱלֹהִים לַעֲשׂוֹת.

The heaven and the earth were finished, and all their array. On the seventh day God finished the work that He had been doing, and He ceased on the seventh day from all the work that He had done. And God blessed the seventh day and declared it holy, because on it God ceased from all the work of creation that He had done.

Religion and Environmental
Responsibility

AN ADDRESS TO JEWS AND CHRISTIANS

A S A PERSON PRIVILEGED to be nearing the end of his eighth decade on this beloved planet, I am able to take a somewhat long view of contemporary history. I was raised in the mid-twentieth century, the child of a fully secularized and rather militantly atheist household, like those of many American Jews in that era. Of course, my atheist father was himself the grandchild of hasidic Jews, but that belonged to the distant and mostly forgotten past. Religion itself, as a force in human affairs, was seen as a thing of another era. Jews coming out of eastern Europe thought of religion as an ultra-conservative force on the world stage; its image was that of the Russian church in the latter days of the czar, or of the hapless rabbis who stayed behind in old-world small towns and with their values, as thousands of Jewish young people moved off to the cities and to new continents, engaging the bold new world of the twentieth century. Secularization was seen as a constant and unstoppable process.

No one, looking ahead from the mid-twentieth century, would have predicted the tremendous role that religion would play in the twenty-first. No one, that is, except the embattled people of faith. To everyone's surprise but their own, Christians, Muslims, Jews, Buddhists, Hindus, and others fill the front pages of contemporary newspapers, which document us as a tremendous—and sometimes, indeed, frightening—force in world affairs. The question before us is whether we can make this be good news, even redemptive news, for the history of human civilization. As a religious person who does not anticipate the direct interference of a divine hand in history to save us from ourselves, I have come to ask the question of such salvation differently. Will the resurgence of *faith* in God, or a rebirth of religion, bring about the deliverance of our so urgently threatened planet? Needless to say, there is plenty of evidence to the contrary. We have seen Buddhists slaughtering Muslims in Myanmar recently, and Muslims slaughtering Christians and Yazidis on the battlefields of Syria. But it was not so long ago that we heard of Christians slaughtering Muslims in the refugee camps of Lebanon, and of a certain Jew, cheered on by others, who did the same to Palestinian Muslims, thereby desecrating the holy grave of our shared ancestors. All this hate and slaughter keeps these so-called religious folks too busy to confront the most serious challenge of our age, the environmental crisis that threatens to overwhelm us all, exacerbating every other crisis as it rains down death and destruction upon everyone, without distinction. But is there also a good, possibly even salvific, side to this new power of religion, one that might lead us to together face, rather than ignore, that challenge? How do we bring such a committed and shared religiosity to birth? Let me propose another way of asking the question. Is it coincidence that the first species to have the ability to destroy our biosphere as a fit habitat for all higher forms of life is also the first to be equipped with the moral conscience and perspective that might prevent us from doing so? Religions, despite all their limitations and narrowness of vision, serve humanity as the great vehicle for that moral conscience. To say it in classical Western theological language: might it be that the rebirth of religion is emerging from a divine call that is welling up within us, stirring us to repent of our collective abuse of this planet, and of one another, before it is too late? Is God seeking to protect that last shred of moral conscience in humanity? Is religion itself being given the gift of this awareness and power to stir conscience by the One it worships in order to awaken humanity from its dangerous self-serving slumber before the earth is pillaged to the point of utter destruction? Or, if you are more comfortable with Gaian than with biblical language, might you say that Mother Earth is offering all of us renewed access to the sacred in our times, as the need increases—viewable from the Sierra Club poster, audible in the silence of the meditation retreat—to arouse even the most avowedly secular among us to come to her defense?

The coming together of religious leaders in America—primarily Christian and Jewish, but embracing others as well—around this issue is evidence that such an awakening is happening within all of our traditions. The pope's leadership in this cause, expressed in his remarkable document of moral courage entitled *Laudato Si*, to which I will return later, is a clarion call to all people who call themselves religious. It is taking place in Buddhism as well, especially due to the commitment of the Dalai Lama and the growing influence of Buddhists in the Western world. And it is taking place in what may be more unexpected places as well. I read a remarkable interview with the abbot of a mountaintop Taoist temple in rural China, quoted in the *New York Times*: "China doesn't lack money; it lacks reverence for the environment. . . . We all live on the earth together—we are not isolated," he said from his remote monastery. "As Taoists, we have to work to influence people in China and overseas to take part in ecological protection."[1] Is there a universal process of *teshuvah*, of return to awareness of the One, or of the holiness of existence, happening here?

We Jews and Christians have a shared language for stirring environmental awareness. That is the language of Creation. We are religious communities based on our shared faith in this being a created universe, emerging from the word of God. This means that our world, including all that has happened in the several billion years of its existence, is attributable to God, however we may understand that. While far from being a literalist or fundamentalist in my reading of Genesis 1 or the psalmist's magnificent hymns to Creation, these remain essential to my spiritual life, binding it inexorably to my loving concern for the fate of this planet and those who dwell upon it, and hence calling me to environmental activism.

In placing the weekly Sabbath at the center of our devotional lives, we Jews have always lived in awareness of Creation. Our Friday evening ritual calls for three readings of Genesis 2: "Heaven and earth were completed, they and all their hosts." Before we recite the *shema'* each morning, we bless God, who "renews each day the work of Creation." When we put on our *tallit* in the morning, we call out the verse from Psalm 104, the greatest of the Creation psalms, "He spreads forth light like a garment, stretching out the heavens like a curtain," as though repeating or taking part in the very first act of Creation. In the last several years, I have been urging Jews everywhere to take up our ancient but long-neglected tradition called *ma'amadot*, concluding each morning's prayer service with the appropriate day of the Creation narrative in Genesis 1, on Sunday saying: "In the beginning," on Monday "God said: 'Let there be a firmament,'" and so forth through the days, thus completing the cycle every week. (See the final section of the preceding essay.) This serves as a daily reminder that we live in God's world, and thus we bear responsibility for working to maintain it. I invite Christians, as fellow bearers of the same sacred story, to join in this practice as well. The divine voice of Creation is an unceasing one, and so it should be in our lives.

This call to moral responsibility is all the more vital in the specific times in which we live. We are Christians and Jews, but we are also citizens of the country in which some of the gravest threats to the future of this planet are taking place. Decisions made by our government, led by officials we have had a hand in choosing, have been heading in some remarkably bad directions lately. We are all responsible. The cynical trampling of any concern for the environment on the part of political leadership in our society cannot be tolerated in silence. The idea that our political life is dominated by a conflict between "business-friendly" forces and "survival of the earth–friendly" forces is ridiculous. How well will "business" thrive on a scorched planet? The conflict is not about "friendliness" to business, but rather between those with foresight and those lacking it, or those willing to dismiss it for the sake of short-range profiteering and vote grabbing.

Let me return to our shared faith in Creation. We proclaim that the world was created by the word of God. The original witness to this faith is the narrative of Genesis 1, but it is repeatedly invoked in the prophets and psalms as well. "By the word of God were the heavens created, and by the breath of His mouth, all their hosts" (Ps. 33:6). It is a formula widely attested in the rabbinic sources, as well as in the famous opening of the Gospel of John.

What do we mean when we evoke such language today? "Word," for us, does not refer to language in any conventional sense, but to a deeper sense of what language is. Language is a system of sounds that convey meaning to fellow speakers of a particular tongue. The relationship between the specific sound combination or, in writing, group of letters, and the thing intended is mostly arbitrary, the very beginning of symbolism in the development of humanity, repeated in the life of each verbal individual, no matter what language will emerge from his or her mouth. In saying that all of Creation is by the divine word, we are saying that all existence is potentially *meaningful*, translatable into categories of speech. The Word, the great conveyer of meaning, lies within it, waiting to be discovered. Bringing ever more dimensions of existence into God's presence, or discovering that presence within them, is, from our point of view, the human quest for meaning, for turning phenomena into language. It is from the articulation of our encounter with the world that meaning arises. Turning this process around to see it from God's point of view, however, our discovery of meaning is the ongoing, ceaseless process of divine self-revelation, the speaking of the divine Word. We discover, God reveals; God reveals, we discover. We listen, God speaks; God speaks, we listen. *Shema' Yisra'el:* "Listen, strugglers!" It's all about listening.

I engage us in this little exercise of what you might call mystical theology because I want to make a point. *Laudato Si* has rendered a great service by its author's insistence that concerns for our environmental future and the relief of poverty are not to be separated from one another. The ongoing concern of the churches for the poor of this world, both Christian and not, is one of the great moral beacons shining forth in these dark times. The focusing of concern upon the people of the Southern Hemisphere—Africa, Latin America, and South Asia—and the dangers to them of rising tides and progressive drought and desertification, is all terribly important and too much ignored by the temporal powers that be. We of the overprivileged wealthy societies consume vastly more than our fair share of earth's resources, yet those who will "foot the bill" for our overconsumption are likely to be the poorest, hence those least responsible for the planet's devastation.

But this linkage between preserving our resources and serving the poor also contains another message, the reason that some political figures have denounced the pope's good words. Their concern with what they call "the bottom line"—"How much will it cost?"—blinds them from seeing the real bottom line that God and nature have placed before us. We cannot allow economic interests to be juxtaposed to environmental concerns. A dead planet, one without pure food to eat, water to drink, or air to breathe, a thousand Mar-a-Lagos overwhelmed by rising tides, will not be much of a reward for the wealthy elites who hold onto power and flee from responsibility. What will happen to all those tax-sheltered fortunes once the Cayman Islands are submerged? (Or will they survive on a purely digital "Cayman Islands"? And will the poor Cayman Islanders be able to live there?) With so many sophisticated tools of planning and prediction in our hands, we need to think of a future that at once protects the natural world and relieves the suffering of impoverished humanity.

To this exemplary concern for economic justice in the papal document, I want to add another dimension, emerging from the Jewish experience. I speak of the concern for freedom and liberation. God speaks to us through all the wonders of Creation, but we hear that voice only when we are ready. God is *revealed* to us only when we are ready to *discover,* and only then can we *respond.* "Every day," we are told, "a voice goes forth from Mount Sinai."[2] In the language of our sacred story, you can come to Sinai only when you are freed from Egyptian bondage. A thousand comments on the word *mitsrayim,* "Egypt" in Hebrew—especially those of the hasidic masters—tell us that this word literally means constriction or narrowness. Each person's "Egyptian bondage" is that which constricts his or her vision or ability to see God's handiwork. Only when that constriction is removed can we hear the divine voice—the same voice that speaks through Creation—saying: "I am Y-H-W-H your God who brings you forth from the Land of Egypt, the house of bondage" (Ex. 20:2).

What is that house of bondage, that place of inner constriction, that keeps us from hearing and responding to the word of God? Pope Francis is certainly right in saying that it can take the form of poverty. I'm sure the Israelites in Egypt were all living on less than a dollar a day, like so many of the poor throughout our world today. How can you respond to the call of God to save the earth when you are struggling in each moment for your own food and shelter? But this "Egypt" also means political oppression, enslavement to the whim of the powerful and mighty, thus having no control over your own fate, no sense of fairness in human affairs. "Let them go make their own straw![3] Let them go find their own health insurance!" are kinds of things that Pharaoh and his like enjoy tweeting out.

But there are other forms of Egyptian bondage as well, things that constrict us from responding freely to the divine call. Addiction is such a prison of the mind and spirit, not leaving us free enough to hear God's word. It is a terrible plague in today's world, adding another level of bondage to so many already caught up in the chains of poverty. So too is sexual obsession, the inability to control one's passions, distorting God's greatest gift, the ability to love. But so too are subtler addictions, including the endless drive for high achievement and success, seemingly the drug of choice for too much of our middle- and upper-class Jewish community. Are you free to respond to the divine call to save our world when you are wholly given to climbing the corporate ladder, or making quick millions from your latest app? Will you teach your child to listen and respond to God's voice in the wonders of nature if it will distract her from the getting the grades it takes to make it into the Ivy League? Or will you quickly figure out how to turn that love of nature into a summer seminar in Costa Rica, something that will surely look good on that young person's growing CV?

We need the spiritual freedom to reorder our priorities. We Jews are terribly concerned about our demographic survival, and about the future of Israel, divided by many opinions. Christians are very given to concern about legislation around issues of morality, and they too are deeply divided among themselves. Muslims are caught in the tensions between Sunni and Shia, over which some are ready to kill one another, and around challenges of modernization. Eastern religions, too, suffer many a divide. All of these are important and legitimate concerns, whatever one's point of view on them. But all of them are also distractions from the single most urgent issue of our times. How do we remove the blinders, first from our own eyes, then from the eyes of our faith communities, to help everyone to see this clearly? How will we influence change in government policies when "the environmental issue" is not issue number one, even for those who support us? Surveys of voters in recent U.S. elections, both presidential and congressional, showed that survival of the planet was far down the list among voters' priorities. A decade or two ago, we were saying that it would take clear evidence of the effects of climate change to move people to act. Now we see the rising seas, the increase of hurricanes and other climate oddities, but nothing has changed in the behavior of those in charge. The rollout of climate change–denial politics seems to outstrip the pace by which the good Lord, or Gaia, can thunder out warning signals to us of the great disasters to come.

We people of faith need each other, my friends, and the world needs us to realize how much we need each other. We have to show that we can stand together in awareness of the miraculous nature of our existence. We need to share and give expression to a sense of divinity that penetrates every moment of our lives, enlightening even their darkest corners. We need together to form the core of a new resistance to the brutalization of humanity in our era, the disregard for the sacred quality of each human life and of the created world of which we are a part. In the growing strength of religion as a factor in human affairs, we have been given a great gift, a salvific opportunity that we cannot allow to slip between our fingers.

Many of us who are people of faith today are survivors, having remained faithful to God and to our traditions, despite the multiple attacks on religion over the course of the past two centuries. Others are returnees, people who rediscovered the sacred and the power of our traditional languages for accessing it in response to the spiritual vacuity of secular and materialistic Western culture. But in order for this old/new religiosity emerging in the postmodern context to have staying power, we will need to reach out to a new generation, one very much concerned with the environmental challenge, and to make common cause. This will mean putting an end to the remaining elements of religious triumphalism that sometimes still divide us, as well as articulating shared commitments to some of the values that the next generation takes for granted: democratic governance, gender egalitarianism (including full respect for the LGBTQ community), concern for the oppressed, and acceptance of science as a legitimate source of knowledge about our lives. Each of these arouses questions that are painful and problematic to some elements within each of our communities. These need to be treated with understanding, patience, and delicacy. But acceptance of these values is crucial to constructing the community we need to build. Not only should all religious communities be able to find common ground in working on the environmental issue; religious and conservation groups, with their overlapping sense of appreciation of this world and its many gifts, should work together to bring forth a youthful coalition for progress around it.

The contemporary religion we articulate will need to be based upon a fully nature-embracing spirituality, one that sees the divine presence as embodied within the physical world. This can be hosted by a great variety of theological views within both the Jewish and Christian traditions. But we must move away from the legacy of Platonism that we Westerners all bear, distinguishing between a "true" spiritual world and the "merely" physical. A creation-inflected spirituality means that we celebrate the divine presence within all of God's creatures, however we spell out the details of that presence. A sense of spirituality is precisely that which brings us closer to an appreciation of nature and a sense of awe before its wonders.

That awakening of wonder and its renewal is the most important message that we religious folk—all of us—have to bring to the postmodern world. My chief mentor in recent years is the Rabbi of Chernobyl, who died in 1797. I have just completed a translation of his great book of homilies, *The Light of the Eyes*. (Chernobyl was once known for a very different kind of bright light than that for which it is remembered in history!) In speaking of the Exodus from Egypt, he says that *our* Exodus has already taken place. The real enslavement of Egypt was that of mind and spirit, leaving its victims unaware of the reality of God. Unlike the enslaved Israelites of old, we have our faith; we are aware of the divine presence that fills all the world. The challenge, he says, is how to make our actions, our moral selves, live up to our spiritual awareness.

Our situation is a bit different. We, too, live in an "Egyptian bondage" of mind and spirit. In our case, it is the secularized consciousness of our society, along with too much pursuit of success and comfort, that blinds us to the wondrous quality of existence that surrounds us in each moment, if only we could open our eyes to it. As the hasidic master knew so well, the first task of religion is the *liberation of the spirit*. As we attain that freedom and reawaken our souls, we need to act, both individually and as a collective force, in ways that fulfill our sacred vision.

We religious folk represent a tremendous potency for change in our world. Religion is still the language that moves the hearts and minds of most of humanity. We religious leaders of the West need to find a way to reach out to our counterparts throughout the world, including Christians, Muslims, Hindus, Buddhists, and others. We need to make common cause in defense of a truth that we all share, however varied our nuances in ways of expressing it. All that exists contains the power or presence of the One who created it. Therefore, we must walk through this world with love and reverence, doing all we can to preserve its glory for future generations. This shared vision needs to be translated into real political action, both within national voting campaigns and in international forums, perhaps new ones that we should create together.

The great power of religious faith in our world must be seen as a divine gift and a sacred opportunity. In it may lie humanity's greatest hope for liberation from self-destructive forces that will cause terrible harm in times already upon us, both to our own offspring and those of all the other species that depend upon us for survival. But what we do with this gift is in our hands, especially those of our religious leaders. Only in working together, embracing this earth as divine Creation, will we be able to move forward.

Judaism as Counterculture

Why is Abraham called *ha-'ivri* (Gen. 14:13)? Because the entire world stood on one side, and Abraham on the other.

—BERESHIT RABBAH 42:8

WE JEWS HAVE SEEN ourselves as a counterculture, standing over against the values of the broader society in which we live, for a very long time. The word *'ivri*, traditionally rendered as "Hebrew," was first applied to the people of ancient Israel in the context of their Egyptian bondage. Joseph, when imprisoned by Pharaoh, is referred to by one of his fellow prisoners as *na'ar 'ivri*, "a Hebrew lad" (Gen. 41:12). Scholars have long debated the relationship of this word to the Ḥapiru tribes who migrated into Egypt during the second millennium BCE. But it is clear that Joseph is being designated by the Egyptians as somehow different, not "one of us." The single rather obscure reference cited above ties the name back to Abraham, giving the midrashic tradition a chance to offer this comment on the term's meaning. Rather than ascribing it to the ancestral name *'ever* (Eber), which seems most likely, they take it literally, to mean "side" or "crossing." "The entire world" presumably referred to the idolators whom Abraham defied. Ever since then, we Jews have understood ourselves as a countercultural force, swimming against the tide of every mainstream civilization amid which we lived.

Abraham is called to leave Mesopotamia, a place of rather high, sophisticated culture, wandering off to "the land that I will show you"

(Gen. 12:1). It is a wild, "unsown" land, says the prophet (Jer. 2:2), but a place where he will be free to create a new religious civilization, rooted in his own emerging tribe, that will offer the world a different set of values and perspectives on living. Already in antiquity, even prior to the mid-rashic *bon mot* about the ʿ*ivri*, Israelites saw themselves as set off from all others, a sense generated by (or projected onto, depending on your understanding) the God whom they worshipped. Hear the Second Temple psalmist, in verses still familiar to the Jewish worshipper:

> Eyes have they, but they see not;
> Ears, but they hear not,
> Noses, but they cannot smell. . . .
> Neither do they utter sound from their throats.
> Like them are those who make them,
> And all who trust in them. (Psalm 115:5–8)

For better and for worse, that was how the Israelite in the ancient world was taught to regard the religion—but that included the art and culture—of the world outside. It was all vanity, worthless. We worshipped the only true God, the unseen and mostly unknowable Creator of all. Human conversation with that God had begun with the call to Adam, still in the Garden. *Ayekah*, "Where are you?" This is the first word addressed to humanity by the One, the Great Nothing, or the Mystery out of which we emerged. As such, it is the beginning of revelation, maybe even its core. Because it addressed Adam, we see it as calling to every person, each of whom exists in the image of God and our single universal ancestor.[1] Yes, this is still the unique tribal God of Israel. But He is also the only true God, Creator of heaven and earth.

The voice of that God came to Abraham in a uniquely demanding way. Go forth and be different. Stand out from, and stand up against, the world around you. Hebrew scripture is the record of what Abraham's tribe created, a religious civilization existing in response to the repeated call of God. That divine voice, liberating Israel from Egypt as it had called them forth from Mesopotamia, made them stand up on their own, defying and denying the two great centers from which they had in fact derived much of their culture. The little kingdom of Israel, later Judea, a minor player on the stage of political and military history, was to create a culture and system of values all its own, standing over against those of both Egypt and Mesopotamia.

The God of that civilization never let the Hebrews forget that they had once been slaves. He demanded that they treat strangers with welcome and compassion. He called for the dignity of rest for every human being, even for beasts of labor. Above all, He demanded justice: justice for the downtrodden, for widows and orphans, for the poor and needy of every sort, no matter whether they were members of His chosen tribe or not. Yes, He also demanded worship, first in the form of sacrifices, later transferred to the "inner altar" of the heart in terms of prayer and acts of ritual devotion. But it was always clear that the demands of justice and human decency came first. If you forgot these priorities, the prophets—and later, their writings—were there to remind you.

Then, for a period of about seventeen hundred years, virtually all the world's Jews came to live under the rule of civilizations that were defined as either Christian or Islamic, both traditions that viewed themselves as superseding Judaism. Tolerating the presence of Jews in their midst to varying degrees (often their presence was economically beneficial), they uniformly viewed the teachings of Judaism as anachronistic and essentially without value, serving only as a foil to their respective and exclusive claims of truth. Their stereotypes about Judaism—a narrow, exclusivist, and excessively legalistic faith—were widely believed, and reflected defensive strategies of survival that emerged in rabbinic Judaism partly in response to pressures from without.

Conversion to Judaism was viewed as more or less insane, but was still enough of a threat that it was legally forbidden, often on pain of death. The countercultural threat of Judaism was well noticed, and always considered somewhat dangerous, potentially a corrupting influence on the broader populace. Haman's line to the king, in the probably fictional tale of Esther (written perhaps as early as the third or fourth century BCE, but defining what would be the situation of the Jews for millennia to come) says it all: "There is a certain people scattered and dispersed among the peoples. Their practices are different from those of any other people, and they do not perform the rites of the emperor" (Esth. 3:8).

Yet the Jews persisted. A certain number gave in, many converting in response to the social advantages it offered, but some undoubtedly also convinced by what seemed to be overwhelming evidence, loudly trumpeted by the majority cultures, that the God who governed history had clearly abandoned the Jews, turning His favor elsewhere. Why remain faithful to a God—or teachings about a God—who had obviously rejected His people? Those who did keep the faith were at pains to demonstrate that this abandonment, punishment though it might be for their ancestors' sins, was not permanent, and that in the end they would be vindicated. No text points to this more poignantly than the comment by RaSHI (1035–1105) on the opening verse of the book of Lamentations, bemoaning Jerusalem's destruction: "How does she sit solitary, the city once so filled with people! She has become like a widow." RaSHI comments: "*Like* a widow, but not truly a widow, because *her* Husband is going to return to her."[2] Both the belief in chosenness and the messianic dream were essential to the tenacity with which we held on to our existence.

Jews lived in a great variety of relationships to the surrounding majorities over the long history of the premodern diaspora. Often their cultural creations took on a certain coloring that recent scholarship has seen to be influenced by their surroundings. But neither the Jews nor their neighbors saw it that way at the time. Jews were a foreign body, and a problematic one, throughout that long era. Generally, but not always, Islamic societies were somewhat more hospitable than Christians, who saw Judaism as a more directly rival faith. Some states—Russia prior to its acquisition of Polish territories in 1772 is the biggest example—excluded Jews entirely, partly out of an ancient fear that their very presence might serve to undermine the dominant faith.

Modernity, washing as a wave over Jewish communities beginning in the late eighteenth century, welcomed Europe's Jews as full participants in a partially secularized and open society. Success, largely economic and educational, became the Jew's card of acceptance into the upper echelons of that society, a place where she or he had no prior roots. Progress on this front was slow and by no means uniform in the long period between 1780 and 1933, but a great deal was achieved, and Jews contributed mightily and enthusiastically to the cultures of modernity and cosmopolitanism that were emerging throughout the Western world.

With modernity, the nature of Jewish counterculturalism shifted significantly. The remaining traditional Jewish communities, whether in Germany or in the eastern European *shtetl*, had lost much of their countercultural dynamic. Struggling desperately to hang on, they had no interest in serving as an opposition to the often hostile Christian majority. Jews who entered the modern world, including those who chose to remain observant, sought to quietly make themselves acceptable to the broader culture, not to stand as thorns in its side.

It was from among the assimilating and Western-educated portion of Jewry that a new sort of cultural criticism began to emerge. By the turn of the twentieth century, Jews were highly overrepresented in the avant-garde, whether in literature, the fine arts, or political movements. Jewish tastemakers in the Western world, in such highly varied roles as revolutionary activist, literary critic, art dealer, and political funder, tended to support movements that gave expression to outsider voices, undoubtedly reflecting their own experience as somewhat insecure newcomers to the broader cultural and political realm. This was true both in late nineteenth-century and interwar Europe, as well as among the children of immigrant Jews in North America, usually representing the first generation in their families to encounter higher education in the modern sense. The highly assimilated Jews who were the leaders of all these countercultural trends in the modern world often failed to notice—or occasionally openly denied—the typically Jewish character of their stance with regard to the general society. But anti-Semites were well aware of it and did not fail to point it out.

Hitlerism, the raging, genocidal rejection of the Jew, was also a rebellion against modernity and cosmopolitanism, values with which Jews were correctly identified. Its "Aryan" nativism demonized all those diverse movements that had so attracted Jewish intellectuals newly liberated from the ghetto mentality. Its seemingly ridiculous linking of Jews to both Bolshevism and capitalism in fact was onto something. Karl Marx and Leon Trotsky represented one face of the supposedly threatening Jew, Rothschild another. The international banker and the international Communist conspiracy both reeked of internationalism, opposed to the nativism of the ethnic-based nation-state. Jews were overrepresented in all the movements of transnational modernity, no matter their political stripe. The battle against world Jewry, degenerating into the unspeakable horrors of the Holocaust, was a cry for a "purist" ethnic nationalism, one that would exist precisely to exclude unwelcome strangers. That is why it is so horrid to see it rear its ugly head again today—even, unbelievably, among Jews.

For the surviving remnants of European Jewry, the Holocaust was the ultimate watershed event. With the exception of small minorities at each end of the spectrum (a few extreme ultra-Orthodox and the most highly assimilated), European Jewry acknowledged that the Nazis had proven the political Zionists to be correct. Anti-Semitism was so utterly endemic to Christian society that Jews could no longer tolerate the pain and danger of living in its midst. The creation of a Jewish state, one in which our traditions would dominate and where we could create our own culture, was the only alternative. The "displaced persons" surviving in postwar Germany, the silently suffering Jews in the Soviet Union, and nearly all the other survivors became fully committed Zionists in the short period between 1945 and 1948, joined rapidly by their brothers and sisters living in the Islamic world.

Meanwhile—Living in America

North American Jewry, an ocean away from the events of 1933–45, was much less transformed by them. Most Jews here continued to live in a society defined more by 1780—emergence from the ghetto—than by 1933. Our question was still that of how to live as a Jew in the context of modernity, in an open and increasingly borderless society. Zionism was a good idea, worth supporting for European and Near Eastern Jews, but not for ourselves. Despite some minor disturbances, we continued to live the good life here, and were not interested in exchanging it for the insecurities of life on the edge of the desert and in a very unstable part of the world. Progress continued to be made in our degree of acceptance into the American (white, of course) elite, and the worship of the gods of success and high achievement became the true faith of most American Jews. This faith was garbed—lightly so, for most—in some version of liberal Judaism, a religion that taught much about doing good for others (as long as these didn't threaten one's own status) and a certain bourgeois respectability. It seemed—especially in the eyes of its children—to have very little of counterculture about it. It is hard to be seeking acceptance by the majority culture and to stand in challenge to it at the same time.

Noble attempts at constructing a secular Jewish identity in America were stepped up in the early postwar years. Most of these were built on a combination of Yiddishism and leftist politics. Unfortunately, the disappearance of the Yiddish-speaking reservoir of Jews in eastern Europe (mostly due to Hitler, but also to the rapid Russification of Jewry in the Soviet Union) made the former become an increasingly dead-end street. Leftist politics, as well, were hardly a good strategy for identification in the Cold War period. It also became clear that in the United States ethnic identities alone would not long survive. Assimilation, and eventually intermarriage across ethnic lines, were the price of living in our open society—at least for those "privileged" to have skin color that eventually could allow them to be defined as "white."[3]

As the Jews' place in America became ever more secure, our religious life became ever more shallow and trivialized. Many essentially secular Jews joined synagogues just as a statement of affiliation, with minimal interest in Jewish tradition or spiritual life. Although our community professed a will to continue, Jewish ignorance became rampant and widely accepted within it, even as our general educational level soared to new heights. A special creation of American Jewry was the secularly well-educated Jew who got up at a relative's Bar/Bat Mitsvah and read the blessings from the transliterated card, pronouncing *baruch* as in the "ch" sound in "cheese-steak." The gap between the generally high level of education among Jews and the virtual Jewish illiteracy of many became scandalously wide. The synagogue of the 1960s and later was regularly mocked in literature and film, mostly created by Jews, as ultimately devoid of religious content, a kind of country club with services.

But then something began to stir beneath the surface within American Jewish life. By the mid-1960s, American Orthodoxy was coming back to life, and small but significant numbers of Jews from nonobservant families were being attracted to it. The Havurah movement, originating in the late 1960s, showed the possibility of a more intense Judaism within a liberal framework, based on small communities of commitment. The Jewish Renewal movement joined the younger generation of Reconstructionists in pushing the boundaries in favor of religious creativity and open, welcoming communities. Reform Judaism, long committed in theory to the social justice agenda, took inspiration from the civil rights movement and turned the slogans of "prophetic Judaism" into a strong activist tradition. The leading roles of support that Jews played in the early civil rights movement, the rebirth of Jewish activism in the Soviet Jewry movement, and the very significant presence of Jewish voices in the emerging feminist movement all had significant effect upon the self-image of American Jews. There began to emerge a new pride in being different, partly legitimized by the "black is beautiful" movement of the 1970s. This allowed for a sense that Jewish distinctiveness was a part of the "Rainbow Coalition" that made America truly great. In more recent decades, this spirit has brought forth and filled the ranks of a whole host of new Jewish do-good organizations. Graduates of day schools and Jewish summer camps, following the example of the 1960s Havurah movement, have established new *minyanim*, or prayer groups, independent of professional leadership, competing with the established congregations. Some of those young people are now causing great awkwardness in liberal Jewish establishment circles as they express their good Jewish counterculturalism by challenging policies of the Israeli government or American Middle East policy. Gap-year programs for high school graduates (often in Israel) and short-term stints for young adults in Jewish-based movements for social change (some including a dollop of Jewish learning) have begun to change the landscape significantly.

The American synagogue began to change as well. New translations of the liturgy were less pretentious; the atmosphere, including the dress code, of the synagogue became much more informal. Cantors became less would-be opera performers and more guitar-strumming song leaders in a worship service that strove for participation. Rabbis and cantors sought ways to infuse the ancient liturgy, often quite remote from contemporary Jews and their concerns, with commentary, poetry, and music that might help to open the hearts of those attending. Synagogues came to be judged more for their warmth and welcome than for the wealth displayed by magnificent architecture or decoration.

All this happened, of course, against the background of continued assimilation, declining birth rates, sky-high intermarriage figures, and the simple disappearance of large numbers of Jews into the American melting pot. Despite lots of hand wringing and much investment, there was relatively little that could be done to reverse this natural process. Compared to all other mostly white-raced ethnics in the United States, Jews, due to the overlay of religion and ethnicity, were doing remarkably well, even though it often has not felt that way.

In the course of this revival within the conventional synagogue-based Jewish community, a sense of Jewish counterculturalism has also begun to reemerge. The great social upheaval of the 1960s had a remarkable array of Jewish heroes (and a few villains, depending on your point of view). Well remembered from that era is yuppie leader Abbie Hoffman yelling out to his Jewish judge in Chicago (also coincidentally named Hoffman), on hearing his sentence: "You're a *shandeh* for the *goyim!*" Cultural critics and progressive political voices, having survived the red-baiting years, began to reemerge. The generation of Irving Howe and Max Lerner has been replaced by newer voices. Jews in the news media—think of Wolf Blitzer, Jake Tapper, and Chuck Todd—are highly represented among those who call for truth and personal integrity in the political sphere. Jewish columnists in the *New York Times*—Tom Friedman, Michelle Goldberg, Paul Krugman—while representing diverse views on certain questions, stand together for a sense of human decency. Political voices on the left, ranging from such Jewishly educated Jews as Michael Lerner and Arthur Waskow to bearers of Jewish name and memory of Jewish suffering like Bernie Sanders, are all important social critics in the name of higher, typically Jewish, values. While the center of American comedy seems to have shifted from Jews to blacks, the leading Jewish comedians—Jon Stewart, Billy Crystal, Susan Silverman—are people who stand for universalist and liberal values that seem familiar to most of their Jewish hearers.

To be a Jew in America is still to stand out, to be different. Americans, even those without a shred of anti-Semitic animus, are still aware of the Jews as a group within American society, and can generally recognize Jewish family names. The question is whether being Jewish means not only *to stand out*, but also *to stand for* something. If it does, just what is it that our Jewish identity calls upon us to stand for? Is there a Jewish ethos that runs across the spectrum of diverse Jews and Judaisms, embracing the Orthodox, the secular, and everyone in between? That takes us back to Abraham and the countercultural role of the Jew. Our ancestor was reputedly the first iconoclast, smashing the gods in his father's workshop. Are there idols and idolatries against which we together can stand up today?

Where Do We Jews Stand?

You might guess that I think there are—or I would hardly be writing this essay. But they are not as easy to identify as they were a generation ago. Liberal politics were then practically a sine qua non of Jewish existence. That is hardly the case today. The shift of voting patterns toward the right, especially within the Orthodox community, presumably the greatest bastion of Jewish loyalty and knowledge, has been deeply shaking to all of us who take our Jewish identity seriously. Witnessing the willingness of Jews who should know better to overlook obviously unacceptable statements and behavior, extending support even to the presidency of Donald Trump, leaves those of us in the Jewish liberal majority feeling stunned and wounded. It feels as though some of what we thought to be our most precious Jewish values are being abandoned by Jews who should understand them well. It is in the face of this challenge that I take up an attempt to call attention to three of these values, and to insist that they do indeed unite us, even when self-interest—including that of defending (or should I say "denouncing all criticism of"?) Israel—stands in their way.

The Memory of Slavery

Every Jewish child is brought up on this one. It is the answer to the four questions that we rehearse for the *seder*—whether Orthodox, Reform, or secular—at a very young age. The fact that we were slaves in Egypt is supposed to affect the way we treat strangers and fellow victims of slavery and oppression. The many biblical verses attesting to this are too well known to need to be quoted here.

The problem with this obvious value of Jewish tradition and experience is that the ancient—and presumably edifying—memory of slavery is mixed with the more recent, and much more searing, memory of oppression. "Egypt" is easily overshadowed by Auschwitz in the Jewish imagination. The terrors engendered by that more recent enslavement are still very real. Both in Israel and in the American Orthodox community, where the presence of survivors and their descendants is significantly higher, the natural urge for self-protection outweighs all other considerations. Recent anti-Semitic attacks on ultra-Orthodox Jews in America have rightly reinforced this concern for security above all. But the result is that biblical verses can get to be interpreted more narrowly, or other scriptures brought forth to stand against them, reinforcing old ghetto-era stereotypes about the non-Jewish world. Palestinians, Syrian refugees, and sometimes even African American neighbors in changing neighborhoods get turned into Nazis and "Pharoahs." And suddenly we hear Jews saying: "We need a tough guy—whether Meir Kahane or Donald J. Trump—to stand up against them."

While we need to listen openheartedly to the fears that still plague a large part of our community, we also must not give in to them. We need to trust that the very real memory of trauma will fade with time. We need to take an active role in helping with the socioeconomic integration of the ultra-Orthodox community. This is not a simple process, but hopefully it will ultimately diminish the moral influence of its extremist fringes. Even regarding Israel, where the problems are likely to remain unresolved for a long time, the ability to see the suffering of the other must not be set aside. The small sproutings of humanitarian concern, even within some settler communities, need to be nourished.[4]

"Remember that you were slaves in the Land of Egypt" has to create a natural sense of sympathy for oppressed groups, wherever they are. A Jew who remembers Egypt cannot simply turn aside on learning the fate of the Darfuris in Sudan or the Rohingya in Myanmar. It means that we care about statements like the Universal Declaration of Human Rights, and believe that governments should act in accord with it.[5] It does not necessarily drive us all toward socialism, but it does insist that unbridled action in favor of one's own self-interest, whether economic or political, is wrong, and needs to be checked by another set of values. This applies both to individuals and societies.

The Image of God

Our Torah begins not with the story of the Jewish people or God's covenant with Israel, but with the creation of the world. Its universalism regarding the divine image in all human beings, male and female, is stated unequivocally in Genesis 1, and repeated several more times in the Genesis narrative. Most significant, it is given as the reason for the abhorrence of shedding blood, as the cornerstone of God's covenant with Noah after the flood (Gen. 9:6).

The preeminence of this teaching within Judaism is underscored by a well-known passage in the Jerusalem Talmud recording a debate between the great second-century Rabbi Akiva and his friend ben Azzai.[6] They were investigating the question "What is the *klal gadol*, the greatest underlying principle, of Torah?" Akiva said it was "Love your neighbor as yourself," echoing a view that had already been recorded just a few years earlier in the Christian New Testament. "But I know a greater principle," said ben Azzai: "On the day when Elohim created humans, He made them in the image of God; male and female He created them" (Gen. 5:1–2).

We are not certain as to the nub of the argument between these two sages. Ben Azzai might have been saying that "love" is too high a standard to demand as a universal principle. Some neighbors, as Jews have long learned from experience, are not easy to love. Nevertheless, ben Azzai insists, they too must be recognized as created in God's image. Or perhaps the question of universalism and particularism lay at the center of their debate. The "neighbor" of the Leviticus verse might be read narrowly, referring only to your Israelite neighbor. Perhaps, indeed, it meant only your properly observant Jewish neighbor, at that. Ben Azzai's principle, deriving directly from Creation, necessarily embraced every human being ever to exist, even the most lowly or despicable in behavior.

The Mishnah, recorded in the generations immediately following this debate, codifies this universalism in the following formula: "See how much greater than human deeds are those of God! A human king stamps out many coins from a single press, and all of them look the same. But the King of kings, the blessed Holy One, stamps every human in the press of Adam, and each one looks different." To this is added, very pointedly: "Why was Adam created singly? So that no person be able to say to another: 'My father was greater than yours!'"[7] The rabbinic tradition so celebrates human diversity that it ordains a blessing to God each time one sees a physically nonconforming person. "Blessed is Y-H-W-H . . . who has diversified His creatures!"[8]

Yes, there are also passages that can be found in the vast rabbinic corpus that seem to read the other way. Most notoriously, a passage in Numbers 19:14 regarding ritual purity and contact with the dead, says that "a person" in the text refers to Israelites, not to other nations.[9] This statement was taken out of context and expanded in later ages, when xenophobia emerged as the Jewish response to persecution. Especially in the mystical tradition, this sense of Jewish uniqueness, almost biological, was put forward. It is now carried as a banner by certain fringe elements within the Israeli national-religious community, used as a justification for asserting the primacy of Jewish claims. It needs to be combated firmly and openly. Similarly, "Esau hates Jacob," taken to mean that anti-Semitism is endemic to all non-Jewish populations, is still widely quoted in some traditionalist circles, especially those closer to Holocaust memory.[10]

Commitment to faith in humans as the image of God does not resolve all our ethical questions. Regarding two of the great moral dilemmas of our time, abortion and assisted suicide, concerning the beginning and end of life, believers in the divine image, hence the sacredness of human life, could be driven by that faith to take either position. But it is vital that this be the ground on which they are decided, and that human life not be violable for reasons of economy or convenience.

The essential humanitarian message of Judaism stands on these two pillars: the memory of our own enslavement and the universality of the divine image. The countercultural imperative of these values stands out clearly in our own day, perhaps more than at any other time in the postwar era. We live in an age of aggressive capitalism and flight from social responsibility, a time when gaps between rich and poor, between native and stranger, and between racial groups within our society are growing ever more severe, strained to near breaking point. Caring about the humanity of the other and identifying with the plight of outcasts and strangers are not values by which our society lives. They certainly do not seem to be the criteria by which we choose our leaders.

To be a Jew means to stand up for these values, even when they seem to run against our narrow self-interest. A Jew has to be willing to pay higher taxes, if that will help to provide health care for the poor and elderly. A Jew needs to support high quality of public education, even if one's own children are in Jewish day schools. Jews need to stand for the value of human life, opposing the soul-numbing violence of Hollywood, television, and video games—areas where some Jews are making lots of money—as well as the obscene cynicism of the gun lobby. Jewish men and women need to stand up against the insulting degradation of the human body in the vast industry of pornography, including the "soft-core" pornography that so penetrates the world of advertising and entertainment. We do not need to be prudes, but the values of Judaism do include something called *tseni'ut*, "modesty," today translatable into concern for the cheapening of the human, especially the female, body for commercial gain.

As escapees from both Egypt and Auschwitz, we need to stand with the oppressed and those who need to flee their homes, whether in Guatemala or El Salvador, Syria or Afghanistan. This does not mean that Jews need to oppose all restrictions on immigration, but it does lean heavily upon us to tend toward the compassionate and to actively work toward solutions for truly agonizing problems.

Nor should our sense of Jewish compassion stop at the borders of Gaza. To stand with Abraham, defying the world, is also to stand with the same Abraham who defied God and risked his own life for the sake of some ill-behaved Palestinians in a place called Sodom. Yes, caring for the people of Gaza and the West Bank may seem to run counter to Jewish self-interest, even to Jewish security. But we are playing for higher stakes than just another hilltop in Judea or Samaria, or just a little more pressure to assert over those miserably poor Arabs in Gaza. Too often, Israel's looking out for economic advantage, as well as old-fashioned land hunger, are cloaked behind the label of "security." We are playing for higher stakes indeed—the very highest. If we lose the moral message that is the very reason for our existence, along with the loyalty of our children, we will have lost it all.

Responsibility for God's Creation

Here you may say "the natural order" or simply "the planet," if you prefer. That is not the argument we need to have at this moment. An ancient rabbinic source teaches that "the blessed Holy One set a condition with all He had made in heaven and earth. 'If Israel accept My Torah,' He said, 'all will be well. If not, I will return you to primordial chaos.'"[11] The statement can be read as Israelocentrism at its most rampant. "Only we matter! We are the sole purpose of existence!" But read it instead as a declaration of ultimate moral responsibility. "This beautiful world will survive only if we—*and communities like ours*—take ultimate responsibility for it." Another well-known text, more universalist in its focus, says that soon after creation, God walked Adam around the Garden, which he was commissioned "to till and to guard." "Take good care," he was told, "because if you let it be destroyed, there is no one to come set it right after you."[12]

We Jews exist in the United States largely as a *religious community*. Each of those two terms has significance in terms of this conversation about counterculture. A community is a voluntary group of people who choose to live in a face-to-face encounter with one another. I have been a member of intense communities of only twenty or thirty members, and I am also a member of the American Jewish community, numbering some 5 or 6 million, depending upon how you count and whom you believe. This definition holds true for both. A fellow member of my community is someone I take seriously. I care about her or his opinions, even if that means being particularly horrified by them. I need to look that person in the eye and respond to those opinions, because that is what it means to belong together as members of the same community. I want that person, more than others, to get to know me and to hear my views, because we share community. For us Jews, that community begins in Egypt, at Sinai, and in wandering through the wilderness together. That is our teaching, our Torah. You may be a *ḥasid* in Brooklyn, an utterly assimilated Jew in the wilds of Montana, an extremist settler in the Hebron hills, or a committed atheist in a philosophy department. As long as you have not fully opted out of defining yourself as a Jew (which you have a right to do, of course), we are members of the same community. We need to look at one another and hear what the other has to say. That all falls within the rubric of even a narrow reading of Rabbi Akiva's "Love your neighbor as yourself" as the basic rule of Jewish life. We Jews all live in the same moral "neighborhood."

A *religious* community is one that shares a language, including both words and symbolic gestures, for talking about all the important things. These include God, truth, existence, mortality, ethics, and lots more. We do not all need to agree on any of these issues, but we speak the same language when we talk or even argue about them. That language derives from an ancient canon that we consider to be sacred, however we define that term. Our conversation is enriched by our long history of reinterpreting that canon, both as a whole and down to every word and letter, over and over again. As it happens, our particular legacy is strengthened by the fact that it embraces a diversity of views, somehow always able to say "both these and those are the words of the living God."

Because of America's status as a trans-ethnic polity, and because religion plays such a large role in the self-definition of most Americans, we as a religious community are in a position of potentially great influence in this society. Whether you call it providence or happy coincidence, this is also the country where many decisions vital to the future of the planet and humanity as a whole are being made. It is important that we stand together in articulating these key values of the Jewish tradition and experience, seeing to it that they have a hearing in our political life and on every level where decisions are made. To speak with such a voice, we will need to overcome some serious inner differences in the way we read those values. Our efforts in doing so will be well rewarded.

Now we need to turn to Israel. Counterculturalism in a situation where Jews have sovereignty, and where the majority culture is itself Jewish, is different than that afforded by our diasporic quasi-outsider status. The very powerful model we have for it, of course, is that of the prophets of ancient Israel, and the way they saw much of their mission as that of standing up to Israel's kings. Philosopher Yeshayahu Leibowitz was such a figure, reviled by much of the public almost as much as Jeremiah had been a couple of millennia earlier. Writers like Amos Oz and David Grossman have worn something of the secularized prophet's mantle in criticizing both governmental actions and public values. Israel has not yet had a rabbinic figure who rises to those countercultural heights.

Surprisingly, one of the things Israel needs most is a *Jewish community*. Because the state that David Ben Gurion conceived was itself said to be Jewish, the idea of an organized Jewish community never quite took hold in Israel. There are synagogues on every corner, of course, and now community centers as well. But none of these takes the role of an organized Jewish community, standing for certain values and poised at midpoint between the individual and the state, challenging both when needed. Without it, the state is in constant danger of becoming *totalitarian*, a total entity that brooks no challenge from within, except that of frustrated lone individuals. Political parties, often corrupt and unprincipled because of the needs of coalition politics, cannot take the place of civil society.

Those of us who love Israel from abroad desperately want to help create these communities, but also know that we cannot impose them on an unwilling society. The current government fights any such attempts as undue foreign influence, because it feels that its policies of acting in favor of what it perceives as Jewish self-interest will be challenged if such communal institutions emerge. But the prophetic urge never departs from the Jewish people. We await its voice. "A lion roars; who can but fear? Y-H-W-H has spoken. Who can *not* prophesy?" (Amos 3:8).

Wandering Jews

I F THERE IS A new Kabbalah to be revealed among diaspora Jews in our age, I have long suspected that its biblical basis will be the seemingly obscure concluding chapters of the book of Numbers, which open this way: "These are the journeys of the children of Israel who went forth from Egypt in their multitudes, by the hand of Moses and Aaron. Moses wrote their goings forth to journey by the mouth of God; these are their journeys as they went forth" (33:1–2). The chapter then goes on to list the various stopping places in the course of Israel's forty-year journey through the wilderness. The Torah reading tradition, as practiced in the Ashkenazic synagogue, recognizes a mysterious quality in these place-names, chanting them in a special lilting tune that is used only here and at the Song of the Sea.

Imagine Moses writing them down as he completes the Torah, just as he is getting ready to deliver his great final speeches. He knows that he is not to enter the Promised Land, that he will have no part in the "glory of battle" that lies ahead. Instead, he chooses to leave his people with a list of all those places in which they had camped along the way, back when they were still just wanderers. But this record of travels, seemingly meaningless and perhaps confused meanderings around the desert wasteland, is not written down just as a memento for future generations. There is something sacred in the list of place-names—a secret yet to be revealed. "They journeyed from Elim and camped at Yam-Suf. They journeyed from Yam-Suf and camped at Midbar Sin. They journeyed from Midbar

Sin and camped at Dofkah. They journeyed from Dofkah and camped at Alush. They journeyed from Alush and camped at Rephidim, where there was no water for the people to drink. They journeyed from Rephidim and camped at Midbar Sinai. They journeyed from Midbar Sinai and camped at Kivrot ha-Ta'avah ('the Graves of Desire')" (Num. 33:10–16).

Journeys, wanderings. We diaspora Jews have been wanderers for a long time. How did Moses know that this was to be the fate of his people, thousands of years into the future? He gave us a zigzagged, back-circling map of forty-two places where we had camped. This is a holy number, say the mystics, corresponding to the hidden forty-two-letter name of God.[1] Each camping site—some lasting for days and others for years—represented its own holy letter. "They journeyed from the Graves of Desire and camped in Hatzerot. They journeyed from Hatzerot and camped in Rithmah. They journeyed from Rithmah and camped in Rimon Paretz" (Num. 33:17–19).

The reason we will write our own Kabbalah around them is because we continue to be wanderers. In the private religion of our own inner lives, we all have such sacred lists, all the important stopping places in our journeys. Our generation wanders as none before it, perhaps not since the days of our hunter-gatherer ancestors. Yes, we always were wandering Jews. But the truth is that many of our ancestors lived for quite a while—perhaps five or ten generations—in the same city or *shtetl* somewhere in the old-world diaspora. It was the twentieth century, with its great upheavals of population, that broke that bond and set us loose. Some went first from small town to city, then from eastern to central Europe, then (those who were lucky) on to America. Others had unfortunate stops in Siberia and the DP camps—or much worse—along the way. We new-world Jews, born in places where our families had only the shallowest roots, felt free, sometimes almost *called*, to wander, to cover territory across the country and around the world, before settling down. The decision to stop wandering is a hard one; many of us never quite come to peace with it. When we do settle, it is often in yet newer places. Each generation of wandering Jews, so it begins to seem, seeks out a new place to call home and make its nest.

Some of the old desert place-names seem to have meaning, and might be translated that way: "They journeyed from Community and camped at Mount Beauty. They journeyed from Mount Beauty and camped at Trembling. They journeyed from Trembling and camped at Choirs. They journeyed from Choirs and camped at the Bottom (or maybe at 'Asshole'; anyway, it was a terrible place)." But we're not quite sure of those meanings. Perhaps we need another set of tools, not yet discovered, to really decipher them. That will be the new Kabbalah.

Meanwhile, lay out your own family's journey this way, in as much detail as you know of it. Go ahead; try it. "They journeyed from Berdychiv and camped in Hamburg. They sailed from Hamburg and landed in Ellis Island. They ferried from Ellis Island and camped on Rivington Street. They journeyed from Rivington Street and camped in the Bronx, on the Grand Concourse. They journeyed from the Grand Concourse and settled in Teaneck, a place of much traffic."

Now do your own travels, key stations along your road of life. "I journeyed from Teaneck and camped in West Philadelphia. I journeyed from West Philadelphia and backpacked in Europe. I journeyed from Europe and camped in Ann Arbor." Go ahead, do your own. Write it down, just like Moses did. Once you have your list, try chanting it aloud.

It is not only we American Jews who seem to have this special desire for wandering. Our Israeli cousins, just a generation after having announced an end to Jewish exile, are out on the roads again, among the world's most intrepid travelers. "I parted from Petaḥ-Tikva and went to Amsterdam. In a puff of smoke, I flew to Dharamsala. From Dharamsala I trekked to Katmandu, gathering-place of the tribe. I fled to Bali, then to Morro de Sao Paulo, and settled in Los Angeles."

There is something of the nesting instinct that belongs to our feminine side; the man-soul within all of us often struggles with the desire to keep wandering, to see life as an endless journey rather than as the history of a growing home. Even when settled and loving our families, there is something in us that still hankers for the open road. That's how Jack Kerouac became the hero of an entire male generation, readers of his *On the Road*, mostly guys who had long given up such travels but still wanted to hear and dream about them. Maybe the film *Thelma and Louise* became some of that for female companions on the road.

We even have a word for it, an English term derived from the old German—*wanderlust*. What is it within us that still desires, against all reason, to cut loose from ties and hit the road? How many good relationships have we ended, how many hearts lie broken, because we just couldn't "stay put"? Perhaps it is that old tribal wanderer, the one who has not quite left behind the "hunter-gatherer" stage of human history, who remains alive somewhere deep within us.

The ancient memory is embedded in our lives as Jews. Look at two of our oldest rituals and ask where they really come from. On the spring full moon, we used to sacrifice a lamb and then, for a week, eat only nomads' bread. We still eat that thin, crunchy stuff, bread like that which people made before we settled down, before we had ovens. The dough was carried on our backs, so we're told, baked only by the sun. At the fall full moon, we leave our houses and live in wanderers' huts for a week, covered with palm fronds or pine branches or whatever our climate provides. Only later did these rites come to be associated with one specific journey, that which took us out of Egypt. But their origins go back to the most ancient of human memories.[2] What are they, if not nostalgia for the freedoms of that ancient age, passed by so many centuries ago, but not quite fully left behind? The farmer, tied to his own patch of land and the cycles of its cultivation (not too unlike the office worker on the 9 to 5 treadmill), dreams of being freed from it, back on the road "like in the good old days."

Of course, we have lots of precedent for this nostalgia from within the tradition, beginning with Abraham and Moses, both of whom found God in the course of lone journeys. Elijah, off on Mount Carmel, Rabbi Simeon and his son in the cave. The later Rabbi Simeon, the hero of the Zohar, teaching his little band of disciples as they wander about the Holy Land. Rabbi Naḥman of Bratslav's holy beggars, living out in the forest. One senses that there is something universally human, not just Jewish, about this instinct. Both the Buddha and the Desert Fathers could easily be added to our list of wanderers and seekers.

Exile and wandering do not begin with the destruction of the Temple, neither the First nor the Second. Humanity—all of it—is in exile since the expulsion of Adam and Eve from the Garden, since the punishment of Cain: "a wanderer shall you be in the earth" (Gen. 4:12). We are descended from Cain's brother Seth, but we seem to still have some of that mysterious wandering uncle within us. The exile of Israel is a dramatic repetition, on a collective level, of the whole human condition. After all, if a people dares to call itself "a kingdom of priests," it has to have undergone the great suffering of those whom it serves. If Israel wants to serve in a priestly role to the whole human community, our exile and wandering show that we identify with the eternal human pain of homelessness.

The kabbalists understood that the wandering of Israel was at once both tragic and holy. They took seriously an ancient teaching that said, "Everywhere Israel were exiled, the *shekhinah*, or divine presence, was exiled with them."[3] Originally, this meant that God had never abandoned the Jews. Just as in Christianity (a religion of the individual), God had come down into human form in order to experience death, the individual's greatest trauma, so in rabbinic Judaism (the religion of a people) did God take on the greatest form of collective suffering, that of exile and wandering. Wherever Jews went, *shekhinah* followed, often described as a Mother following Her beloved children.

The kabbalists, however (as so frequently), preserved the metaphor but transformed its meaning. *Shekhinah*'s exile came first. Something of separation and alienation penetrated the divine realm itself, from the very beginning of existence. Perhaps it was a flaw in the universe, a by-product of the very existence of a separate, seemingly nondivine realm. Or maybe it was caused by the emergence of human individuation, the sense of need to separate from one's parents (and divine Parent) in order to become oneself. In any case *perud*, or separation, entered the Godhead. This tragic fate is not just the human tragedy, but that of God as well. We Israelites, as a holy people, recapitulate that primordial event in our history as wanderers. Destruction and exile, to carry the symbolization to its fullest hasidic expression, were not punishment for our sins, but a holy opportunity, causing us to be scattered through the world so that we could raise sparks of holiness, even from the most remote of places.

Here there seems to be a sort of split within the kabbalistic imagination. Some saw that uplifting as an effort to redeem *shekhinah*, to end Her exile. We, Her devotees, are Her bridal attendants, ever preparing for the great wedding. Or perhaps we are Her children, longing to see Her reunited with Her Spouse. We are forever busy beautifying Her, adorning Her with the devotion of each commandment we fulfill. All this is for the purpose of *ending* Her exile, and with it our own. Each Shabbat is a foretaste of that, when we sing and pray for the Holy Apple Field, as She is called, to have Her Master enter Her once again. But other voices were less sanguine about the possibility of *shekhinah*'s imminent redemption. The most we could do, they felt, was to share in Her wanderings, to support Her in Her suffering. There were traditions of kabbalists and *ḥasidim* undertaking voluntary periods of exile, going penniless from place to place, in order to partake of this cosmic drama. (The image will not be unfamiliar to those who know tales of wandering Buddhist monks.)

Shekhinah wanders with us wherever we are exiled. Even when we think we are making a positive choice to wander forth, responding to a new love or a new career opportunity, there is something of exile about it: loss of friends, loss of familiar patterns and places. As She wanders with us through all those forty-two mysterious stopping places, so do we wander with Her in the big one, the single exile that is our life here on earth.

Scholarship Is Not Enough

IN 1945, GERSHOM SCHOLEM published a scathing and somewhat sensational article entitled "Amid Second Thoughts on the Science of Judaism."[1] Accusing Leopold Zunz and Moritz Steinschneider, the founding fathers of the *Wissenschaft des Judentums*, or the historical/critical study of Judaism, of having "danced amid the graves" of the Jewish past (one to which they sought only to offer a "decent burial"), Scholem cut himself off from the post-Enlightenment traditions of Jewish scholarship in central Europe, of which he was very much a product. In contrast to the old *Wissenschaft*, notably still referred to by its German name, Scholem puts forth the renewal of the scholarly enterprise in the context of the Jewish national revival, a scholarship conducted in Hebrew and centered in the Land of Israel. Scholem, both scholar and Zionist, might have wanted a truly Zionist renewal of Jewish studies, one in which the drama of Jewish national rebirth would be accompanied by truly dramatic breakthroughs in historical self-understanding. Thus far he finds only disappointment:

> Is this what we were longing for? Is this the inheritance? Is this our destiny? Where is that building we had promised to erect, that house of so deep a foundation in our shared existence that it would reach into the skies? . . . Or might we have seen wrongly? Could it be that we blew the shofar when the time had not yet come, like those fools in Jerusalem of old?[2] The spiritual air is still

polluted, and there is no renewal. Then we would have announced something that never happened, a redeemed Jewish scholarship that has not yet come to be.[3]

A great deal has happened in Jewish scholarship in the last seventy-five years, both in Israel and in the diaspora. The acceptance of Scholem's own work and the far-reaching implications it has had for our understanding and definition of Judaism in several periods is but one of several earth-shattering—or perhaps I should better say "stereotype-smashing"—events that have happened in Judaic studies in the postwar period. Foremost among these is the placing of Jewish religious and intellectual creativity in the context of the broader cultural realms in which it existed. Even the Talmud, long kept aloof from contextual study, is viewed as a literature reflecting Jewish life in late antiquity. In recent decades, the interest has shifted from the Greco-Roman context to that of the Persian Empire, within which the Babylonian rabbis lived.[4] Parallels to contemporary Christian creativity are also widely examined.[5] In any case, the Talmud is no longer treated as the abstract creation of trans-historical schoolmen. The impact of the social sciences on every aspect of historical research has also had a revolutionary effect on Jewish studies in the course of these decades. Controversies once described as theological in nature have been examined for their social and economic implications, as far back as the 1930s.[6] An era of socialist-tinted Jewish historiography has come and gone. The tendency toward Zionist lenses in Jewish historiography has been more persistent, but it too has been challenged in recent decades. Sophisticated historians of Jewry now face, along with their colleagues in other historical fields, the difficult questions raised by the sociology of knowledge as to the nature and unspoken assumptions of historical judgments. As psychoanalysis sought to assert itself as the most profound of sciences (or most compelling of myths) in the late twentieth century, both heroes and villains of Jewish history were, and continue to be, subjected to psychohistorical investigation.[7] Over the past two or three decades, feminist scholarship and gender theory have had a tremendous impact both on the selection of materials investigated from the Jewish past and the ways in which they are analyzed.

The growth of history of religions, including both phenomenological and comparative studies, has revolutionized the way scholars read Jewish religious literature of prior ages. The works of such highly respected early twentieth-century masters as Solomon Schechter on the rabbinic sources or Simon Dubnov on Hasidism now seem to us hopelessly naïve. Jewish mystical studies, a field that has come into its own only once liberated from Scholem's sole dominance, is shaped by all these currents.[8] The influence of the Christian and Islamic settings in which the kabbalists and *hasidim* lived can no longer be ignored,[9] nor can the value of typological comparisons to religious phenomena in figures and cultures with which there is no historical connection. The introduction of methods originating in literary criticism, including much of postmodern discourse, into every field of Jewish studies, from biblical to modern studies, has often been quite spectacular.

There remain some important differences between Judaic scholarship in Israel, conducted entirely in Hebrew, and that produced abroad, mostly in North America. In Israel, the field is now dominated by people who grew up and were educated in the world of religious Zionism. For them, immersion in the world of Jewish text is entirely self-justifying and taken for granted. The breadth of their knowledge, now augmented by electronic research methods, is often quite breathtaking. Methodological sophistication, of the sorts mentioned above, is somewhat more spotty. The fact that one can still get along without it leaves it as a matter of personal inclination. When it is joined to the high level of textual knowledge found in Israeli scholarship, it can be truly groundbreaking.

In the diaspora, there seems to remain much self-consciousness regarding any crossing of boundaries between academic scholarship and personal involvement with the materials, more so than in Israel, somewhat a reversal of the case in Scholem's day. University departments of religion, literature, or history, the settings in which most Judaic scholars live, are often not comfortable places in which to admit such interests. Religion departments in particular, once peopled by a slew of former ministers or escapees from Christian fundamentalism, spent many years demonstrating to the university that their approach was quite antiseptic, lest they be accused of being proselytizers in disguise. Some Judaica faculty at universities have been at pains to insist that they are not to be seen by the community as "Jewish educators," meaning that the university-based academic can take no responsibility for the propagation of a Judaism that might be supportive for the future of the Jewish people. Here there is an important distinction to be made between university- and seminary-based scholars. The latter obviously are encouraged to think and teach beyond their "purely" scholarly interests. While fully trained within academic canons, the nature of their teaching mission and audience changes the purpose of their enterprise, making it more deeply and self-consciously integrated with the task of building a Jewish future.[10]

The truly incredible growth of Jewish studies as a field, both in North America and in Israel, can also hardly be dismissed. There are now many times more working scholars, positions, monographs, and journals devoted to such research than would have been dreamed of just a generation or two ago. It would seem that in America and Israel—places offering a freedom from apologetics unknown to the early *Wissenschaft* scholars and a range of scholarly sophistication far exceeding that of nineteenth-century Germany—Jewish scholarship has finally come into its own. Still, there are causes for concern in both centers. Tenured positions in the field are drying up in Israel, due to the lack of undergraduate interest, partly the result of the great emphasis on STEM and especially on high-tech studies in that country, with the tremendous economic opportunities they offer. In the United States, the decline of Jews as percentages of undergraduate student bodies (largely due to a great influx of foreign students) is added to this attraction to the sciences, creating severe downward pressure on student enrollments. One could create a great Purim skit based on the titles of courses Judaic scholars have to whip up in order to stimulate undergraduate enrollments.

Yet Scholem's challenge still seems to haunt Americans as well as Israelis. Has there yet been a true renewal of Jewish studies? Is the intellectual and spiritual life of our communities truly enriched by what is being produced by the academy? Think of Scholem, a true cultural Zionist, as a disciple of Bialik and as an early fan of Agnon. Bialik's *Sefer ha-Aggadah* (*The Book of Legends*) indeed did have a transformative effect on the *yishuv* of his day, and on early Israeli culture.[11] Taught in the schools for many decades, it became the secular Israeli's chief conduit of knowledge about the rabbinic tradition and the society's best sourcebook for "Jewish values." Agnon tremendously enriched both the language and the love for tradition of a whole generation of Jewish readers.[12] Scholem's first major student, Isaiah Tishby, did the same for Kabbalah with his *Wisdom of the Zohar*.[13] Adin Steinsaltz's edition of the Talmud made that work accessible to new generations of learners both in Israel and beyond, having tremendous impact on the growth of Talmud study throughout the Jewish world.[14] In our own day, we might point to Daniel Matt's great translation of the Zohar as having such a role for English-speaking Jewry, and of Tzvi Mark's complete edition of Rabbi Naḥman's tales as rendering that cultural treasure accessible to the contemporary Hebrew reader.[15]

But presenting the sources in accessible form is only a first step. What would Scholem's "redeemed Jewish scholarship" look like in our day? And what would be its relationship to the critical-historical method, to which he always remained wedded as well? What seems to be needed is a step Scholem would never have dared to take, a semi-secular reclaiming by the Jewish people of the old value of *talmud torah*, Torah study as a sacred act, so central to Jewish life throughout the ages. To reach this, one must go beyond the critical, accepting its legitimacy, but also learning to again read Torah, in its broadest sense, as a source of inspiration and wisdom.[16] In terms that would be familiar to Rosenzweig as well as Scholem, we will need to reattach the Tree of Knowledge to the Tree of Life.[17]

The Western academy and its tradition of humanistic learning are deeply imperiled in our day. This threat began with the separation of the acquisition of knowledge, largely driven by the advances of science, from what might be called the quest for wisdom. The university became a bastion of knowledge, often technical knowledge and skills that would qualify one for a particular professional role within society. Attention to the human being who was being thus prepared was mostly set aside, dismissed as too much of a luxury in a budget-constrained collection of academic departments, none of which saw education of the whole person as its priority. Sometimes it was also dismissed as dated, a leftover of the old religion-dominated medieval university, one that needed to be set aside in the name of scientific rigor and intellectual freedom.

It would be laughable to hear a prospective student in today's world proclaim: "I am going to university in order to become wise." The pursuit of wisdom, or of spiritual refinement, was long ago pushed aside in the Western university. You might learn how to think critically in a university, if it is doing its job. But it is hardly a place to become wise, a place where the two trees of knowledge and life might be brought together. One might still go to an *ashram* to pursue such wisdom, perhaps even to a Benedictine monastery, but hardly to a university.

But how about a *yeshiva* or a *bet midrash*? Can we, a people who believe in *Torah min ha-Shamayim*—(translation: that our teachings contain a transcendent truth)—present them in such a way that Jewish learning becomes the setting for a personal quest after wisdom and spiritual growth? And can we do so while at the same time being intellectually honest, not hiding anything that we have learned from critical inquiry? Here "*redeemed* Jewish scholarship" also has to become "*redemptive* Jewish learning," a kind of intellectuality that transforms the lives of individuals, encourages them to build new communities of such learning, and thus helps to transform the world around them as well, a pursuit of wisdom connected to life itself.

Scholem's call was issued in the context of a great national revival. He wanted the newly emerging people and its culture, a Jewry coming back to life, to be deeply rooted in the knowledge and wisdom of the past. Our present call begins more in an age of individual spiritual quest and its fulfillment, but with implications for the collective culture of the future Jewish people as well. Ours is a time when the value of Jewish continuity, including the study of the textual tradition, is no longer taken for granted by younger generations of Jews. This is true of those who have grown up in the liberal movements in the diaspora, as well as of Israeli youth from secular homes. It is also the case for increasing numbers of *datlashim*, the Israeli term for the formerly Orthodox, or the *hozrim bi-she'elah*, those again asking questions, some still within the observant world, a growing and important group of Jewish seekers.

Our age calls for a new way into the sources. Yes, they were written whenever they were, by whoever wrote them. We know all that, but leave it behind us. The historical-critical approach had served to distance us from the text, always surrounding it by historical context. We seek to be close, even intimate, with the sources, and with the Source hidden within them. There is something tremendously exciting about being engaged in a living, ongoing conversation with a text written in ancient Judea, maybe in the fifth century BCE, a Midrash on it from the Galilee in the second century, expanded by a Babylonian sage in the fifth, reinterpreted first by a philosopher in twelfth-century North Africa, and again by the mysterious Zohar in Christian Spain, then spun in a completely surprising way by a Ukrainian hasidic master two hundred years ago. In good Jewish learning, they are all present to you around the table, as you are to them. We are told repeatedly to see each of them as though speaking his words before you.[18]

Of course, what you have to offer in this conversation is different. That may be because you are a woman, newly invited into this long-ongoing process. Or it may be because you know some Semitic philology. Or perhaps because you've studied Buddhism and seen some interesting parallel. Or you are a gender-queer person who sees things through a previously repressed or unexplored lens. Or maybe you're a scientist, and that gives you a different take on the text. Or . . .

This conversation is made possible because of our shared acceptance of the text as sacred, as part of the sacred canon of Israel, meaning that we allow ourselves to be *called* by it, to hear the divine voice that may speak to us through it. This is the case not because of divine *authorship* but because of divine *presence*, found within the sources and attested to by countless generations of Jews. We affirm it as sacred canon, a place within which we seek that presence. The text becomes a *mikra kodesh*, a place from within which we are called *to and by* the holy. The text is opened up for us; in the famous hasidic understanding of the Zohar's *patah Rabbi Shim'on*, "Rabbi Simeon opened" the verse. But we too are opened in this encounter, one of deep mutuality.

The key to such an approach lies in creating a space for personal encounter between the learner and the text. The new *bet midrash*, just emerging in our day, should be one that makes this explicit as one of its goals. Its *hevrutot*, or pairs of learners, should be encouraging and challenging one another on this level, beyond simply figuring out the meaning of the words or following the argument.[19] Whether Torah or Talmud, theology or poetry, Zohar or *Hasidut*, the value should be one of opening to deeper hearing of the text, allowing oneself to be called, even by particular words or phrases that appear within it. Such learning should be little interested in "covering ground" and much more attuned to deep exposure.

This is not an entirely new approach to learning. It is the kind of close reading-based learning that once engaged the teachers of Aggadah, the authors of the Zohar, and the early hasidic masters. They engaged deeply with the text, savored it slowly, and then, surprisingly often, came forth with new and startling readings of it. This is what the hasidic sources mean when they read the phrase *Torah li-shmah* (literally, perhaps "learning for its own sake") as *le-shem heh*, "for the sake of the letter *heh*," representing the *shekhinah*.[20] Contemplate those words and letters until you encounter the divine presence within them, *until they come alive to you, and you become newly alive in them*. Bring with you, of course, any tools you may have to enrich that encounter, including those learned from history, philology, and all the rest. But also gain the ability to set them aside at some point, to stand quite naked before the text.

"What does this sort of reading have to do with scholarship?" you might ask. How can the scholar, who has trained so hard in the very different direction of critical perspective, allow him- or herself to move in this direction? Exegesis, reading out of the text, was a positive step, the scholarly tradition taught us (such medievals as Ibn Ezra or RaDaK were praised for it), while eisegesis, reading *into* the text, was to be avoided. It might, after all, wind up being *merely drash*, homiletics, a dirty word in the scholarly pantheon.

But the truth is that *drash* is where Jewish creativity has always lain. In our world, given the level of both ignorance and distance from the textual tradition, we need the help of scholars in order to renew it. They are the only ones, having both textual mastery and the sense of having worked through the critical questions, who can lead us into this post-critical moment of a new *ahavat Torah*, love of learning, love of our teachings, which includes the ability to read them with a creative eye.

As one who has been around Jewish scholars for a long time, I am beginning to see, both in Israel and in the diaspora, the emergence of a younger generation of scholars in the field of Jewish mysticism who are openly admitting that they are engaged in a quest that has personal/spiritual as well as academic/intellectual dimensions to it. This circle, many of whom I have been privileged to get to know well, unselfconsciously refer to themselves as the *ḥevrayya*, with an understated implication that they are the Jewish mystic wanderers of today, the spiritual descendants of Rabbi Simeon and his band in the Zohar—which they know well to be a work of fiction. That awareness exists side by side with their desire not only to understand and analyze the profound thought of the Zohar, but to touch the sublime through their own involvement with it. This admission is quite new—and still somewhat daring—within the world of Judaic scholarship, something that would never have been tolerated a few decades ago. Theological writing, reflecting on the truth or insight value of the old sources, has not yet emerged from these circles, but it is not far from the surface.

We must not allow this sort of study to remain the elitist exercise of such small circles. If the American synagogue is going to survive, it will have to structure itself to be a *bet midrash* at least as much as a *bet tefillah*, and one open to the sort of study described here. There, of course, much of it will have to be carried on in English, with key terms and value-concepts preserved in Hebrew. It is essential that rabbis and other adult Jewish educators be trained in this approach to higher Jewish learning. Much of that training will be the result of their own participation in it, but there are particular pedagogical aspects of it that should be taught as well. (Parallel *battey midrash* have begun to emerge in Israel. The names *Elul*, *Binah*, *Oranim*, and others are well known, and have collectively begun to have a major impact.)

Paradoxically, there is something quite American about this approach. If Jewish learning is to speak to future generations in America, it will have to find an American voice. Such a voice is neither than of Volozhin nor that of Berlin. The former is to say that we cannot pretend that we are a direct copy of the eastern European or contemporary *ḥaredi yeshivah*, with only gender egalitarianism added to the mix. We need to create a *bet midrash* for a very different age, without being overwhelmed by nostalgia. As for the latter, such a *bet midrash* will have to recognize history, but be willing to go beyond it in response to a search for meaning that is couched in essentially religious terms. America, the country of such great material success and opportunity, is also, it turns out, a place of endless spiritual quest and search for meaning. Judaism will be important to American Jews because it has something to say about God and the meaning of one's own life, because it offers a way of being human in a deeply dehumanizing age.

There is also something of the postmodern spirit in this call for an old-new sort of Jewish learning. The melting away of the self-confidence that characterized modernist readings of ancient texts, when history and philology seemed adequate tools to unpack what the sources "really" meant, has opened a door of great opportunity for us. Unfortunately, there are too many alternative systems of interpretation trying to rush into that doorway, uniting to create a sometimes impossibly abstruse style of thought and expression, rendering postmodernism a curse rather than a blessing. But if we can resist these temptations, allowing that doorway to remain open, we clear a path to multiple readings in which the reader is a full participant, engaging deeply and mutually with both the text and its authors.

I have lived my entire intellectual life at the nexus between these two eras and sorts of reading. I am not willing to give up on either of them. I will tell you about them through a tale of two Levi Yizḥaks, figures with whom I happen to be engaged as I write these reflections. The first is the famous one, Levi Yizḥak of Berdychiv (1740–1809), rabbi of that Ukrainian town and a major figure in the spread of Hasidism in the late eighteenth century. I am currently writing a study of Levi Yizḥak's life and thought, to appear in a monograph on him and a series of articles. Here, my insights are most significantly historical. I am interested in Levi Yizḥak's role in the formation of the hasidic movement, his interactions with fellow members of the Mezritch circle within Hasidism, and his stance regarding particular issues that arose in his time. I engage in this through close reading of the sources, comparing and contrasting his writings with those of others in his day, and a carefully controlled, but significant, bit of personal insight as to what it means to be a leader in a new and struggling religious movement, how one influences disciples while letting them follow their own inner paths, and so on. All of this is focused on understanding Levi Yizḥak in the context of his own time and place.

The other Levi Yizḥak who accompanies me these days is much less well known. R. Levi Yizḥak Bender (1897–1989) was a leader of the Bratslav sect within Hasidism. Born in Poland, he became engaged early with the teachings and person of Rabbi Naḥman of Bratslav. In 1915, he made the daring move across the war-torn Russian border, choosing to be close to his master's grave in Uman, Ukraine. Living in the Soviet Union for the next thirty years, he suffered great persecution, but became a leader within the small surviving community of Bratslav disciples. He arrived in Israel, having survived in Uzbekistan and then in displaced persons' camps, in 1949, and was a key figure leading up to the great revival of Bratlsav Hasidism in Israel.

I am now reading Yiddish-language transcriptions of his oral teachings in Jerusalem.[21] He repeatedly tells his hearers that every word you read in the teachings of our master is addressed directly to you. The same is true, he makes it clear, of every word in the Torah itself. Were it not for the message it has to deliver to you alone, you would not have noticed it, but would have moved on to the next word or teaching. The true spiritual master, he believes (and for him Rabbi Naḥman is clearly the greatest of these), knows intimately the soul of each of his disciples, even those who are to be born long after his day. If the text did not have something to say to you, it would not be there before you. Only in opening your heart to that possibility will you truly know what it means to engage in Torah. I have no scholarly stake in reading his memoir; I only want to listen to his wise counsel.

Yes, there is a prophetic voice that calls out to me, saying: "How long will you be leaping back and forth between these two fences?" (1 Kings 18:21). But I hear also the cooler voice of Kohelet, who taught: "Hold fast to this [way of thinking or reading]—but don't let go of that one, either!" (Eccles. 15:18). Which of these two readings is to be primary, and which secondary? That, of course, my dear postmodern reader, you will have to decide for yourself.

Dear Brothers and Sisters

A LETTER TO ISRAELIS

I AM WRITING TO YOU as an American Jew, one who loves Israel and is gravely concerned about its future. That future is inseparable from the future of the Jewish people as a whole, a matter to which I have devoted most of my life. There are things that I need to say to you about our collective condition, things that I feel you need to hear, and can only hear from a Jew who loves you and yet has chosen to live outside the land.

Why should you listen to me? Since when do Israelis listen to American Jews, after all? I have three reasons to offer. The first is that I do not see myself as an outsider to you. I am part of "Israel" in the sense that I mean it here. The name *Israel* refers to the entire Jewish people, wherever they are. In premodern Hebrew, including the halakhic literature, "Israel" is a name given to every Jew. I therefore think of myself as "Israel," a Jew (or, in older English usage, an "Israelite") living a full and rich Jewish life, even though I am not an Israeli, which is a matter of citizenship, and indeed does not require one to be a Jew. (I state these obvious facts because there is confusion about them. That confusion was inevitable from the moment David Ben Gurion decided that the state would be called "Israel." It becomes increasingly hard to tell the visitor from Burma or Mongolia that "Jew" and "Israeli" are not the same thing, especially if you do not want to define Judaism solely as a "religion" in the Christian sense.

If you insist, as I do, that the term *Yisra'el* applies to every Jew, it becomes almost impossible.) A Christian Arab citizen of Israel is an Israeli, which I am not, but does not belong to *'am yisra'el*, the Jewish people, which I do. Throughout the Arab and Muslim world, "Jew" and "Israeli" seem to be almost fully interchangeable, often in an anti-Semitic context. But even people who should know better confuse these categories, sometimes intentionally. Israeli political figures often speak of *'am Yisra'el*, meaning the Israeli nation. But I too, not an Israeli citizen, belong to *'am yisra'el*. The politicians probably should say *ha-'am ha-yisre'eli*, meaning the Israeli people, but that subtlety is lost on them. In any case, I am not sure that they always mean to include non-Jewish Israelis as part of their "people." And that is part of the problem.

I am also a Jew who has a very strong personal connection to Israel—and here I mean the country. I visit there once or twice each year. I am now making a habit of spending several winter months there every year. I have many dear friends and colleagues there. I am very proud that several of my books have been published in Hebrew, and I have many readers there. Since I love the Hebrew language and I believe that the most long lasting of Jewish cultures is that which is written and discussed in Hebrew, I am especially happy about that. Although I choose to live outside the land, I feel I have a very small place within the new Judaism that is being created in the minds and hearts of many Israeli Jews.

The second reason is that Israel can no longer afford to refuse to learn from American Jewry and the Judaism we have created here. For many decades of both the Zionist movement and the early State of Israel, Israelis viewed American Jews with disdain. We were dismissed as Jewishly ignorant, naïve about anti-Semitism, and indifferent to the difficult issues facing Israel. American Jews were a source of money and (the great dream!) potential *'olim* (immigrants), but not of ideas or models of Jewish living. The attitude has changed slowly over the past several decades, but it remains deeply entrenched. But on two crucial issues, that of *where we stand in Jewish history* and the nature of *Jewish identity*, I believe that we represent the wave of the future, one that is catching up with you very quickly. It is therefore urgent that you listen to what we have to say and begin to pay attention to models and interpretations of our shared Jewish legacy that we have created here.

Finally, there is an important lesson that you have to learn from the history and experience of America itself. This is not about our specifically Jewish experience, but about what we have learned from being Americans in the early twenty-first century. The United States continues to suffer, sometimes nearly feeling torn apart, by the unlearned lessons of its history. The sooner you face these realities, I believe, the wiser you will be in handling them.

Where We Stand in Jewish History

We Jews, wherever we live, are heirs to one of the great spiritual legacies that humanity has created. Judaism is universally recognized as one of the seven or eight major religions in the world, and the people of Israel, all of us, are its bearers through history. That treasure is itself the result of the Jewish people's struggle to both maintain faithfully and develop creatively what they saw as its unique religious message. The greatness of the first portion of that historic legacy, the religious and especially the prophetic message of ancient Israel, has been universally recognized, largely through its influence on Christian, and hence Western, civilization and values. But Judaism as created by the sages of Israel, in post-biblical times, is also seen as one of the world's great spiritual legacies. At its best, it teaches a great universal message about the oneness of God, and hence the unity of all being as divine creation, for which we humans bear responsibility. It teaches that each human being is a unique and precious embodiment of the divine image, hence insisting on the dignity and preciousness of each human life. It insists on the primacy of moral law and on the subjugation of all human authority to the divine demand that we create societies based on compassion and justice. It also teaches that ancient traditions, even those thought to be divine, can be reinterpreted and reshaped by sages throughout the generations.

The paradox of Jewish existence is that this universal message is borne by a very particular people, one that has been struggling to preserve its own existence, often not an easy task, for the past two thousand years. The Jewish people has always understood that its continued existence is directed toward a purpose, that of teaching and bearing witness to our greatest values. It is to teach and witness these that the people Israel was created, whether by the faith of Abraham who followed God's call, or at the foot of Mount Sinai when we said: "We shall do and we shall listen." Jewish existence is therefore also a *conditional* existence, as the Torah makes clear many times. If we lose sight of this mission, it is not clear that we will, or even should, continue to exist. We might be wiped off the earth by those who hate us, as nearly happened in Europe. We might disappear and be assimilated among others, as could happen in America, where assimilation is so easy. Or we might morph into something new. For example, we could turn into an Israeli nation-state, one bearing no particular value other than that held by all nations, to continue to exist and thrive, and to protect its citizens. Any of these fates, I believe, would destroy the sacred mission of the historic Jewish people. As a believing Jew, I am committed to the continuity of *purposeful* Jewish existence. For this reason, I am completely opposed to what is called the "normalization" of Jewish existence by its transformation into Israeli nationhood. Any religious Jew, whether living here or there, whether Orthodox or Reform, has to oppose that transformation. I do not believe that the State of Israel is "the solution to the Jewish problem." The striving to be "like all the nations," as the people said to Samuel when calling for a king, is not the reason we have survived so long.

Having said that, I should make it clear that I also believe fully in the legitimacy of the State of Israel, as a nation of all its citizens. Of course, Israeli citizens, Jews and non-Jews alike, have much reason to take pride in their country. (I, too, as a fellow Jew, take great pride in the best that Israel has created.) I hope they will share still greater pride and dignity in the future, in a more just and equal society. But that is completely separate from the purpose or meaning of Jewish existence, which has a meaning that transcends politics, for Jews both inside and outside the state.

In order to bear our message for humanity, however, we Jews need to survive, and to live with a sense of dignity and security. That was not the case for a very long period of our history, when we lived as an oppressed minority among peoples who denied the continuing validity of our teachings and even cast doubt upon our full humanity. Jews were portrayed as demons or wicked subhumans throughout the Middle Ages, sometimes even complete with horns and tails. Over the course of 150 years, ranging from 1780 to 1933, we increasingly thought—and dared to hope—that we had moved beyond that era, into a time when our right to exist would be taken for granted and we would have the freedom to express our truth, even to share it with others. The emergence of Jewry from the ghetto, that imposed from both without and within, began in the closing decades of the eighteenth century, continuing for the next century and a half. Jews became equal citizens in emerging new nation-states, ideally free both to participate fully in the political and economic lives of those societies, and to celebrate our own traditions, both cultural and religious, as we chose.

We Jews in North America still live in an extension of that period; we are essentially *post-1780* Jews. We see ourselves as living in the modern—or now postmodern—world, and have been involved for nearly two centuries in creating a Judaism fitting to that era. That means, above all, an era of freedom, one in which we can choose our degree and style of Jewish self-expression, without compulsion either from without or within. That freedom and the open society it fosters also means that the door to total assimilation, and hence Jewish disappearance, stands wide open. We are well aware of that.

Most of us American Jews are Ashkenazim, our ancestors having arrived from eastern Europe between 1881 and 1924. A minority among us—but a culturally important minority—are Jews from German lands, including some who came as early as 1848, as well as others who fled to these shores during the Nazi era. It was these earlier German Jews who established the patterns of Jewish living in America, including the primacy of the (mostly unattended) synagogue as our key institution, the strong sense of mutual responsibility among Jews, and the generous concern of Jewry for the civil betterment of American society, including the spreading of those values mentioned above. The second-generation children of eastern European immigrants, anxious to assimilate to America in many ways, largely stepped into the patterns of Jewish living that had already been created here.

For a while, there were attempts to create forms of secular Jewish identity in America, not completely unlike the secular identity created in *erets yisra'el* in the early twentieth century. A strong sense of ethnic and cultural identity, but a very minimal level of religious observance, characterized many of the first generation of eastern European Jewish descendants to be born here. Yiddish was the main linguistic bearer of that secular culture, but knowledge of it did not survive into the third generation, and it could not bear the obliteration of its eastern European homeland. Those among the children and grandchildren of mostly secular Jews who did not assimilate and disappear completely from the Jewish community (and many did) have rediscovered more of Jewish religious life to varying degrees, as a way of Jewish self-expression. This has come about partly because we live in the most religious of all advanced countries. To be American is largely to be religious, or "spiritual," or "seeking," in one way or another. The more American that Jews became, paradoxically, the more some sort of religious self-identification became part of their lives.

But there was another reason why secular Jewish identity did not thrive well here. The United States, as you have surely noticed, is a country defined by its racial history. Race is a significant marker of difference for Americans. So too is religion, which is so highly respected here. But Americans of the mainstream simply do not get why ethnic difference and identity should be so important to people who are, after all, fully welcomed into the privilege of being "white." It is somehow expected here that by the third generation, Italian Americans will eat bagels and Jews will eat pizza, or they will all go together to a Tex-Mex restaurant. Other languages are meant to be forgotten in this very monolingual culture. The Hispanics are now challenging that, but they are a very large (and partly racially distinctive) group. For Jews, always anxious to see anti-Semitism fade away, acceptance into the "white club" came rather late. But once it did, they were elated, and willing, to some extent, to pay the price. Most American Jews, now fifth or sixth generation since immigration, don't even know enough Yiddish to get the punch lines of Jewish jokes, certainly don't know any Hebrew, and feel themselves quite fully American. Their markers of Jewishness, if they exist at all, are mostly religious forms: Pesaḥ seders, Ḥanukkah candles, a brief appearance at synagogue on Yom Kippur, and celebration of life-cycle events.

But most Jews in this country, even half- or quarter-Jews, still live within a social circle that includes other Jews as well. Jews continue to seek each other out as friends, even though their circles are somewhat mixed. Many of these Jews, though far from immigrant memories and having little connection to Israel, have a great curiosity about Judaism and a thirst for Jewish knowledge of all sorts. This is true even among the very many who do not join synagogues. They are still post-1780, post-Enlightenment Jews. By this I mean that their first question is still "What is the meaning of Jewish existence in the modern (or postmodern) world?" How can Judaism be interpreted so as to fit in with modernity? What does the wisdom of our tradition have to teach us, living in the context of such very different times? Does it have anything interesting to say about the great questions facing us as citizens of the United States and of the world today?

That makes us very different from our brothers and sisters in Israel. Israel is not a post-1780 Jewish society, but a post-1933 one. It is built on a premise that says, *"They're trying to kill us! All of us!"* and asks: *"How are we going to survive?"* This left no room for the post-1780 question "How is Judaism meaningful today?" In fact, the verdict of the post-1933 analysis, at its sharpest, is that 1780 was an illusion. "Look! It was Germany—or Prussia—where the Jews were first emancipated. And look what happened to them there!" "Trust no one," the more extreme version of this ethos, that of Menaḥem Begin and Bibi Netanyahu, says, "because under their skin they are all anti-Semites." This analysis was sold by rightist Ashkenazim to Jews of Near Eastern origins, who had long felt themselves degraded by the Muslim majorities amid whom they lived, and to post-Soviet immigrants, who had much experience with real anti-Semitism. As a result, it has become the dominant perspective within Israel.

Of course, this worldview does not exist without good reason. The Holocaust killed more than half the Jews living on the Eurasian landmass and made the others into a tribe of survivors. Anti-Semitism, as we continue to see, still exists as a strong force, even in places where there remain almost no living Jews. Most of the survivors deeply committed to Jewish life, along with many others, went and helped to build the State of Israel, a venture dedicated first and foremost to the survival of the Jewish people. Their primary question was: "How can the Jewish people survive, rebuild, and live securely?" From the early years, all Jewish Israelis were engaged in a great struggle for survival, against real Arab enemies and against severe economic conditions. There was no room in the psyche for questions of ultimate meaning. The "Why?" of Jewish existence was put on the shelf for a future time. It was seen as best not to raise such questions, with all the complexities they might call forth. The various differing "tribes" within Israel might have very different answers to these existential questions, and the new state could not allow such division to come to the fore. Israelis in the early years of the state needed most to believe in the future, in the possibility that the new state could survive and thrive, and that its highly diverse Jewish population could unite around the ideal of that survival, embodied, for both the Labor and National Religious parties, as a semi-deification of the state. The deeper questions could wait.

That was sufficient "meaning" for the first two or three generations of Israel's existence. The ingathering of exiles and the forging of a single nation became its greatest pride and purpose. Despite all its problems, this achievement has been a great success, one of the most marvelous historical happenings of our era. But in the rush of celebrating that success, we (yes, all of us Jews) did not fully realize how deeply our values would be put to the test as we employed them to bring forth this new social and political reality. We failed to notice that the return to Zion and the creation of a Jewish state in the aftermath of the Holocaust was also taking place at the very moment of the breakup of the colonial era in world history. This co-incidence (I use the term without judging whether it is of divine or accidental origin) surely calls upon us to think about the meaning of those events in both of those contexts, the Jewish and the world-historical, simultaneously. From a Jewish point of view, we see the return to Zion as the fulfillment of ancient prophecies. It is hard to deny this, reading the prophets and seeing both the dispersed people gather and the desert bloom. Even for a Jew like me, who wants to find nothing messianic in Zionism, witnessing the rebuilding of Israel makes the echoes of Isaiah's prophecies resound in my ears. The sense of historical "rightness" of Jews returning to our ancient homeland, one of which we had always dreamed, is very strong. But the other narrative, that which sees a Western people coming to what they proclaimed "a land without a people for a people without a land," when it in fact did have a native population, also cannot be ignored. A colonial society is one in which a self-defined "superior" population imposes itself upon, and appropriates the resources, including the land, of, a "native" human group, whom it then deprives of freedom. This is not only the perception from a Palestinian point of view, but the way much of the world, itself only recently liberated from colonialism, inevitably views the Zionist enterprise. We cannot ignore it, nor can we dismiss it as simply the failure of our own public relations campaign, as we so often do. Our Jewish values and our own memory of historical oppression cannot permit us to be or to create a colonial society. This is the great pain of Israel, the historic moral flaw in its creation, without which it would not exist as it does today. The New Historians in Israel are forcing us to examine these questions in more open and honest ways.

Any discussion of this subject has to be marked by compassion for all the sufferers and by awareness of the historical context. A third of our people were slaughtered in a series of horrific events that came to define the term *genocide* for the entire human community. Those European Jews who were left after 1945 wanted more than anything else to leave that bloodstained continent and to go to the Land of Israel, to build a state or community of their own, free from gentile domination. Who could oppose such a morally justified will? As Elie Wiesel used to say, Europe was glad to get rid of the survivors, so as not to have to look them in the eye and be reminded of its own guilt. We were not like British, French, or Belgian colonialists who were out to rob the colony of its resources for the benefit of the mother country. We had no other country! That was the whole point. We wanted to make a mother country (*moledet*) for ourselves right there in Israel, our own ancient home, so long the object of our prayers and dreams. As any reader of the Jewish prayer book knows well, we had never given up on our claim to the land and the dream of restoration to it. Zionism was successful as a political movement among the Jewish masses precisely because it tapped into those ancient and long-sustained messianic dreams.

So here we are, placed by history (or might it be divine providence?) in an untenable situation. The colonial era is collapsing, and we come to form a state, to re-create Jewish sovereignty after two thousand years. We know we are not colonialists, but much of the world does not. Were we put in this situation for some reason? Are our deepest values being tested? How are we doing in that test?

"But let us be reasonable," you might say. How could anyone expect the Jewish refugees, first from the pogroms of eastern Europe and then from Hitler, soon to be joined by a mass flight of Jews from Arab lands, to stop and consider that their new homeland was being built at some-one else's expense? The myth that the Holy Land was "a land without a people," waiting to receive these "people without a land" fitted the needs of the moment too well. While according the Arab fifth of its popula-tion nominal equal rights, Israeli society has mostly tried to ignore their presence, creating a Jewish state in which the welfare and security of its burgeoning Jewish population was the primary concern. The moral di-mensions of Jewish/Arab relations were put off for another day. But so too were the bigger philosophical and religious questions of Jewish existence and its relation to the emerging new identity of "Israeli."

This situation became significantly more critical following the victo-ries of 1967, including both the conquest of old Jerusalem and the occu-pation of the West Bank and Gaza. This new map forced a new perception onto the Israeli mindset, one quite different from that of those who had first anticipated and then created the Jewish state. Suddenly there were new territories open before the Israeli population, one that had felt sig-nificantly hemmed into a narrow space, especially around the country's midsection. But there was also a new, large, and deeply unhappy Arab ci-vilian population that was inherited along with these territories, a people that had been raised on resentment against Israel for usurping many of its former homes. What was Israel to do about both of these, land and people?

Although the great military victory of the Six-Day War was won mostly by second-generation secular Israeli fighters, including many *kibbutz*-based children of 1948's Palmachniks, it was celebrated and ulti-mately overtaken by two groups who had previously been largely margin-alized in Israeli society. First were the *yeshiva* students of the national reli-gious movement, originally called Mizrachi. These were centered around the disciples of Rabbi Zvi Yehudah Kook, son and heir of the famous first chief rabbi Avraham Yiẓḥak Kook, whose mystical ideology of Jewish rebirth involved a strong sense of the Land's unique holiness and its ability to transform the Jewish soul. Much of this was adapted from the theology of twelfth-century poet-philosopher Yehudah Halevi, as filtered through the later mystical tradition. It saw an ontological difference between the Holy Land and all other earthly places, a distinction perceptible only to the unique Jewish soul. The younger Rav Kook and his followers saw the 1967 victory as a true miracle, one that called upon them to act by settling and thus sanctifying the entirety of the country, as defined by biblical borders. In short: the land calls to us; never mind the people living there.

The other group that supported them in this view, large enough to bring about a new electoral majority, was the previously marginalized Sephardic/Oriental Jewish population originating in the Near East and North Africa. For them, immigration to the Land of Israel had always held great religious meaning. The 'Emeq Jezreel and Tel Aviv visions of what Israel meant (see the "Tish'ah be-Av" essay above) had been purely those of European Jews, from which they had felt excluded. Now the old sense of sacred places and the urge toward pilgrimage, ever a key factor in Oriental Jewish life, welled up within them. Suddenly there were large pilgrimages being organized to the Wall and to the tomb of the patriarchs in Hebron, and even to such more dubious sites as the tombs of Joseph, Samuel, and others. Visits to the alleged burial places of Rabbi Simeon ben Yoḥai in Meron, Maimonides in Tiberias, Rabbi Isaac Luria in Safed, and many more figures from the rabbinic and kabbalistic past came to take a large place in Israeli religion.

Because this new movement was led by both Sephardic and hasidic Jews, it took on all the characteristics of folk religion. The national/religious *yeshiva* types, though perhaps not really believing in the authenticity of some of these tombs and the blessing associated with visiting them, acquiesced readily to this folk religion in order to build a coalition of support for their own project of broader settlement in the newly acquired territories. The secular Ashkenazic Jewry that had created the Jewish state came to feel itself an embattled minority, increasingly so following the right-wing electoral revolution of 1977.

That situation, in increasingly aggravated form, remains Israel's political and demographic situation today. The large Russian immigrant population, badly wounded by Communism, was quickly pulled toward the right, despite its secularity. This condemned any attempt at a left-leaning government to near impossibility. The right, with strong national/religious participation, took great advantage of its status, especially in the realm of education, where "national" often took the lead, religion being used to buttress strongly nationalistic views.

But a day of great *ḥeshbon nefesh*, self-examination, is about to come for Israeli society. The ultimate questions can no longer be left aside. There is a new generation of Israelis who will insist that the questions long neglected be placed on the table. This has come about for a number of diverse reasons. First and foremost is the sacrifice required for this Jewish survival in the context of an Israeli nation. Will new generations continue to offer the lives of their sons for an ideal no greater than that of survival itself? Not a few have begun to seek an alternative, either of emigration or of at least holding a second passport "just in case." That "just in case" refers partly to the dangers of Arab attack, but partly also to an Israeli society that turns too ugly and racist. "Will I want to raise my children there?" is a question heard among not a few younger secular Israelis. How large will the communities of former Tel Avivim and *kibbutzniks* now living in Berlin, Miami, or Los Angeles need to get before Israel takes notice? Yes, the economic success of "High-Tech Nation" will bring some of them back. But will it make them ready to send their children to serve and risk their lives? They or their children will ask, "For what is it, exactly, that we are offering our lives?" Is it for survival—that post-1933 narrative that one side insists so vehemently is the only truth—or is it for the sake of holding onto the post-1967 territories and the settlements? Is that enough reason to sacrifice so many lives, if there might be another alternative?

But there is also a moral price being paid along with the terrible price in lives and insecurity. A large part of the Jewish population in Israel—mostly but not exclusively in "secular" circles—has come to question the exclusive truth-claim of the Zionist narrative. The sense that the Palestinian population is the victim of our great success becomes harder to deny, both when we see the large number of civilian deaths on both sides in clashes between Jews and Arabs and when we look at the ever-increasing gaps between us and the Palestinians in economy and resources, including use of the land itself. Then these two questions begin to merge: Am I willing to sacrifice the lives of my children for a settlement project that I know in my heart to be wrong?

There is a growing sense that if Jewish survival is going to cost so great a price, it must have some more profound meaning. This is part of the reason for the rediscovery of what is called "the Jewish bookcase" among secular Israelis, looking back toward classic sources once ignored in order to seek greater meaning. This includes a greater interest these days in the enterprise of Jewish theology, especially in the writings of such non-Israeli Jewish thinkers as Levinas, Heschel, and Soloveitchik, who were at one time ignored in Israel. My own readers, too, are a small part of this. In national/religious circles, the profound thinking of Rabbi Avraham Yiẓḥak Kook dominated the ideology for more than half a century. But now, partly because they see that Rav Kook's son used that teaching to pull toward what may be a dead end in Israel's future, there is much search for alternatives, including both the revival of Bratslav[1] and the interesting postmodern writing of Ha-Rav Shagar. These are all people dealing with the ultimate meaning of Jewish existence, or presenting Jewish approaches to the meaning of human existence itself. These are the post-1780 questions, so long postponed in Israel.

This is what I mean by the historical reason for paying attention to American Jews. We are a strong and proud Jewish community that was not essentially transformed by the events of 1933–45. Over our long period in America, we have developed a body of thought, diverse ways of teaching, passing on, and practicing Judaism, and an array of communal institutions that are made to suit the needs and respond to the questions of Jews living in the modern world. Pay attention. Of course, not all can or should be copied or directly imported. Indeed, there is much lacking in the American model, especially for an Israeli population that begins with Hebrew, and therefore has much greater access to the sources than their American cousins will ever have. Still, there are things to learn. I have seen quite a few Israelis who have discovered Judaism in the course of visiting or living in America. Once the wall between "secular" and "religious" was taken down, much interesting discovery could happen. That wall of rigidly needing to choose one such identity label or the other needs to come down in Israel as well.

There is another side as well to the new urgency of dealing with the once-delayed questions. Both travel and the internet have made our world much smaller. Israelis travel everywhere, especially to the Far East. There a whole generation of post-army Israeli youth have been exposed in India, Nepal, and Thailand, especially, to a spiritual culture entirely different from the one their parents or grandparents rejected. Without the built-in defenses they had against "being religious," many have discovered the life-enhancing qualities of meditation, yoga, and spiritual teaching derived from one Eastern school or another. On returning to Israel, some have simply opened Hebrew-speaking yoga or meditation centers based on Eastern tradition. Others have quickly translated the spiritual hunger that was opened up in them into the language of a Judaism from prior generations, joining Breslov, Chabad, or some other form of premodern Judaism. But not a few are looking for something within our own tradition that will not demand of them that they reject either modernity or universalist consciousness and will still give them a spiritual Judaism of depth and integrity.

A new Israeli Judaism is beginning to emerge. It is far from strictly Orthodox, and it combines elements of ethnic memory, national pride, and spiritual search. It is very important that this new emerging Judaism be built on the best of Jewish values, listed above, and not carry forth the exclusivism ("God has chosen us alone") and the xenophobia ("All non-Jews are secret anti-Semites") that represent not freedom, but the worst of *galut* Jews' defense mechanisms and nightmares. This Israeli Judaism will not be the same as American liberal Judaism. It will contain a large amount of Sephardic/Oriental legacy, not just that of the eastern European *shtetl*. Love for the Land of Israel and the Hebrew language will have a large place in it. But it too, in an Israeli context, will have to face the post-1780 question: How is Judaism meaningful for today? What are the essential truths that we need to preserve and pass on to future generations of Jews? How do we express these ancient truths in language that can speak to the current generation? Here Israeli Jews can learn much from the diaspora Jewish thinkers who have been working on this question for a very long time.

Jewish Identity

The nature of Jewish identity itself was once viewed quite differently from the North American and Israeli perspectives. Precisely because America is such a melting pot of religious, ethnic, and racial identities, each person claims the right to choose the elements of identity that are important to him or her. Identity is seen primarily as individual rather than collective. Yes, we are all Americans, loyal to our government and Constitution. But for most of us that sort of generic "Americanness" does not form the basis of our chosen identities. It is not surprising in America to hear somebody named Krakovsky say: "I am only one-quarter Irish by ancestry, but I identify as Irish American." Most members of some American Indian tribes have only a quarter or less of Indian ancestry. In recent years, other sorts of identity markers have supplanted the ethnic and religious. So a Ms. Cohen might easily say: "I identify as a lesbian, a Yankees fan, and a lover of country music. The origin of my family name means nothing to me." There is an ever-growing sense in American society that each person can, and even should, choose the markers of his or her own identity, and that these may legitimately change more than once over the course of a person's life. Ancestry is one among many possible factors in such chosen identities, and one is free to leave it behind—unless, of course, it is racially visible. It seems taken for granted in America that race and gender (including orientation) are inevitable identity markers; the rest is up for grabs.

This means that Jewish identity is increasingly seen as a matter of choice. Many Jews, including partial Jews (whether on the maternal side or not) take great pride in their Jewishness, wanting also to pass that identity on to their children. They struggle with finding a means to do that, especially if the synagogue does not appeal to them. Their children will go through the same process as they mature. Some will want that Jewish identity; others will leave it behind. That is the nature of our open society. Therefore, those of us who care about the future of both Judaism and the Jewish people are charged with the tremendous task of answering the question: "Why remain Jewish?" This was a question you never heard in my generation. Of course you were Jewish; your grandparents spoke with Yiddish accents! That was quite enough. Like it or not, that's what you were. You knew that, and so did the anti-Semite around the corner. But that is no longer the case. This is an age in which you choose identities, and Jews need a reason for holding onto this one. Indeed, the recent upturn in anti-Semitism will probably cause some to flee their Jewish roots. Why burden my children with a heritage that means nothing to me? We therefore constantly seek to make the Jewish heritage interesting and stimulating, whether in spiritual, intellectual, or emotional ways.

In Israel (as in the former Soviet Union, by the way), Jewish identity was taken as a collective given. It was marked on your identity card and was not something you could cast away. But this too is changing, partly because of the greater role demanded by the rabbinate in matters of personal status, thus alienating a great many Israelis from the term *yehudi* when applied to them. Many secular Israelis now question this unchosen identity marker that either means nothing or has negative associations for them. Recently there have been some attempts—so far unsuccessful—by secular Israelis to insist that their nationality be listed as "Israeli" rather than "Jewish." Israel is burdened by its inability—again, due to the power of the rabbinate—to assert the Jewishness of several hundred thousand immigrants from the former Soviet Union. Most are either partly Jewish or married to Jews, raising Jewish-Israeli families. Others just used Israel as a way of escape—but they too are now living as Israelis. Can they also be Jews?

But this question affects not only these immigrants. As more Israelis travel abroad and more Europeans visit Israel, mixed marriage will be a growing prospect for many Israelis. Will the children of those marriages be raised in Israel and identified as Jews? There will need to be some good reason to convince the non-Jewish spouse to agree, both to a difficult conversion process, if they choose that, and to the idea that those children will be subject to dangerous army service. What resources will the Israeli spouse have to draw on to help in that conversation? Does she or he know why their kids should be identified as Jews, other than to please the grandparents? For these reasons, too, it becomes urgent to deal with the greater questions of Jewish identity and the ultimate values of Jewish existence. Is there greater meaning, besides loyalty to the past, to holding onto defining oneself as a Jew?

As a religious Jew, I can respond to this only in religious language. While I do not identify with the *dati* community in Israel, or with Orthodoxy in America, I understand that Jewish identity is meaningful because of its religious roots. All my work is about translating the language of tradition into a new spiritual self-understanding that Jews, both Israeli and diaspora, might find plausible and attractive today.

I begin with a bit of traditional language that is bedrock for me: "I will dwell amid the Children of Israel and become their God. Then they will know that I am Y-H-W-H their God who brought them forth from the Land of Egypt *to dwell within them*. I am Y-H-W-H their God" (Ex. 29:45–46). Y-H-W-H seeks Israel out as a dwelling place in this world. We Israelites are a living parallel to the *mishkan*, a wandering sanctuary for the divine presence. This is the purpose of the whole enterprise, the reason God brought us forth from Egypt. We are liberated from human bondage in order to become an earthly dwelling for Y-H-W-H, the ever-living force that redeemed us.

But what does this mean to a person of my religious mindset? I do not believe literally in a God who chooses Israel as His own from among all peoples. Does a phrase like "Y-H-W-H seeks Israel" retain any meaning?

But I do believe that there exists something like a divine call or outreach toward each human being. The One, present within each human soul, as within every creature, calls upon us to be aware, to become an embodiment of holiness in the world, a *mishkan* for the *shekhinah*. This is true of every person. The human quest for meaning is universal; Judaism is one of many languages in which it may be undertaken.

But we *as a nation*, from our beginning, committed ourselves to that task. We are called *Yisra'el*, which means that we have collectively taken on the identity of our ancestor who wrestled with God, who struggled to understand. In declaring ourselves a *goy kadosh*, a holy nation, we insisted that our *collective* identity, the purpose for which we continue to exist in each generation is that of spiritual awareness and moral living. We would make no distinction between our national identity and our spiritual values. We would never prioritize the national over the spiritual and moral truths we are here to witness. The purpose of our ongoing existence as Israel would be the transmission of those values.

A time is coming when a new generation of Israeli Jews will ask what those values are. If Jewish identity is to remain important to them, in an age when the freedom of identity choice reaches Israel as well, much collective soul-searching will be needed. We think we have something to say about those questions, and we hope you will be able to join with us in a conversation about them, reformulating them for your own context.

A Nation's Sins Are Not Forgotten

Like the Jewish people, the United States sees itself as a society created on the basis of ideals and teaching. The principles of freedom and democracy are seen by many, both conservatives and liberals, as the meaning of American existence. The Constitution is revered, treated like a holy text, given not by God, but by the wisdom of our ancestors. But American society was brought forth on the backs of two great sins: the taking of the land from its original inhabitants, who were banished, degraded, and massively killed, and the importation of African slaves, who contributed greatly to the American economy (especially, but not only, in the South), without reward.

Two hundred and fifty years later, American society is still riven by those sins. Racial injustice, carried on first through law, then through social discrimination, has never left us. Mistreatment of blacks by police and other authorities makes for daily headlines in the American press. So too do the violence, poverty, and social disarray within the African American community, its people never fully recovered from the terrible degradation brought upon them. Native Americans, living both in remote reservations and in cities, suffer terrible poverty and disease, including the plague of hereditary alcoholism, a gift from the white man. We hear less about their plight mainly because more of them were slaughtered, not because their fate is any more just.

America pays a price for these sins every day of its existence. The degradation of nonwhites in America causes endless suffering, first and foremost for its victims, many of whom have never recovered from its trauma. But the rest of American society also pays a seemingly never-ending price. Just read the headlines any day, and you will see it staring back at you. But the greatest damage to America lies in the moral sphere. How can we claim to represent the values we do while still wearing these two garlands of shame around our neck? Every dictator and enemy of democracy, from Hitler to Stalin, from Putin to Xi, knows this and makes use of it. How can we criticize the Chinese for their treatment of the Tibetans and the Uighurs, without having the fate of Native and African Americans thrown in our face? How can we stand up against racism and ethnic violence around the world—as we feel we should—with these original sins still pursuing us?

I say this to you for what should seem like obvious reasons. The Palestinian people are not going anywhere. Neither is the memory of their victimhood. Yes, *of course* a vast propaganda machine has been used to increase that sense of victimization. Yes, their leaders have been cynical and corrupt. Yes, the Arab states could have done more to absorb them, and chose not to do so. All of that is true. But the victimhood is real nonetheless. The crushing poverty in Gaza is real; so too are the daily degradations suffered by the Arab population in the West Bank, in sharp contrast to the ever-growing settlements of Israelis that were built to surround them and to create "facts on the ground" to avoid any possibility of their independence.

We do not know what resolution the future holds. Will there eventually be a Palestinian state, perhaps forced by international pressure? Will annexation lead to one state, followed by a long struggle for equal rights, in which the world's sympathy (including that of a great many diaspora Jews) will be with those struggling for equality? Neither option looks terribly promising right now. But whatever happens, the conduct of Israel and Jewish Israelis toward their neighbors will not be forgotten. If not handled well, it will pursue this country, *and the image of the Jewish people*, for hundreds of years. That is a lesson to be learned from the history of America.

The warning here is that the sooner we improve this situation, the better off we will all be in the long run. Israeli governments have been much too shortsighted, holding off inevitable decisions to gain another year or another few hundred dunams of land. They ignore the long-term effects of their efforts to hold onto as much as they can. Since Israel is the more powerful party on the ground, it gets to hold onto nearly everything. But at what cost? We have to learn to treat this relationship less like hagglers in the market, holding on for every penny and bit of advantage, and instead conduct ourselves like healers in a post-trauma hospital unit, where generosity and caring for the other's plight is the order of the day.

Over 150 years after the end of slavery, black leaders in America are still demanding reparations. They surely deserve this, although working it out will be extremely complex and painful for all. How much easier it would have been to have done this earlier, perhaps avoiding all those years of seething bitterness, perhaps allowing for a much more positive buildup of family and social life within the African American community itself. The long delay and resistance to this reflects a deep moral blindness in American society, one that (as we see more clearly these days) continues to divide the entire nation.

Do you get what I'm saying? Israel, and with it much of the Jewish people, is stricken with that same moral blindness. We have *won* the war with the Palestinians. We have won it over and over again! It is time to declare victory, and to do what a noble victor does: to act generously, to open our hearts to the wounds and needs of the other, with whom we are destined to live side by side.

The moral truth of what I have said here is so obvious that it needs no further justification. Nevertheless, let me buttress it from the viewpoint of Jewish self-interest as well. The Jewish people emerged from the Holocaust with a tremendous amount of moral credit in the eyes of the world. We had been the hapless victims of a regime that defined evil for the world. Indeed, much of the world was ashamed to look at us. That moral credit did tremendous things. It got the United Nations to declare support for a Jewish state. It got the churches, including the proud Catholic Church, to completely change their view on Judaism, as well as on other religions. It made anti-Semitism disgraceful throughout the Western world, including the United States. It was epitomized by the awarding of the Nobel Peace Prize to Elie Wiesel.

Israel, in its treatment of the Palestinians, has used up much of that moral capital. The Jewish people, and Jewish influence on international affairs, are again treated with suspicion. Some of this is old anti-Semitism, but some of it is justified. Israel has acted cynically, as though Palestinian suffering were merely a public relations issue. The world is smarter than that. Some of what is called "anti-Semitism on the left" is indeed that, just dressed up in new clothing. But not all criticism of Israel's policies should be dismissed as that, or just combated with public relations campaigns. To do so would be a grave mistake.

The Jewish people needs that moral capital restored. Some of that happens on small-scale levels, when Israelis or Jews help others in need around the world, in the face of disaster. IsraAID, American Jewish World Service, and many others are doing great work; I am a total fan of such efforts. But the moral capital of the Jewish people will not return to us until we are able to look the Palestinians in the eye, as a people as well as individuals, and to be seen as acting toward them with decency and humanity, treating them as fellow *tselem Elohim*, images of God. *'Am Yisra'el*, the Jewish people around the world, have the resources to help make this happen, and would be happy to join in the effort. But that effort needs to begin with Israelis. You will first require new leadership and new vision to do that. We are waiting for such leadership and vision to arise.

To return to the question with which I began: Why should you listen to us? Since when have Israelis ever listened to diaspora Jews? The simple reason is that *ahavat yisra'el* is still alive within us. We love you, despite all that has come between us. We urge you, with all our hearts, to realize that your truest friends are not the evangelical Christians, for whom you are pawns in a narrative that we Jews do not share. Nor are they the Trumps of the world, who tolerate and coddle racists who are on the edge of anti-Semitism, and will be drawn into it easily. The ones who really love you are these troubling and sometimes annoying cousins from across the sea. We are still *family*. Listen to us.

American Jews after Pittsburgh . . .
and Monsey . . . and . . .

WHERE DO WE STAND?

S OMETIMES THERE IS NOT much that all of us Jews seem to have in common. We are of the right and left, loving Bibi and despising Bibi, Orthodox and secular, committed to two-state and one-state solutions, and all the rest. So let me try this on for size. We are all (with the exception of the tiny Indian Jewish community) descended from people who lived for seventeen hundred years as despised minorities in Christian and Islamic countries, both traditions built around the belief that ours was outmoded, inferior, and sometimes even demonic. We learned to live with our heads down, always ready for a blow to fall, often responding with understandable hostility toward our oppressors.

We Jews in North America, as well as in postwar western Europe, dared to think that was over. We lived in essentially secularized societies, where neither ethnic origins nor religious faith was supposed to cause you pain. We learned to hold our heads high, proud of our many achievements. We in the United States knew this country had a terrible and unresolved racial problem, but we (mostly white-looking) Jews were told, from the 1970s on, that we were white after all, something previously denied by many. We were welcomed to live in previously restricted suburbs, break through Ivy League quotas, work in previously excluded "white-shoe" professions, and even to marry into *Mayflower* families. "It's over," we said to ourselves. "Serious anti-Semitism in America is a thing of the past."

Yes, we knew there were a few kooks still out there. Old stereotypes die slowly in the backwoods, we told ourselves, but we didn't take them seriously. But then came the deadly combination of Trump, Bannon, and the anonymity of social media posts—and *boom!*—here we are after Pittsburgh. A nice, safe Jewish neighborhood like Squirrel Hill. And suddenly all of us know that it could have happened in Flatbush, Scarsdale, West Orange, Brookline, Lower Merion, West Rogers Park, West LA, or any of a dozen other "safe" places for Jews. And any of us, or the people we love, could have been in the synagogue that day.

At once, an ancestral voice, long repressed, pipes up within me. "How can you trust them?" it says. "Behind every *goy* lies an *anti-semit*," said with just that Yiddish inflection. "How do you know what they're really thinking?" After all, we've had Menaḥem Begin—and lots of his followers—whispering this in our ear for a long time, hoping it might stir us toward *'aliyah*. We desperately don't want to believe it. "Some of our best friends," after all—and, by now, not a few of our spouses and in-laws—are gentiles, people evincing not a shred of anti-Semitism. How do we help them understand this deep Jewish instinctual fear—trained by all those generations of bitter experience—that has been awakened within us?

In terms of immigration history, I am a rather typical American Jew. My mother's parents arrived in 1903/4; my father's in 1906. Both my parents were born here, shortly after my grandparents arrived. But my mother's father, a very important figure in my life, had grown up an orphan. His father was killed when he was three months old, shot by a drunken peasant, I was told, back in his town in Latvia, where lots of Jews were killed for no particular reason. He came from a world where there were two kinds of people, *yidn* and *goyim*. The hatred was mutual, but the Jews were always the victims. The only other thing I know about that town is that it is located near a cliff overlooking a river. In 1941, the year I was born, the Nazis and their local helpers lined up all the Jews and shot them into the river, to avoid the effort of burial. This included Grandpa's stepfamily. I was there on the day after he was told.

For the not small percentage of Jews who are at least in part descended from 1930s refugees, Holocaust survivors, or former Soviet Jewish communities, the memory is even clearer. "You foolish *Amerikaner*," they say to us descendants of the 1900s immigrants. "How could you not have known?" For them, the event in Pittsburgh recalls the face on that old small-town Czech Jewish woman shopkeeper during the Holocaust in *The Shop on Main Street*, in the moment when she realizes what's happening and calls out the half-forgotten word: "Pogrom?"

Where do we go from here? It is clear to us that we do not want that terrified, xenophobic utterance from the back corner of our brains to dominate our lives or our view of the world. We have come too far for that. These were not pogroms, after all; each was the act of one man, his mind addled by filth spewed by others, but still just a single individual. In contrast to them, we have seen, and need to acknowledge, the many thousands of genuinely caring friends and neighbors, including political and religious leaders, Christian and Muslim, who came out in what feels like genuine support and empathy.

These events force us to think hard about who we are within American society, and what sort of future we are seeking here. Let me say something very obvious, but hardly mentioned out loud anymore: we Jews are a minority group. Under 2 percent of the American population, seeking to maintain a distinct identity, devoting tremendous energy and resources to warding off total assimilation, we hope to survive here in the long run as a distinctive subgroup. Despite our mostly white skin and our mostly high earnings and achievements, we are, like any minority, *different*, subject to being seen and treated as alien to mainstream America, misunderstood and stereotyped—yes, and occasionally even killed. Understanding that anti-Semitism or anti-Judaism is a disease that has infected Christianity (and even "post-Christian" circles in the West) for many centuries and cannot disappear overnight, we also have a vital need to engage in positive dialogue with members of the majority Christian religious culture here, as well as other minorities, including both racial and religious groups, especially Muslims.

The word *minorities* in current American political discourse is a shortening (dating perhaps from the 1980s) of the phrase "underrepresented" or "underprivileged" minorities. We were not that, and therefore we came to be excluded from the "minority" status. Of course, in ever race-conscious America, *minority* also seems to be applied only to those who look different, especially because of color of skin. But Muslims are a minority in this country—regardless of skin color—Sikhs are a minority, with or without turbans, and Jews are a minority, with or without *kippot* (skullcaps) or dangling *tsitsit* (fringes). We, of course, know and feel that status. For another film statement, think of that Woody Allen moment in *Annie Hall*, when he sits down to dinner with the girlfriend's family in Iowa. That's a scene most Jews remember well.

A major factor that explains the surprising success of sometimes hateful populist politics in the United States as well as Europe is the fear of white-skinned Christians of European descent, highly privileged until now, that they are about to become a minority. Hence the desperate fear of immigrants "overrunning" our countries, bringing with them alien values and cultural forms, "replacing" the current population. Suddenly, so it seems, Jews, especially Jewish liberals (George Soros seems to represent us best in that, but it could be any one of many others), are being depicted as a vanguard of such an "invasion." But here we are: committed by our Torah, as well as by our legacy of past oppression, to welcoming these strangers. It was Jewish sympathy for immigration, embodied by HIAS (Hebrew Immigrant Aid Society), that triggered the Pittsburgh atrocity.

This is a decisive moment. It is time for us to speak up unambiguously for those values, indeed to decide where we stand in American society altogether. We are a highly successful minority, but a minority nonetheless. We need to stand clearly for a diverse, multi-ethnic, multi-religious, multi-gendered United States. We should want to be part of the emerging rainbow. We have no place among the builders of walls, among the threatened and fear-mongered white phalanxes that we have seen in Charlottesville and elsewhere. Shame on those Jews who do not understand this. No, thanks. We do not want to hide behind the "Judeo" label of the "white Judeo-Christian society" that some are proposing to us. We do not want to be on the wrong side of history, either morally or demographically.

Like every other stripe in that emerging rainbow, we too have our own vital interests. Our need to survive means that we need to support an America that recognizes diversity in education and celebrates citizens, cultures, and languages of many sorts. Some of us want to raise and educate our kids knowing and speaking Hebrew or Yiddish; we need to support the right of Latinos to do the same for their own cultural heritage. While identifying with other minorities, we do not always agree with their politics. We will not be told that we must oppose Israel's right to exist in order to conform with the views of some people's versions of political correctness or "intersectionality." We need to be aware of anti-Semitism on the left and in "progressive" circles as well as on the right. We achieved much in this country as it became more of a background-blind meritocracy. We believe in, and should actively support, aid to presently disadvantaged and historically victimized groups, including both African Americans and Native Americans, but we should not give up on ultimately seeking a merit-based standard of achievement for all Americans.

At the same time, while choosing to identify with the new minority-majority America, we should not see ourselves as turning our backs on the great number of good, democracy-loving, white Christian Americans whose ancestors did so much to create this great country and so many of whom welcomed us to these shores and today welcome others. On the contrary, our in-between status as a now-privileged white-skinned group that chooses to identify with minorities should make us ideal bridge builders between those two Americas. The values for which we so long have stood: *ahavat ha-ger* ("loving the stranger"), *tsedek* ("justice"), and *ḥesed* ("compassion") should be the foundation stones on which that bridge is constructed. *Maybe that is why we are here.*

All of this must be seen, as must everything else in world affairs, as taking place in the shadow of the great environmental crisis that is soon to engulf our world, in significant part due to the moral and political failure of this country's elites. In decades to come, I fear, there will be millions fleeing drowning and starvation. Today's growth in xenophobia and racism may be a foreshadowing of that greater crisis to come. Ironically, those most likely to proclaim themselves deniers of climate change may actually be acting in anticipation of it. The way we behave now, and the America we create, will set the tone for the way we respond to much that lies ahead. We know where, and with whom, we Jews must stand.

Jewish Mysticism and
Its Healing Power

I FIND MYSELF SURPRISED to be addressing this subject. For many years I have been a student and teacher of the Jewish mystical tradition. This is a body of lore to which many people have turned for healing over the centuries. They have often seen teachers of this tradition as holy men, *tsaddikim* who have some special closeness to God, resulting in an ability to pray successfully for the healing of the sick. There is a whole realm called "practical Kabbalah," still very widely practiced in Israel, especially among Jews of Near Eastern origin (but also among some *ḥasidim*), that deals almost exclusively with the curative power of blessings, amulets, and holy names. I have always kept myself quite distant from this aspect of Kabbalah. I think it important, for the sake of full disclosure and honesty, that I explain why that is the case.

The crucial event of my psychological life, that which determined more of my future biography than any other single occurrence, was the death of my mother when I was eleven years old. She died of a terrible cancer, one the doctors in 1952 were unable to cure and one that even today, if allowed to advance as it did then, would be beyond medical help. The fact that my sister and I have now long ago made our fiftieth *yahrzeit* pilgrimage back to the New Jersey cemetery where she lies buried allows me to speak about it, but of course it does not complete the healing. I came to understand many years back that there was no healing for such a wound, and that my emerging personality would form as scar tissue over it and around it.

A child already attracted to religion before this shocking event, one for which I was quite unprepared, I spent the next seven years seeking the solace of intense religiosity, the assurance that this death was not without meaning and somehow not final, and the embrace of God as a surrogate parent. My life as an adult began only as I broke free from the near suffocation of this self-imposed embrace. I had to accept the arbitrariness of natural processes that determine life and death, as well as our inability to control them either by medicine or by appeal to divine mercy. This left no room for claims that the right *rebbe*, prayer formula, or amulet might have made the difference. More significant, I had to come to the realization that nothing I could have done would have prevented it. My being somehow "better" in the eyes of God would not have saved my mother's life. This meant that I had to deny particular providence, the faith that I had tried so hard to hold onto through those years. I needed to confront the possibility that life and death are indeed without meaning, other than that which we construct out of our own aspirations and longings.

In those crucial years, I crossed the desert peopled by the likes of Friedrich Nietzsche, Franz Kafka, and Albert Camus. Nietzsche taught me of the death of God, even of the initial joy and exultation at that discovery. But Kafka came right behind him, teaching me that the Nietzschean celebration of the death of God lasts but a moment, leaving you quite alone in an absurd and horrifying universe. From Camus I learned that meaning happens in that universe only as you fashion it for yourself. I came to understand Torah as the language of meaning we Jews collectively have fashioned—or discovered, or had revealed to us—as we traversed that desert, a wilderness that Rabbi Naḥman of Bratslav, I learned later, calls the "void" or the empty space, from which God is necessarily absent, in order that we can become ourselves. Although I have tried to follow R. Naḥman's invitation to jump across the abyss with him, the leap of faith allowing one to live on the far side of that void, I cannot do so with innocence or simplicity. For me (as for him, I believe) both the void and its far shore are always there, and neither negates the other.

There is no naïveté in my faith, no room for pretending. My theological enterprise has been about articulating what I sometimes call a "Judaism for adults," which means those who stand with me in having abandoned—or, perhaps more accurately, having been abandoned by—the naïve religion of childhood fantasy. We have been expelled from Eden, as were

Adam and Eve, by the force of our own curious minds. This necessary departure from childhood causes us to stand with Cain, the original absurd hero. Yet we seek meaning, rising up in *defiance* of the void.[1] I understand that defiance to be the opposite of pretense.

My quest has been one of making meaning while staring absurdity in the face. In the course of this journey, undertaken first for my own survival, but then also to share with others, I have sought to marshal the rich resources of Jewish texts and symbols, including teachings of the mystical tradition. To this all of my theological writing and much of my scholarly and educational work have been devoted. My early attraction to the language of Kabbalah and Hasidism had to do both with the profundity of its religious ideas, some of which I first encountered in the writings of Gershom Scholem, and the richness of metaphor and poetic imagination with which these teachings are sometimes graced. Later I came to appreciate the unitive mystical consciousness that underlay these and the ways the kabbalists used all of Judaism as a path toward deeper rungs of inner experience. All of these I have tried to reinterpret in our own language, hoping to render them accessible to today's seekers.

While engaged in this process, one that has now stretched over more than half a century, I was of course aware that other uses were being made of the kabbalistic tradition as well. Jerusalem taxicabs and market stalls adorned with pictures of a Moroccan or Baghdadi Jewish saint told me that popular Kabbalah was alive and well among certain sectors of the Jewish community. Over the years, various tales would come to my ears of someone who was cured from illness or saved from disaster by the blessing of the Lubavitcher or another hasidic *rebbe*. These, of course, echoed a great deal of what was present in the sources I studied, but I remained uninterested in—and somewhat dismissive of—the alleged curative powers of either kabbalistic amulets or the blessings of hasidic rabbis. I considered this popular use of Kabbalah a betrayal of the deeper mystical tradition, that which saw all worship as an act of pure giving and devotion, not seeking even such reasonable earthly rewards as health and longevity.

Following in the tradition of Martin Buber and other neo-hasidic writers, I tended to skip over such promises when seeking materials for translation or teaching. For years I listened to the late Shlomo Carlebach make a very different selection from the hasidic teachings than I did, one that sought out and glorified naïve faith, while I was trying to pick up and paste together shards of meaning—"broken tablets," as I called them—on the far shores of its destruction. While I might have enjoyed the account of childlike faith in the tales of one hasidic master or another, any move in that direction on my own part felt dishonest, as though I were abandoning the hard-fought truth that I had come to know.

Decades of involvement with mystic teaching do have their effect, however. I am engaged with a realm of human understanding that by definition goes beyond ordinary rules of reason or scientific explanation. By temperament as well, I am not a scientist. I am not much attracted to those experiments that try to lend greater credibility to mystical experience by measuring the alpha waves of meditators or analyzing the brain chemistry of apocalyptic visionaries. Even academically, my approach is rather more phenomenological: I seek to take the mystic's testimony seriously, to analyze it in its own terms, perhaps to compare it with language heard elsewhere, and to be especially wary of reductionist or dismissive explanations. This means that I have to *listen* to the mystics of prior generations, allowing myself to become open to the reality they describe. I cannot cut them off when they begin describing something—a miraculous healing, for example—that my modern mind and my own life experience want to deny as absurd.

This involvement with the realm of inner mystery has forced me to admit how much there is that I—dare I say "we"—do not understand. I certainly cannot judge whether the visions or recounted experiences of mystical teachers throughout the world are "true" or not on the basis of my meager ability to explain them. I have come rather to accept them as strivings to express the ineffable, as attempts to describe an inner reality that makes powerful claims, both on the original visionaries who describe them and on later generations of faithful readers, sometimes including myself, who are inspired by them.

I have come to accept that there are forces or energies present in the world that we have not yet found ways to measure or describe. In ways we do not understand at all, there are people who have the psychic ability to "tune in" to the frequencies of these energies and come to see or know things that are otherwise beyond explanation. The field of psychic research is as yet very young and overwhelmed by both charlatanism and the excessive skepticism that comes in its wake. But I believe we still have much more to learn in this area than we know at present, and humility behooves us in our ignorance. This does not mean, of course, that we are to become patsies for the many spurious and suspicious claims in this area that appear every day.

The same has slowly come to be the case with regard to accounts of healing, whether based on the blessings of a *tsaddik* or simply the power of prayer. As I have become aware of the defensive role that a certain cynicism about such claims plays in my own psychic life, I have been forced to become more open to the reality of experiences recounted by others. This was best brought home to me in a conversation with a group of rabbis that I had the privilege of teaching a number of years ago. I went to them for help in preparing for my appearance at a conference on Jewish healing called "Mining the Tradition." I wondered whether I could speak there about Kabbalah and healing (they were not seeking a purely academic lecture) without somehow pretending to be a mystical healer, or without, at least by implication, lending support to something that I might consider quackery.

"Suppose," I said, taking a worst-case scenario, "there are cancer patients in the audience, having come to listen in hope of finding a cure. What shall I say to them? If I give them a sense that Kabbalah and its teachers do have healing powers, I'll be sending them off to buy holy water from someone I consider to be a quick-buck phony. If I tell them I think it's all nonsense, I'll be unfairly destroying their hopes, something I surely have no right or desire to do!"

Had I looked around for a minute at that group of ten or twelve rabbis, most of whom I knew quite well, I would have recalled the presence of two cancer survivors among them, one other whose spouse had just survived a heart attack, and yet another who had lost her husband to illness at a terribly young age. Yet all of them wanted to tell me of the power of prayer in their lives and in confronting illness or loss, while none of them sought to make a naïve claim that it was prayer alone, rather than medical intervention, that stopped the cancer's growth or saved the life.

Our conversation brought forth all kinds of important thoughts, some previously stored in my own memory, that belong to such talk. The Talmud's declaration that "outcry is good for a person, whether before or after the decree has been issued" makes it quite clear that what is "good" about outcry or prayer is not its ability to change the decree.[2] A distinction that was crucial to our conversation is that between "healing," or making whole, restoring a broad sense of health, and "curing" the actual medical condition, one surely familiar to many readers. The fact that we cannot offer a cure should in no way stop us from seeking to offer healing. This applies even to the use of materials from the mystical sources that indeed did claim to have curative powers; we may find them valuable resources for healing even without being literal believers in their curative effects.

This healing begins with a gift of empathy, companionship, and being present. It shares an awareness of the pain, suffering, or fear experienced by both the patient and those who love the patient, that whole man or woman who is now designated by that unfortunately clinical term. The caregiver also suffers from fear of experiencing the approaching loss of a loved one. How I know that, from my own long period of caregiving for a now departed spouse! Teachings that speak of a deep, unitive faith, where the gulf between the divine and human, the temporal and the eternal, is transcended, are an important part of the healing resources our mystical tradition has to offer. We should indeed mine that aspect of Jewish teaching, using it in this context as a tool of healing, without any pretense to curative powers.

A most striking comment offered by one of the rabbis was a rereading of the 'amidah phrase refa'enu ha-shem ve-nerafei to mean "Soften us up, O Lord, so that we may be able to receive healing."[3] Open our hearts so that we can receive the gift of those who seek to heal. Help us to break down our own resistance to Your healing love! This was a message I needed to hear then and still could use to listen to more fully today. It also stimulated in me a memory of an old reading of my own of another passage in the 'amidah: ha-merahem ki lo tamu hasadekha—"You are compassionate, Lord, even when Your love is not simple."[4] Help us to accept Your compassionate presence, Lord, even when compassion means just that—You are present with us in our suffering—and not that You will "avert the decree."[5]

Not long before that conversation, I had written in a book:

> I do not know much about the power of prayer to affect others: to heal the sick, to bring home the lost, to protect those we love from harm. I remain somewhat neutral to the claims now being made again, on this far edge of the age of skepticism, for the efficacy of prayer in the external world. But I know that prayer heals the one who prays, restoring a wholeness or a balance that can be lost when we are beset by concern or worry. And since the One who lies within us, to whom we give the words of prayer, lies as well in the heart of the one for whom we pray, we would indeed be setting false and unnecessary limits to say that the energy of our love, expressed in that prayer, *cannot* reach the other.[6]

After that conversation, I would probably add the line: "Listen to the testimony of those who have been healed no less carefully than you listen to the outcry of those who have not."

But the conversation with my rabbi friends led me somewhere else as well, and that brings us closer to my subject. Our healing, as important as it is to us and those who love us, is ultimately a small matter. The world will go on without us. We are all mortals. "The days of our lives are but seventy years, or eighty if by strength" (Ps. 90:20). Anything beyond those, so common in our age, is pure gift. Generations in families will come and go, some longer and some shorter. The real healing that is needed is not only of the sick and the bereaved, but of the whole human situation. This leads me back to some of the great ideas of Kabbalah that I mentioned earlier.

The kabbalists understand that the world itself is a broken place. Somehow, in the flow of energy from its boundless Source into the finite beings that populate the world as we see it, there was a break, a flaw, or a moment of painful separation. There are various versions in kabbalistic lore as to how this loss of wholeness came about, and much of the myth-making creativity of the kabbalists is devoted to this question. Judaism is not primarily a religion based on the need to atone for an original sin. The rabbis mostly believed that the struggle with evil and temptation begins over again with each person. But the tale of Eden does belong to our scripture, and the faint memory of a lost paradise haunts our tradition. Indeed, one way of reading the entire Torah is to see it as a response to our expulsion from Eden. The sin for which we were expelled, according to the kabbalists (and later also discovered by Kafka), is that of having separated the two trees, having broken off the Tree of Knowledge from its own root in the Tree of Life.[7] The quest to satisfy curiosity leads us to make that separation. Knowledge that is about mere curiosity, "just the facts," unaccompanied by a commitment to *live* the truth learned, to transform our lives into vessels that serve such truth, leads us down the path that will take us to "evil," knowledge in the service of self-promotion, and aggression, "my" truth arrayed against "yours." Torah as the new Tree of Life is given to us as the antidote to this alienation, a way of learning, a path of spiritual awareness combined with moral living that leads us toward a new Eden, toward our Promised Land.

There is something within the human being that longs to feel fully at home in the universe, to celebrate life as we once did in Eden, but this is not given us; the gates to paradise are closed. Even more, the human heart longs to return to the single Source from which it came, to unite with the wholeness of Y-H-W-H, but it cannot, at least not for more than brief interludes. Paradoxically, our very longing for God, or oneness, or an undivided heart, shows us how far away we are, at the very same moment that it whispers to us how close we truly could be, indeed truly *are*, if that broken heart could only be healed. Nobody in Jewish literature, and indeed few among the world's religious teachers, has described this aspect of the human situation with the poignancy of Rabbi Naḥman of Bratslav:

There is a mountain, and on that mountain there stands a rock. A spring gushes forth from that rock.

Now everything in the world has a heart, and the world as a whole has a heart. The heart of the world is a complete form, with face, hands, and feet. But even the toe-nail of that heart of the world is more heartlike than any other heart.

The mountain and the spring stand at one end of the world, and the heart is at the other. The heart stands facing the spring, longing and yearning to draw near to it. It is filled with a wild yearning, and constantly cries out in its desire to approach the spring. The spring, too, longs for the heart.

The heart suffers from two weaknesses: the sun pursues it terribly, burning it because it wants to approach the spring. The second weakness is that of the longing and outcry itself, the great desire to reach the spring. The heart ever stands facing the spring, crying out in longing to draw near.

When the heart needs to rest a bit or catch its breath, a great bird comes over it and spreads forth its wings to shield the heart from the sun. But even at its times of rest, the heart looks toward the spring in longing.

Now if the heart is filled with so great a desire to draw near to the spring, why does it not simply do so? Because as soon as it starts to move toward the mountain, the mountaintop where the spring stands would disappear from view. And the life of the heart flows from seeing the spring; if it were to allow the spring to vanish from its sight, it would die. . . .

If that heart were to die, God forbid, the entire world would be destroyed. The heart is the life of all things; how could the world exist without a heart? For this reason the heart can never approach the spring, but ever stands opposite it and looks at it in longing.[8]

To be human is to be distant from God, so very distant as one end of the world is from the other. Our deepest desire, our greatest need, is to stare into the divine face, to drink at the deep well of God's presence. Yet we cannot do so; we cannot come any closer than we are. Every prayer we utter, every time we say the vital word "You" in prayer, proclaiming God our beloved, we are also confirming our separation from the One that we hope would (and, on some level, *does*) embrace us all. The longing itself, the hasidic masters understood, can serve as a bridge between our distance from God and our renewed intimacy.[9]

This is what needs healing, and it is to this work of healing that religion, in the profoundest sense, must address itself. This is the true message of redemption, the promise to bring us forth from the *mitsrayim* (Egypt) or narrow straits of *galut ha-da'at*, the "exilic" perception of our ordinary consciousness, and to give us a taste of the "breadth" of the wide open spaces whence YaH responds to us (Ps. 118:5). This is the One reaching out to us from the far side of the void, where the oneness of being is total and where the "Thou" of our prayers gives way to the single silent sound of the divine *anokhi*, "I am."

To be a healer is to evoke a sense of this redemptive embrace in the ones who need healing. This is a message Rabbi Nahman understood so well, urging us to find "bits of goodness" in each person, including ourselves.[10] The healer does this by being present to the one(s) in need, by listening to the cry of pain—rather than seeking to hide behind often trivializing blandishments—by giving love. The religious healer comes to understand that this is not his or her own love that is being given, but that he or she has been offered the privilege of conveying the love of God, the wordless but very real call coming from the other side of the void. In the patient near to death, this may be perceived as a final call homeward, even welcomed as that. But it does not come only in that form; more often, it is a call to renewed life.

The general healing of human alienation cannot, of course, gloss over the unique situation of any single human being. Each of us needs to seek out and come into the arms of this wholeness in ways that are appropriate to who we are, to our needs, to our particular pains in life's journey. There is a need for as many healers as there are such varieties in human needs. Ultimately, healing must be offered on a "retail," not a "wholesale," basis. That is why I have found it meaningful, alongside my writing, to have spent much of my life training rabbis, who will work with people one-on-one.

But each of us also needs to learn how to step beyond our individual situation and to see the ongoing process of healing, called *tikkun* by the kabbalists, in its fullest ramification. It is the process of individuation—that which makes each of us into the unique self that we are—that separates us from our deeper root in being as a whole, which we later seek to recover. Yet individuation itself should also be seen as a holy process: the emergence of a healthy, balanced ego is as much a revelation of God's image as is the conquest of that ego and its dedication to a higher purpose. The whole cycle of human life is thus nothing but the intake and outflow of selfhood, transported in the flow of divine, cosmic breath. Our healing lies in our becoming aware of that all-pervasive underlying truth.

The commandments of Torah, the forms of religion, are there to provide shared outward structures within which this dual quest, the true 'avodah—a rich word embracing "work," "service," and "devotion"—is to take place. Each in our unique way, we become ourselves and transcend ourselves, over and over again. This work is nothing less than a transformation of the self into a mirror of divinity. To say it in a way more familiar to the Western mind: each human being may realize the potential to truly become the image of God. This process of self-transformation requires *investigating and discovering* the deeper truth, *realizing* that truth in the way we live, both individually and in community, and *communicating* the value of that work to those around us. This three-part task is the true purpose of religion, the healing of our wounded humanity.

The Jewish esoteric tradition offers a particular set of tools through which this work can be done. Although Kabbalah is often presented as an abstract metaphysics or theosophy, it is best understood as the hasidic masters did, as a form of religious 'avodah, a way to do our inner "work." All reality, according to the kabbalists, is constructed according to a ten-fold pattern, a divine structure that unfolds from within the most hidden recesses of divinity. We humans can understand that reality primarily through our own inner experience, since the cosmic pattern is repeated in the soul-life of every person. That is the hasidic understanding of the kabbalists' ten *sefirot*. While here is not the place to explicate this system in full, a very general outline can be offered.[11] The following may be considered my own neo-hasidic understanding of Kabbalah's inner structure, as applied to the inner life of the individual.

Within your deepest self (connected to the single Self of Being, or God) there are infinite resources of energy, first emerging in deep, preconscious stirrings. Slowly they begin to filter into consciousness.[12] In doing so, however, they necessarily become constricted, as the conscious self is so much smaller, narrower in focus, than the infinite realm of preconscious potential within. As self-conscious mind begins to emerge, aware of these inner energies, they begin to coalesce around two poles.

One is a center of love-energy; we feel loved and blessed by the Source of our energy and seek to pass that blessing on, whether to partner and offspring through the physical love-act or in sharing love with those around us. The other center feels the energy as a surge of strength, a way to build up the self, to stand securely as an individual. Sometimes this demands a holding back of love, a defense of the vital borders between self and other, as in the initial process of individuation. Human life involves a great struggle between these two, a tension between the impulse to give, to be generous and outflowing in spirit, and the impulse to hold back, to stand firm, to build the self into a bastion of strength, even if that means withholding giving. The adult self needs the fortitude that can only be created by a degree of holding back. As we mature, we need to resolve that tension, to find a way of proper balance between the two.

As we do so, however, a second great tension appears, that between the demands of perfectionism and the grace of self-acceptance.[13] One side of us wants to accomplish it all; it is the "type A" personality within us, striving for great accomplishments, improving our lives, maybe even saving the world and bringing the messiah. The other pole in this struggle is that of humility, a virtue too much neglected in our aggressive culture. (Indeed, how can humility assert itself, after all?) This means accepting yourself for who you are, loving yourself (and knowing that you are loved by the One that ever flows into you) even if you can't transform the world, cook like a Cordon Bleu chef, or write the great American novel. When we resolve these two tensions—love versus self-assertion and demand versus acceptance—we are ready to be proper givers and receivers of the divine energy that continues to course within us.[14] We learn the dynamic of giving/receiving also from our sexual roles as male and female, although the experienced lover always learns to play the other role as well as his or her primary biological one. Thus we are all "male" and "female," givers and receivers of love. (Even so-called straight people have to learn this lesson, though it is often hard for them.)

This is the essential kabbalistic system, read here as a textbook of religious psychology. The seven "lower" of the ten *sefirot* (primal numbers), known as the *middot* (personal qualities), function as a set of tools for doing our inner work, for achieving balance, for making sure that one or another of these inner drives has not run amok, as they so often do. This achievement of proper balance is the healing work that each of us needs to do. While we must take great care never to blame the victim and imply that "your illness has come about *because* your spirit was out of balance," those who do this work know how much better illness can be managed and wholeness achieved by a person who is set on the course of proper balance among these forces.

What I am suggesting here is that Jewish mystical teaching does indeed bear a great healing message, and that we who have been privileged to study it have an obligation to share its wisdom in the context of helping broken spirits to become whole again: our own and those of others, the healthy and the sick. This has little to do with esotericism or magic, but everything to do with the charism, the true divine gift, of human caring and relationship.[15]

Here I am forced to return to the personal confession with which I opened this essay, and to confront the real reasons why this topic is such a hard one for me. By the time I was eighteen years old, I understood that no prayer, incantation, or righteous behavior on my part would have saved my mother's life. Her physical wound was not one that could have responded to those attempts at a cure, any more than it did to the doctors' best efforts.

The real question was not her wound, but mine. The brokenheartedness with which I have lived for what are now sixty-seven years was also not subject to cure, but definitely responded to healing. I have been blessed by endless gifts of such healing over these decades, blessings of heaven conveyed to me through the vessels of human love. For forty-nine of those years, I was married to a woman who had lost both of her parents in adolescence; that choice of partner was not coincidental. The depths that attracted me to her were born of our shared sense of loss, and we offered much healing to one another in the life and love we shared.

It surely is also not coincidence that I was drawn to the figure of Rabbi Naḥman of Bratslav, whom I depicted as the great wounded healer of the Jewish tradition, in a book I called *Tormented Master*, back in 1979. The accounts of Rabbi Naḥman, uniquely among hasidic sources, depict a childhood of great psychic pain, marked by loneliness, doubt, and a constantly gnawing sense of inadequacy. His disciples claimed that he had overcome all of these, becoming the greatest of hasidic masters, one to whom countless thousands, both in his lifetime and even more today, turn for blessing and healing. As his biographer, I understood that he had not truly "overcome" any of this pain, but that he had learned to turn it around and use it as a tool of empathy, allowing him to soothe the pain of so many others, "to pull them out of hell by the *peyos* ['forelocks']," as he once said.

The broken heart, if not embittered and hard-crusted, becomes the open heart. People who feel great pain may develop a special openness to the pain of others. That doorway to healing has not closed in the transition from the medieval to the modern world. It was told of the Ba'al Shem Tov, the great-grandfather whom Naḥman was so anxious to emulate, that someone who had been healed by one of his amulets opened it up and found nothing written in it but the healer's own name: Israel ben Eliezer.

This wisdom of healing, and of using the resources of one's own self, life, and pain to heal others, has largely passed from the domain of hasidic masters to that of humanistic psychologists, more than a few of them Jews. Such therapists are well known to engage with hasidic stories as tools of healing. Some of them, Reb Shlomo would be sure to remind us, are probably great-grandchildren of hidden *tsaddikim*.

But teaching, too, as well as writing, can be a wounded healer's path. Through both of these vehicles, I seek to offer healing not only to wounded souls like my own, but also to the deeply wounded heart of the Jewish people, still not recovered from the terrible slaughter of one-third of our brothers and sisters. Such brutalization does not pass out of the system quickly or easily. And the heart of the world—now manifest in the overheated body of this poor, abused planet—it too cries out for healing, now more than ever. All of them—all of us—need the sweet balm of hasidic teaching.

My Own Jewish Education

A MEMOIR

IN THE RABBINICAL SCHOOL I helped to found some eighteen years ago, we require that students entering the program have the equivalent of two years of college Hebrew under their belt, so that they can begin reading rabbinic texts in the original. Otherwise, they are first required to do a year of preparatory studies. We quickly discovered, however, that the Hebrew language as known by diaspora Jews comes in an infinite variety of packages. There is the Hebrew of those who attended day schools until sixth—or eighth—grade, and then began forgetting. There are those who spent a year in Israel after high school. Some did so in *yeshiva*, others worked on *kibbutz*. The Hebrew of each of these groups is entirely different. Such also is the case with those who spent a few summers in a once-upon-a-time Hebrew-speaking summer camp, those who actually took college courses, and so forth. Each of them, it seems, had his or her own Jewish and Hebrew education. Shaping a class out of these is not an easy undertaking.

But I, too, am one of those American Jews. My own Jewish educational story is, on the one hand, quite familiar, but it is also like no other. Since, in the end, it seems to have worked out fairly well, I thought I would like to share my story with you, even in some detail, combined with a bit of reflection along the way.

My formal Jewish education began when I was eight years old. My father took me aside, in a rather grave manner, and told me that there was

something I had to do for Grandma, his mother-in-law. I had to go to Hebrew school, three times a week for the next five years, so that there could
be something called a Bar Mitzvah. If I hated it too much, he assured me,
I would be allowed to quit.

Informally, however, my Jewish education began earlier. Not in my
own home, to be sure, which was completely devoid of any shred of Jewish
knowledge or observance, but in the home of that grandmother, the little
apartment above Grandpa's tailor shop in Paterson, New Jersey. I remember the Shabbos candles (a four-branched candelabrum, Grandma told
me, because she had four children), and especially the aroma in the air after each candle went out, perhaps my first memory of special smells. Next
to the candles on one side was something mysteriously called a *pushke*,
where you put some coins for charity before candlelighting. On the other
side was a photo of my grandmother's aunt, Tante Shushke, the paragon of
true piety in our family. (I remember especially liking the rhyme of *pushke-
shushke*.) I knew that there were things Grandma didn't do on Saturdays,
like writing and sewing, even though the tailor shop downstairs was open
and busy. I thus knew the word *shabbos* when I was a little kid. I learned that
you couldn't ask for a bacon and tomato sandwich at Grandma's house,
and that you had to watch which fork you were using to eat. I remember
the great event of the Sunday before Passover, when all the grandchildren
would gather and help carry the Passover dishes down from the attic. (My
dear sister, who never received a day of Jewish education, knows how to
correctly pronounce *peysekhdike* from the memory of that annual event.) I
recall the special foods, including rock-hard *teygelekh* for Rosh Hashanah
and *kneydlekh* at the *seder*. I also recall my father, a committed atheist, furi-
ously annoying his in-laws at that *seder*, when he came up with a question
of his own: "How can you eat gefilte fish without rye bread?"

I have a memory of being seven or eight years old and going, somewhat regularly, to Friday evening services at Newark's Temple Bnai Abraham with my mother. I was the one who initiated those visits, but Mom
seemed quite happy to go along. Whether it was a desire to do something
with her son, an escape from Dad's cigar smoke–filled Friday night bridge
games, or perhaps a need for religion in the face of her recently diagnosed
cancer, I do not know. Might she have been less of an atheist than her very
ideological husband? In any case, the memory of being there together is
a strong one.

Let me describe the scene. Bnai Abraham at Clinton Avenue and
10th Street, a huge, round synagogue building, with a sanctuary hold-

ing twenty-four hundred seats. Well over a thousand are filled on Friday nights. People are not there to pray; few even open their books. They have come largely to hear Dr. Joachim Prinz speak. He is a fiery orator, known to be highly intelligent, a committed Zionist, and an outspoken liberal, quite as he is depicted in Philip Roth's *The Plot against America*. Some may also be there to hear the cantorial concert. Abraham Shapiro was one of the grand cantors of his day. The choir (paid professionals, mostly non-Jews) is hidden from the congregation in a box above the ark. Their voices float down, to this child's ears, like those of angels. When the ark is opened (by a seemingly magical push-button on the rabbi's desk), indirect lighting shines on the pink tufted cushions behind the gold- and silver-adorned Torah scrolls. Combined with the music, it's like a little bit of heaven on view. I recall turning my head down and then looking up to see those angels singing at the top of the ark.

Now another memory. I am thirteen years old, just back from my first summer at Hebrew-speaking Camp Ramah. (More on how I got there below.) We had Hebrew school classes on Saturday mornings (but no writing!), followed by Junior Congregation. Being a big kid now, I decided to go instead into the main sanctuary. I arrived during the Torah reading and stood up silently to recite the morning *'amidah*, just as I'd learned to do at camp. After the service, I went to up to say *Gut Shabbos* to Rabbi Prinz, whom I quite revered. There was also an elderly rabbi emeritus in the congregation, who had served there for many years. He said to me, in a booming and condescending rabbinic voice: "Are you the young man who was standing during services? We don't do that sort of thing here." I never walked into that sanctuary again. Rabbi Silberfeld had sealed my choice of my grandparents' *shul* over the Temple, and probably had given me a strong push in my journey toward adolescent Orthodoxy.

My grandparents' *shul* had a formative place in my Jewish education. Once Grandpa retired from the tailor shop, when I was six, he started going to *shul* every Shabbos, then every day. I spent many a weekend and Jewish holiday with my grandparents, going to *shul* with them. This became more frequent after my mother died when I was eleven. My grandparents were emotionally ravaged by that loss (compounded terribly when their only son died two years later), and I was their great consolation. Everyone in the family (except for my father) thought it was great for me to spend lots of time with them. They reaped in endless *nakhas* ("pleasure") from their increasingly Jewishly devoted grandchild, and I learned from and imbibed their Old World *yiddishkeyt* ("Jewishness").

Let me tell you something about that *shul*, the Clifton Jewish Center. It was an unaffiliated traditional synagogue. Men and women sat together, but the liturgy was entirely in Hebrew and *davened* in Old World style. Almost everyone who attended was over sixty and east European–born; Yiddish, or half Yiddish, was the lingua franca of the place. I was one of three kids who somehow were regulars in this mostly elderly congregation. That *shul* bears with it lots of pleasant memories of sitting with Grandpa, listening to the half-understood Yiddish conversations, and giggling together at Mr. Leimetz, a Galician Jew (undoubtedly from Passaic, as Grandma would say, where they were all *galitzianer*) who would say *ein keleheinee* when the rest of us said *ayn kelohenu*.

The rabbi there, Eugene Markovitz, was encouraging about my religious life, but did not make a strong impression on me. A postwar immigrant and *yeshiva* graduate, he was still somehow acclimating to his new country (he later wound up being a student of American Jewish history). His Judaism was Orthodox, unbending, but did not come across as particularly deep or thoughtful. His sermons were predictable and unimpressive, certainly no comparison to those of Dr. Prinz. He had made his compromise over serving in a congregation with mixed pews, but clearly would have been more comfortable elsewhere. With a little effort, I imagine he could have pulled me more fully into the Orthodox realm, but he never made the effort. I think my dad probably scared him.

But my strongest memories of the Clifton Jewish Center are those of Yizkor days, the four times a year when memorial prayers for the dead are recited. On Yizkor days the focus of all attention was on two elderly women, my grandmother and Mrs. Markovich. Grandma was, as always, dressed up, probably having been to the beauty parlor the day before. But she arrived in tears and cried, somewhat audibly, through the entire service: Hallel, Torah reading, and all the rest. Various women would come over to greet and console her. Mrs. Markovich, thin as a rail, dressed in old-country simplicity, was white as a sheet. She was quiet and stoical throughout. But everybody knew that as Yizkor proceeded, the rabbi would read all the names (a fairly short list in this new congregation) from the memorial tablet on the wall. When he came to Mrs. Markovich's husband's name, she would scream. We all knew it; she did it every time. You could feel the collective holding of breath when he got to a name or two before his. She let out her little scream, and then it was over; Grandma went on crying and Mrs. M. retreated into herself.

On the High Holy Days, an elderly cantor (a friend of the rabbi's family, I think) came out from Brooklyn. All I remember is that his voice cracked with tears when he came to the passage "Cast us not off in old age" in the Yom Kippur liturgy. The point of all this, I am trying to say, is that I sensed something emotionally "real" about religious life as I experienced it in that *shul*. The place was totally unpretentious, Old World in style, and authentic to the only modestly educated people who had built it. Unlike Bnai Abraham, which felt showy and religiously shallow, this little place was simple and honest. Nobody but the rabbi and perhaps one or two members were strictly observant, and no one pretended otherwise. But showing your feelings, even pouring out your heart, was something that seemed to belong there, quite naturally. That made a great impression.

Formal Jewish education is said to begin with the alphabet, and those were indeed the opening lessons in my first year of Hebrew school, using a book simply called *Ha-Sefer*, "the book." But Hebrew letters were there already in my childhood, because Grandma and Grandpa read a daily newspaper called *Der Tog*. I began putting them together during that first year of Hebrew school. The only Hebrew sign one saw on the streets in our neighborhood read בשר כשר, which I recall first sounding out as *bosher kosher*, taking *bosher* to be a Yiddish way of saying "butcher." A bit later, a bakery opened up (at Clinton Avenue and 11th Street, for any Newarkers who happen to read this) that had a neon sign reading ביאליסטאקער קוכען. That was a big chunk of Hebrew letters all at once, but I was proud to figure out that it advertised *Bialystoker Kuchen*, better known as *bialys*. Thus I also learned of Bialystok, a city not far from Grandma's place of origin in what she and Grandpa still called *der heym*, "back home."

Perhaps to my father's dismay, I took to Hebrew school immediately. Partly, it offered an entrée into secret things that only adults knew about, and that held great promise. Another part was that the tough kids from public school were not there (many of them were being punished for their sins at catechism across the street, at a place called Blessed Sacrament), and that meant you did not have to play dumb and pretend you didn't know the answers. My first teachers there were clearly eastern Europeans, grandparent figures to me. But after a year, we started getting Israeli teachers, first Mrs. BetHalahmi and then Aryeh Rohn. I think it was Mrs. BetHalahmi who first got us hooked up with pen pals in Israel (of course she must have rewritten everything we wrote!), and that was especially exciting to me.

Aryeh Rohn was my first significant Jewish teacher. I was in his classes for probably six of the eight years I studied, thrice weekly, at Temple Bnai Abraham Hebrew and Hebrew High School in Newark. Aryeh, Viennese originally, had lived for a number of years in pre-state Palestine. Like many other middle Europeans, he did not quite find himself there, and wound up settling in the United States. A committed Zionist/Hebraist, he taught each morning at a Conservative day school in Brooklyn, then "moonlighted" in Newark, quite a long commute in those days. His approach was what was called *'ivrit be-'ivrit*; from a very early stage, no English was spoken during class. We went on from studying the Torah text (narrative sections only; I don't think we ever read Leviticus) to the historical prophets, describing "Israel in its land," key to the Zionist narrative. We kept up with our pen pals, we planted trees in Israel for many occasions, we distributed and collected little blue boxes for the Jewish National Fund, we sang Hebrew songs, and all the rest. Once we were beyond the Bar Mitzvah year, an event that filtered out the indifferent, the classes consisted of only six or seven students, all of whom were serious and seemingly happy to be there.

Many decades later, sometime around 1990, I was sitting in my office as president of the Reconstructionist Rabbinical College when our receptionist rang up and said: "There someone here who says he was your teacher, and wants to visit you." In walked an elderly Aryeh Rohn, along with his wife and another Israeli couple they'd been visiting in Philadelphia. In that conversation, Aryeh said to me (in Hebrew, the only language we ever spoke), "I still remember your father. He's the one who said to me [here he switched to English]: 'Over my dead body he'll go to Camp Ramah!' But I defeated him."

That's the story. Dad was a militant atheist who thought all this involvement with Judaism was utter nonsense. He didn't like it in his in-laws (his own parents were secular Jews, having rebelled while still back in Poland against their hasidic upbringing), and he liked it even less in his son. Mom had died when I was eleven, which surely had increased my own attraction to and need for religion. When I was twelve, Dad had begun to date, and the thought of having his kid away in camp for the summer was quite a temptation. I would not consider the sports camps he was pushing. Thus Aryeh got me into Ramah and the Conservative movement's educational orbit. I think Aryeh was quite happy when I told him that I considered him entirely responsible for my involvement in Jewish life.

My Bar Mitzvah is a scene worth recording here. Although I was prepared in Newark, the event took place in Clifton. The instructors at Bnai Abraham refused to teach me cantillation, since I was hopelessly nonmusical. They said, "You will *declaim* your Haftarah." But nobody in my grandparents' *shul* even knew what that word "declaim" meant, so I memorized the Haftarah with my best imitation of the proper chant. I sailed through it (Rabbi Markovitz commented only that I had failed to look down at the book). In those days we were not trained to do any more than that and the speech, which apparently also went well. Dad sat there looking terribly unhappy, glowering out from under a broad-brimmed fedora hat. He refused to put on a *yarmulke*, since that was a religious symbol, so he thought. He had no idea, this being his only time in a synagogue during his adult life, that he looked somewhat *frum* ("pious") in that big hat. My grandparents beamed at me and glowered back at him, since he had brought along his then fiancée, which they thought was totally inappropriate. The reception was held at my aunt's house in nearby Fairlawn on Saturday afternoon. (She had "a finished basement" with a bar, all in knotty pine—a big deal in 1954.) Dad had promised to pay for part of the reception, but then never came through, as my mother's parents often reminded me, even many years later. They were a family that didn't forget.

I spent three summers in Ramah, one in Connecticut and two in the Poconos. During the latter two summers, my teachers in camp were Yosef Yerushalmi and Gerson Cohen, on their way to becoming leading Jewish historians. Because my Hebrew was good, I was placed in classes together with the day school students (mostly from Akiba in Philadelphia, where I later sent our daughter). But in Newark, our education was more secular, and I had never opened the Talmud. "Don't worry," said the warm and kindly camp librarian, the summer I was sixteen, "I'll teach you some Talmud." His name was David Weiss Halivni—widely known as the world's greatest Talmud scholar, and the only one of my teachers still among the living.

During those two adolescent summers, I began taking Judaism quite seriously. I devoured Heschel's *The Sabbath* and much of his *God in Search of Man*. These felt like books of incredible profundity to me, and my future outlook was beginning to be shaped by them. The level of learning and intellectual conversations taking place in camp was utterly beyond anything I had experienced in my rather mediocre public high school in New Jersey. It thus became clear to me that exploring Judaism was the most intellectually stimulating and personally satisfying thing one could do.

At the same time, I had also discovered a book called "Guide to Jewish Law," known in Hebrew as the *Kitsur Shulhan 'Arukh*, and began rather compulsively observing anything I possibly could. This was a source of constant strife between my father and myself. I think it is fair to say that religion, and especially the question of observance, was the field on which we fought out most of our father/son battles during my adolescence. Needless to say, there can be no real victor in such struggles. We both lost a lot. I, at sixteen, was ready to leave home forever in order to lead a fuller Jewish life. Dad was in some ways glad to be rid of me.

That summer, before going off to college, I read the first whole book in Hebrew that I completed, after all the language books and simplified versions that had preceded it. I was extremely proud of myself! The book was a little paperback of Agnon's *Bi-Levav Yamim*, "In the Heart of the Seas." Needless to say, I was carried away by the romantic Zionism of that work. I probably could have sailed across the seas to *erets yisra'el* on a handkerchief, just as did the hero of that tale.

I was sixteen years old when I started Brandeis University, where my career of Jewish learning began in earnest. Before taking you there, however, I want to offer a generational reflection. I was a young American Jew precisely the right age to gain maximal benefit from the large group of Jewish intellectuals, including many teachers and scholars, whom Hitler cast upon American shores in the late 1930s, and, in some cases, as postwar survivors. We can begin in Newark with Joachim Prinz, whom I have mentioned already. Prinz was famous as a rabbi who had defied Hitler and was forced to leave Germany earlier than most. Dad chose that Hebrew school because of him; Prinz was known as a fiery left-wing and Labor Zionist orator. When I became too pious for Bnai Abraham, I switched my loyalty to Prinz's brother-in-law, Max Gruenwald, formerly rabbi of Mannheim, Germany, but by then in Milburn, New Jersey. I've already told you about Aryeh Rohn, a Viennese.

I shall presently say more about my most important mentors at Brandeis, Nahum Glatzer and Alexander Altmann. I arrived at Brandeis in 1957, in the shadow of the sudden death of Simon Rawidowicz, Russian/German Jewish philosopher and scholar who had founded Brandeis's unique Jewish studies program. I never met Rawidowicz, but his presence was still deeply felt. I studied German with his widow, Esther Klee Rawidowicz, and I spent many a memorable Shabbat afternoon at their home in the adjoining Cedarwood section of Waltham with her son Ben, who became a friend and later a colleague. I went on to study at the Jewish Theological Seminary (JTS) with Abraham Joshua Heschel. Among my other significant teachers at Brandeis were philosophers Aron Gurwich (a disciple of Edmund Husserl) and Herbert Marcuse. All of these were middle European intellectuals, educated in Germany in the interwar period. At JTS, Saul Lieberman, Weiss Halivni, and others all fit the bill as well. I think it fair to say that I didn't take any teacher seriously who didn't come with a middle European accent. (That may be why, incidentally, I never had much attraction to Mordecai Kaplan's thought. It was just too *American*, in the Pragmatic sense. Where was the existential *Angst?* Where were Nietzsche and Sartre in his rather too-well-tied-up "Reconstructionist Answers" to "Questions Jews Ask"? I had already been taught that the only *real* questions were unanswerable.)

Brandeis University was only nine years old when I arrived as a very young freshman in the fall of 1957. Still, it had already achieved a remarkable reputation among people like my parents, Jewish moderate left-wing intellectuals. Founder Abe Sachar had brought people like Max Lerner, Marie Syrkin, and Irving Howe to the Brandeis faculty, labeling it as existing somehow in continuity with left-leaning Democratic and Labor Zionist politics and cultural outlook. Avant-garde art and music were part of the scene. Guests at Brandeis included Eleanor Roosevelt, Adlai Stevenson, and David Ben-Gurion. Norman Mailer and Allen Ginsberg read from their work. "Beat" identity and early-day smoking of marijuana were present on campus by 1959 or 1960. So too was political activism. By 1960 we were "sitting in" at Woolworth lunch counters in Roxbury, trying to rouse Boston blacks to identify with the emerging civil rights struggle in the South. In addition to the American Jewish (but not always Jewish: witness John Roche, Irish American historian) left-liberal faculty for whom Brandeis was known, there was also a significant group of middle European émigré intellectuals, including those I have just mentioned.

Impressed by Brandeis's liberal credentials, my father had no awareness of the small corner of Brandeis that was to serve as well as a hothouse for the development of my own Jewish intensification. Liberated finally from the rules of home, I was able to become fully observant in the areas of Shabbat, *kashrut,* and regular daily prayer. Such behavior was pretty rare on the Brandeis campus in those days, I should add. There was a "kosher line" in the cafeteria, but most of those who ate there were from traditionally observant homes. No one wore a *kippah* around campus in the late 1950s. When the first *kippah* wearer (it was a bright plaid with a buckle in the back—remember those?), a graduate student in music, appeared on the scene around my junior year, we "Hillel kids" found him embarrassing. We constituted a bare *minyan* on Shabbat and felt a strong sense of alienation from the dominant campus culture(s). Another exercise in alienation!

During my freshman year, I started to become deeply committed to Jewish learning on a regular basis. Although Brandeis had extensive Judaica offerings, no Talmud was taught in university classes, supposedly at President Sachar's insistence. His Brandeis was to be quite a Jewish place in cultural character, but that meant American Jewish liberal, with a strong dose of Judaic scholarship, but kept at arm's length from being anything like the only other Jewish-sponsored university, Yeshiva University. Brandeis was very definitely not to look or feel like a *yeshiva* in any way. That meant no Talmud. This ban was broken (by Baruch Levine) only in my junior year. I began to plunge into studying rabbinic sources on my own. (My old friend Herman—later Hayyim—Shapiro, with whom I shared an apartment the summer after freshman year, recalled later that I was never interested in going to the beach or anywhere that college kids might want to go on a summer afternoon. I always had either *mincha* to *daven* or some Talmud to learn.) I was gently encouraged in this path by a young, dynamic Hillel director who had just come to Brandeis, Yitz Greenberg. He and his wife, Blu, immediately became important personal models. Yitz and Blu were only five and seven years older than I am; he was a very young Hillel director and I was a very young freshman. But I sensed a warmth and caring in both of them that was very important to me at the time. Although too young to be surrogate parents and too "old" (in our status, not in years) to be friends, they occupied an important place in the life of an essentially very lonely and confused kid.

Placing out of Brandeis's language requirements with my Ramah/ Newark Hebrew, I immediately entered a course on the book of Isaiah taught by Nahum Glatzer. Glatzer had been a leading disciple of Franz Rosenzweig and a key figure in the Frankfurt Lehrhaus circle. Both a scholar and a translator/popularizer (of which he was by no means ashamed), Glatzer was the key figure, through Schocken Books, in making both Rosenzweig and Franz Kafka known in early 1960s America. A shy and somewhat formal person, Glatzer did not develop close personal relationships with students. Nevertheless, he became a key teacher for me. After freshman year, I took mostly graduate courses with him. (The second whole Hebrew book I read, after the Agnon, was Ibn Verga's sixteenth-century *Shevet Yehuda*, an account of the expulsion from Spain, for a Glatzer course on Jewish historiography. This was, in retrospect, a unique Jewish education!)

Glatzer was significant to me in several ways. While maintaining a professorial stance throughout, it was obvious that he was deeply moved, in a personal and religious way, by the sources he taught. We students, who always sought out information on the personal Jewish lives of our teachers, came to know that he led the *Ne'ilah* service at Harvard Hillel

each year on Yom Kippur. In my mind, at least, this picture fused with
the tale of Rosenzweig's experience of Yom Kippur in a Berlin Orthodox
synagogue, the event that had "saved" him from an imminent conversion
to Christianity. There was an aura of spiritual mystery around Glatzer,
heightened by his own silence on the subject. I was also much impressed
by his daring to publish on a variety of seemingly unrelated subjects,
choosing his own pattern of interests even if they did not quite constitute a conventional area of specialization. Other scholars (including some
Brandeis colleagues) derided him for it, but I took it as a positive example.
I was also very much taken with Glatzer's commitment to making classical
Jewish sources available in translation, presented in a somewhat poetic
framework. His Midrash anthology *Hammer on the Rock* and his collection of prayers *The Language of Faith* were especially important to me. I
made much use of them, especially the former, in my early years of teaching. My first book, *Your Word Is Fire: The Hasidic Masters on Contemplative
Prayer* (translated together with my friend Barry Holtz), followed quite
consciously in their path.

During my third year at Brandeis, Alexander Altmann came, first on
a one-semester trial basis and then full-time, to occupy what had been
the Rawidowicz position. Altmann, possessing a masterful knowledge of
Jewish thought, both philosophy and mysticism, ranging from late antiquity to modernity, also had a rabbinical degree from the Orthodox
(Hildesheimer) Seminary in Berlin. He had been saved from the Nazis
(unlike his parents, who died at Auschwitz) by a rabbinical appointment
in Manchester, England, where he stayed for nearly two decades. He had
come to disdain the active rabbinate, especially that of a singularly non-
intellectual community, and longed to enter the academic world. Turned
down for the succession to Professor Julius Guttmann in Jerusalem, he
was delighted to receive the Philip W. Lown Chair at Brandeis.

I well recall Altmann's first Brandeis course, held during a one-
semester trial visit in 1959. It was called Classical Jewish Thought, and
in it he surveyed four topics (God, Creation, revelation, and messianism,
if memory serves me rightly), including biblical, rabbinic, philosophical,
and kabbalistic treatments of each. I was quite "blown away," by the profundity and richness of the materials, and also by the breadth and depth of
Altmann's knowledge. I must confess that I have retaught that course, or
some variety of it, many times, to both undergraduates and future rabbis,
over the past five decades. In the following year he taught The Jewish
Mystical Tradition, the first serious course on this subject ever taught in

an American university. I was in that class too, and my fascination with it set the course of both my personal life and my future academic career.

I will digress here to tell the story of how I learned that the Zohar, of which I first heard in Altmann's classes, was a truly holy book (indeed, it is always referred to in traditional settings as The Holy Zohar, *ha-Zohar ha-Kadosh*). During his trial-year course, Altmann always taught bareheaded, as in those days seemed appropriate to the university setting. He read and quoted from both the Bible and Talmud quite regularly. As he lectured, Altmann often paced back and forth across the front of the classroom, peopled by perhaps twenty or thirty students. As we first came to discuss Kabbalah, I watched as he paced a little farther, peering out into the hallway through the small clear-glass diamond in the otherwise frosted window door. Seeing no one coming by, he deftly slipped a hand into his pocket, donned a small black *kippah*, and picked up the Zohar volume on his desk. He read a brief passage, closed the book, and the *kippah* disappeared. That must be a *really* holy book, I learned in that moment—a far more memorable lesson than the passage itself, or anything he might have said about it.

During my freshman year, Yitz Greenberg invited one of his few Orthodox colleagues in Hillel, Rabbi Zalman Schachter, Hillel director at the University of Manitoba, to lead a *shabbaton* at Brandeis. Zalman, still a faithful Lubavitcher, was the first living *ḥasid* I had met, and he made a tremendous impression upon me. He felt like "the real thing," unlike the various American imitations. Again, it was the accent, the extensive amount of Yiddish (which I loved) that peppered his speech, the seemingly vast store of Jewish knowledge he had, all wrapped up in a great blanket of warmth and openheartedness. I was deeply touched by the encounter with him, and when I was a senior, then president of Hillel, I invited him back. That was the true beginning of our lifelong friendship and mentorship. Although we diverged in some important ways, I owe him more than I can say. More on Zalman below.

An important part of my life as a budding Jewish scholar was lived in the bowels of the old Brandeis University library. For two years I supported myself with a part-time student job as an assistant to the Judaica librarian Al Greenbaum. A onetime student of Simon Rawidowicz, Greenbaum still carried the torch for his much-lamented mentor and his Hebraist philosophy, although he was Orthodox, unlike Rawidowicz. He was a kind of walking bibliography, a lover of Jewish books of all sorts as well as a constant chatterer and sharer of information. I learned a great deal from him.

In the summer of 1959, I was employed at my first full-time job, working my way into the role of assistant Judaica cataloguer at the library. Huge numbers of Jewish books were being donated to Brandeis in those years, a very large percentage of them in Yiddish, leftovers of the immigrant generation's passing. These were the days before the National Yiddish Book Center, and Brandeis seemed the natural place to send such things. Part of my job was to sort through these unsolicited gift collections and see what was worth adding to the library's holdings. Probably thanks to Rawidowicz's influence (he was a rare lover of both Hebrew and Yiddish, and supposedly a great orator in both), Brandeis did collect Yiddish books. Its policy, however, was not to catalogue or accession translations from world literature *into* Yiddish. Hence multiple sets of Guy de Maupassant, Tolstoy, Henrik Ibsen, and nearly everyone else in nineteenth-century European literature were heaped on the discard pile, along with seemingly endless editions of Shalom Aleichem, Peretz, and other Yiddish classics. (My very favorite title among the translations was Nietzsche's *Azoi Hot Geredt Zaratustre!*) From left-wing families came copies of *Das Kapital* and histories of the Jewish labor movement, both in Europe and in the United States. These were often accompanied by a single brown-paged *siddur* and high holiday *mahzor*, usually published in Vilna or Piotrkow, left over from the prior generation, telling a whole multigenerational family narrative, much like that of my own father's family. From more pious quarters there tumbled in *humashim* from Lemberg, *Mishnayot* from Vilna, occasionally a whole Vilna *Shas*, and endless prayer books from the Hebrew Publishing Company in New York.

In addition to working through these mostly unwelcome gifts, I began to get involved with cataloguing more serious acquisitions. This led to an involvement with Hebrew bibliography and an appreciation of early works. Catalogues and bibliographic tools by such as Steinschneider, Zedner, and Friedberg became regular companions. I was still several years away from considering myself a book collector, but I was developing knowledge that would eventually lead me in that direction. My fascination with all things old and eastern European continued, so the discovery of Hebrew books printed in such obscure and wonderfully interesting-sounding places as Minkowicz, Bliezorke, and Nowy Dwor certainly began to catch my attention. There I was, back in the Ukraine or Poland, the "old country" that had fascinated me since childhood.

About midway through college, my Orthodox period came to a crash-and-burn end. I decided I was no longer a believer, and that I had been hanging onto religion for all sorts of neurotic reasons, left over from the death of my mother and a rather awful adolescence with my angry father. On the eve of my eighteenth birthday, I went out to a local diner and ate two non-kosher hamburgers. (I used to say that after the first I might have still repented, but the second sealed the deal.) I gave up observance suddenly and quite completely.

Yet I remained very connected to Jewish life, in a cultural way. I was committed to the study of both Hebrew and Yiddish. Having been fascinated by Jewish learning ever since those summers back in camp, I was not about to give it all up. So I went in search of a secular Jewish identity, trying out both Zionism and Yiddishism. A single memory stands out that will tell you something of what it was like for me in those days. As a rare bird in intensely seeking a secular Jewish identity, I quickly became chair of Brandeis's small Student Zionist Organization, actively supported by Boston's Zionist House and the local Israeli consul. During the summer of 1959 or 1960, word came down from the consulate that an Israeli couple in town was hosting a "party," meaning (to them, but poorly communicated) an evening to talk with young American Jews who might be considering 'aliyah. In the course of hanging around the Bick (Harvard Square's Hayes-Bickford cafeteria, the main "beat" hangout in those days), I responded to the usual "Where's the party?" query by handing out the couple's address. Needless to say, within hours this earnest young religious couple were overrun by hundreds of half-drunk or stoned kids, most of them not Jewish, who had no idea they were attending a very different sort of "party." Not my best hour of leadership, one might say, but it speaks volumes about my identity confusion at that particular point. Needless to say, I didn't last very long as a budding Zionist leader.

Another piece of secular Jewish identity I tried on in that period was that of Yiddishist. During my junior year, Brandeis for the first time offered regular courses in the Yiddish language. They were taught by Michael Astour, a recent immigrant from the Soviet Union, where he had spent many years in a Siberian prison camp as a non-Communist Jewish intellectual (originally from Vilna). Astour was actually at Brandeis to study antiquity with Cyrus Gordon, but he was happy to teach Yiddish, a personal love that he shared well. The "advanced" Yiddish class had all of two students, a young woman named Esti, who had graduated New York's Peretz School, and myself, armed with my own unique blend of my grandparents' broken-Yiddish conversation, many childhood hours spent trying to decode their daily Yiddish newspaper, some high school and college German, and my fairly good Hebrew and traditional knowledge. The latter meant that what was hardest or most esoteric for Esti was easiest for me. We had a great time reading the Yiddish classics, being the youngest attendees by half a century at some lectures of Boston's Yiddishe Kultur Klub, and meeting poet Itzik Manger when he came to speak, finally watching him pass out drunk on the Astours' living room couch.

By my later years in college, the very beginning of interest in Eastern religion was also stirring around campus. We'd all had our first exposure to an idealized and spiritual East through Hermann Hesse's *Siddhartha*, a big book during my freshman and sophomore years (it went along with *The Little Prince* and Erich Fromm's *The Art of Loving*), but now we were on to D. T. Suzuki (followed later by the authors of the various "Zen and the Art of . . ." books). The Zen ideals of attaining perfection through silence and meditation were attractive to us partly for their countercultural valance. They represented the utter rejection of the fast-paced (but not nearly as fast as now!) struggle-to-get-ahead careerism of America, and perhaps of American Jews in particular. These Eastern teachings, as presented to us, did not seem much like "religion" as we knew it, bearing little of either dogma or guilt-producing moralism. (Of course we had never met young people who had grown up Buddhist, but that did not occur to us.) I shared much of this attraction to a different sort of experience-based spiritual teaching and read and thought a good deal about it, though I was never significantly drawn to Eastern practice, except for the love of silence itself, especially when shared with others.

It was in the midst of this questing that I came back to the realization that I was, in fact, a religious person after all. This did not mean that I accepted the conventional religious "answers" I had once tried to give myself to the great challenges confronting belief. Nor had I come to aspire to the sort of bourgeois-*balebatish* lifestyle enjoyed by the Orthodox as I'd come to know them at Young Israel of Brookline, for example. Not at all! "Being religious" to me meant that the quest for infinity and even for intimacy with the infinite was somehow still real in my life, that the sacred was still a quality of life that I knew to be real and sought to encounter. This persistence of my self-identification in religious terms, even after the big break with observance and various experiments in both social and ideological realms, was certainly due in significant part to the influence of my teachers, especially Altmann and Glatzer. I still recall a sermon Altmann preached (or was it a guest lecture?) at Young Israel in 1959 or 1960, shortly after his arrival. It was on the origins of the *kedushah* prayer and its roots in the Merkavah mystical tradition. I felt that I was witnessing this very proper and conservative scholar transcend himself at the climax of his talk, rising up to enter the angelic chorus calling out, "Holy, holy, holy!" I was ready to join him. Significantly, it was the religious enthusiasm that came out in his teaching that impressed me, not his piety as expressed in prayer or observance.

During my senior year, either Altmann or Zalman gave me an essay by Hillel Zeitlin called *"Yesodot ha-Ḥasidut,"* "The Fundaments of Hasidism." As I read it, I had a compelling sense that I knew Zeitlin was speaking the truth, even *my* truth, in a way that was quite shocking to me. His discussion, opening with Being and Nothingness (I had been reading Sartre's book with the same title not much earlier), put Hasidism into philosophical terms that rendered it entirely acceptable to me. I began to see a hasidic Judaism as a response to the alienation and absurdity that had come to open such a gaping hole in my intellectual life, probably best epitomized by my involvement with Sartre, Camus, and especially Franz Kafka. It was not about "believing in God," and was certainly not about renewed authority of *halakhah*. Rather, it was focused on plumbing mysteries of existence, of reaching toward the infinite, but doing so through the very beautiful gateway of kabbalistic symbolism. I was hooked. I knew this would be my religious language for the rest of my life, and I promised that I would translate that essay into English. I did so only fifty years later, when I edited a collection of Zeitlin's writings.

At about the same time, Professor Altmann also introduced me to the world of phenomenological *Religionswissenschaft*, getting me to read Rudolph Otto and Mircea Eliade, among others. These lent an intellectual respectability to my interest in mysticism, a sense that I did not have to choose between religious seriousness and academic honesty. No such choice seemed necessary, especially because my models of religiosity, Altmann and Glatzer, were themselves academics. I was already on the course of looking toward religion for a deeper truth and perspective on life than anything that had been offered by my newfound secularism. I understood, as one already post-Orthodox in experience and orientation, that this was a truth to be found across the diversity of human religious cultures, rather than as the exclusive property of my own religious tradition. A vague sense that this mystical Judaism might emerge as my Western alternative to Zen was beginning to take hold. By the time I graduated Brandeis, I would say that there was a small cadre of friends there who were beginning to treat me as a serious religious thinker/scholar in the making.

By my senior year in college I was starting to build a library of Hebrew books, especially those of the mystical tradition. I discovered Biegeleisen's Hebrew Book Store, then still on the dying Lower East Side. I developed the habit of writing my name, in Hebrew, on the flyleaf of those books, and (in the early days; I dropped it afterward) the year of acquisition. My copy of the *Sefer Ba'al Shem Tov* says 1959/60. By the time I graduated college, I was regularly attempting to study both Zohar and Hasidism on my own. I was also finding great meaning in the Yiddish and Hebrew poetry of the postwar years: Glatstein, Leivick (I read them with difficulty, but I struggled to do so), Uri Zvi Greenberg, and others. Their outcry against heaven bore witness to an ongoing religiosity, a religiosity of protest, to which I fully subscribed. A pretty odd twenty-year-old, I guess, but it didn't seem so in those days.

Graduating college, I knew I wanted to become a scholar of the Jewish mystical tradition. This was both a personal and academic passion. In order to do this, I knew, I would have to first gain a knowledge of classical Jewish sources, especially Talmud, as well as great fluency in medieval Hebrew and Aramaic. There were only two places to engage in such study, as far as I was concerned: Jerusalem's Hebrew University and the Jewish Theological Seminary in New York. I took them on in that order.

In summer of 1961, this newly minted BA in Jewish studies went off to Jerusalem for a year. I sat in on Professor Scholem's lectures (the topic was "Origins of the Kabbalah" that year, if I recall rightly) and I took a readings course in Zohar with Dr. Rivka Schatz. There we read through a section of Zohar (*shelaḥ lekha*), which I found utterly fascinating, and where I gained some significant skills. To support myself during that year, I got a job teaching English at a night school run by an organization called the Religious Working Youth. My students were almost all teenagers growing up in immigrant homes from the East: Iraq, Kurdistan, and Persia (the North Africans went to a different school, for some reason). This, too, was an important Jewish educational experience for me, exposure to a whole world of Jews and Judaism that had nothing to do with Yiddish or eastern Europe. I probably learned as much from my students that year as I did from my teachers. Of course, I also fell in love with Jerusalem, to which I have never ceased returning.

The following year, I enrolled in a five-year course of study at the rabbinical school of JTS. From the outset, I found the place disappointing and even wounding to my own sense of self as a serious adult student. I found that teachers "took attendance" in class, something that no one had done in that way ("reading the roll," they used to call it) since junior high school. Some of my fellow students were bright and serious, but others were distinctly immature, reading newspapers (sports pages, mostly) during Talmud class and being openly disrespectful in other ways as well. An aura of cynicism hung over the more intellectual students, a sense that we had "seen through" the primitive claims of tradition (biblical literalism, revelation, the authority of *halakhah*) and were just "playing the game," partly to maintain our place in the institution, partly to appease either parents (hardly true in my case!) or some unenlightened corner of our conscience. While I shared some of that sense, particularly with regard to *halakhah*, a garment I chose to wear rather lightly, I also continued to understand myself as a spiritual seeker, one nourished increasingly by my readings in hasidic sources, with which I filled many hours. Most of the seminary's faculty, a solidly nonspiritual lot, had very little understanding or appreciation of this. I like to say that I walked around JTS with a copy of Allen Ginsberg's *Howl* in one pocket of my jeans and the *Kedushat Levi* (a well-known hasidic classic) in the other; both were equally unwelcome at the seminary.

My first Talmud teacher at the seminary was Seymour Siegel. A well-trained Talmudist, he was just becoming interested in the mystical tradition. He therefore chose to teach the tractate Ḥagigah in that year, the text containing much of early Jewish mystical lore. This was a great boon to me, and Siegel and I achieved a certain rapport over our interest in it. By the end of the year he saw how deeply unhappy I was at the seminary, indeed that I was seriously considering leaving. Siegel did me two great favors. First, he convinced Abraham Joshua Heschel to take me on as a special student, his first in quite a few years. I was to undertake a research project under Heschel's guidance and was also to enroll in a small weekly seminar taught in his cluttered, smoke-filled office, with four or five (later a few more) other students. I was exempted from all "practical rabbinics" classes and was placed in an advanced Talmud group, all indicating that the seminary recognized me as one training for a career of scholarship, rather than the pulpit. I was most gratified by this arrangement and decided to stay. Siegel also introduced me to Rivka Horwitz, a onetime Scholem student living in Teaneck, New Jersey, who was looking for a partner in the weekly study of Zohar. Rivka, later a leading scholar of Buber and Rosenzweig, taught me much as we read Zohar across her kitchen table, and she became a lifelong friend to my wife and me. We had many significant conversations across multiple kitchen tables over several decades.

During those seminary years, I was beginning to take my own spiritual life more seriously. Annoyed by the seminary synagogue (faculty only were permitted to sit in the front rows, students at the rear; in 1964 that felt a little like a Birmingham bus), I usually spent Shabbat mornings at what was called Rabbi Vorhand's *shtibl* on West 90th Street. Although the plaque on the building read, "Chief Rabbi of Prague," that meant only that he had been the head of the hasidic survivor community in that city briefly in about 1947. Actually he and most of the Jews there were from Munkatch (Mukachevo), a very different part of onetime Czechoslovakia, all Holocaust survivors and their children. The little room was a hothouse of spiritual intensity. I remember one Reb Shia who would bang on the wall and seemingly holler at God as he prayed. Others paced back and forth, praying at their own pace, only coming together for *kedushah* or other communal moments in the prayer service. A fine Hungarian *cholent* followed the service, something that probably also helped me to become a regular. For a while there was a little boy, a recent immigrant from Romania, who used to sing *zemirot* in an incredible soprano voice at *se'udah shlishit* in the *shtibl*. (On Shabbat mornings he sang in the all-male choir of a nearby fancy Orthodox synagogue.) If you ask me where I really learned to *daven*, it was first in my grandparents' *shul*, as a child, and then again in Rabbi Vorhand's *shtibl*. At the same time, I began to ask myself questions like "Why can't there be a *shtibl* for non-Orthodox Jews?" Why do liberal synagogues have to be big, formal, and pretentious, when real *davening* is so intimate, personal, and completely informal? Here was the *ḥavurah* being born.

JTS was known, of course, for its fine Talmud faculty and its devotion to classical rabbinic legal studies. During my years there I did develop a degree of skill at reading and explicating Talmudic dialectics, now long neglected. I also developed an appreciation for the keen minds and verbal skills of those who could engage in and clearly articulate the complex web of argumentation that appeared on nearly every page. Chaim Zalman Dimitrovsky was the great master at this; I enjoyed his classes as a kind of exquisite demonstration of dialectical brilliance. There was true aesthetic pleasure in seeing him outline a *sugya* in his mind, and sometimes on the blackboard. He also spoke a particularly beautiful Hebrew. My personally favorite Talmudist, Weiss Halivni, was less clear an expositionist. He was always six steps ahead of the argument and assumed we were all there with him, an error in judgment regarding his students. Other Talmudists on the faculty were less impressive to me, especially arousing my ire by the way they treated less successful students. I had a classmate who was very dear to me, a very bright fellow, but afflicted with a dyslexia that made it almost impossible to read Hebrew sources aloud (let alone Aramaic!). His teachers made his life miserable, and I watched in silent anger and chagrin.

Although I took some pleasure in the skill of mastering Talmudic texts, I never became a serious Talmudist. I just did not have enough interest in the subject matter to stay with it. I was not engaged by questions of the civil code or by property law. Had I not been "bitten by the Jewish bug," I never would have thought of becoming a lawyer. (Maybe a literature professor, maybe an antiques dealer, maybe a chef—but never a lawyer.) What I liked best in Talmud were the tractates of *Mo'ed*, the discussions of ritual, and of course the Aggadah, which some of our teachers insisted on skipping. I remember peeking ahead on the page to see where some interesting Aggadah might show up and offer relief from the legal discussion.

The section of the Talmud called *Nashim*, "Women," was more difficult than the civil code. Although I cannot claim to have yet been a feminist in the mid-1960s, those sensibilities were already stirring both within and around me. Something was deeply wrong with the serious and unquestioning way we were being taught this. Once, I recall, several of us were preparing for Professor Saul Lieberman's class on the first chapter of the tractate *Ketubot*, dealing with marriage contracts. The text opens with, "A virgin should get married on Wednesday, so that if the husband claims that he did not find evidence of her virginity, he can go directly to the court, which meets on Thursdays." How convenient for the husband! There is then a long discussion of when and how virgins are to be married. A few pages on, the Talmud asks about virgins getting married on the Sabbath eve. The question then becomes whether one is allowed intercourse with a virgin on the Sabbath, since breaking the hymen might be considered an act of tearing, which is forbidden by Sabbath law. In the discussion, the rabbis suggest an analogy to breaking open a pimple on the Sabbath, bringing along the following question: "Does he break the pimple in order to have it broken (i.e., to improve appearance) or to remove the pus that lies within it?" If it is the pus he is after, this act might be considered "work for a sake other than its own," which, although technically forbidden, is not a punishable Sabbath violation. Once we had stumbled through the Aramaic and realized (with the help of RaSHI and Adin Steinsaltz) just what a *mursa* ("pimple") was, I recall getting up, slamming the *gemara* shut, and announcing to my fellow students, "Sex is not like picking pimples!" I stalked out of the room.

I stayed and spiritually survived at JTS largely because of Heschel. Now it's time to say something about him and our relationship. Let me begin it this way. People used to say that JTS in those days was a train running on the Vilna–Berlin–New York express line. It couldn't decide if it was a Lithuanian *yeshiva*, a Berlin *Institut fuer die Wissenschaft des Juden-tums*, or a training school for New York–area rabbis (anything west of the Hudson remained essentially unknown and uninteresting). The problem for Heschel was that he was not on that train. He was a *ḥasid* from Warsaw, with roots in the Ukraine. True, he had gone through his Berlin period. But now, in the face of the Holocaust, he was most interested in being a spokesman for the vanished world of prewar east European Jewish spiritual life, featuring a passionate relationship with a personal God fraught with strong mystical undertones, the religion of Hasidism. This religion was not welcome at the seminary; it was not yet considered "mainstream Judaism." Heschel's regular teaching assignments consisted of alternating courses between Maimonides and Judah Halevi, two classical figures of medieval Judaism. Heschel knew this material well, but resented the assignments and taught poorly, not preparing for classes and paying little attention to his students. His little seminar on Hasidism, taught on his own time, was quite different. Though here too he could hardly have been described as a pedagogue, he led the group with enthusiasm and offered personal insights and stories that we considered gems. It was a privilege to be in his presence, even during the year or more when he read to us from the long, rolled-out galley sheets of his *Torah min ha-Shamayim*, about to be published. I remain tremendously indebted to the Jewish Theological Seminary for having given me the opportunity to study so closely with him.

Heschel gave me the huge assignment, over the course of two years, of reading through Rabbi Meir ibn Gabbai's *'Avodat ha-Kodesh*, a sixteenth-century kabbalistic summa, and writing a paper on it. I did so (about eighty pages in Hebrew), but could never be sure that he had read it. I came to realize that Gabbai's main theme, that our worship fulfilled a divine, and not just a human, need, was the key to Heschel's own philosophy, indeed encapsulated by the phrase *God in Search of Man*, title of his theological magnum opus. In giving me Gabbai, he had in a sense proffered to me the key with which to open the treasure house of his own understanding of Judaism, a fact it took me many years to fully discover. No matter (this too took years to accept!) that he never read my paper; I had been shown a way inside.

But distance remained between us. He was still the great theologian and seminary professor, while I was the student. Unlike some others, I was not ready to be a fawning disciple. In different ways, I should note, I turned away from discipleship with both Heschel and Zalman, two figures with whom many others sought just that sort of relationship. I was too independent for that. Or perhaps too ornery. Or perhaps too frightened of submission. I wrote a paper for Heschel, "The Possibility of Petitionary Prayer," that he found disturbingly questioning; my emerging theology, even then, was significantly to the "left" of his. Along with many seminary students, I found Richard Rubenstein's newly published (1966) *After Auschwitz* to be a breath of fresh air, someone daring to say what we were all thinking. He was early in saying that post-Holocaust Jewish theology could not go on pretending that nothing transformative had happened. It was now fully clear that God did not act in history, and we needed to admit that truth. You could not mention Rubenstein's name in Heschel's presence. He was a *talmid she-sarah*, a onetime Heschel student who had "gone bad," blaspheming by uttering the phrase "God is dead." Although Heschel was himself a Holocaust survivor, having lost his mother and sisters in the Warsaw ghetto, he did not let anything but love of God and beauty of both creation and Torah emerge from his lips. Only at the end of his life did he dare let out that the Kotzker skeptic was as strong a voice within him as the Miedzybozh (i.e., Ba'al Shem Tov) devotee.

In our last conversation, several months before his sudden death (in 1972, five years past my ordination), I found myself saying to him: "Professor Heschel, it never quite worked between us. When I needed a professor (as in reading and commenting on my papers) you wanted to be a *rebbe*. And when I needed a *rebbe* (on the edge of pouring out my heart), you kept to the role of professor." And then he was gone.

But I was wrong. I had learned a tremendous amount from him, and I have continued to do so, teaching him over and over again (especially his *Torah min ha-Shamayim*), respecting him greatly, and arguing with him (now unfortunately one-sidedly) for over half a century. Heschel taught me how to read both *aggadah* and *ḥasidut*, taking note of their own careful interpretations of the biblical sources, but then also mining them for the rich spiritual insights that emerged from their language, sometimes even from half-stated assumptions to be found between the lines. There was no one like Heschel for offering a deep insider's appreciation for the native language of this Jewish narrative theology, and I was greatly privileged to learn it from this unique master. Much of the skill that I have passed on to my students—and demanded of them—was a gift from him.

On graduating rabbinical school, I returned to Brandeis for doctoral studies with Professor Altmann. An alternative plan had been to go to the University of Chicago to work with Mircea Eliade, applying his methodology to Jewish mystical texts. But I heard from my friend Max Ticktin, the Hillel director at Chicago, that Eliade had little interest in Judaism, and was not likely to be sympathetic. (This was years before Moshe Idel devoted so much energy to uncovering Eliade's pro-fascist past.) I decided Brandeis was the safer course, but that decision clearly kept me inside the world of Jewish learning, rather than in the broader history of religions field. I also briefly considered going back to Israel to work with Scholem, but was advised by many that he was notorious for his bad relationships with students, and that he had low regard for most Americans. I knew that Altmann was a wise, generous teacher and always a gentleman. It made sense to go back to him.

When I got to Brandeis, Professor Altmann laid out his plan for me. "If you want to be a Kabbalah scholar," he insisted, "you will need to acquire medieval Latin and Arabic, in addition to the Jewish languages. Eventually you will do the same sort of dissertation as several others among my doctoral students, editing one of the Hebrew writings of Rabbi Moses De Leon from manuscript, and producing a critical edition."

It was 1968. The world was burning around us. Vietnam had poured out into the streets of New York and Cambridge. The Six-Day War had just passed, and a renewed concern for Israel's survival was much on our minds. The cultural and spiritual revolution, partly spurred on by our generation's discovery of psychedelics, was transforming our consciousness. This was not an easy time to concentrate on learning Latin and Arabic for a future career as a medievalist.

It was during that first year as a doctoral student that I, along with several others, developed plans for Havurat Shalom, a story that does not belong here. When we opened the Havurah, in the fall of 1968, I was there in the role of teacher. The sort of learning we did together in those first years at Havurat Shalom has been the model for all my teaching ever since, especially in the two rabbinical schools that I have had the privilege to lead. The aridity of the university classroom was something we sought to leave behind. Yes, we accepted the various conclusions of critical scholarship, and at times were enthusiastic in learning about them and discussing them. There was no resistance to historical method. But we also understood, almost instinctively at first, that it did not suffice for us. We sought—and often found—in the sources, despite all that we knew of their origins and authorship, something of *divrey Elohim ḥayyim*, the living

word of God. This transformative way of learning and teaching continues
to this day—just over fifty years later—to be one from which I continue
to learn and be nourished, on a daily basis. This, too, was a gift from my
teachers—even though in 1968 it felt like a rebellion against them.

After four years of devoting much more energy to the Havurah than
to my doctoral studies, I went back to Professor Altmann and said: "I want
to write a book on Rabbi Naḥman of Bratslav. Will you accept that as a
dissertation topic?" To my great joy, he agreed. Hence was born *Tormented
Master*.

In recalling the Havurah years, I want to go back to Reb Zalman and
try to convey something of what I feel I learned from him. Although never
my teacher in a formal way, he gave me a great deal, and I feel that much
of who I am and what I do in Jewish life has everything to do with our
relationship and what he taught me.

In about 1964 Zalman published an article in *Judaism* magazine called
"Toward an Order of Bnai Or." In it he proposed establishing a Jewish monastic community, consisting of couples and families that would take vows
of commitment to one another and to God's service. In this first iteration
of Bnai Or (quite far from what it later came to be), these people would
live in close community, serve as a laboratory of Jewish liturgical and spiritual creativity, and would lead retreats and publish materials leading toward a neo-hasidic spiritual awakening among American Jews. Zalman
had been inspired toward this vision by a number of influences, including
frequent visits to Catholic monastic communities, the call to Yavneh, or a
new Hasidism, by Hillel Zeitlin in interwar Poland, and especially, so he
said, by the rediscovery of the Dead Sea Scrolls. The dream of Qumran—
or his fantasy of what Qumran had been—held great fascination for him.
The name Bnai Or ("Children of Light") was of course taken from the
ancient scrolls. Behind all this was the intensity of his memories of youth
among Lubavitchers (especially a brief period in Antwerp), reworked in
the years when he knew that his own final break with that community was
becoming inevitable.[1]

Zalman and I were first really close in the years between 1965 and
1970. This closeness had much to do with my increasing love affair with
the hasidic sources, his move away from Lubavitch in quest of a more contemporary setting for his spiritual quest (something to which I fit in per-
fectly), and both of our discoveries of psychedelics. Zalman first tripped in
1963, I in 1965. Both of us were bursting, in those days, with insights into
the parallels between things we had experienced and muted testimonies

to such experiences in the sources of Hasidism that we both read, taught, and loved. We would send each other copies of our holy books with underlinings and exclamation points in the margins, and we exchanged tapes where we spoke with great intimacy about things we had seen and heard, touchings of the upper (or "inner," as we both insisted) worlds.

In 1964, Zalman introduced me to my beloved and now much-lamented wife, Kathy, known to us then as Sister Kreindel, another candidate for that Bnai Or community. Zalman officiated at our wedding in 1968, and we remained very close to him throughout the nearly fifty years of our marriage. We last saw him at Kathy's seventieth birthday celebration, just two weeks before his passing. While that Bnai Or community never came to be, my involvement in founding Havurat Shalom had everything to do with a transposition of Zalman's original dream into the context of the 1968 counterculture, something in which he too was by then an enthusiastic participant (in some ways more than I).

I was especially delighted that Zalman was able, due to a sabbatical, to spend the first year of Havurat Shalom with us in Cambridge, along with his new wife, Malka. The four of us were very close, and spent many wonderful *shabbatot* and holidays together. He taught several people at Havurat Shalom how to *daven*, leading the traditional *tefillah* with great openheartedness and passion, a style that they in turn carried into the world of the Jewish counterculture.

Above all, I think, Zalman represented to us a deep sense of Jewish authenticity. He was of the youngest generation possible to still remember pre-Holocaust Europe; that was of great significance to us *Amerikaner*. Although his family had in fact spoken German at home in Vienna (Galician Jews seeking some small degree of assimilation), and he had gone to what was something like a "modern Orthodox" school there (the Chajes Gymnasium) rather than *yeshiva*, Zalman had taken on, during his Chabad years, a very Yiddishized way of speaking, and he spouted forth endless quotations of biblical and rabbinic sources, most of them learned from their settings in the many Chabad texts he had committed to memory.

Not only did Zalman possess that authenticity, he was happy and willing to share it. He was the one who allowed me to speak of the *ribboino shel oilem* or *der aybershter*, rather than of "God," and of Moishe Rabbenu and Avrohom Avinu rather than Moses and Abraham. These symbolic changes in language in fact made a tremendous difference, not only for those whom I taught, but upon my own ability to feel like an "insider" in conveying the tradition. That was who I wanted to be, and Zalman, more than anyone else, saw that in me, shared the goal, and enabled it to happen. It was that desire to teach from within, conveying the tradition, however updated, from one generation to the next, that determined my pattern—carried out three times in the course of my lifetime—of leaving behind the university and its insistence on (at least a pretense of) outsider stance toward the tradition. Instead, I sought out more intimate and informal settings, communities in which I could carry forward the gift he had given me of passing on Torah as a living torch to ever-new generations of disciples and future leaders.

In choosing to conclude this narrative here, I by no means intend to say that my Jewish education ended in 1975, when I received my PhD. I continue to learn, of course, and every student, every class, and every publication project has been part of that ongoing education. I continue to be intrigued by the fact that in premodern Yiddish (unlike Hebrew) there is no separate verb that means "teach." *Lernen* is the act in which both "teachers" and "students" are engaged together. I tell my students that the rabbinate is the original career of lifelong learning. It has been a great privilege to engage in it with them over the course of these many decades.

My Rabbinate

A FIFTIETH-ANNIVERSARY REFLECTION

An abbreviated version of this text was delivered at Hebrew College's
Rabbinical School *semikhah* ceremony on Sunday, June 4, 2017.

TODAY MARKS THE FIFTIETH anniversary of my ordination as a rabbi. I was ordained on June 4, 1967—the day before the outbreak of the Six-Day War. It was a moment of high drama for all involved. Elie Wiesel was the graduation speaker; the air was thick with tremors of a new Holocaust, while we as a community were just beginning to fully absorb the shock of the last one. America was deeply engaged in the Vietnam War, and all the great social traumas that were to burst forth the following year were already cooking away, ready to boil over.

I had come remarkably close to missing that event. I was a pretty radical young man in those days. Within weeks of graduation, I had been ready to tell the institution that I wanted no part of its degree, that the rabbinate had become so corrupt an institution, and the title so debased, that I would not be able to accept it. That was 1967, after all. Even two years later, I published a now embarrassingly self-righteous piece in a *Judaism* magazine symposium, where I complained about the vacuousness of synagogue life and railed against rabbis who shared the bourgeois lives and values of their congregants. If you want to be generous, you may call it my Heschelian prophetic period.

Yes, I was young and foolish. But not quite *that* foolish. I did accept the degree and promptly began to make good use of it. Without it, I could hardly have founded Havurat Shalom, which in some ways served as the cornerstone of what has become a lifelong involvement with teaching rabbis and other leaders as a step toward reconceiving a future North American Jewish community. Three times in the course of my career I have turned away from a relatively successful career in the secular academy to work in smaller and more intimate settings, training future rabbis. My wife, Kathy, used to say that some guys, when they reach a certain age, get a little red sports car every few years. "Green gets a little red rabbinical school." My response has been that the *red* in that sentence refers mostly to the color of the ink in the ledger books of those rabbinical schools (someone please explain that reference to the young people), but also to the politics of some of the students who apply to them.

Why have I been doing this? I decided at some point, while in the midst of my first university teaching job, that I cared deeply about the future of the Jewish people. I felt that Judaic scholarship, fascinating as it was to me and to a few others whom I saw at Jewish studies conferences, would have little value in engaging new generations of Jews in the creative project of building that Jewish future. As American Jews grew ever farther from the memory of the immigrant generation, they were naturally ever more open to total assimilation and absorption within an increasingly welcoming American melting pot. We would need to create a new way of explaining Judaism that would speak to these generations. History itself would just not do it for them, nor would appeals to tribal loyalty or to the martyrdom of the Holocaust. I began teaching and writing that vision, something in which I am still deeply engaged. But a crucial part of what I could do for the future of Jewry and Judaism (I cared about both) was to train leaders who shared something of my vision, who could at least open and read the texts from the Jewish past that I considered most vital and exciting, and who would engage with me and after me in the questions of how to live both as a Jew and as a religious human being in what we would later come to call the postmodern world.

The texts to which I refer are those of the Jewish mystical, especially the hasidic, tradition. These had not been taught in regular courses in any modern rabbinical school, all of which had been nurtured by the traditions of *haskalah* and *Wissenschaft* (modern rationalist "enlightenment" and critical scholarship), which had openly rejected them. I knew that it was only these sources and their reading of the tradition that had saved Judaism for me. Without them, I would have sought and found my spiritual nourishment elsewhere. I suspected, already in the 1960s, that I was not alone in that need. As the decades have gone forward, I am happy and proud to have played some small role in the recovery of those sources for the Jewish mainstream, including the *nakhas* of seeing my own students writing about them, translating them, and teaching them to future generations of rabbis and others.

The shaping of the Jewish future as I envisioned it required attracting certain types of people to the task of Jewish leadership, including precisely some of those I saw turning their backs on Judaism—often for good reason—and seeking their truth elsewhere. After some experimentation, I saw that this could not be done in a denominational setting. The denominations' constant struggles over self-definition and defending turf—usually around points of ritual practice—was simply too wearying and alienating to the sorts of Jews I hoped to attract. We needed a new, informal, and intimate learning environment where those souls could flourish, finding both the nourishment and the freedom they needed to grow. Because each future rabbi is unique and has to find his or her own distinct Jewish path (translating "the roots of each soul in the Torah"—and here I was following the best of hasidic teaching), pluralism and openness were essential to the vision. That explains many of the choices I have made, especially in the founding of the Hebrew College Rabbinical School, the faculty who teach in it, and our response to questions that have emerged in the course of its existence. Of course, I wanted to help bring forth (not "produce," please) Jewish leaders who were deeply rooted in the tradition, who felt at home among the original sources. I also wanted rabbis to have the skills they needed, as educators, pastors, and communal leaders, to do their work successfully and without too much frustration. But in these things my approach was not unique. Essentially, I wanted to train rabbis who had three qualities: I wanted them to be *seekers, devotees, and lovers*. From here on I want to unpack what I mean by each of these three terms.

In the opening paragraph of my book *Radical Judaism*, I said that after fifty years of teaching and passing on the tradition, I still see myself primarily as a *seeker*. That is still the case a decade later. This means an ongoing quest to live in God's presence, to become ever more aware that "the whole earth is filled with God's glory," and to share that insight with others in ways that are stimulating and awakening, rather than dogmatic and dulling. An "ongoing" quest is one that indeed never ends, following the psalmist's advice to "seek His face always." Each day and each moment is there to offer a new opportunity to seek the face of Y-H-W-H, the ever-elusive One that stands behind all the masks that hide and reveal God at once.

I want *seekers to become rabbis* and *rabbis to become seekers*. For seekers to become rabbis requires their striking deep roots within the tradition, becoming immersed in Jewish sources, learning to speak as insiders to Judaism, while still in the course of seeking. They do not have to conclude that Judaism has all the answers they've been seeking, but they do have to own it as the *language* in which they will go forward, and lead others, in their continuing quest. To be a rabbi, one does not have to sign on to any particular theology or pattern of observance, but one does have to be able to say: "This tradition is my home, the place where I pitch my tent."

For rabbis to become seekers is the reverse, but sometimes a more difficult process. It requires a reduction of self-assurance, finding room for more questions and fewer answers. Too many rabbis have thought they need to resolve the seekers' questions, much as their ancestors engaged in *teshuvot*, responsa, to questions of religious law. In taking on this role, they felt that they had to hide their own doubts and confusion, feelings unseemly for a rabbi who was supposed to be in authority. But all that is gone now. This is a new sort of rabbinate, one in which you are qualified to be a rabbi and teacher not because you have the answers, but only because you have been seeking a little harder or a little longer, perhaps with more access to the original sources, than those around you. Your authority stems precisely from the honesty with which you admit how much you don't know.

Shmuel Yosef Agnon's *Days of Awe* recounts the following parable by Rabbi Ḥayyim of Sanz:

> A man had been wandering about in a forest for several days, not knowing which was the way out. Suddenly he saw a man approaching him. His heart was filled with joy. "Now I shall certainly find out which is the right way," he thought to himself. When they neared one another, he asked the man: "Brother, tell me which is the right way. I have been wandering about in this forest for several days."
>
> Said the other to him: "Brother, I do not know the way out either. But I too have been wandering about here for many, many days. But *this* I can tell you: Do not take the way I have been taking, for that will lead you astray. And now let us look for a new way out together."[1]

That's the kind of person I would like to see in the rabbinate, and I have spent my life creating centers of rabbinic training that would welcome them. *Brothers* and *sisters* to the seekers who surround them, not authority figures who seek to quell or dismiss their doubts. I like to think of such rabbis as faithful descendants of our father Abraham: the original iconoclast, spiritual adventurer, and religious experimentalist, who set us all off on an endless journey.

Finding God or truth cannot be put off to the end of that quest, since it never ends. But we come to learn that *the finding takes place within the seeking*, that they are indeed one. This discovery is the cause of great celebration and gratitude, an oft-repeated moment of awareness, *da'at*, that leads us from seeking to *devotion*.[2]

Every observer of Jewish life knows that rabbis are not a daily presence in the lives of most liberal Jews, including those who belong to their congregations. But rabbis do play a crucial role in essential moments in the life cycles of those Jews, when they are called upon, completely out of context, to "make meaning" in a profound and personal way. To do this in an authentic manner, the rabbi her- or himself has to be rooted in the ongoing quest of which I speak. A key part of being a rabbi is one's own engagement in the great challenge of our lives as mortals, the significance of our brief moment of existence, and the meaning of our inevitable encounters with death, first of our loved ones, then our own. A rabbi has to find something to say about these weighty matters, based on Jewish tradition, and has to learn to articulate it well, and with great sensitivity, to each unique moment, family, and situation. To this we have to add reflection on our place in the ongoing history of our Jewish and Western civilizational journeys. In our day, we need to add also thoughts on our relationship to the natural environment and the evolutionary journey of which we are all a part.

The rabbi as *devotee* should begin each day with a prayer of gratitude for the great privilege (and responsibility) of serving as spiritual guide to others. The life of quest has to become one of service, both to God and to the community. The phrase *ana 'avda de-qudsha brikh hu*, "I am a servant of the blessed Holy One," is not an easy one for people like us to utter. Modernity has made us too self-assured for that, too proud of our many accomplishments. Some of those are indeed quite impressive: fighting back disease, lengthening the human lifespan, instant cross-global communication, living in relative peace with so many diverse sorts of people. Other things about our age are terribly condemning: the ongoing rape of the planet's resources, the terrible widening gap between rich and poor, the idolatries of money, success, and superficial beauty. Realizing that mortality is still with us, that we understand very little, and that each of us is here only for an instant in planetary history, should humble us and help us to understand that *we were placed here to serve.*

Being a devotee means cultivating one's own inner life, a necessary step in being able to serve in such a role for others. The ability to be present as a full human being in such moments of need can only come out of the rabbi's own inner religious or spiritual life. To live a life of giving to others, you need to be nourished by God's presence in your own life. Otherwise, your well will quickly run dry. To *hold* people, in their pain as well as in their joy, to pastor in an almost literal sense, you as a rabbi have to be able to draw on a great—indeed, endless—reservoir of strength, which is really not your own at all, but God's, in which you are rooted by your own faith. For a rabbi, cultivating and probing the depths of spiritual life is nothing less than a survival skill.[3]

So teaching students to become rabbis, helping each one grow into his or her own rabbinate, as we like to say it, includes instructing them on how to become devotees in their own inner lives. This includes prayer, both communal and personal. Spiritual direction and counseling also have a place. Continuing all of these throughout your rabbinate should help keep you open to that reservoir of strength and inspiration. But in our tradition the inner life is also very much nurtured by study of the sources, learned and discussed in openhearted ways, so that each rabbi's spiritual life is rooted directly in the text and language of the ages. The rabbinate is the Western world's original tradition of lifelong learning. Staying close to Torah as a great font of living waters should be an ongoing source of nurture to our own inner gardens, and hence to the rich plantings we can pass on to others.

All this begins, however, with cultivating a life of prayer. Prayer, in the broadest sense, is the best tool we have for this cultivation of inwardness. Prayer is not easy for the newcomer and is *too easy* for one used to it, who wears it like an old shoe. We have to grow constantly in our life of prayer. So too in our ongoing learning. In this way, *seeker* and *devotee* live together in our hearts. The text of our prayer book is a great help in this, if we learn to open ourselves to it. There are moments, however, when its language gets in the way. Silence, with or without special training in meditation, is also a resource to be welcomed and cultivated. So too walks in the woods or around bodies of water. Spiritual friendship, ḥevruta in the deepest sense, is also a great boost to the devotional life. Don't be without it.

Our tradition calls us to a devotional life of great simplicity. Celebrate life by singing about the daily miracles of dawn and dusk, the call of the weekly Sabbath, on which we were first told to neither light fires nor gather sticks, two beautifully Stone Age markers of a special time. We worship throughout the year by such acts as waving branches, blowing horns, lighting candles, living in huts, eating crackers. Of course these have to be the *right* branches, the *right* horns, the *right* huts, and the *right* crackers, each on the proper day of the year. But they are still acts of utter simplicity, and we must take care that this simplicity not get lost amid the welter of details about how to do them "right." They are there to show us how the most ordinary of human deeds may become filled with holiness, invoking God's presence, causing us to bow down in awe while our hearts fill up with joy. Openness to this devotional life is essential to the rabbi, as it should be to every Jew, to every human being.

And now to the third point. Here comes the bumper sticker for it: *Rabbis are great lovers!* (But I *do not* recommend that bumper sticker for your synagogue parking lot!)

The Ba'al Shem Tov said that his soul had come into the world because of three loves: *the love of God, the love of Torah, and the love of all Israel.* The first neo-hasidic teachers, more than a century ago, already insisted on widening "Israel" to embrace all of humanity, everyone created in the divine image. Of the love of God we have already spoken. More on love of Torah below. But the real test of love lies in our ability to generously and unselfishly love people. Yes, that continues to mean loving Jews in a special way, because that is the community we are here to serve. There is no being a rabbi without becoming comfortable with that. We are here to be leaders of the Jewish people. We are here to stand up for the best of our tradition's moral teachings, and to guide Jews toward them. When our community turns away from those values, the failing is ours; we have not succeeded in our role as leaders. Our sages referred to themselves as *neturey karta*, guardians of the polis, of the community, many centuries before that title was grabbed by a small, self-righteous sect within the Jewish people. But our teaching is one of love that extends to all humanity, and indeed the kingdom of all God's creatures. Only that way do we give flesh and bone to *ve-ahavta et ha-shem elokekha*—"Love Y-H-W-H your God"—by manifesting it in *ve-ahavta le-re'akha kamokha*, loving one another as we love ourselves.

Ahavat Torah: For us as Jews, God's love is manifest in a special way, in the form of teachings. "You so loved our ancestors," we say each morning in *Ahavah Rabbah*, "that You became their Teacher. Give us that same grace; be our Teacher as well." We rabbis, as faithful students of divine teaching, are here to help share it with others, to pass on the teaching— and the love. God shows us love through the act of teaching. We spend our lives learning to do the same. In a sense, love is all we have to offer: our love of God, of Judaism, and of Jews. The Judaisms motivated by authority, by fear, and by guilt are all gone for most Jews. All we have is love. Everything else derives from that. But that love is *plenty*, if we know both how to share and how to replenish it in ourselves.

That is our essential truth. "The rest is commentary," as Hillel taught so long ago, so early in the formation of what was to become Judaism. But of course commentary is where all the fun is, as we Jews have known so well. We have fun in discussing, arguing over, and stretching our understanding of Torah. We've been doing that for a very long time. It must be that we enjoy it! Our way of having fun means loving, living, and learning Torah. That is the Ba'al Shem Tov's *ahavat Torah*. And it should indeed be fun, undertaken with lots of joy and even a bit of levity. That is the essential process of *talmud torah*. "Read that verse one more time. Find new meaning in it. Use it to gain an insight you never had before. Stretch your mind and a heart a little wider open. Go for it! Have fun!"

All this talk of love sounds very like Rabbi Akiva, the one who taught that "Love your neighbor as yourself" was *klal gadol ba-Torah*, the most basic rule of Torah. On this particular matter, however, I am a disciple of his friend R. Simeon ben Azzai, who insisted that "Every human is created in God's image" is a still more basic rule.[4] Seeing to it that more and more people are treated with the fullest of human dignity, and are thus enabled to discover the divine spark within themselves, is what it's all about. That is our mission as people of love. All our daily interactions with others must make this an ever-growing reality.

Love and caring for people requires involvement in lessening human suffering and injustice in our world. Never forget that the rabbinate is a lifetime dedicated to moral leadership, not just a career devoted to promulgating Jewish tradition. These two have to become inseparable in all the work you do, as well as in the image you project within your community and beyond it. This begins with highest standards of personal morality, but extends to involvement in some of the great moral causes of our day. The needs are many. All the social and political platforms that enhance this possibility must be our own. There is no separation possible between the call for love and the demand for justice. Life will tell you in which causes you need to be involved. Choose your causes wisely, but work for them vigorously and with courage.

Who would have believed, back in June 1967, that fifty years later I would be standing before a class of new rabbis who are being ordained in no less threatening times. Then it felt like there was a vital challenge to the existence of Israel, maybe even to the Jewish people. Now we stand before an existential threat to our values, to our sense of human decency, to honesty and integrity in public life, to principles of democracy and care for the poor and underprivileged that we thought could be taken for granted in our country. All this with the fate of humanity and our planet hanging precariously in the balance. "Take nothing for granted" is what we are learning again in this hour.

In such an hour, we are in need of leaders. They have to be *anshey mid-dot*, a wonderful biblical phrase that can mean "people of values," but also "people who measure up" to the needs of the hour. They need to be *seekers* of truth, *devotees* to God and to community, and *lovers* of God, Torah, and humanity. I have sought and found quite a few of those over these years, bringing them along to join in the task of building a Jewish future. I am proud that you are among them.

Becoming a rabbi is a deeply humbling moment. Looking back on one's rabbinate fifty years later is no less humbling. May we all be worthy to be called "rabbi" someday.

Pilgrimage 2019

I N THE SUMMER OF 5779 (2019), I made a pilgrimage to hasidic sites in Ukraine, accompanied by a wonderful *minyan* of dear friends and students. I would like to bring you along on that journey, the tremendous effect of which I am still trying to understand and integrate into my life as a neo-hasidic Jew and teacher. Without quite realizing it, I'd been preparing for this visit my entire life. For you to understand that, I'll have to prepare the way by sharing with you with some pieces of my memory, going all the way back to childhood.

I grew up in Newark, New Jersey, in the 1940s–50s. It was a city that then had sixty thousand Jews living in it, and some thousands of Ukrainians as well. Because my very progressive-thinking father did not want to live in what he called the all-Jewish "ghetto" of the Weequahic section, we lived in adjacent Clinton Hill, a white working-class neighborhood that included, along with many others, a hefty sprinkling of Ukrainians, as well as some Jews. Our two-family house was owned by our Ukrainian peasant neighbors upstairs, Prokip and Doshka (they had the English names of Peter and Sophie, but these were never used) Chomiak. The Chomiaks, low-skilled factory workers in Newark, had immigrated after World War I. They were salt-of-the-earth old-country peasants—and not anti-Semites. Mrs. Chomiak, my first babysitter, was especially protective of me, even telling me which other Ukrainians on the block *were* anti-Semites, and hence to be avoided. I grew up sitting at her kitchen table, listening to endless conversations in Ukrainian, watching her make endless *pirogies* (*piruheh*, in her dialect) and stuffed cabbages (*kholipches*).

My own grandparents were just as eastern European as were the Chomiaks. For reasons unknown to me, I was always attracted to the Old World. I cherished every bit of Jewish practice my grandmother told me about from tales of her home back in Lomza, in northeast Poland. My grandparents' *shul*, where Yiddish was still the lingua franca among the elderly *daveners*, was a place where I felt entirely at home. As a stamp collector—that was my chief preoccupation as a child—my very favorites were stamps of Poland, Ukraine, and Bosnia-Herzegovina (surely because of its wonderful name!).

As a young adult, I found my own way into a more serious Judaism through the portal of Hasidism, a movement that originated in that very same part of the world. A coincidence? I think not. I began by reading Heschel and Buber, but by age twenty I was deeply engaged with the original sources of Hasidism in Hebrew, books that had originally been printed in such wonderful-sounding places as Slawuta, Korzec, and Berdychiv. I began to know the names of *shtetlekh* in Ukraine and Belarus better than I knew the twenty-one counties of New Jersey, which we'd had to memorize in elementary school. My teachers, in the university and seminary worlds of the 1960s, were all ultimately from eastern Europe, overlaid with academic study somewhere to its west. Each of them, I knew, was what we called "a brand saved from the fire," a rare escapee from blood-soaked Europe.

From the time I first read it (perhaps fifty years ago), I knew that my ideal religious community was that described by Rabbi Naḥman of Bratslav in his tale *The Master of Prayer*: "He dwelt away from inhabited places . . . in that place was a river, with trees and fruit. They would eat of the fruit. They paid no attention to clothes—anything you had was all right. . . . There they would engage in prayers, songs, and praises to the blessed Holy One, along with confessions, fasts, mortifications, and the like." (In my version, of course, there'd be no mortifications or fasting, only learning, intense conversation, and soulful singing.) The woods in which this took place, of course, were the thick forests of Ukraine—the only woods R. Naḥman knew. My re-creations of that community took place in urban settings like Boston and Philadelphia, and were never quite the same.

When I became deeply involved with the study of Hasidism, those towns with the wonderful names—Miedzyrzecz, Shepetivka, Kopyczenice, and all the rest—were mythical places, existing only in the Jewish imagination. They had disappeared from the earth, cut down by the horrors of the Holocaust, and in many cases already by prior destruction under the Soviets. The fact that there were still physical locations bearing those names was irrelevant to us. They were behind the Iron Curtain, and almost certainly devoid of Jews. The *Encyclopedia Judaica*, our guide to contemporary Jewish reality in the 1970s, had an article on each such place, often paying more attention to the community's destruction than to its entire prior history. It ended its account of each place with the ritual-like sentence: "The Jewish community of X was not reconstituted after the war." End of story.

After the breakup of the Soviet Union, groups of hasidic pilgrims, along with Jewish families in search of roots, slowly began making journeys back to the old homeland, especially from Israel, which is much closer. They discovered that there were, in fact, small communities of Jews still living in many of those towns, although they, the visitors, were there more out of interest in the dead than in the living. They rediscovered gravesites of hasidic *rebbes*, great and small, and often erected new *ohalim*, small shelters, to be used as places of prayer, over their graves.

Among North American Jews, such trips were much rarer, with the exception of occasional families of Holocaust survivors. For most American Jews, Israel became the place of our ethnic pilgrimages. Irish Americans went back to visit "the old sod" in Ireland, Italian Americans went back to Italy, Greek Americans to Greece, and Jews went—and sent our kids—to Israel.

I am one of those American Jews. I love Israel; I've been back and forth thirty or forty times; I lost count long ago. But Israel is not where we come from. The truth is that I was never particularly excited, on tours with Israeli guides, to learn that we were in a place where King David had defeated the Philistines, or where Ahab or Manassah or some other king of ancient Israel had built a palace. Those connections always seemed quite distant, and rather forced, to me. Archaeological remains—including those of Galilean synagogues—were interesting, but did not really touch my soul. Similarly, I never came to think of hummus or falafel as Jewish food. Israel was a locale of forcibly transferred identity. It was fascinating and attractive, as it still is to me—but it is definitely not "where we come from," not in the sense of immediate family roots or accessible memory.

I don't know why it took me this long until I made this trip. I'd been to Soviet Ukraine once in the bad old days—in 1973, my wife and I were among the young couples sent to witness to Soviet Jews that the world had not forgotten them. But that was only a quick trip to a few major cities. (In fact, I'd been quite involved in the early years of the Soviet Jewry movement—another piece of my ex–eastern European identity.) I'd also been to Warsaw and northeast Poland once, including some hours of digging about in the Lomza cemetery, vainly seeking my great-grandparents' gravestones. But the longer trip, and especially to the Ukrainian sites I'd so long taught of and studied, took much too long to happen.

When it did, it took place in two stages. A group of Israeli academics, including some friends of mine, decided to schedule a conference on the history of Hasidism, to take place in Uman, Berdychiv, and Miedzybozh, the home of the Ba'al Shem Tov. I signed on, and Hebrew College became a co-sponsor of the conference. But I immediately felt that I wanted my first contact with these places to be of a quality unlikely in the midst of an academic conference. Hence I invited this group of some of my closest friends and students to join me on a five-day pilgrimage prior to the conference itself. We had the great good fortune of the participation of Yohanan Petrovsky-Shtern (now professor of Jewish history at Northwestern University), a native of Kyiv and also my former student, who served as our guide, native speaker, and overall helper throughout our visit.

Flying in from various places, nearly all of us first gathered at the Kyiv airport. Our flights, via London, Paris, Amsterdam, New York, and Tel Aviv, all converged to arrive within an hour of one another. We greeted one another with much love; *anpin nehirin*, shining faces, were clearly going to be a key part of this journey. Stay with me for a moment within that circle at the airport, opening up for hugs as we greet each new arrival. This will give me a chance to tell you something about our remarkable little *minyan* of happy pilgrims, and to try to share a bit of the deep feeling of love for one another that colored and deepened so much of this journey.

First let me say how it happened. Several years earlier, Yohanan invited me to take such a trip with him. I suggested that perhaps Ariel Mayse, my dear student and partner in loving and writing about Hasidism, might join us. In the end, that two- or threesome would wind up becoming a *minyan*, as other dear friends and students asked to come along. (Endless thanks to Yohanan for his patience and generosity about all this!) My old friend Allan Lehmann, with whom I have been learning *ḥasidut* since *ḥavurah* days, decided to come along. So too his son Elie Lehmann, a student whom I've seen develop from childhood through rabbinic ordination. Ebn Leader, my dear student and colleague, and a great *talmid ḥakham* in his own right, also decided to come. He brought his own very close *talmidah*, Lee Moore. When Mimi Feigelson from Jerusalem decided to join us, I'd not remembered that she and Ebn had a friendship going back many years. (It was great to see them sometimes acting like Israeli teenagers together!) Jordan Shuster is a more recent student, someone who also feels very close to both Ebn and Ariel. Getzel Davis, a graduate of our program, has been my student since Brandeis days, and is also close to both Allan (once his Hillel rabbi) and Ebn. (Ebn, Allan, Getzel, and I, along with a couple of others, study the holy Zohar together each week.) Avram Mlotek—a last-minute addition to our *minyan*—turned out to be a dear friend of Getzel's. I too had caught a glimpse of his soul listening to him as a wonderful *ba'al tefilah*. The fact that Avram, Jordan, and I are all lovers of Yiddish also created a special bond and helped warm up the group.

All ten of us are rabbis, though none of us in a conventional synagogue setting. (That's a comment in itself!) Among us, three have Orthodox *semikhah*, one Conservative (that's me!), one Reconstructionist, two private nondenominational, and four Hebrew College, also with no party label. (Yes, that adds up to eleven—one has double-dipped in *semikhah*s.) Eight men, two women—we *davened* together as a *minyan*, without any objections. In our own lives back home, we represent a fairly wide spectrum on observance, as well as lots of other things. But none of that kept us apart in any way. Poor Yohanan was the only non-rabbi in our group. We threatened to give him *semikhah* at some point—but with his teaching appointments stretching from Chicago to Munich to Lviv to Kyiv, he hardly needed our *gushpanka* ("seal of approval").

In describing us as "happy pilgrims," I mean to say something about the nature of our journey. We were there to *celebrate* the hasidic masters, to share our love for them, for their teachings, for their melodies, and for the tales about them. Although we spent most of our time visiting cemeteries and ruins, this was not meant to be a mournful journey. On the bus, during interminably long rides between places, we sang *niggunim* and studied hasidic Torah. Unlike most of the hasidic and other *ḥaredi* pilgrims we met along the way, we were not there to stretch out in supplication on the graves of the righteous, begging them to intercede for us before the Throne of Glory, seeking healing or help from some affliction. Not at all! We were there to tell them how much we loved them, and to thank them for having already blessed us so richly with their teachings, over all these years.

But, as Jews traveling in eastern Europe, we quickly discovered that you can never leave the mournful side behind on such a visit. After checking in for a night of luxury at the best hotel in Ukraine (the Ukraina, for those who want to go), we proceeded to what had to be our very first stop—the ravine at Babi Yar, where nearly thirty-four thousand Kyiv Jews were shot down in the course of two days in 1941.

We had not come to Ukraine to commemorate the Holocaust. Our focus was on Jewish life here 150 years earlier. But we knew, of course, that there would be no escaping it. Standing in the forest at the edge of that terrible ravine, now filled with the luxurious but tangled growth of trees and vines—clearly nourished by all that Jewish blood—we found ourselves far beyond both words and tears. How loudly do you need to sing that *El Malei Raḥamim* here, to awaken all those dead—and perhaps also the silent God who was present watching on that day? How slowly do you need to say *kaddish*, listening for fifty thousand—including others slaughtered here later in the war—to say their *amen, yehey shmey rabbah*s?

Minḥah in an old Kyiv synagogue, a quick dip in its *mikveh* for a couple of our guys, and then dinner at a luxurious kosher restaurant (a lot better than you can get in Boston!) made up the rest of our first day together.

The next day, Wednesday morning, we knew we wanted to start our day with *shaḥarit* together. It was *rosh ḥodesh Tammuz*. We had not, however, reserved a hotel room in which to do it. To the side of the hotel's front entrance, there was an outdoor patio with some chairs and sun umbrellas, so we *davened* there. Standing in an outdoor public place in Ukraine, there we were, eight men and two women, most in *tallit* and *tefillin*, not afraid either of anti-Semites or of some militant *ḥasidim* who might come along! It was a beautiful morning and a very powerful *davening*, a kind of "Here we are; this is who we are!" maybe addressed both to God and to the world around us, witnessed by quite a few surprised Ukrainians who happened to walk across the plaza. As it happened, the easterly direction was a glass wall of the hotel, where the sunlight caused a mirrorlike effect. I was *davening* toward the rear of the group, watching the *anpin nehirin*, the shining, happy faces of our pilgrims, and feeling terribly blessed and grateful. A *davening* moment I won't forget!

We had two destinations for that day: Chernobyl and Berdychiv. The former was the home of R. Menaḥem Naḥum, author of the *Me'or 'Eynayim*, my very favorite of the early hasidic classics. My full translation of it was to appear the following year (*The Light of the Eyes*), and three of the young folks on this journey had at some point served as my research assistants during my five years of work on it. Berdychiv was the home of R. Levi Yizḥak; I am currently working on his biography, hopefully to be completed in the coming year.

A visit to Chernobyl, as you can imagine, is no simple matter. Our minibus took us several hours northward from Kyiv, while we read some of the master's teachings together. About ten miles out of Chernobyl, we had to transfer to a special vehicle to take us inside the contamination zone. The old town of Chernobyl, I should quickly add, is in the least contaminated section, several miles away from the power plant that was named for it. We were assured that there was no danger in the couple of hours we spent there. Our special guide was disappointed—even hurt— that we did not want to see the abandoned city of Pripyet and the remains of the plant itself. In his year or more of daily guiding, he had met only one other group interested in the Jewish memory of Chernobyl—but we were the first ones he'd met who wanted to see *only* the Jewish graves and the ruined synagogue—and not the world-class attraction that draws tens of thousands of visitors each year! Strange tourists, we were!

The Chernobyl cemetery did not survive the Soviet era and the Holocaust. There are a few remains of graves on the edge of a forest. Attached to the wall of an abandoned building there is a locked, rusted metal door with a chalked-in Hebrew notice "This is the grave of the *Me'or 'Eynayim.*" Nothing more. Inside, there is a rectangular area to mark the gravesite, dominated by a large receptacle for *kvitlekh,* or petitions for prayer. We stood around it, prayed a little, sang a little, danced a little—all with lots of love and wistful sadness. This tomb—in contrast to several others we were soon to see—obviously had been neglected, probably because the nuclear accident was still fresh news when the *ḥasidim* began coming back and fixing things up in the early 1990s—and nobody wanted to do it in Chernobyl, where they were then told it was still too dangerous to visit. This work still needs to be done, and I hope to call upon the *ḥasidim* to do it.

The other Jewish site to see in Chernobyl—aside from houses peering out from amid now overgrown woodlands along the road—is the abandoned synagogue. This *shul* was that of R. Aaron, the *Me'or 'Eynayim's* grandson. That would date it from somewhere around 1850, perhaps a bit later. At that point, Chernobyl was still a major hasidic pilgrimage center, and the large synagogue was erected partly to serve those pilgrims. Perhaps R. Aharon was even competing a bit with his better-known brothers in places like Tolne and Skvira. After a particularly bad pogrom in 1920, however, R. Aaron's descendants left Chernobyl for Kyiv. There was never again a hasidic *rebbe* in Chernobyl. The Jewish community, already diminished by migration to the West, was further reduced by the pogrom and its aftermath. Although Jews remained in the town, the *shul* was closed down, probably in the 1920s, by the Soviet authorities. A faded red star on the worn façade shows that it was used in later years as a Soviet army recruiting center.

The synagogue building, surrounded by woods, is the ultimate example of a *ḥurvah*, an utterly ruined building. You can still tell which room—the one with the big windows—is the *shul*, which the *beys medresh*, with the built-in bookcase; you can follow the stairs down toward the *mikveh*, though you don't dare go down all the way. In some places, trees are already growing into the building. Floors are caving in, walls have big gaping holes, and the whole structure seems on the eve of imminent collapse. If you are looking for miracles on this little journey of ours, first on the list is the fact that I survived walking across those floors without their falling in beneath me.

We don't know if there were any Jews who came back to Chernobyl after 1945. Among those few people who returned to live there after the accident in 1986, there are surely no Jews. Nevertheless, it was a very important place for us to visit, both because of our great love for the *rebbe* and *ḥasidut* that once were centered here, and as a way of experiencing the utter destruction of what was once such a thriving center of Ukrainian Jewish life.

From Chernobyl, we got on the road to Berdychiv. These two places are worlds apart (as symbolized by the incredibly bumpy and slow roads between them!). One is a mostly abandoned townlet, with the woods growing farther and farther into it; the other is a city of about eighty thousand. Berdychiv remains something of the sleepy backwater it had already become in the nineteenth century, as the major railway lines bypassed it, and as the once famous commercial fairs moved on to Brody and elsewhere. But it is still a small city. As it happens, the world expert on Berdychiv's history was on our bus, so Yohanan told us a great deal about the place. Once the most prosperous *shtetl* in the Ukraine, the town still had about an 80 percent Jewish population at the turn of the twentieth century, and sixty or seventy houses of prayer and study. Haskalah and Yiddish literature flourished here once, alongside Hasidism. There was a Jewish population here after the war years and in independent Ukraine, mostly *shtetl* Jews who had survived the war in central Asia and had come back, perhaps to a larger and safer Jewish community than their own original towns. Even in 2000, there were a few thousand Jews. That number, following a new wave of emigration due to political and economic instability in Ukraine, is now down to a few hundred—except for small Chabad and Satmar communities (the latter running a school for girls) from outside the country. (The low cost of living in Ukraine has proved attractive to hasidic visitors, and even to a few who have chosen to stay.)

The academic conference took us back to Berdychiv the following week, including a visit to the one *shul* still left in use, something of a pathetically rundown hovel. I had the great undeserved privilege of giving a talk about Levi Yizhak right there in what had been his community. Walking around the central square of the town, one could see other former *shul* buildings, onetime Jewish homes (our guide pointed out roof-lifting *sukkah* porches to us!), and the site of the former market square, now built over by a department store. All somewhat pathetic.

Berdychiv was one of the first mass-murder sites of the Holocaust, a proving ground for what was later to take place in Kyiv. About seventeen thousand Berdychiv Jews were herded out of the ghetto and shot at what had been a military airfield outside the town.

We did not get to that site. Generally speaking, those murder sites are hard to reach, requiring lots of walking through the fields. There are now memorial tablets there, but they are seldom visited. Much more visited is the huge Berdychiv Jewish cemetery, in continual use from at least the early nineteenth century up the present, for the few Jews who remain. At its center is the *ohel* of R. Levi Yizhak, a major visiting site for groups from Israel. Levi Yizhak did not create a dynasty, but his reputation is such that his grave is probably the third most visited in Ukraine, after those of R. Naḥman and the Ba'al Shem Tov.

Arriving at the rather spacious *ohel,* we found it occupied by a group of some thirty *ḥaredi* women, engaged in a combination of prayer and singing. Most of the guys in our group immediately huddled behind the *meḥitsah,* making much of what it felt like to be on the other side of the separation barrier. I confess that I did not join them there, but just sat quietly at the back of the room. When the women left, we had the place quite to ourselves, except for a couple of locals seeking donations toward the upkeep of the place. We spent an hour or more there, mostly in silence, interspersed with a little learning and singing, eventually getting to *minḥah.* None of us felt like we were praying to Levi Yizhak, but it felt important to be praying in his presence, to be able to almost count him as one of our *minyan.* There were prayers and stories about Levi Yizhak on large posters on the wall, some in Yiddish, read aloud to us very nicely by our R. Avram.

Toward the end of that hour, I suddenly felt something was wrong. I heard Levi Yizhak calling out to me (not literally, of course): "Get out of here! Stop venerating me! You want to see a *tsaddik*—go find Hayyim Shmerl in the far corner of this *beys oilem,*" just as he would have said about

Jews in his lifetime. I felt very strongly that there was something wrong with this singling out of the tomb of one holy man to visit, when there were so many other holy Jews out there in surrounding graves whom no one was visiting at all. So we all spent some more time, maybe up to another hour, wandering around the Berdychiv cemetery. It was not easy to walk around there, and my sense was that we really needed a whole day to "cover" it well. Another reason to go back.

Leaving Berdychiv late in the day, we drove on to Zhitomir, a larger city. Sadly, we did not have time to visit the grave of Levi Yizhak's disciple, R. Aaron, who is buried there. Instead, we were headed for the very surprising location of a Chabad-run summer camp at the edge of the city. There we had our kosher dinner and night's lodging. At the coffee line and over the *netilat yadayim* sink I ran into a bunch of Chabad youth, teenagers from Brooklyn and Australia, who were there as counselors to Jewish kids from Ukraine and elsewhere in eastern Europe. *Very* impressive. Where are our *tikkun ʿolam*–infused liberal Jewish kids in that lineup?

A gorgeous morning *davening* that second day of *rosh ḥodesh*, still at that camp, overlooking a river. We were watched by a group of very *frum*-dressed teenage girls, who were terribly curious at our mixed-gender, female-led Hallel. Scandalized, perhaps, but they did not run away too quickly! We like to think we did a bit of an educational *mitsvah*.

Thursday was a day of many stops, with many bumps along the way. We wanted to take in lots of places, not staying too long at any single one. First was Polonne, to the *ohel* of R. Yaʿakov Yosef, the disciple of the Baʿal Shem Tov, the one he called "my Yossele." He was the great scholar who made his master's innovative teachings acceptable to the educated rabbinic elite, the same group that he constantly excoriated in the pages of his books. Not an easy personality, as far as one can tell from his writings, but an important figure in Hasidism's early history.

Polonne, a really small town both then and now, was an interesting visit. While most of the gang stayed in the *ohel*, talking and thinking about R. Yaʿakov Yosef, Getzel, Avram, and I wandered outside, spending our time instead looking at the more recent graves. Polonne, now almost devoid of Jews, had an active community into early in the twenty-first century. This seems to have been one of those little places (like Shargorod and others) where some traditional Jewish life survived during the Soviet era, even in the decades after the war. Until the 1980s, we could tell, there was still someone who knew how to carve tombstones in proper Hebrew; we could see when that art died out. But it was also clear that some of these fenced-in plots were still being visited and tended, at least until recently, and that touched us deeply.

But there was another, more personal, reason why the visit to Polonne and its graveyard was important to me. Here in Boston, the tracts within Jewish cemeteries were mostly owned by *landsmanschaftn*, Jewish "hometown societies" that functioned mainly as burial agencies. Even though Boston Jewry thinks of itself as mostly *Litvak* (Lithuanian) in origin, in fact many of these *landmanschaftn* bear the names of Ukrainian towns. When the members of those groups died out over the course of the past several decades, the remaining plots were sold to other groups. Our Newton Center Minyan bought land for burial from the Polonne Society. Thus it is that my beloved wife, Kathy, who left us behind nearly two years earlier, lies in the Polonne section of the Baker Street Cemetery. One day I expect to be there next to her. It thus meant an awful lot to be in the real Polonne, looking at the graves of our "cousins" in the old country part of our shared *beys oilem*, "eternal home."

This was one of the many moments in the trip that made me think about myself and our beloved companions as essentially eastern European Jews, who only happen to have got to America, thanks to the courage and enterprise of our immigrant grandparents. Without them, of course, all of us would be lying somewhere in those murder pits, or maybe as bits of ash in Sobibor or Treblinka. Perhaps, by some lucky escape to the war years in Uzbekistan, we might have wound up back in one of these Soviet cities or towns. The point is that we are *the same Jews* as those who stayed behind. We American Jews tend to think of ourselves as having an entirely separate history, we grandchildren of *shtetl yiddelekh* lining ourselves up as noble little American descendants of Haym Solomon or Rebecca Gratz. We certainly heard more about them in what passes for "Jewish education" in this country than we did about the greats among our own ancestors, whether the *Kedushat Levi* or Shalom Aleichem, to name two Berdychiv-based Jews. It is time we see ourselves for that part of who we are.

From Polonne we went on to Shepitivka and Slavuta, two more large towns that were well known in Jewish history long ago, but now are mostly forgotten. In Shepitivka we visited the tomb of R. Pinhas Korzecer, a contemporary of the BeSHT. Here, too, we studied some of his Torah on the way into town. R. Pinhas, whose teachings are mostly preserved in epigrammatic form, is author of two of my favorite sayings, which I of course need to quote for you here. One is about prayer. "People think," he said, "that you pray *to* God. But that is not the case. Prayer itself is of the essence of divinity." When people are really praying from the heart, God is not "over there" somewhere, perhaps in heaven, either listening or not. God is right here, inside their prayers. "You, O Holy One, dwell amid the prayers of Israel" (Ps. 22:4). The other is more directly relevant here. He said: "I thank God that my soul came into this world after the holy Zohar was revealed, because the Zohar kept me a Jew." I feel the same way about the teachings of the hasidic masters themselves, as well as about the Zohar. I can't imagine what my Judaism would be like without the Ba'al Shem Tov and his disciples, if it would exist at all.

I was therefore especially grateful we made it to his little domed shrine, right there in the middle of Shepitivka. His *ohel* and one single particularly beautiful gravestone are all that are left of the old cemetery in that town (there is a newer cemetery, but we didn't get there). I was also especially grateful to some of the more agile and daring of our little *ḥevrah* who dared to climb over the fence—before we discovered that all you had to do was push the gate right open.

In Slavuta, we all listened patiently as Yohanan told us in great detail the story of R. Pinhas's son, the founder of the local printing press, and all he suffered at the hands of the czarist authorities. This was clearly a story Yohanan loved, and was prepared to share with great gusto. Both the story and the performance of it were well worth the time—especially to Reb Getzel, whose own family comes from Slavuta. He, in fact, had been there once previously, on a family pilgrimage.

During the conference, we were much helped by a wonderful fifty-some-year-old Jew, a native and resident of Slavuta. Having grown up there, the son of local Jews returned from surviving in the Soviet East, he tried *'aliyah*, but found that Israel was not for him. He came home, and now, with his fluent Hebrew, works with groups like our own. He let us in on the secret that there is still a little Jewish community in Slavuta. Not knowledgeable, not *shul*-going, but very much aware of and caring for one another. Such little groups probably continue to exist in many other such places as well.

Our final stop for the day was possibly the most powerful of the entire trip. Anipol (or Hanipol) is a really small town, in that same west-central Ukrainian district called Volhyn. I cannot even find it on my Soviet-era map. For reasons not entirely clear, it was where R. Dov Baer, the Maggid of Mezritch (or Miedzyrzecz, if you insist) moved just a few months before his death. It was the home of two of his disciples, R. Zusha and R. Yehudah Leib. The Maggid, really the founding figure of Hasidism as a historical movement, died and was buried there in 1772. R. Zusha lived there eighteen more years and finally was laid to rest next to his master, along with his friend R. Yehudah Leib.

Sometime after 1990, when Ukraine became independent, an organization called Ohaley Tsaddikim started to operate, rediscovering gravesites, cleaning out neglected cemeteries, and erecting these *ohalim* over the graves of the *rebbe*s. They did a particularly good job in Anipol, where almost all the gravestones in the cemetery are gone, leaving a large, nearly empty grassy field around the *ohel*. At the far end of the field stands a large *menorah*, a memorial to the town's martyred Jews. All of this is in a beautifully pastoral setting overlooking the River Bug.

We entered this *ohel* in total silence, staying there a long time. For Ariel, who has spent years studying, loving, and struggling to understand the Maggid, this was the highlight of the trip. For both of us, thinking constantly about that group of disciples in Mezritch, what the Maggid taught them, and what they talked about with one another, this was a terribly powerful and holy place to be. For all of us, seeing master and disciple lying side by side, especially the highly intellectual master and the seemingly "simplest" of his disciples, this was a tremendously touching place. I will go there again.

Since we are in Anipol together, I will share with you a little teaching we found along the way. It comes both in Zusha's name and in that of R. Pinhas. Learning Torah, he said, is hard for many Jews; it takes both time and patience. But everyone can do *teshuvah*, returning to God. "What is *teshuvah?*" he asked, and responded by using the word as an acronym.

> The Tav of *teshuvah* stands for *Tamim tihyeh*, "Be wholehearted with Y-H-W-H your God."
> The Shin represents *Shiviti Y-H-W-H le-negdi tamid*, "I place the divine name ever before me."
> The Vav stands for *Ve-ahavta le-re'akha kamokha*, "Love your neighbor as yourself."
> The Bet is *Be-khol derakhekha da'ehu*, "Know God in all your ways."
> The Heh is for *Hatsne'a lekhet*, "Walk humbly with your God."

Not bad, we thought, as a summation of our own religious values. What is this Neo-Hasidism of ours trying to convey? Wholeheartedness, constancy of devotion, love of neighbor, seeking God everywhere, and humility. Pretty close! All I might want to add would be a *Sin* for *simḥah*, to be sure to do it all with joy.

Thursday night was spent in a country inn in Ostrog, a town right on what had once been the Polish-Soviet border. This town was long ago the intellectual capital of Jews in the Ukraine. Such great pre-hasidic figures as the MaHaRSHA (R. Shmuel Edels, Talmud commentator) and R. Yeshaya Horowitz, author of the SHeLaH (Two Tablets of the Covenant, a great spiritual compendium) had both been rabbis there. Ostrog has a huge fortress-type sixteenth-century synagogue, but almost no Jews. The *shul* is now undergoing reconstruction, a great effort undertaken by one capable and caring individual. It will someday soon be a wonderful tourist attraction.

Friday morning took us on to Miedzybozh, the home and burial place of the Baʻal Shem Tov, and hence the unofficial capital of the hasidic "empire." This too is a small town. The houses here, as in most of the smaller places, look just like they must have in the eighteenth century, except that the thatched roofs have all been replaced by corrugated tin. (Hopefully running water and indoor plumbing have been added as well—although my guess is that it is not universal.) Old women still wear babushkas, which are named for them. Chickens run across the road, and goats are seen in many a yard. Each house is surrounded by gardens, containing both flowers—obviously much loved here—and vegetables. They look like little jungles by midsummer, just the way the Chomiaks' yard looked back in New Jersey. It all seemed quite familiar.

The conference gave me four more days—including a Shabbos—in Miedzybozh, so I felt I got to know it well, and I fell in love with it. The old cemetery, where quite a few lovely old stones are preserved, is on a hilltop, with the Baʻal Shem Tov's *ohel* in the middle. There his two grandsons are buried with him, along with R. Abraham Joshua Heschel of Apt (yes, the ancestor of my own revered teacher), who settled in Miedzybozh in the early nineteenth century. The view from the cemetery is quite spectacular, overlooking fields and farms for as far as the eye can see. Someone had left a single old metal chair out in the graveyard, behind the *ohel*, and I will confess to several hours of lovely *hitbodedut* there.

There is a visitor center, hotel, tourist shop, and kosher restaurant near the *ohel*, along with a big yard for tour busses to pull up, park, and turn around. All of this must be very odd to the residents of the little town. Whether they love it, bringing in as much income as it does, or hate it, because of ancient anti-Semitism and the way it disrupts their quiet lives—or, most likely, both—I am not privileged to know. I can say that I think things have been done with some degree of taste there, but I worry about what will happen if development continues, which it seems like it will. It is not yet too late for Miedzybozh to get it right.

The synagogue of the Ba'al Shem Tov has been beautifully reconstructed, based on photos taken by the Anski ethnographic tour, just before the First World War. Though obviously new, it was an especially lovely place to pray. A few feet up the cobblestone street from it is the *beys medresh* of the Apter, an old brick building that half survived, and is now beautifully refurbished as a place of prayer and learning.

Both Anipol and Miedzybozh came quickly to feel like holy places for me, and I need to tell you a little bit about that. Like many of us, I have always had certain private holy places in my life, mostly places where something significant had happened to me in the past, especially in the context of relationships. Jewish holy places have never worked very well for me. The *kotel*, or Western Wall, was once an important place for me to visit each time I went to Jerusalem, but no more so. It has become too tied to politics and clashes around the place of women. Its use for military ceremonies, its centrality to Yom Yerushalayim marches, and its serving as background to the cursing, shouting, and spitting at the Women of the Wall has simply ruined it for me. I find it very hard to go there any more. Of the other holy places in Israel, some just seem ridiculously inauthentic—the tomb of King David on Mt. Zion or that of Joseph in Shechem. Others, like the tomb of R. Shim'on ben Yoḥai at Meron, are so busily dominated by the pious of a different sort that I have difficulty finding my place there. The historian in me takes over, greeting them with a good deal of skepticism. But here, in Miedzybozh and Anipol, there is no question of authenticity. These graves are 250 years old, and sustained by almost continual memory, rather than being ancient sites "discovered" a millennium or more after the person was buried. And these are also the burial sites of those people who most connect me to Torah, those who "kept me a Jew." They are very powerful and very real. Yes, I still go to them more to celebrate than to supplicate. But there is a sense of sacred presence I feel in them that I have no need to deny.

For me, as a committed diaspora Jew, it is also significant that these holy places exist outside the Land of Israel. I have always known that God is present everywhere, and that where the *shekhinah* rests has an awful lot to do with where we open our hearts. Let's just say that Anipol and Miedzybozh were two places where mine cracked right open.

There were two more stops on our journey before pilgrimage met conference. These both have to do with a unique sort of Hasidism, one to which I have a special sense of connection, both as a historian and as a seeker: Bratslav (or Breslov, in the hasidic pronunciation) and Uman.

The drive from Miedzybozh to Bratslav takes about six hours. The Breslov *ḥasidim* inhabited a different district, quite far south and east from the larger centers of hasidic life. This geographic separation, made real to us by our journey, probably has something to do with their ability to create a different style of Hasidism, based on the teachings of their unique master, R. Naḥman. That Hasidism, which I have described at great length elsewhere, has much to do with spiritual struggle, longing for a sometimes absent-feeling God, and especially with the effort to overcome *meni'ot*, obstacles in one's path toward living a life of spiritual joy and fulfillment. Indeed, we were to encounter some special such *meni'ot* in this part of our journey.

Before "arriving" with you in Bratslav, I want to say a word about the scenery you encounter along the way. This part of west-central Ukraine is a land of endless farms and fields. Podolia, the area around Miedzybozh, is rolling hill country, though farmed as well. As you go south and east, the land becomes flatter. You go from field to forest, then back to fields again. The main crops seem to be wheat and sunflowers, grown for their oil, used in cooking. Huge fields of sunflowers are quite beautiful. (Here and there, in the course of our six hours, we even engaged in the *mitsvah* of helping them to grow!) Driving through the forests, your mind turns toward both parts of the past. Could this be the kind of place where R. Naḥman prayed in the woods? Would these marigolds and sunflowers be those he talked about in his teaching on the field of prayer, where you gather bouquets of words in blessing after blessing? Then, almost at the same time, you ask: Is this forest thick enough for partisans to have survived here? Is this a place I might have fled to, had I run away from a local *Aktion?*

Bratslav is a rather untouched old town, still looking much like it did long ago. Once a district capital, it is now a nearly forgotten place—except for its name being so famous among Jews. The poor farmers and shop-keepers of Bratslav must be in utter shock to see the people who come to visit their little town from Jerusalem, New York, and Boston.

There is no synagogue left to visit, and the Jewish graveyard is high on a hill, out at the far edge of the town, next to an abandoned old mill overlooking the river, again the southern branch of the Bug. It is probably a blessing that this spot is separate from the town itself. You climb up the

hill along a wooden walkway and come to the *ohel* of R. Natan, succes-
sor to R. Naḥman and leader of the Breslov community after his death.
R. Natan is the faithful disciple, the one who really shaped both the message and the community called Breslov for future generations. The spot
of his burial, amid townspeople killed in the pogroms following the First
World War, is quite beautiful, leaving you with a sense of what hasidic life
must have been like in this bucolic setting, while always under threat from
a long series of enemies: czarist police, rival (and stronger) hasidic groups,
pogromchiks both local and roaming, the Soviet anti-religious regime, and
finally the Nazis, actually here in the form of Romanian fascists who occupied this area they called Transnistria. It is hard to believe that anything
could have survived here. Only a hardy band like R. Natan's could have
made it.

Departing from Bratslav for Uman, another couple of hours away,
was actually a very touching moment for me. As we got back into our bus
and rode through the town, I could not help but think and speak of R. Naḥman, in the moment when he decided to make the same journey. Let me
tell you a bit about it.

The young R. Naḥman had come to Bratslav some seven years earlier, in 1802. After nasty fights in some other places, here he seems to
have come into his own. The townspeople accepted him, and groups of
disciples from various other nearby places—Tulchin, Nemirov, Dashev—
came on pilgrimage to visit him three times a year, but especially on Rosh
Hashanah. R. Naḥman dared to dream the biggest of all Jewish dreams:
he was going to help bring the messiah. His great-grandfather the Ba'al
Shem Tov had not succeeded at that, but now the time was right. He was
going to transform the minds and hearts of Jewry with his brilliant teachings, his soulful instructions for private prayer, and his wonderfully fan-
tastic stories, tales that would capture the Jewish imagination and rescue it
from the clutches of the evil urge.

While allowing himself these grand dreams, however, Naḥman was
also a person who struggled constantly against depression and a sense of
unworthiness. These were the "obstacles" of his religious life, and he did
mighty battle against them, teaching all those around him to judge themselves generously and always to strive for a life of sacred joy. But then
another obstacle was put in his path: tuberculosis, a disease very common,
highly feared, and usually fatal in the early nineteenth century. His wife
died of it in 1807, and he knew that he was already infected. A year later,
he compromised his own principles and made the long journey to Lem-

berg (now Lviv), to consult a modern doctor. When that failed to help, he heaped curses on the medical profession. Now, thirty-seven years old in 1809, he knew he was most likely about to die. He decided he wanted to be buried among the martyrs in Uman, where the terrible Haidamak pogroms of 1768 had slaughtered thousands. He knew he had to go there, to prepare for the end, but did not know when. Then a fire broke out in Bratslav, burning his house to the ground. That was the final sign, he said, taking his few remaining belongings and putting them up on the wagon.

This was the moment I thought of as we began to drive out of Bratslav, heading toward Uman. How filled with despair he must have been, knowing that he had nothing left to do but die! This was one of those moments when he surely must have cried out to himself: "*Zeyt zikh nisht meya'esh*—Never despair! There is no such thing as despair in the world!" He must have seen it all coming to naught. Here he was, still just a small-town *rebbe* with perhaps a hundred disciples, all in the same little obscure corner of the world. Almost no one had even heard of him. Yes, he had taught that "somewhere" there is a person in the world known to no one, who yet has secret rule, even over the mighty. He was that someone, but now it was getting too late for it to be revealed.

Could R. Naḥman have imagined that those same words against despair would be hanging from the wall of the Breslov *shtibl* in Warsaw in 1941, where Emanuel Ringelblum recorded them, inspiring Jews to hang on and survive, never to give in? Could he have pictured thirty thousand Jews from all over the world pouring into Uman on Rosh Hashanah to visit his grave? Could he imagine his teachings, translated into many languages, reaching the hearts of Jews whose way of living is so far from his own? Could he have dreamed that his tales would one day be printed not only in English but in a *Ukrainian* edition, now about to appear? How right he was, never to give in to despair! Even at this moment, when there seemed to be almost nothing left for him, an unimaginably grand future lay before his enterprise!

Of course, this message is so powerful for me because I say it to myself as well. At age seventy-eight, blessed with many more years than R. Naḥman, but now somewhat weakened by decades of physical self-neglect, I too ask what is left. Yes, I have several more great projects under my belt (my newly acquired *gartel*, dare I say). I very much hope to bring them to completion. But this enterprise to which I feel so committed—building a bridge between the memory of Hasidism and the needs of countless Jewish seekers in our own time—how few have walked across it! How narrow—hard to access, complicated by ambivalence, and all the rest—it is! Will it have any future? Is there reason to hope it will go somewhere? Here I look to R. Naḥman, thinking about how he must have felt on that journey to Uman . . . and the great surprises that were still to come.

Uman. The hardest part of our journey. First the city, then the *tsiyyun*, the grave of R. Naḥman. Uman is the biggest city we visited, other than Kyiv. It has over one hundred thousand people, and is the major commercial and industrial center of its area, more or less midway between Kyiv and Odessa. It has been known as a center of military industry, both under Soviet and Ukrainian rule. In fact, the two old large synagogue buildings (one for local Jews, the other built by the Breslovers in the mid-nineteenth century), cannot be visited, as they are still in use as part of the military-industrial complex. The city, although built over several hills, feels like a gritty, industrial place, with nothing particularly beautiful about it.

That is true with one very major exception. Uman is famous for a large and very beautiful park, known as the Sophia Garden. It was created by the local Polish nobleman Stefan Potocki for his wife around the turn of the nineteenth century. Its designers copied gardens in London, Paris, and Warsaw, and came up with a very lovely design, reaching across hills and fields, filled with ponds and artificial waterfalls. Surprisingly, it was maintained all through the Soviet years, the famine of the 1930s, and even the war, without being destroyed. It is considered one of the major tourist attractions in Ukraine; schoolchildren, vacationers, and picnickers from all over the country come there. We, too, the conference attendees, enjoyed a very lovely day there.

The conference tour bus also took us out to the edge of town for that long walk in the woods, leading to a monument inscribed in Ukrainian and Yiddish (over an old Soviet-era Russian memorial), saying that here, in September 1941, twenty-five thousand Uman Jews were shot and dumped into this ravine. Here we were again, back in the Holocaust. Today there are at most a few hundred "native" Jews living in the city, with no organized community. In 1941, the Jews were still a little more than half of the city's population.

I asked the friendly and helpful Ukrainian local museum director, who was guiding our tour: "What was it like the day after? Are there are written records, oral histories? Did anybody talk about it? Perhaps write a poem or a diary entry about it?" "No, we have nothing from those war years," he quickly assured me, obviously wanting to move on to some less painful subject. But, of course, the question stuck in my mind. Your kid is a third grader in a local Soviet public school. One day, more than half his class disappears. You know what has happened to them, but what do you tell your kid? What do you tell yourself? Or are you too busy accumulating abandoned furniture, or moving into a nicer, suddenly available, apartment, to think about such things?

And how are we visitors supposed to relate to these questions, still somehow hanging in the air in a place like this? To be sure, great-grandchildren do not bear guilt for what was done seventy-five years ago. But . . .

Well, Uman, the Jews are back. This year, thirty thousand pilgrims, mostly Israelis, showed up for Rosh Hashanah. The numbers do not yet seem to be diminishing. Even when we were there, in early July, there were multiple busloads coming in and out. They were an incredible combination of traditional *ḥasidim* (actually rather few of those), Jews of North African heritage, both men and women, seemingly in separate groups, national-religious types (*tsitsit* but Western dress), and spiritual hippies, day-old returnees to Judaism, and lots in between. "Our brethren, the whole house of Israel," as the prayer says. For some of these visitors, R. Naḥman has been made over into a Near Eastern Jewish saint. For others, he is a Jewish version of an Indian holy man; one could imagine people coming to his festival in Uman and then going to worship with another such figure on the banks of the Ganges. In complete contrast to Chabad, there is not a shred of discipline or control in Breslov. Everyone is welcome. Indeed, like that little group in the woods, it is still a "come as you are" party. But thirty thousand Jews romping around in the woods could be quite a nightmare, even for R. Naḥman.

The healthy instincts of both hasidic and Near Eastern Jewish spirituality dictate that partying, indeed, is part of the pilgrimage. Yes, you may come to supplicate at the grave of the *rebbe*, asking him to "pull you out of hell by the *peyos*," as he has promised. Here at Breslov is a religion that very much responds to the human need for personal salvation, a kind of religious language not much heard in Jewish circles. But while you're here at this holy place, you also want to drink to the *tsaddik*'s soul, hang out with likeminded Jews, and see the sights. The Sophia Garden seems to have made it as part of the tour.

One thing these pilgrims are decidedly not about, however, is getting to know the local populace. The high-hill district where the gravesite is, around Pushkin Street, is a totally separate enclave within the city. Most signs there are only in Hebrew, not in Ukrainian or English. It is now a high-rent and high-value district; the Ukrainian families who happen to own apartments there are considered lucky. Unfortunately, there seems to be no local planning or control over building in that area, and it has gotten to look quite awful—like some of the worst neighborhoods of Jerusalem or Bnai Brak, but without any of Jerusalem's charm. I'm told there are now eighty Israeli families living in Uman year-round, catering to the tourist business. They, too, I suspect, have little interest in meeting their neighbors. I fear for what might happen there one day.

The *tsiyyun*, or grave marker, of R. Naḥman is also different than any of the others I've described. Indeed there are old photos from the 1930s of a very nice-looking little *ohel* there. But the old cemetery was plowed over by the Nazis, and the site was built into apartment blocks by the Soviets. Now the place of R. Naḥman's burial has been "rediscovered," and it is a large synagogue building, with the tomb built into the wall between two different rooms for worshippers (both male, of course; the women's section is off to one side). The place is covered with fancy gold-embroidered curtains and hangings, bearing the names of various well-meaning donors. Unfortunately, it is terribly overdone in that way. It feels like the body of R. Naḥman has been wrapped up in so many prayers, curtains, and walls by his disciples that it is almost impossible to get to him in Uman.

There is an active life of real Jewish piety around the *tsiyyun*. Reb Mimi went into the women's section at 2 a.m. and discovered over a hundred women sitting there, tearfully reciting psalms. Among the men, there seem to be many *minyanim* each morning and afternoon, some screamingly loud, but giving one a sense of a Breslov version of the notorious *shtiblekh minyanim* of Jerusalem, where you can pop in any time "for a quickie."

As you can tell, it was not much for us. Our Shabbos in Uman was lovely because we were with each other, having our own good *davening* (*Kabbalat Shabbat* led by Avram in my hotel suite), enjoying one another's company and endless rounds of good kosher food—but spending very little time at the *tsiyyun* itself. If you want to meet R. Naḥman, I would say, meet him first in the pages of his teachings. Then do try a Breslov *minyan* somewhere in the world—anywhere but Uman, at least for your first encounter. Save Uman for later.

The truth is that I still feel that way about all the *rebbes*, even after this wonderful pilgrimage. I love them most for their teachings, which indeed did save Judaism for me. Yes, I know those teachings include lots of versions of "I want to watch how the *rebbe* ties his shoes"—which mean that the person and his behavior are more important and unique to Hasidism than anything that can be found in books. By now, however, those anecdotes themselves are also mostly to be found in books. The *rebbes* who are still alive in our day, tenth- or twelfth-generation descendants of the authors, can show you little more than the *style* of Hasidism, the forms in which it all took place. It is no accident that the two most thriving forms of Hasidism in our day are those that have no living masters.

As for visiting the dead in all these holy places—I found it a surprisingly rich and invigorating experience, especially with this wonderful cadre of neo-hasidic faithful around me. I hope soon to do it again, with God's help. But the *neo* part of that term does remain very important to me. In this I am a disciple of R. Levi Yizḥak, when he asked: "Why does the Talmud hint (in the word *teyku*, 'let it stand') that Elijah the Tishbite will one day resolve all the outstanding questions? Why not Moses?" Elijah, after all, was not a man of Torah. The Torah is called that of Moses, not of Elijah! "Moses," he replied, "died and was buried. You can't learn Torah from a dead man." Torah needs to be reinterpreted afresh for each generation. Only an Elijah, one who never died, can come back to answer all our questions. Meanwhile, until Elijah comes, we have to do it for ourselves.

The Ba'al Shem Tov himself knew that as well, of course. He was a genius at throwing out novel interpretations of well-known biblical verses and rabbinic sayings, meant to stir up the mind and lead people beyond ordinary ways of thinking or believing. In a certain sense, Hasidism from the outset was a *neo*-hasidic movement. Its very essence was opposition to conventional piety, a quest for something deeper.

The *rebbes* who are present in those *ohalim*, scattered across the towns and hilltops of Ukraine, are all dead men. There they lie, along with millions of other, more recent, Jewish dead. But the sparks of holiness that they uplifted fill the air, and can still be recovered by new generations who seek them out. Yes, those sparks fly pretty far. They are accessible wherever souls open up to them: we encounter them here in North America, and certainly in Israel as well. But something of those sparks continues to hover in a special way over those places where the words were first spoken and the deeds first done. Some of us seem to need to go there—maybe even are being sent there—to see what we can retrieve, and to raise up their spirits—and our own.

Glossary of Hebrew and Yiddish Terms

Aggadah. Literally "narrative." The nonlegal portions of early rabbinic literature, included within Talmud and Midrashim. Replete with theological and moral teachings, considered authoritative but massively reinterpreted by later generations.

Ahavah. Love, the same term used for both interpersonal love and that between Y-H-W-H, the world, and humans.

'Akedah. The binding of Isaac on the altar, described in Genesis 22.

Aleph. First letter of the Hebrew alphabet, unpronounced. Also signifies the number one.

'Aliyah. Literally "ascent." (1) In the synagogue's public reading of the Torah, an invitation to rise and recite the blessings before and after each section is read. (2) Immigration to the Land of Israel, considered the "highest" of all places.

Anokhi. "I am," the opening words of the decalogue in Exodus 20:2 and Deuteronomy 4.

'Avodah. Literally "work" or "service." Also religious devotion, service to Y-H-W-H.

Ba'al tefillah. Leader of public prayer. Distinguished from a professional and musically trained *ḥazan*, cantor.

Balebatish. Yiddish, from Hebrew *ba'al bayit*, "householder." Comes to mean "respectable" or "decent." *Balebatishkeyt* is a sort of middle-class respectability.

Bet midrash (Yiddish: **beys medresh**). House of study, typically attached to a synagogue, lined with books and set out with tables across which people engage in *ḥevruta* ("partnered") study of texts.

Beys oilem (Hebrew: **Bet 'Olam**). Literally "eternal home." Cemetery.

Binah. Literally "understanding." The third (by hasidic count second) of the ten *sefirot*. Depicted in mostly feminine and maternal images; the womb out of which the personal male and female God-figures, the blessed Holy One and the *shekhinah*, are born.

Da'at. Literally "knowledge," but used in Hasidism to refer to spiritual awareness, wakefulness of mind. *Da'at* is also a quality within God, representing the third *sefirah* in the hasidic count. It is symbolized by the letter *vav*, elongating the flow of energy packed into the primal point of *yod*, drawing it "downward," into the world.

Daven, davnen (Yiddish). Praying, specifically the recitation of daily liturgical prayer.

Erets yisra'el. The Land of Israel, defined in the Torah by various sets of borders.

Etrog. Citron, used in the ritual of Sukkot.

Eyn sof. "Endless." The undefinable reservoir of divine energy or potential that exists prior to and beyond the self-defining and self-limiting gradations (*sefirot*) that constitute the process of emanation.

Frum (Yiddish). Pious.

Gartel (Yiddish). A rope belt donned prior to prayer, according to hasidic custom, "girding one's loins" for the spiritual struggle ahead.

Haggadah. The text of the Pesaḥ *seder* or ritual banquet.

Halakhah. The path of normative Jewish religious praxis, covering all areas of life. Sometimes rendered as "law."

Hallel. A group of psalms (113–18), recited on festive occasions, often sung with joyous tunes.

Ḥaredi. Literally "trembling" (might well translate "quaker"!). Especially pious, trembling at the word of God. Sometimes called "ultra-Orthodox"; living according to the strictest interpretation of *halakhah*, often rejecting modern Western education and values.

Ḥesed. Compassion, representing the boundless flow of divine love. Juxtaposed to *din*, divine judgment, sometimes demanding the temporary withholding or redirection of that love.

Hitbodedut. Literally "self-isolation," often used as a term for lone meditation. Among Breslov *ḥasidim*, there is a special technique of spontaneous verbal prayer also called by that name.

Hosh'anot. Literally "salvations," a collection of special festival prayers recited on Sukkot while circling about the synagogue, imitating the rite of pilgrims in the ancient Temple.

Kavvanah, kavvanot. Intensity or religious passion, especially in the act of prayer. In the plural, refers to specific mystical directions regarding prayer.

Kelim (singular **keli**). Vessels. Used in Kabbalah to refer to the vessels within which Y-H-W-H sent light into the world in the act of Creation.

Kelipot (singular **Kelipah**). "Shell," referring (see preceding entry) to the fragments of smashed vessels, after the divine light proved too intense to bear the emptiness of worldly existence. These fragments hide the light, thus turning demonic. Hence *klipe* means "demon" in Yiddish.

Kippah (plural **kippot**). Skullcap.

Kodesh kodashim. "Holy of Holies," referring to an item or locale of extreme holiness. Primarily refers to the innermost sanctum of the desert tabernacle.

Kreplekh (Yiddish). Dough pockets, usually stuffed with meat (ground beef lung was best, my grandmother insisted). Traditionally eaten on the eve of Yom Kippur and Hoshana Rabbah.

Meḥitsah. Separation barrier between men and women in the traditional synagogue.

Meni'ot. "Obstacles," used in Breslov Hasidism to indicate doubts or other feelings, but sometimes also physical circumstances, that keep one far from God.

Middot. "Qualities" or "measures." The term is used regarding both the inner divine and human selves; in the human world, it especially refers to moral qualities. A *bal mides* (*ba'al middot*) is Yiddish for "a person of refinement and decency."

Midrash. The process and literature of investigating scripture in search of deeper meanings, often resulting in eisegesis. Also the books (plural *midrashim*) containing this sort of interpretation, compiled between the fourth and twelfth centuries.

Mikveh. Ritual bath or bathhouse.

Minḥah. Literally "offering" or "gift"; the afternoon service, usually recited at dusk.

Minyan. A quorum of ten adult Jews required for public prayer and certain ritual occasions. The inclusion of women in the count is a recent (heterodox) innovation.

Mishkan. The tabernacle erected by Israel during its wanderings in the wilderness, described in Exodus 25 and elsewhere. Later Jewish tradition spiritualizes it to refer to the inner tabernacle of the soul.

Mitsrayim. "Egypt," an ancient designation also meaning "straits," based on the Nile Delta. Later readings read it as any place of inner constriction, keeping one from the breadth or freedom of divine encounter (cf. Ps. 118:5).

Mitsvah. "Commandment," but also understood in the broader sense of "good deed."

Nakhas (Hebrew: **naḥat**). Pleasure, especially a parent or grandparent's pleasure with children.

Netilat yadayim. Ritual washing of hands, performed before prayer or prior to breaking bread at a meal.

Ohel, ohalim. Literally "tent," here referring to small enclosed structures at the sites of graves of *tsaddikim*.

'Olam ha-ba. "The Coming World," in common parlance referring to the afterlife, but used by the Zohar to refer to a world that is ever about to be revealed; also related to *binah*.

Peshat. The simplest, most obvious, level of interpretation (although not necessarily literal).

Pushke. Yiddish for "box," referring particularly to a metal box with a slit to insert coins, used for collecting charitable gifts.

Rebbe. Literally "teacher," used to refer to a hasidic master.

Rosh ḥodesh. The first day(s) of the new month, considered semi-festivals.

Seder. Literally "order"; the ritualized home banquet held on the first night(s) of Pesaḥ.

Sefirot (singular **sefirah**). Literally "ciphers." The ten aspects or stages of divine self-revelation, manifest in a process that began prior to Creation, but is repeated endlessly. The ten *sefirot* collectively constitute the divine Self in its dynamic unity.

Seliḥot. Penitential prayers recited before dawn during the month of Elul preceding Rosh Hashanah, and on public fast days throughout the year.

Semikhah. Rabbinic ordination, given from teacher to student by way of passing rabbinic learning across generations. Offered by institutions, as distinct from individual rabbis, only from the nineteenth century.

Shabbat (or Yiddish **Shabbes**). The weekly Sabbath, beginning Friday at sundown, extending into Saturday evening.

Shaḥarit. Morning service, named for its original timing at dawn.

Shekhinah. The indwelling presence of Y-H-W-H. In Kabbalah, the feminine partner of the blessed Holy One, She who receives His blessing as seed to be poured forth to sustain Her children, the souls of those who dwell in the lower world, understood by some as dwelling within Her.

Shema'. "Hear!" The daily recited proclamation of divine oneness, beginning with "Hear O Israel, Y-H-W-H our God, Y-H-W-H is one," continuing with three passages of Torah text.

Sho'ah. Holocaust.

Shofar. Ram's horn, blown during Elul, at the Rosh Hashanah service, at the conclusion of Yom Kippur, and upon the arrival of messiah.

Shtetl (Yiddish). Small town, typically those Jewish-majority towns of eastern Europe.

Sod. "Secret"; the esoteric, often kabbalistic, meaning of a scriptural passage.

Sukkah. Booth used as a temporary dwelling during the harvest festival of Sukkot.

Tallit. Prayer shawl, adorned with ritual fringes on its four corners.

Talmud. The great compendium of Jewish praxis and teachings, two recensions of which, the *bavli* ("Babylonian") and *yerushalmi* ("Jerusalem" or *erets yisra'el*) were composed in the third to sixth centuries.

Talmud torah. The process of learning, integrating, and interpreting Torah. The term is also used to designate traditional elementary schools of Jewish learning.

Tefilah. Prayer, referring to both the entire phenomenon of praying, both spontaneous and liturgical, and the specific recitation of the *'amidah* prayer.

Tefillin. Phylacteries, leather boxes containing Torah passages, worn on the arm and forehead during weekday morning prayers.

Teshuvah. Penitence, but used in the broader sense of return to God, attraction to the Source.

Teyglekh (Yiddish). Honey-soaked bits of dough, eaten on Rosh Hashanah as tokens of a sweet year to come.

Tikkun 'olam. "Restoring the World," a Jewish designation for doing good in worldly ways.

Tsaddik. Righteous one, a designation also for leaders of hasidic groups.

Tsitsit. Ritual fringes.

Tsiyyun. "Designation," here referring to the designated burial spot of a *tsaddik*, or the marker over such a grave.

Yarmulke (Yiddish). Skullcap.

Yiddelekh (Yiddish). "Little Jews," a term of affection for ordinary Jewish people.

Yiddishkeyt (Yiddish). "Jewishness." Among the religious, the term might be rendered as "Judaism," but used also by secular Jews to designate values and character traits associated with proper Jewish living.

Yir'ah. "Fear" or "awe," veneration of Y-H-W-H. Seen to stand in balance and tension with *ahavah*.

Yizkor. Memorial prayers for the dead, recited on four festival occasions during the year in the Ashkenazi synagogue.

Notes

Neo-Hasidism

1. This truth is stated with remarkable clarity by the hasidic master R. Yehudah Leib Alter of Ger (1847–1905), author of *Sefat Emet*. "The proclamation of one-ness that we declare each day in saying *Shema' Yisra'el* and so forth really needs to be understood as it truly is. . . . 'Y-H-W-H is one' means not only that He is the only God, negating other gods (though this too is true!), but . . . that there is no being other than He . . . everything that exists in the world, physical and spiritual, is God Himself." Yehudah Leib Alter, *Otsar Mikhtavim u-Ma'amarim* (Jerusalem: Machon Gahaley Esh, 1986), 75–76.

2. From the daily morning service. See as well the reading of *eyn 'od*, "there is none other" (Deut. 4:39) in the second section of Tanya by R. Shne'ur Zalman of Liadi, the "Bible" of Chabad Hasidism.

3. Bereshit Rabbah 68:10. On my reading of Canticles 2:9, see Sifre Be-Midbar, ed. H. S. Horovitz (Leipzig: Gustav Fock, 1917), no. 115, p. 125; and the comments by R. Zevi Hirsch of Nadvorna translated in Arthur Green et al., *Speaking Torah: Spiritual Teachings from around the Maggid's Table* (Woodstock, VT: Jewish Lights, 2013), 2:25–30.

4. Note that I am not trying to claim Maimonides as a panentheist or a monist. That would betray the strong transcendentalist bent of his negative theology. For all but the philosopher, Maimonides's God is surely more absent than present, beyond knowledge or experience. But the First Cause that is revealed to the pro-phetic imagination, and with which the philosopher's mind can become united, is testimony to a divine presence that was there to be *discovered* all along. Nor do I mean to say that Maimonides was the first to think philosophically about God. He represents the culmination of a long tradition, beginning several centuries before him. We should also note the confusion caused by the absence of a neuter pronoun in Hebrew and other Semitic languages. Neither philosophers nor kab-balists had a way of saying "It" about the One. However abstract their intentions, the pronoun used was always that misleadingly translated as "He."

5. See further in my *A Guide to the Zohar* (Stanford: Stanford University Press, 2004). Here the debate revolves around the nature of *eyn sof*, God as the unknowable

endless. If all existence is in a constant state of flowing forth from and being quickened by that source, as R. Moshe Cordovero understands it, we are indeed very close to a monistic view, though one veiled by all the constant "activity" in the symbolic realm of the *sefirot*. See some brief but striking formulations by Cordovero as quoted in Daniel Matt's *The Essential Kabbalah: The Heart of Jewish Mysticism* (San Francisco: Harper, 1995), 27–28, 38–49.

6. I have seen an essay of that era entitled "Die Judenthum in ihre Hauptstroemun-gen," probably the first instance of that term, but am now unable to locate it.

7. In some ways, my own project has been the construction of a modern Jewish theology that is rooted in eastern, rather than western, Europe. On my quest for spiritual ancestry, see my "Three Warsaw Mystics," available on my website artgreen26.com.

8. *M. Avot* 4:1.

9. Of course there are important exceptions. Within Judaism, Alan Brill has surveyed the range of approaches in the Jewish tradition in his *Judaism and Other Religions: Models of Understanding* (New York: Palgrave Macmillan, 2010) and *Judaism and World Religions: Encountering Christianity, Islam, and Eastern Traditions* (New York: Palgrave Macmillan, 2012). See also *Jewish Theology and World Religions*, ed. Alon Goshen-Gottstein and Eugene Korn (Oxford: Littman, 2012); and Alon Goshen-Gottstein, *Same God, Other God: Judaism, Hinduism, and the Problem of Idolatry* (London: Palgrave Macmillan, 2016).

10. See my essay below, "Religion and Environmental Responsibility," for further treatment.

11. This is a lesson I learned from my great teacher Abraham Joshua Heschel. His magisterial *God in Search of Man* begins with a hundred-page treatise on what it means to develop religious awareness and to ask religious questions; only then does he turn to the answers of Judaism.

12. For further discussion, see my essay *"Da'at:* Spiritual Awareness in a Hasidic Classic," in *Religious Truth: Essays in Jewish Theology of Religions*, ed. Alon Goshen-Gottstein (London: Littman, 2019).

13. The hasidic masters knew this well. It is most clearly articulated in their speculations around Abraham, and how he discovered the Torah (i.e., "the path" or "the truth") from within himself, before it was given. See my discussion of this in *Devotion and Commandment* (Cincinnati: Hebrew Union College Press, 2015).

14. This phrasing is adapted from the "Prayer of Elijah," part of the introduction to *Tikkuney Zohar,* and recited daily by Sephardic Jews. Available in translation in Daniel Matt, *The Essential Kabbalah: The Heart of Jewish Mysticism* (San Francisco: Harper, 1995), 50–51.

15. Abraham Joshua Heschel of Apt, quoted in *'Ateret Tsevi, aḥarey mot* (Jerusalem, 1960), 25a. See my *Ehyeh: A Kabbalah for Tomorrow* (Woodstock, VT: Jewish Lights, 2003), 51–52.

16. On this point, I am clearly a "Bratslaver" and not a "HaBaDnik." Bratslav (or Breslov) Hasidism, founded by Rabbi Naḥman of Bratslav, sees spiritual growth as full engagement with one's emotional life, marked by much inner pain, outcry, and longing. The original teachings of ḤaBaD preferred an attempt to transcend the emotional morass by attaching oneself to higher thoughts and entering into

a state of contemplative detachment, leaving the broken self behind, to be dealt with later.

How I Practice Judaism—and Why

1. Both the philosophical and mystical traditions devoted a great deal of attention to *ta'amey ha-mitsvot*, the search to find meaning in the commandments. This literature, widely popular from the twelfth to the seventeenth centuries, is largely ignored today in the curricula of both *yeshivot* and seminaries.

2. In nineteenth-century Hungary, I would have been called a *status quo ante* Jew. I rather like that name. It belonged to rather fully observant Jews who rejected the emerging term *Orthodox*, as do I. Obviously adopted from Christianity, it refers to a faith based on a fully laid-out doctrine, deviation from which is not permissible. I have long believed that ours is a generation that eschews all orthodoxies, Jewish or Christian, Marxist or Freudian. We are one of those generations for whom the broken tablets were placed in the ark alongside the whole ones (b. Berakhot 8b), as we are able to digest truth only in small bites.

3. See Ariel Evan Mayse, "Tree of Life, Tree of Knowledge: Halakhah and Theology in *Ma'or va-Shemesh*," *Tradition* 51:1 (2019): 3–26; Maoz Kahana and Ariel Evan Mayse, "Hasidic Halakhah: Reappraising the Interface of Spirit and Law," *AJS Review* 41:2 (November 2017): 375–408; Elliot R. Wolfson, "Walking as a Sacred Duty: Theological Transformations of Social Reality in Early Hasidism," in *Hasidism Reappraised*, ed. Ada Rapoport-Albert (London: Littman, 1997), 180–207.

4. See "Judaism and 'the Good'" in my *The Heart of the Matter: Studies in Jewish Mysticism and Theology* (Philadelphia: Jewish Publication Society, 2015), 55–72.

5. B. Berakhot 45a.

6. See my translation of *Me'or 'Eynayim* (*The Light of the Eyes* [Stanford: Stanford University Press, 2020]), *bereshit*, n. 241. He is broadening RaSHI's comment to Exodus 20:1, which sees the ten commandments spoken in a single word. In his comments to Exodus 24:1, RaSHI states that all 613 commandments are included in the ten commandments, noting that Saadia Gaon had sought to spell out this connection in his liturgical poem about the 613 commandments (a genre known as *azharot*). See Be-Midbar Rabbah 13:16 for a series of creative *midrashim* that assert that all of Torah was included in the ten commandments. Similarly, the *Tikkuney Zohar* 20, 63b–64a states that all of the commandments of the Torah were included in the first two commandments, being the utterances that all of Israel heard directly from God; all positive commandments are seen as rooted in "I am Y-H-W-H your God" and all negative commandments in "You shall have no gods before Me."

7. A derivation widely found in hasidic sources. See those listed in Menahem Nahum of Chernobyl in Green, *The Light of the Eyes*, *bereshit*, n. 156.

8. The source for this reading is *Tikkuney Zohar* 29, 73a and 70, 131b.

9. Rabbi Akiva's view that the Song of Songs was said at or of Sinai is discussed by Saul Lieberman in "*Mishnat Shir ha-Shirim*," in Gershom Scholem, *Jewish Gnosticism, Merkaba Mysticism and Talmudic Tradition* (New York: Jewish Theological Seminary, 1965), 118–19. See further discussion below in "Judaism as a Path of

Love." On the reading of this verse in the Sinai context, see b. Shabbat 88b. There the Talmud takes "came forth" either as "passed out" or "died" and needed to be resurrected.

10. In contrast to all the neo-Kantians, from Hermann Cohen to Yeshayahu Leibowitz, it is precisely the heteronomy to which I object. I find that it undermines the joy of spiritual spontaneity, which I continue to find in familiar forms, freely chosen. I have deeper objections to this as well, based on my rejection of limited Western definitions of the self.

11. See the interesting parallel in the teachings of Levi Yizḥak of Berdichev, *Kedushat Levi, Derush le-Pesaḥ.*, 180b, s.v. '*Inyan pesaḥ*. There he notes that the king or emperor's word is law, once he has finished pronouncing it. But as long as he is still speaking it, there is a possibility of affecting his will and changing it. Y-H-W-H, who is beyond time, has never ceased pronouncing the *mitsvot*. See the discussion in my "Hasidism and Its Response to Change," *Jewish History* 27:2/4 (December 2013): 319–36, esp. 332–34, or on my website artgreen26.com.

12. See Rosenzweig's essay "The Builders: Concerning the Law" in his *On Jewish Learning*, ed. N. N. Glatzer (New York: Schocken, 1955), 72–92, esp. 85: "Law [*Gesetz*] must again become commandment [*Gebot*]. . . . It must regain that living reality." See the discussion of this theme in Rosenzweig in Paul Mendes-Flohr's "Law and Sacrament: Ritual Observance in Twentieth-Century Jewish Thought," in *Jewish Spirituality II*, ed. Arthur Green (New York: Crossroad, 1997), 317–45, esp. 327–29. That "how," of course, was a spiritual/devotional "how," not one of practical detail. One could find instruction on it in the tradition of *ta'amey ha-mitsvot*, theological "reasons for the *mitsvot*," much more than in the legal codes themselves. This was continued later in such devotional classics as Elijah De Vidas's *Reshit Ḥokhmah* and the anonymous (and partially Sabbatian) *Ḥemdat Yamim*.

13. The kabbalists also understood this to be the case. In the Zohar's bold assertion that the blessed Holy One, the essential male God figure of biblical/rabbinic tradition, was *born* of mysterious forces that reached beyond Him, and was energized constantly by a flow of blessing from that unknowable Source, they were admitting that devotion to such a "God" is a bridge to a higher and deeper truth. The crucial difference is that they believed that this figure was generated from "above," while I am describing it as one of human projection. As will become clear presently, however, I am willing to say that it is only our constricted human consciousness that limits us to seeing it that way. Still, my theological "heterodoxy" is partly defined by this admission.

14. This phrase occurs several times in the Talmud. See, e.g., b. Nedarim 8a.

15. The inner process of halakhic creativity, especially in the premodern era, was complex, often highly creative, and open to both circumstance and personal subjectivity. There was objection to codification all along, and I do not mean to reduce all the legal tradition to the presence of codes. Great awareness of these dynamics is found in the fascinating and surprisingly far-reaching critique of contemporary *halakhah* as found in the writings of Orthodox rabbi Nathan Lopes-Cardozo. See especially his *Halakhah as Rebellion: A Plea for Religious Authenticity and Halachic Courage* (Jerusalem: Urim, 2018).

16. *Sefat Emet, emor* 5634 [1874], and the final paragraph for *shavu'ot* 5638 [1878]. Some of the derivation from these sources is possibly my own.

17. See especially the texts by Meir Ibn Gabbai and Yeshayahu Horowitz quoted at length by Gershom Scholem at the conclusion of his landmark essay "Revelation and Tradition as Religious Categories in Judaism," in his *The Messianic Idea in Judaism and Other Essays on Jewish Spirituality* (New York: Schocken, 1971), 282–303.

18. See the long note in my "The Hasidic Homily: Mystical Performance and Hermeneutical Process," in *As a Perennial Spring: A Festschrift Honoring Rabbi Dr. Norman Lamm*, ed. Bentsi Cohen (New York: Downhill, 2013), 261–62, n. 26.

19. B. Berakhot 6a.

20. See the teaching of Ze'ev Wolf of Zhitomir translated in Arthur Green et al., *Speaking Torah: Spiritual Teachings from around the Maggid's Table* (Woodstock, VT: Jewish Lights, 2013), 2:159–60.

How I Pray

1. See the wonderful array of sources on this subject presented by my revered teacher A. J. Heschel in *Heavenly Torah* (New York: Continuum, 2006), 93–103. See especially my very favorite of these, the cave at the shore of the sea, in Shir ha-Shirim Rabbah 3:15. For the true *mevinim*, I call this the "Thunder Hole" *midrash*.

2. God is at once the knower, the known, and the knowledge. Maimonides, *Mishneh Torah: Yesodey ha-Torah* 2:10.

3. The psalmist's (147:3) image of God as "healer of the brokenhearted" is deeply touching to me. So too the hasidic/Sephardic version of the prayer for healing in the *'Amidah*, expanding it to include "all our pains and all the blows we've suffered," and calling forth *arukhah*, or "scar tissue," to grow over them.

4. Here I am living with R. Naḥman's *Likkutey MoHaRaN* 64.

5. From the prologue to his *Tale of the Seven Beggars*.

6. *Sifre* on Deuteronomy 11:13; Maimonides, *Mishneh Torah*, Laws of Prayer 1:1.

7. These and related hasidic teachings on prayer are translated in my *Your Word Is Fire*, coedited with Barry W. Holtz, rev. ed. (Nashville: Jewish Lights, 2017).

8. *Ḥovot ha-Levavot, Sha'ar Ḥeshbon ha-Nefesh* 9, available in English as Bachya ibn Paquda, *Duties of the Heart*, trans. Moses Hyamson (Jerusalem: Feldheim, 1970), 2:211.

9. Zohar 2:206a. Quoted in the synagogue service as the Torah is brought forth for reading.

10. Adapted from the chapter on prayer in my book *EHYEH: A Kabbalah for Tomorrow* (Woodstock, VT: Jewish Lights, 2003).

11. See Yehoshua Avraham ben Yisrael, *Ge'ulat Yisrael* (Ostrog: n.p., 1821), 2:15a. Also in Midrash Pinḥas (Lvov: n.p., 1874), 1:8b; 2:6. The teaching is based on a reading of Deuteronomy 10:21. It is cited by Martin Buber. See "He Is Your Psalm," in *Tales of the Hasidim* (New York: Schocken, 1947), 1:125.

12. Judah A. Joffe, "The Etymology of 'Davenen' and 'Katoves,'" *Proceedings of the American Academy for Jewish Research* 28 (1959): 77–92.

13. See Jon Levenson, *The Death and Resurrection of the Beloved Son: The Transformation of Child Sacrifice in Judaism and Christianity* (New Haven: Yale University Press, 1993).

14. A more literal reading renders it: "As for me, my prayer is to You, O Lord."

15. See *Ba'al Shem Tov 'al ha-Torah* (Jerusalem: Nofet Tsufim, 5757 [1996–97]), 1:233–34, *parashat noah*, no. 133.

16. B. Yebamot 64a, b. Hullin 60b.

Barukh Atah

1. Isaiah 44:6: "I am the first and I am the last; besides me there is no God." Cf. the New Testament's "I am the alpha and the omega" in Revelation 1:8, 21:6, 22:13.

2. It is this need to make myself vulnerable to being called upon that leads me to say *atah* in prayer, rather than an inherent conservatism or resistance to change, as was claimed by Marcia Falk in an early response to my *Seek My Face* (Woodstock, VT: Jewish Lights, 2003). See her *Book of Blessings* (San Francisco: HarperCollins, 1996), 418–23, esp. 420–21. See also her earlier "Toward a Feminist Jewish Reconstruction of Monotheism," and Lawrence A. Hoffman's "A Response to Marcia Falk," *Tikkun* 4:4 (July/August 1989): 54–57. See further discussion below, as well as in the preceding essay "How I Pray."

3. So too I note the absence of a human *hineni* in response to God's *ayekah*, "Where are you?" in the Garden. This, it seems to me, is the true sin of Adam.

4. Yair Lorberbaum, *In God's Image: Myth, Theology, and Law in Classical Judaism* (Cambridge: Cambridge University Press, 2015).

5. For a (relatively) succinct summary of his view of ethics as rooted in the absolute "otherness" (alterity) of the other, see Emmanuel Levinas, *Alterity and Transcendence*, trans. Michael B. Smith (New York: Columbia University Press, 1999), 3–37, 99–106.

6. See my fuller treatment below in "Judaism as a Path of Love," and the sources from *Reshit Hokhmah* quoted there (*ahavah* 6:10, 8:10–14, 9:5).

The Seeker Returns

1. This theological sensibility is beautifully evoked in the section from the introduction to the *Tikkuney Zohar* (17a–17b) known as *Patah Eliyahu*—"Elijah opened up." Thus, "Besides You, there is no unifier in the supernal and lower realms. . . . Regarding all the sefirot, each one has a particular, known name . . . but You have no particular name, for You are the One who fills all of the names." This mystical prayer has been included toward the beginning of many prayer books for hundreds of years.

2. Zohar 3:224a.

3. The best-known depiction of the *sefirot* is, of course, the figure of Adam Kadmon, or primordial man. This is God's great act of *imitatio homini*, dressing up the divine rungs as though in human form.

4. Much of this shift from "up" to "in" takes place already in the sources of Hasidism, the earliest modern manifestation of Jewish spiritual quest. That is part of why I find it so nourishing for the seeker of our day.

5. The Talmud (b. Makkot 24a) refers to the prophet Habbakuk having reduced all the 613 *mitsvot* to a single principle, "The righteous one lives by his faith" (Hab. 2:4).

6. *Shulḥan Arukh, Oraḥ Ḥayyim* 5:1 notes that one should have this intention in mind when reciting this divine name in prayer.

7. *Hokhmah* as the primal point of divine emanation reflects a long history within pre-kabbalistic Jewish thought, beginning with the hymns to primordial wisdom in Proverbs 8 and Job 28 and proceeding through the identification of *ḥokhmah* with primordial Torah, the eternal word of God, in the rabbinic imagination, etc. On the images associated with *ḥokhmah* and *binah* in the Zohar, see Isaiah Tishby, *The Wisdom of the Zohar*, trans. David Goldstein (Oxford: Littman, 1989), 269–307, and the Zohar selections translated in that section, 309–70.

8. Bereshit Rabbah 27:1, citing Daniel 8:16, and see the alternative source text cited there in the name of Rabbi Yehudah bar Simon.

9. As quoted by R. Zvi Hirsch of Zydachov in *'Ateret Zvi, aḥarey mot*.

10. See Rabbi Naḥman of Bratslav's tale of the king and his counselor, to which my *Seek My Face* may be read as an extended comment. The original tale is available in English translation in *Nahman of Bratslav: The Tales*, trans. Arnold J. Band (New York: Paulist, 1978), 113–19.

All about Being Human

1. In the words of hasidic master R. Uri of Strelisk: "When an ordinary Jew says the words of the blessing, *barukh atah adonay*, the word *adonay* signifies the divine name Y-H-W-H. But when the *tsaddik* says a blessing, every word is a divine name. *Barukh* is a name, *atah* is a name, and so forth. That is why the prayer book says *barukh she-amar ve-hayah ha-'olam, barukh hu*, which should be translated: "A *barukh* you say that creates a world—now *that's* a *barukh!*"

2. This is the position of Simeon ben Azzai in his famous dispute with Rabbi Akiva, recorded in Y. Nedarim 9:4 (30b). See the more extensive discussion in my *Radical Judaism* (New Haven: Yale University Press, 2010), ch. 4.

3. Thus Targum Pseudo-Jonathan on Genesis 1:27, and compare on Genesis 5:1–3. Note that on Genesis 5:3, where there is less cause for theological concern, this Targum uses the more direct *ikon* rather than the derivative form *diyukon*. See the discussion in Yair Lorberbaum, *In God's Image: Myth, Theology, and Law in Classical Judaism* (New York: Cambridge University Press, 2015).

4. This is found in the story of the first day in "The Seven Beggars." See *Nachman of Bratslav: The Tales*, trans. Arnold J. Band (New York: Paulist, 1978), 251–82.

5. Rabbi Levi Yizḥak of Berdychiv's first published work was his commentary on the six remembrances: *Shesh Zekhirot* (Mezhirov, 1794).

6. A common phrase in the Talmud. See, e.g., b. Shevu'ot 25a.

7. This is true for classical rabbinic sources. In the Kabbalah of Isaac Luria, there is a conception of Eden as a place of original sin.

8. *Tsava'at Ha-Rivash* (Brooklyn: Kehot, 1998), no. 76, p. 32.

9. Several passages in Rabbi Menaḥem Naḥum's *Me'or 'Eynayim* on *parashat bereshit* refer to Torah study done for ulterior motives as "darkness" that needs to be il-

luminated by the light of the Divine. See also the chapter "Torah Study in Early Hasidism" in Joseph Weiss's *Studies in Eastern European Jewish Mysticism and Hasidism*, ed. David Goldstein (Oxford: Littman, 1997), 56–68.

10. See the fuller discussion of this passage in "The Seeker Returns."

11. "Whoever disgraces [*malbin* is a play on 'whitening'] his neighbor's face in public is like one who has murdered him." b. Bava Metzia 58b. But the biblical text itself seems to highlight the racist reading of Miriam's sin. She spoke against her brother's dark-skinned wife. "You want to be *white*?" God seems to ask her. "Here's some real whiteness for you!"

Judaism as a Path of Love

1. *Agadat Shir Hashirim*, ed. Solomon Schechter (Cambridge: Deighton, Bell, 1896), line 22, and see Schechter's notes there.

2. Of course all of this is based on Akiva as a literary figure, as projected to us by the later Tannaitic and Amoraic sources. For the most recent biographical treatment of Akiva, see Barry W. Holtz, *Rabbi Akiva: Sage of the Talmud*, Jewish Lives (New Haven: Yale University Press, 2017) and bibliography there. Holtz omits most of the mystical Akiva from his portrait, a view with which I disagree.

3. M. Yadayim 3:5.

4. B. Sanhedrin 106b.

5. *Mekhilta de-Rabbi Shimʿon ben Yoḥai*, ed. J. N. Epstein (Jerusalem: *Yeshivat Shaʿarei raḥamim*, n.d.), 143. See the treatment by Saul Lieberman in Gershom Scholem, *Jewish Gnosticism, Merkavah Mysticism, and Talmudic Tradition* (New York: JTSA, 1960), 118–26. See also my prior discussion in "The Song of Songs in Early Jewish Mysticism," included in *The Heart of the Matter: Studies in Jewish Mysticism and Theology* (Philadelphia: Jewish Publication Society, 2015), 101–15.

6. *Yirʾah* is translated as both "fear" and "awe," words derived from the same Hebrew root *y-r-ʾ*. Such Jewish devotional classics as Meir Ibn Gabbai's *ʿAvodat ha-Qodesh* (1:26) and Elijah De Vidas's *Reshit Ḥokhmah* (*Yirʾah* 2:7–15) distinguish "higher" from "lower" (or sometimes "outer" from "inner") *yirʾah*. In its higher form, "awe" is always the proper translation.

7. B. Shabbat 88b.

8. *Guide* 3:53. See the remarks of Warren Zev Harvey: "If Maimonides had no problem speaking of our *ahavah* (or its Arabic analogue: *mahabbah*) for God, he had a big problem speaking about God's *ahavah* (or *mahabbah*) for us. He rarely does so, and when he does it is with reference to a biblical verse. For how could God have *ahavah* for us? *Ahavah* is a bodily passion and God has no body." "Notions of Divine and Human Love in Jewish Thought: An Interview with Warren Zev Harvey," *University of Toronto Journal of Jewish Thought* 3 (2013): 2–3. God's *ḥesed* in the act of creation is mentioned only at the *Guide*'s conclusion.

9. The view of Maimonides, like that of every abstract theology, is confused by the nonexistence of a neuter gender in Hebrew (and all Semitic languages). This word really should be "it," but that was not possible. The language itself (for surely a Jewish theology should be thought in Hebrew!) draws us toward personification.

10. *Guide of the Perplexed* 1:29, 36. But he is about to tell us, of course, in *Guide* 1:54, that all qualities attributed to God, including *ḥesed*, are nothing other than descriptions of divine actions.

11. *Haqdamah*, 17a. This is to say, in kabbalistic terms, that I understand the *sefirot*, and with them all metaphoric descriptions of God, personal and other, as projections from the realm of human experience, and *eyn sof* as eternally beyond the ken of human intellect, though accessible to preverbal intuition.

12. What we experience as the discoveries of human intellect, scientific as well as mythopoeic, may also be viewed from the divine perspective as acts of ongoing self-revelation. This is to be taken as a modification of the preceding note. See further discussion in my *Seek My Face* (Woodstock, VT: Jewish Lights, 2003) and *Radical Judaism* (New Haven: Yale University Press, 2010).

13. *M. Avot* 3:1.

14. Here I express my regret that such biblical and neo-biblical theologians as my own revered teacher Yohanan Muffs, as well as Michael Wyschograd and Jon Levenson, in his recent treatise on the subject, did not go beyond sources from the early rabbinic period in their examination of Jewish reflections on this subject.

15. Menaḥem Mendel Schneersohn (1789–1866), *Derekh Mitsvotekha, ahavah* (Brooklyn: Kehot, 1976), 397. This leads to the rather shocking thought that crossing the Jordan and entering the land (including sustenance by agriculture rather than manna) caused a potential space to emerge between Israel and God, rather than bringing them closer.

16. See my "God's Need for Man: A Unitive Approach to the Writings of Abraham Joshua Heschel," *Modern Judaism* 35:3 (2015): 247–61.

17. Harvey, in "Notions of Divine and Human Love in Jewish Thought" and elsewhere, sets forth three terms for love in classical Hebrew sources: *ḥesed, ahavah*, and *ḥesheq*, suggesting that the last of these is the one best rendered as erotic love. Yet it is interesting that *ahavah*, not *ḥesheq*, is the term used for love throughout the Song of Songs, the primary text for divine-human *eros* as interpreted throughout the later tradition.

18. B. Hagigah 14b. Interestingly, another version of the tale reads "ascended in peace and descended in peace." Here we have the internal and vertical metaphors for the journey to God laid out right before us. See my discussion in *Seek My Face*.

19. See Ann Matter, *The Voice of My Beloved: The Song of Songs in Western Medieval Christianity* (Philadelphia: University of Pennsylvania Press, 1990), and my fuller discussion in "Shekhinah, the Virgin Mary, and the Song of Songs: Reflections on a Kabbalistic Symbol in Its Historical Context," *AJS Review* 26:1 (2002): 1–52.

20. *Mishneh Torah, teshuvah* 10. Here, too, despite the highly passionate description, the term is *ahavah*, rather than *ḥesheq*.

21. Zohar 3:267b. "All" in the Zohar often refers to the entire sefirotic realm. See further the exposition of this text in *Reshit Ḥokhmah, ahavah* 6:10, where he extends the "all" to include the lower worlds. In the kabbalistic sources, including the Zohar, *ḥesed* and *ahavah* refer to the same divine locus. Generally, but not consistently, *ḥesed* is used regarding God's love for humans, while *ahavah* is the term for human love of God. But even earlier, in the Bahir (#185), we encounter the phrase *mitḥassed 'im qono*.

22. See discussion by Isaiah Tishby, *Mishnat ha-Zohar* 1 (Jerusalem: Mossad Bialik, 1957), 158–61 and passages cited there. Available in English as *The Wisdom of the Zohar*, vol. 1, trans. David Goldstein (Oxford: Littman, 1991), 298–302.

23. The kabbalistic symbolism associated with *shekhinah* is drawn from diverse origins, but these include the biblical image of Mother Rachel weeping for her children.

24. Isaiah 50:1 is cited in Zohar 1:22b, 27b, 237a; 2:189b, 255b; 3:8a, 74b–75a, 102b, 115a, 253b, 268a. But see also 1:120b, as well as the passage quoted there by *Derekh Emet* from David ben Yehudah he-Hasid's *Livnat ha-Sappir*, indicating that God has sent His *shekhinah* to be with them in exile *in order to* arouse Him to redeem them! See the very interesting treatment of this theme by Daniel Abrams in "Divine Yearning for Shekhinah," *Kabbalah* 32 (2014): 14ff. There and elsewhere—beginning in "Chapters from an Emotional and Sexual Biography of God: Reflections on God's Attributes in the Bible, Midrash and Kabbalah," *Kabbalah* 6 (2001): 263–86, then in *Ten Psychoanalytic Aphorisms* (Los Angeles: Cherub, 2011)—Abrams has dealt with aspects of family dynamics as expressed in sefirotic symbolism. Although my tastes are less Freudian than his, I find his treatments most suggestive. The Freudian reading of kabbalistic symbols of the feminine is widely expanded in the writings of Ruth Kara-Ivanov Kaniel.

25. See development of this motif in *Reshit Ḥokhmah, ahavah* 8:10–14.

26. See the index to motifs of father-child relationships in Rivka Schatz-Uffenheimer's edition of *Maggid Devarav le-Yaʿaqov* (Jerusalem: Magnes, 1977), 372.

27. See my "Shekhinah, the Virgin Mary, and the Song of Songs: Reflections on a Kabbalistic Symbol in Its Historical Context," *AJS Review* 26:1 (2002): 26.

28. See Reuven Kimelman, *Lekhah Dodi ve-Qabbalat Shabbat* (Jerusalem: Magnes, 2003); and Green, "Some Aspects of Qabbalat Shabbat," in *The Heart of the Matter*, 32–54. It may be that this refrain preceded Alkabetz's composition, as it is found accompanying an entirely different (and less successful) poem in Machir ben Abba Mari's *Seder ha-Yom*. See discussion by Kimelman, 25, n. 155.

29. Referring here to *tsaddik* as an element within God, the ninth *sefirah, yesod*, also symbolized by the phallus, and hence depicted as the male lover.

30. Zohar 2:134a; emphasis mine.

31. *Va-Yiqra Rabbah* 6:1.

32. Here it is clear that De Vidas is influenced by the language of *Avot de-Rabbi Natan*, ed. Solomon Schechter (Vienna: Mordeḥai Knöpflmacher, 1887), ch. 8, p. 36.

33. *Reshit Ḥokhmah, ahavah* 6:16.

34. *Reshit Ḥokhmah, ahavah* 1:25.

35. *Reshit Ḥokhmah, ahavah* 2:16.

36. The first to call attention to the aspect of the Zohar fraternity was M. D. Georg (Jiri) Langer in his *Die Erotik der Kabbala* (Prague: Josef Flesch, 1923). It has more recently been the subject of extensive discussion by several scholars. See Yehuda Liebes's comments in *Zohar ve-Eros, Alpayyim* 9 (1994): 67–119, on 104–5; and *Ha-Mashiaḥ shel ha-Zohar*, in *Ha-Raʿayon ha-Meshiḥi be-Yisraʾel* (Jerusalem: Israel Academy of Sciences and Humanities, 1982), 157–65. In English, see also

his *Studies in the Zohar,* trans. Arnold Schwartz et al. (Albany: State University of New York Press, 1993), 36–43. This subject has been discussed extensively in the various writings of Elliot Wolfson. See, for example, *Through a Speculum That Shines* (Princeton: Princeton University Press, 1994), 368–73; Wolfson, *Language, Eros, Being: Kabbalistic Hermeneutics and Poetic Imagination* (New York: Fordham University Press, 2004), 328–32. See more recently Joel Hecker, "Kissing Kabbalists: Hierarchy, Reciprocity, and Equality," *Studies in Jewish Civilization* 18 (2008): 171–208.

37. See Zohar 3:222b and *Reshit Ḥokhmah, ahavah* 9:5.

38. See sources cited by Abraham J. Heschel in *Heavenly Torah: As Refracted through the Generations,* ed. and trans. Gordon Tucker with Leonard Levin (New York: Continuum, 2006), 105–8.

39. Thus I have interpreted, in my *siddur* commentary, the words *ahavti ki yishma' Y-H-W-H et qoli* in Psalm 116:1. The author is not asking, "What is it that I love?" rendering the verse to mean "I love that Y-H-W-H hears my voice," but rather "How is it that I am capable of loving? What is it that allows me to take that risk?" The answer is "For Y-H-W-H hears my voice."

40. *Sefat Emet, Ki Tavo* 1882, translated and discussed in my *The Language of Truth* (Philadelphia: Jewish Publication Society, 1998), 327–28. I have also cited this text in my *Radical Judaism,* 119; earlier parallel sources are discussed there on 183, n. 65. I have suggested the impossible word *inverbational* for the theology of Hasidism.

41. I thus believe the question goes beyond that of God's lack of body, touching on the very nature of the Maimonidean deity's wholeness or perfection.

42. See my "God's Need for Man."

43. Hillel Zeitlin treated this point most perceptively in his essay "The Fundaments of Hasidism," translating it into philosophical language. See my edition of his *Hasidic Spirituality for a New Era: The Religious Writings of Hillel Zeitlin* (New York: Paulist, 2012), 79–80.

44. He was fond of illustrating this by quoting Leviticus 20:17: "If a man take his sister, the daughter of his father or his mother, seeing her nakedness and having her see his—this is ḥesed. They shall be cut off in the eyes of their people. This is his sister's nakedness; he shall bear his sin." The word *ḥesed* in that verse is what biblical scholars refer to as a contronym, a word that bears the opposite of its usual meaning. It is rendered by the translators as "abomination." But the BeSHT insisted that it retained precisely its original meaning. Even the most absolutely forbidden of sexual loves, that between brother and sister, is a form of fallen *ḥesed.* This interpretation is found both in the *Toledot Ya'aqov Yosef* (once in the BeSHT's name and twice more without citation) and in the *Me'or 'Eynayim* of R. Menaḥem Naḥum of Chernobyl, who was particularly fond of it (quoting it in six places). See discussion in the introduction to my English translation, *The Light of the Eyes* (Stanford: Stanford University Press, 2020). This bold reading is almost "waiting" to be applied to other forbidden loves as well.

45. B. Kiddushin 39b.

46. See the very firm rejection of even any "hope" of reward, especially that of the next world, in such hasidic passages as Menaḥem Naḥum of Chernobyl's *Yesamaḥ*

Lev on *Avot*, in *Me'or 'Eynayim* (Jerusalem: Ma'or ha-Torah, 5758 [1997–98]), 2:587f. Throughout the work, that author consistently interprets any discussion of *'olam ha-ba* in a this-worldly manner.

47. Bereshit Rabbah 35:2.
48. *Pri ha-Arets, shoftim;* emphasis mine. My thanks to Rabbi Ebn Leader for calling my attention to this text, as well as the portion of it quoted below.
49. *Pri ha-Arets, shoftim.*
50. Zohar 1:18b, Schne'ur Zalman of Liadi, *Tanya* 2:7.
51. I owe this formulation to my student Elliot Ginsburg.

Seasons

1. See *Me'or 'Eynayim, shemot* and *va-era*, translated as *The Light of the Eyes* (Stanford: Stanford University Press, 2020).
2. *Kedushat Levi, kedushat Hanukkah* #5. An English translation of this teaching is included in Arthur Green et al., *Speaking Torah: Spiritual Teachings from around the Maggid's Table* (Woodstock, VT: Jewish Lights, 2013), 2:195–97.
3. *Sefat Emet 'al ha-Torah, le-ḥodesh elul, 5659* [1899]. See also his teaching there from *5647–5648* [1887–88], in which he contrasts the first tablets, given through an initial arousal from above but ultimately shattered, with the second tablets, which "came through the power of Israel drawing close—and therefore they remain eternally."
4. Shir ha-Shirim Rabbah 5:3. This statement is frequently quoted in later Jewish literature, including hasidic books, with the ending "and I will open for you an opening the width of a hall." However, this phrasing is never found in classical rabbinic literature. At some point this new ending became popular (it is much catchier!), a change almost certainly drawing upon Rabbi Yoḥanan's statement (in b. Eruvin 53a) that while our hearts are only as wide as a needle's eye, the hearts of the earlier sages were as wide as the opening of a hall, and is thus a contrast already found in a Talmudic statement.
5. A *midrash*—which recurs with many variations—proposes that Israel merited redemption because they did not change their names or language, and avoided slander and promiscuity. *Pesikta de-Rav Kahana*, ed. Solomon Buber (Lviv, 1868), 83b. Against this is the tradition that presents angels objecting to the miraculous splitting of the Sea of Reeds for Israel, since Israel worshipped idols in Egypt just as the Egyptians did. See Shemot Rabbah 21:7.
6. B. Rosh Hashanah 21b.
7. The forty-nine days of counting the 'Omer are there each designated by a combination of two of the lower seven *sefirot*, those born of *binah:* "*tif'eret* within *yesod; malkhut* within *ḥesed*," etc.
8. Cf. Proverbs 1:8.
9. Tanḥuma, Ḥuqqat 8, Be-Midbar Rabbah 19:8, and compare Zohar 3:15a–16a.
10. B. Megillah 7b.
11. In the Idra sections of the Zohar, this endlessly compassionate side of the deity is depicted as male, the figure of *'atiqa*, the Elder, who radiates love into the face of

His Son, *ze'eir*, sweetening the judgment forces within Him. See the remarkable treatment of this aspect of Kabbalah by Melila Hellner-Eshed in her *Seekers of the Face: Secrets of the Great Assembly (Idra Rabba) of the Zohar* (Stanford: Stanford University Press, forthcoming).

12. *Kedushat Levi*, ed. Michael Aryeh Rand (Ashdod, Israel: Mekhon hadrat ḥen, 5765 [2004–5]), vol. 1, no. 413, adapted.

13. In traditional diaspora communities, each of these festivals is lengthened by an extra day, resulting from fear of calendrical error. Hence the number becomes nine versus eight days.

14. RaSHI on Leviticus 23:36, drawing upon Be-Midbar Rabbah 29:36 and b. Sukkah 55b.

15. "At the sea," God "appeared to them as a [youthful] warrior; at Sinai, as an elder teaching Torah." *Pesikta Rabbati* 33, 155b; and cf. *Mekhilta* 20:2. See my discussion in "The Children in Egypt and the Theophany at the Sea," in my *The Heart of the Matter: Studies in Jewish Mysticism and Theology* (Philadelphia: Jewish Publication Society, 2015), 87–100.

16. I have in my possession a letter from my teacher Nahum Glatzer, Rosenzweig's close disciple, responding to my query about whether Rosenzweig was aware of this structuring within the shabbat *'amidot* when he wrote of these three pillars of religion. Glatzer answered that he was not, but was pleased to learn it when it was pointed out to him (presumably by Glatzer himself).

17. Thus the Zohar refers to "the world that is coming, constantly coming, never ceasing." This is Daniel Matt's translation of Zohar 3:290b, and see his note on this in *The Zohar: Pritzker Edition*, trans. and ed. Daniel C. Matt (Stanford: Stanford University Press, 2004), 4, n. 19.

Shabbat

1. B. Shevu'ot 20b. On the kabbalistic uses of this rabbinic claim, see Elliot Ginsburg, *The Sabbath in the Classical Kabbalah* (Albany: SUNY Press, 1989), 102–3, 107–18.

2. M. Ḥagigah 1:8.

Rosh Hashanah

1. B. Rosh Hashanah 8a–b.

2. Here you see me relating to the Torah text within a historical-critical framework. I am comfortable doing that—but I never claim it to be the entire truth. This reading is my version of *peshat*, the surface meaning. I am also happy to read it as *sod*, its secret meaning, where I would just as comfortably say that the Torah chose to keep the name of this festival hidden for some mysterious reason, perhaps to tell us that every day is one on which we can begin again.

3. B. Rosh Hashanah 10b.

4. Some parts of this discussion are influenced by Theodore H. Gaster, *Festivals of the Jewish Year: A Modern Interpretation and Guide* (New York: Sloane, 1953), 107–

23, esp. 113–15. For a more recent brief assessment of the connections between the Jewish and Babylonian New Year, see Uri Gabbay, "Babylonian Rosh Hashanah: Battle, Creation, Enthronement, and Justice," *The Torah*, https://thetorah .com/babylonian-rosh-hashanah/.

5. "The *Hakham* and the *Tam* (The Clever Man and the Ordinary Man)," in *Nahman of Bratslav: The Tales*, trans. Arnold J. Band (New York: Paulist, 1978), 139–61, esp. 154–56.

6. Franz Kafka, *Parables and Paradoxes* (New York: Schocken Books, 1961), 13.

7. B. Shabbat 67a.

8. *Shemu'ah Tovah* (Jerusalem: Ginzey ha-Ḥasidut, 1972), 70.

9. *Or ha-Me'ir, derush le-Rosh ha-Shanah*, s.v. *ve-shama'ti me-ha-magid.*

10. This motif of the child—and especially the royal child—exiled from his father's table, based on early midrashic tropes, is well known throughout later Jewish homiletical sources. In kabbalistic sources, where God is mother as well as father, the motif becomes more complicated, Israel sometimes serving as the sinful child who has brought about separation between the parents, and taking blame for the destruction of the family. See the citations of Isaiah 50:1 in Zohar 1:22b, 27b, 237a, etc., and fuller discussion above in "Judaism as a Path of Love," n. 24. This motif is the source of my late and much-lamented friend Alan Mintz's title *Banished from Their Father's Table: Loss of Faith and Hebrew Autobiography* (Bloomington: Indiana University Press, 1989). His usage makes clear the wide applicability of this legend to the situation of the modern Jew.

11. "The Loss of the Princess," in *Nahman of Bratslav: The Tales*, 51–61.

12. *Beit Aharon* (Brody: Moshe Leib Harmelin, 1875), *likkutim*, s.v. *'od be-shem RaSHa"K*, 292.

13. Mishneh Torah, Laws of Repentance 3:4.

14. I have in mind here an episode within R. Naḥman's "Tale of the Seven Beggars," in *Nahman of Bratslav: The Tales*, 251–82, esp. 260–62.

15. Bereshit Rabbah 10:7.

16. Dov Baer of Metzritch, *Maggid Devarav le-Ya'akov*, 78.

17. See the classic study by Shalom Spiegel, *The Last Trial: The Akedah*, trans. Judah Goldin (Woodstock, VT: Jewish Lights, 1993).

18. *Sefat Emet, yom ha-kippurim* 5655 [1894–95].

Yom Kippur

1. M. Yoma 6:2.

2. A well-known statement in the Talmud (b. Makkot 23b–24a) sees Israel's outcry to Moses, "You speak with us and we will listen, but let not God speak with us, lest we die" (Ex. 20:16), as having followed the first two commandments. This is related to an interpretation of "Moses commanded Torah to us" (Deut. 33:4), noting that the numerical value of *torah* is 611, two fewer than the number of its commandments. "We heard two directly from the mouth of the Power [a name for God]." This latter interpretation, and the language "from the mouth of the Power" (*mi-pi ha-gevurah*), seems influenced by the *Mekhilta*'s reading of Psalm 62:12, as cited by RaSHI in b. Makkot 24a, s.v. *mi-pi ha-gevurah*, and see the entire verse.

3. See the particularly powerful rabbinic interpretation of this narrative in b. Berakhot 32a, where Moses, on hearing God's "Let Me go," "grabbed hold of God as one fellow grabs another by his shirt and said, 'I won't let You go until You forgive them.'"

4. "Statements" is really a better rendition of *dibberot* than "commandments."

5. This is the principle famously illustrated by the debate concerning the oven of Akhnai and its purity in b. Bava Metsi'a 59b, including the rabbi's invocation of "It [Torah] is not in heaven" (Deut. 30:12), and therefore "we pay no attention to heavenly voices" in interpreting it.

6. This should mean, by the way, that it is entirely appropriate—even *more* than appropriate—for women to have a prominent place within the rabbinate that makes such decisions. Oral Torah is *malkhut*, according to the kabbalists—the feminine power that channels and reshapes the divine voice.

7. This call for interpretive and legislative courage goes in both directions, permitting things once forbidden and toughening standards that under changed circumstances now seem to have been unduly lax. Finding solutions to such vexing injustices as the *'agunah* (the "chained" wife, unable to divorce) and the *mamzer* (illegitimate child) belong to the first category; banning of smoking, the hoisting and shackling of animals before slaughter, and deeds that pollute air, water, and soil to the second.

8. *Me'or 'Eynayim, Hayyey Sarah* #6. See my translation, *The Light of the Eyes* (Stanford: Stanford University Press, 2020).

9. B. Yevamot 79a.

Sukkot

1. Va-Yikra Rabbah 30:12, 30:14.

2. *Sefat Emet, sukkot* 5634 [1873–74], included in my *The Language of Truth: The Torah Commentary of the Sefat Emet, Rabbi Yehudah Leib Alter of Ger* (Philadelphia: Jewish Publication Society, 1998), 358–59.

3. B. Sukkah 2a.

4. Zohar 3:103a.

Simḥat Torah

1. The term (*'ahl al-kitāb*) occurs many times in the Qur'an, including a dozen times in Qur'an 3:64–199. In that context, the term refers to Jews as well as Christians and Sabians, and some Muslim thinkers extend the category to include members of other religious groups, such as Zoroastrians.

2. This reading was characteristic of the school of Rabbi Ishmael, a key second-century teacher. See sources quoted and extended discussion by Abraham Joshua Heschel in *Heavenly Torah: As Refracted through the Generations*, ed. and trans. Gordon Tucker with Leonard Levin (London: Continuum, 2006), 370–84.

3. See, for example, *Sefat Emet, le-Shavu'ot* 5638 [1878], s.v. *hashem 'oz le-'amo yitein.*

4. Efrayim of Sudilkov, *Degel Maḥaneh Ephraim*, 6a, *parashat bereshit*, s.v. *o yomar zeh sefer*. See my "Hasidism and Its Response to Change," in "Towards a New History of Hasidism," special issue, *Jewish History* 27:2/4 (2013): 319–36; this source is translated on p. 329.

5. For a good example of such radical readings, see the account of Hannah's outcry against God in b. Berakhot 31b.

6. That is how I translate the blessing *la-ʻasok be-talmud torah*, "to be engaged by the process of learning."

7. I have no objection to "he," if it better suits your need. *The gendering is meant to help open the heart. Use it however it suits that need best!*

8. Zohar 2:99a.

9. See my early treatment of this in "Bride, Spouse, Daughter: Images of the Feminine in Classical Jewish Sources," in *On Being a Jewish Feminist: A Reader*, ed. Susannah Heschel (New York: Schocken Books, 1983), 248–60.

10. Shir ha-Shirim Rabbah 2:17, 3:1.

11. B. Shabbat 105a.

12. See the source from the *Sefat Emet* cited in the next note, and cf. the teaching attributed to the Baʻal Shem Tov in *Degel Maḥaneh Ephraim, parashat ha'azinu*, s.v. *ki lo davar* (Jerusalem, 1963), 266a; and Naḥman of Bratslav, *Likkutey MoHaRaN* I, 19:9, particularly his reading *of ʻosey devaro*.

13. *Sefat Emet, parshat ki tavo* 5642 [1882], translated in my *The Language of Truth: The Torah Commentary of the Sefat Emet, Rabbi Yehudah Leib Alter of Ger* (Philadelphia: Jewish Publication Society, 1998), 327–28.

Ḥanukkah

1. Naḥmanides, *Commentary* on Exodus 13:16.

2. From *ʻal ha-nissim* ("for the miracles") for Ḥanukkah, added to the liturgy of the daily prayers and blessings after meals.

3. From *Modim*, the blessing of giving thanks in the daily liturgy, and traditionally considered one of the two blessings in the standing Prayer, which especially calls for focus and heartfelt devotion; see *Mishnah Berurah* to *Oraḥ Ḥayyim, siman* 101, no. 3.

4. For a book-length study exploring the richness of "light" symbolism in Jewish thought, including kabbalistic and hasidic sources, see Freema Gottlieb's *The Lamp of God: A Jewish Book of Light* (Northvale, NJ: Jason Aronson, 1989).

5. B. Ḥagigah 12a.

6. The verse in Proverbs 6:23, quoted above, is much expanded and commented on in the hasidic sources. See, for example, Menaḥem Naḥum of Chernobyl, *Me'or ʻEynayim, parashat shemot*, s.v. *va-tif'taḥ*.

Purim

1. Esther 9:17–19. The extension to other ancient walled cities—including Jerusalem—is a later innovation. See M. Megillah 1:1 with the commentary of Ovadiah of Bertinoro s.v. *mi-yimot yehoshuaʻ* and b. Megillah 2b.

2. B. Megillah 7b.

3. An association already found explicitly in *Tikkuney Zohar* 21, 57b.

4. See Canticles 4:10, 4:14, 4:16, 5:13, 6:2, and 8:14.

5. B. Shabbat 88a.
6. B. Shabbat 88a.
7. *Kedushat Levi, kedushat Purim* 1. Partially translated in Arthur Green et al., *Speaking Torah: Spiritual Teachings from around the Maggid's Table* (Woodstock, VT: Jewish Lights, 2013), 205–6.
8. For precedents for this approach in rabbinic sources, see b. Meg. 15b and Esther Rabbah 3:10.
9. B. Berakhot 58a.
10. See Elie Wiesel, *Legends of Our Time* (New York: Holt, Rinehart and Winston, 1968), viii.

Pesaḥ

1. The wise son's question in our Haggadah is "What are the decrees, laws, and judgments that Y-H-W-H our God has commanded *you?*" (Deut. 6:20). There is much speculation that the wise son's question originally drew upon an alternative version of the biblical text, one that read *lanu*, "for us," instead of "for you." See Marc Brettler's "Some Biblical Perspectives on the *Haggadah*," *The Torah*, https://thetorah.com/biblical-perspectives-on-the-haggadah/.
2. For examples of this sort of reading of the Pesaḥ narrative, see the early hasidic masters as quoted in Arthur Green et al., *Speaking Torah: Spiritual Teachings from around the Maggid's Table* (Woodstock, VT: Jewish Lights, 2013), 1:197–98 and 2:213–14; and R. Yehudah Aryeh Leib Alter of Ger in my *The Language of Truth: The Torah Commentary of the Sefat Emet* (Philadelphia: Jewish Publication Society, 1998), esp. 391–96.
3. For some interesting hasidic readings of this connection, see the sources in *Speaking Torah*, 2:219–20 and 222–23.
4. Mekhilta, *parashat be-shalaḥ, parashah* 3, s.v. *zeh eli* (Ex. 15:2).
5. Shemot Rabbah 23:15. RaSHI, in his comments to Exodus 15:2, refers both to this and the tradition cited in the previous note.
6. The Targum or Aramaic rendition of the Song of Songs, probably dating to around the eighth century CE, makes much of this; its introductory section briefly describes these ten songs—from Adam's song as the first Shabbat came in until the song of the final redemption. It reads the entirety of the text as a "song of the songs" of sacred history.
7. Sephardim and hasidic Jews read it also every Friday, prior to *Kabbalat Shabbat*.
8. *Shir ha-Shirim Rabbah* 2:14, s.v. *rabbi Eliezer patar*. See also the chapter "The Song of Songs in Jewish Mysticism" in my *The Heart of the Matter: Studies in Jewish Mysticism and Theology* (Philadelphia: Jewish Publication Society, 2015), 101–15, esp. 103–5.

Shavu'ot

1. See the discussion of Sinai in various *aggadot* collected in b. Shabbat 88a–89b. These are recorded there in response to earnest concern in the Mishnah as to

whether Torah was given on the sixth or seventh day of Sivan. Hasidic teachings on Shavuʻot are found, in Hebrew and English, in both Arthur Green et al., *Speaking Torah: Spiritual Teachings from around the Maggid's Table* (Woodstock, VT: Jewish Lights, 2013), 2:215–23; and my *The Language of Truth: The Torah Commentary of the Sefat Emet, Rabbi Yehudah Leib Alter of Ger* (Philadelphia: Jewish Publication Society, 1998), 399–407. For the *hasidim* of R. Naḥman of Bratslav, Shavuʻot was one of the three annual pilgrimage festivals when they visited their master. As a result, some of his most important teachings relate to Shavuʻot.

2. See *The Torah*, specifically Tamar Ross, "Orthodoxy and the Challenge of Biblical Criticism: Reflections on the Importance of Asking the Right Questions," https://thetorah.com/the-challenge-of-biblical-criticism/. See also the volume edited by Tova Ganzel, Yehudah Brandes, and Chayuta Deutsch, *The Believer and the Modern Study of the Bible* (Boston: Academic Studies, 2019).

3. See the opening essay in this volume.

4. "Universe," of course, is an English word based on the Latin, and is conceptually not of Jewish origin. I am using it here to represent the kabbalistic *ʻolamot*, all the "worlds," including that called *atsilut*, the inner world of Y-H-W-H. All those worlds are said to exist in parallel structure, serving as successive "layers" upon one another, coating (and protectively hiding) the innermost truth of oneness. On Torah as a revelation of the inner Self of God, see the passage from b. Shabbat 105a, and the readings of it discussed in the Simḥat Torah essay, n. 12, above.

5. The entire Torah as the name of God is found in Naḥmanides's introduction to his Torah commentary. On the origins and meaning of this claim, see Gershom Scholem, "The Meaning of Torah in Jewish Mysticism," in his *On the Kabbalah and Its Symbolism* (New York: Schocken, 1969), 32–86. The formulation "The soul is part of God above" is first found in the writings of R. Shabbatai Sheftl Horowitz, seventeenth century. On him, see Bracha Sack, *Shomer ha-Pardes: The Kabbalist Rabbi Shabbetai Sheftl Horowitz of Prague* [in Hebrew] (Beer Sheva, Israel: Ben Gurion University, 2002). The discovery of both God and Torah within the human soul—or of the soul's root within both God and Torah—is a mainstay of Jewish mystical theology. This theology is often taught around the Zoharic formula "The blessed Holy One, Torah, and Israel are one." While Isaiah Tishby (*Ḥikrei Kabbalah u-Shluhotehah* [Jerusalem: Magnes, 1982], 3:941–60) claimed that this formula was absent from the Zohar, and an invention of R. Moshe Hayyim Luzzatto in the early eighteenth century, more recent scholarship has questioned that view. See Moshe Idel, *Absorbing Perfections* (New Haven: Yale University Press, 2002), 118. See also Zohar 3:73a, which discusses the binding together of the Holy One, Torah, and Israel, "and each one" (*ve-kol ḥad*). If the final phrase is exchanged for the very close *ve-kula ḥad*, "and all is one," we find one of the formulations in which this idea is found in later mystical literature. A neo-hasidic reading, here as elsewhere, requires a universalization of "Israel." On that point, see the discussion in the introduction to *A New Hasidism*, ed. Arthur Green and Ariel Evan Mayse (Philadelphia: Jewish Publication Society, 2019), 1:xv–xxvii, and various thinkers whose essays appear in that two-volume work.

6. B. Berakhot 45a.

7. Archetypically applied to Moses, the phrase "the Shekhinah speaks from within his throat" appears often in hasidic works—for example, in *Sefer Ba'al Shem Tov* (Lodz, 1938), *parashat be-ḥukotai*, s.v. *im be-ḥukotai* (2), and *Kedushat Levi, parashat va-etḥannan*, s.v. *o yesh lomar va-yered*. The precise phrase is not found in classical rabbinic sources; see Shemot Rabbah 3:15, Va-Yikra Rabbah 2:3, and Zohar 3:232a (in the *Ra'aya Mehemna*). See the long note in my "The Hasidic Homily: Mystical Performance and Hermeneutical Process," in *As a Perennial Spring: A Festschrift Honoring Rabbi Dr. Norman Lamm*, ed. Bentsi Cohen (New York: Downhill, 2013), 261–62, n. 26.

8. B. Berakhot 10a is an oft-quoted source listing five parallels between God and soul. God as the "soul of the universe" is a formulation well known in the comparative study of religion. Plato's description of the "world-soul" (*psyche tou kosmou*) in his dialogue on cosmogony, *Timaeus* (35 A–B) was enormously influential, living on as *anima mundi* in Latin philosophy and theology. The concept of the *Weltseele* was a central topic of German idealism as well. In various ways, all of these traditions are reflecting—with varying degrees of awareness—on the nature of human mind and soul when discussing a divine or universal one.

9. The term *kol* or *kolot* elsewhere in this section refers to thunder. See Exodus 19:16, 20:18. See the fuller discussion of this view of revelation in my *Radical Judaism* (New Haven: Yale University Press, 2010), ch. 3. See also the discussion of this verse in Benjamin Sommer, *Revelation and Authority* (New Haven: Yale University Press, 2015), 36–37.

10. B. Shabbat 88b.

11. See the comment of R. Hai Gaon (939–1038) regarding the *merkavah* ascent to the heavens, recorded in B. M. Lewin, ed., *Otsar ha-Ge'onim*, Ḥagigah (Jerusalem, 1930–31), 14, to Ḥagigah 15a: "He gazes inward, into his [own inner] chambers, like one who see with his eyes the seven palaces." This may be the earliest example in Jewish sources of an internalized reading of "heaven" (unless one counts Deuteronomy 30:12). On this text, see Elliot Wolfson, *Through a Speculum That Shines* (Princeton: Princeton University Press, 1994), 145–46.

12. Of course, "up" and "in" are themselves metaphoric designations. Neither of them makes sense in literal or "geographic" terms.

13. For some hasidic readings of the Torah's tales of well digging, see *Sefat Emet*, *parashat toledot* 5661 (1900–1901), s.v. *be-'inyan ha-be'erot*, and the insistently inwardly-focused teaching in Simḥah Bunem of Przysucha, *Kol Simḥah* (New York: M. Nirenberg, 5715 [1954–55]), 19, *parashat toledot*, s.v. *ve-khol ha-be'erot*. See also my discussion in *Devotion and Commandment: The Faith of Abraham in the Hasidic Imagination* (Cincinnati: Hebrew Union College Press, 1989), 9–24, especially 16–19.

14. Mekhilta on Exodus 20:15.

15. One might understand what is presented here as reflecting the Maimonidean view that it was Moses, rather than all of Israel, who experienced the revelation of Sinai. He is following the tradition reflected in *m. Avot* 1:12: "*Moses* received Torah from Sinai and passed it on to Joshua." The alternative view, that the revelation was to all Israel, is classically seen as that of Yehudah Halevi. Both views

are reflected in the Zohar and the later mystical tradition. There the line from *Tikkuney Zohar* 69, 114a, that refers to "the spreading forth of Moses in each generation" allows for a notion of continuing revelation. Maimonides refers to the prophet as one who has attained perfection of mind and imagination as one: *Guide for the Perplexed* 2:36–37. There is much discussion of the tension between the positive role of the imagination in the prophet and the disparaging way in which Maimonides generally speaks of this faculty. See Warren Zev Harvey, "Three Theories of the Imagination in Twelfth-Century Jewish Philosophy," in *Intellect and Imagination in Medieval Philosophy*, ed. Maria Candida Pacheco and Jose F. Meirinhos (Turnhout: Brepols, 2006), 287–302.

16. As a "*davener*" who follows the Sephardic/hasidic rite, I recite the Torah passage on clearing out the ashes (Lev. 6:1–6) from the altar each morning. It helps.

17. See the fuller discussion above in "How I Practice Judaism."

18. The rabbinic list of basic universal norms for human behavior, the Noahide commandments, are Judaism's closest parallel to "natural law." They are prohibitions against murder, theft, idolatry, incest and adultery, blasphemy or denial of God, dismemberment of living animals even for food, and an admonition to establish a society ruled by law. "Recognizing all humans as embodying the divine image" and these principles of universal law forces me to reinterpret certain norms found within traditional Judaism, notably those regarding the status of women and much of the discussion of sexuality, including the rejection of same-sex physical love.

Tish'ah be-Av

1. B. Yoma 9b.

2. B. Baba Batra 119b.

3. Abraham Joshua Heschel, *The Sabbath: Its Meaning for Modern Man* (New York: Farrar, Straus and Giroux, 1951).

4. See, for example, Yehudah Leib Alter of Ger, *Sefat Emet*, le-pesaḥ, 5637 [1877], s.v. *va-yedaber moshe* and 5652 [1892], s.v. *ita be-gemara ha-mekayem ha-mo'adot*. Heschel, a Warsaw Jew, was educated in Gerer schools, and the influence of Ger upon Heschel's thinking has been insufficiently appreciated. See the succinct discussion and sources cited in Michael Marmur, *Abraham Joshua Heschel and the Sources of Wonder* (Toronto: University of Toronto Press, 2016), 122–23; and my "Three Warsaw Mystics," *Jerusalem Studies in Jewish Thought* 13 (1996): 1–58, also available on my website, artgreen26.com.

5. Arthur Green, "Sabbath as Temple: Some Thoughts on Space and Time in Judaism," in *Go and Study: Essays and Studies in Honor of Alfred Jospe*, ed. Raphael Jospe and Samuel Z. Fishman (Washington, DC: Bnai Brith Hillel Foundations, 1980), 287–305.

6. Yeshayahu Leibowitz, *Yahadut, 'Am Yehudi u-Medinat Yisrael* [in Hebrew] (Jerusalem: Schocken, 1975).

7. Avi Sagi and Dov Schwartz, *Religious Zionism and the Six-Day War: From Realism to Messianism* (London: Routledge, 2018).

8. The single reference in Zechariah 2:16 may indicate that the concept began to develop in early Second Temple times, emerging from a nostalgia for a lost homeland.

9. Exodus 19:13; and see b. Ta'anit 21b.

10. On the whole history of this, see Ron Margolin, *Mikdash Adam* [in Hebrew] (Jerusalem: Magnes, 2005).

11. Thus hasidic masters sometimes compared Sabbath to a *sukkah*, although it is one we enter but cannot walk out of, staying immersed in it throughout the day. However, the trope of "being" Shabbat is occasionally found in the Zohar and hasidic sources, in which the *tsaddik* is Shabbat: Zohar 3:29a; and see *Ba'al Shem Tov al-ha-Torah* (Jerusalem: Nofet Tsofim, 5757 [1996–97]), 1:112–14 and n. 108 there.

12. Similarly, the widely sung *Bil'vavi mishkan evneh*, "In my heart I will build a sanctuary," whose lyrics were composed in the mid-twentieth century by Rabbi Yitzak Hutner, inspired by the lines of a poem in sixteenth-century Rabbi Elazar Azikri's *Sefer Haredim*.

13. I recognize that sometimes it was understood that way in rabbinic literature (see, for example, b. Yebamot 16a). I reject that understanding of *kedushah*.

14. See my treatment in "Three Warsaw Mystics."

15. *Beraita de-rabbi Yishma'el*, from the introduction to the *Sifra*, printed in traditional prayer books following the sacrificial passages toward the beginning of the morning service. Where other classical hasidic books may cite this principle once or twice, Alter places it at the center of this thought—it is quoted over fifty times in *Sefat Emet*. For examples in other hasidic works, see *Kedushat Levi*, 171, *parashat devarim*, s.v. *dibber moshe*; and Kalonymous Kalman Epstein, *Ma'or va-Shemesh* (Jerusalem: Galim, 5746 [1985–86]), 2:52, *parashat hukkat*, s.v. *o yomar zot*.

16. Yehudah Leib Alter, *Sefat Emet* (Jerusalem: Mir, 1996–97), 3:194, *parashat be-har* 5648 (1888), s.v. *ki tavo'u el ha-arets*; translated in my *The Language of Truth: The Torah Commentary of the Sefat Emet, Rabbi Yehudah Leib Alter of Ger* (Philadelphia: Jewish Publication Society, 1998), 204–5.

17. Alter, *Sefat Emet*, 1:69, *parashat va-yera'* 5651 (1890–91), s.v. *be-midrash ve-ahar*, and 1:234–35, *parashat pekudei* 5652 (1891–92), s.v. *be-midrash tanhuma*.

18. Regarding priests or Levites and the rest of Israel, see, for example, Alter, *Sefat Emet*, 3:26, *parashat tsav*, s.v. *be-parshat kah et aharon*. The text in *parashat pekudei* 5652 cited in the previous note applies this thought to Israel and all humanity quite clearly. See Yoram Jacobson, "The Sanctity of the Mundane in the Hasidic School of Ger" [in Hebrew], in *Tsaddikim ve-Anshei Ma'aseh: Studies in Polish Hasidism*, ed. Rachel Elior, Israel Bartel, and Chone Shmeruk (Jerusalem: Mossad Bialik, 1994), 241–77.

19. In the "Polish School" of Hasidism, of which *Sefat Emet* is the apogee, there is much less emphasis on the uniqueness of the *tsaddik*, and more on his serving as an example for the spiritual journey of every Jew. See Michael Rosen, *The Quest for Authenticity: The Thought of Reb Simhah Bunim* (Jerusalem: Urim, 2008).

Creation

1. M. *Avot* 3:1.

2. The best-known version of this tale is found in the opening pages of the Zohar (1:2b–3b), but it existed earlier. The Alphabet of Rabbi Akiva, a text whose

earliest recension dates from the eighth or ninth century CE, contains a longer and more detailed version. See Adolf Jellinek's *Beit ha-Midrasch* (Leipzig, 1855), 3:xvi–xvii and 12–64.

3. Bereshit Rabbah 1:10.

4. Y. Ḥagigah 2:2. God's unwillingness to create with *aleph* for this reason suggests that the letters have some power of their own, and that the Creator has to use them warily.

5. Bereshit Rabbah 1:10.

6. In the spirit of the *Tikkuney Zohar*, I am suggesting that *Elohim*, the God of multiplicity, created *bet reshit*, the origin of duality.

7. As *aleph* opens the decalogue, for the kabbalist the divine name *Ehyeh*, beginning with *aleph*, symbolizing *keter*, the first of the ten divine rungs, opens the process of emanation.

8. Naftali Tsvi of Ropczyce, *Zera' Kodesh* (Brooklyn: Yofi, 1996), vol. 2, *le-ḥag ha-shavu'ot*, s.v. *be-midrash anokhi*, 40a–40b. Warren Zev Harvey, "What Did the Rymanover Really Say about the Aleph of Anokhi?" [in Hebrew], *Kabbalah* 34 (2016): 297–314.

9. Based on Zohar 1:15a. See the elucidation by Daniel Matt on this passage in his *The Zohar: Pritzker Edition* (Stanford: Stanford University Press, 2004), 1:107–9.

10. Both the term and the notion of *tsimtsum* have earlier roots, but only after Luria does it come to play a central role in the drama of the Creation narrative.

11. This is indeed "The Tragic Sense of Life," to steal Unamuno's title, portrayed so poignantly by R. Naḥman of Bratslav in his parable of the heart and the spring, quoted below in the essay "Jewish Mysticism and Its Healing Power." Does poet Azikri's line *nafshi ḥolat ahavatekha*, "My soul is sick for love of You," describe a state where God seems too far from the seeker? Or perhaps too near?

12. This has everything to do with the transition in Hasidism's first generation from the *ba'al shem* to the *tsaddik* as the powerful figure to whom one turned. On this, see my discussion in "The Hasidic Tsaddik and the Charism of Relationship," in *Essays in Honor of Moshe Idel* (Jerusalem, 2021). I realize that I am somewhat overstating the case here, but this is intentional. The early hasidic authors, including the Maggid and his circle, have a more complex and eclectic relationship to the kabbalistic legacy. But I think this is the direction in which they are moving, and a neo-hasidic theology needs to carry that process forward, in part by stating it more definitively than they were able to do.

13. I commend the reader to Hillel Zeitlin's essay "The Fundaments of Hasidism," to be found in *Hasidic Spirituality for a New Era: The Religious Writings of Hillel Zeitlin*, ed. Arthur Green (New York: Paulist, 2012), 71–117. Zeitlin, a founder of Neo-Hasidism, states this more unequivocally than do the hasidic sources on which he draws.

14. *Me'or 'Eynayim, bo*. Typically, comments on this verse ask why the verb "Come" is used rather than "Go." The implication drawn here is partly my own.

15. *Me'or 'Eynayim Bereshit* #5, in my *The Light of the Eyes* (Stanford: Stanford University Press, 2020), 153, based on Zohar 3:29b.

16. *M. Avot* 5:1.

17. Bereshit Rabbah 1:1.

18. Shne'ur Zalman of Liadi, *Tanya* 2:1.

19. The existence of multiple recensions of *Sefer Yetsirah* makes it unwise to speak of the dating of *the* text. Nonetheless, Scholem placed its origins between the third and sixth centuries CE, and Liebes earlier, perhaps even the first century. Gershom Scholem, *On the Kabbalah and Its Symbolism*, trans. R. Mannheim (New York: Schocken, 1969), 167; Yehuda Liebes, *Ars Poetica in Sefer Yetsirah* [in Hebrew] (Jerusalem: Schocken, 2000), 229 and passim.

20. Much is made by later commentators of the fact that 32 is the numerical equivalent of the word *lev*, or "heart," but it is not clear that this was part of the original intent. The *sefirot*, in their more richly developed form, are the subject of most kabbalistic discourse. For an overview of the *sefirot*, including a discussion of the origin of the term in early speculative works, see my *A Guide to the Zohar* (Stanford: Stanford University Press, 2004), 28–59.

21. Liebes, *Ars Poetica*.

22. The quotation is from the daily morning service, based on Psalm 104:30.

23. B. Megillah 21b.

24. This primordial wisdom is most vividly evoked in Proverbs 8, especially verses 22–31, and Job 28. For the influential image of the Holy One looking into the "Torah" and creating the world, see Bereshit Rabbah 1:1, a *midrash* reading the opening verse of Genesis in the light of Proverbs 8:30. Rabbinic literature generally takes biblical references to wisdom (*ḥokhmah*) as referring to Torah, although there are exceptions—see, for example, Solomon Schechter, *Agadat Shir Hashirim* (Cambridge: Deighton Bell, 1896), 5, lines 20–28.

25. Whether that precedence may be considered temporal, if we are in the realm of pre-Creation, deserves some thought. We might rather think of it as logical—derived from *logos*, after all—rather than temporal precedence.

26. Berakhot 55a.

27. The line here from *Sefer Yetsirah* to the thought of Rav Kook is quite unbroken. The divinity of human creativity was not invented by Nietzsche—although Kook is influenced by him, alongside his vast knowledge of classical and mystical Jewish sources.

28. Zohar 3:4a.

29. There is of course a negative side of this, manifesting at times in Jewish rejection of nonreproductive sex and an obsession over wasting seed. See Sharon Faye Koren, *Forsaken: The Menstruant in Medieval Jewish Mysticism* (Waltham, MA: Brandeis, 2011).

30. These terms are loaded with much baggage these days, and this is not the place for a full unpacking of it. Suffice it to say that I refer to a fully consensual sexual expression between two adult human beings who share a sense of love and responsibility for one another, who care enough to want to "know" one another in a full range of that term's meaning.

31. Notice that the root *d-r-sh* has a range of meanings that includes both "to seek out" (as in Rebecca, the first human to "seek God" [Gen. 25:22]) and "to

interpret," as in *midrash*. Interpretation is the constant re-creation of meaning; we create new articulations of meaning in response to our ongoing quest.

32. Yes, I am aware that this contradicts the claim of Rabbi Naḥman of Bratslav (*Likkutey MoHaRaN* 64) that the highest inner places can only be approached in silence. "Both these and those are the words of the living God."

33. See Isaiah Tishby, *Wisdom of the Zohar*, trans. David Goldstein (Oxford: Littman, 1989), 1:292–95. See also the extended discussion associating silence and wonder with pre-verbal divine thought in Joseph Gikatilla, *Sha'are Orah: Gates of Light*, trans. Avi Weinstein (San Francisco: HarperCollins, 1994), 337–42.

34. See my *Keter: The Crown of God in Early Jewish Mysticism* (Princeton: Princeton University Press, 1997).

35. B. Berakhot 12a. From these pressures emerged the understanding of the ten commandments as "containing" all of the 613, as in Be-Midbar Rabbah 13:16. In his commentary to Exodus 24:12, RaSHI quotes this idea and refers to Sa'adia Gaon's *Azharot*, which connects each of the 613 to the ten. *Azharot* are a genre of poetry produced in the medieval period, which list all of the 613 commandments. See further references in n. 6 to "How I Practice Judaism—and Why" in this volume.

36. Pesikta Rabbati 21:18–19; Zohar 3:11b–12b.

37. Zohar 1:15a, and see n. 9 to this chapter.

38. B. Shabbat 88b, and see the hasidic treatments of this source in *Kedushat Levi* (Warsaw: Yitsḥak Goldman, 5636 [1875–76]), 212, *likkutim al-avot*, s.v. *ve-zehu she-ramzu*, and Naḥman of Bratslav, *Likkutey MoHaRaN* 56:7, 173. See also Franz Rosenzweig, *On Jewish Learning*, ed. N. N. Glatzer (New York: Schocken, 1955), 118; and Scholem, *On the Kabbalah and Its Symbolism*, 30–31.

39. See n. 8 above.

40. See my note in Menaḥem Naḥum of Chernobyl, *The Light of the Eyes, parashat bereshit*, 154, n. 241.

41. See the discussion by Harvard astrophysicist Howard Smith in his book *Let There Be Light: Modern Cosmology and Kabbalah* (Novato, CA: New World Library, 2006); and Daniel Matt's *God and the Big Bang*, 2nd ed. (Woodstock, VT: Jewish Lights, 2016).

42. Creation is, of course, one of the three points on a triangle of Rosenzweig's *Star*; but he does not help us to deal with the relationship between religion and science in this matter. It is also perhaps a disservice that Rosenzweig rendered in identifying creation-centered religion with that of classical paganism, thus reinforcing some of the anti-materialist bias of revelation- or redemption-centered religion.

43. This and several following paragraphs are adapted from my *Radical Judaism* (New Haven: Yale University Press, 2010).

44. This reading of *eyn 'od* is based on that of R. Shne'ur Zalman of Liadi in *Tanya* 2:1.

45. Based on a rabbinic reading of Exodus 19:19, found in b. Berakhot 45a. The original passage is somewhat obscure regarding the question of who is speaking and who is translating; see the commentary of Tosafot there, s.v. *be-kolo shel moshe*.

The noun *kol*, throughout Exodus 19, means "thunderclap." See also discussion above in "Shavu'ot: Speaking in Thunder."

46. *Tikkuney Zohar* 69, 114a.
47. See Paul R. Fleischman's *Wonder: When and Why the World Appears Radiant* (Amherst, MA: Small Batch Books, 2013).
48. See the discussion of "hidden miracles" in the chapter on Ḥanukkah in this volume.
49. All translations of biblical passages from here until the end of the chapter are taken from the *JPS Hebrew-English Tanakh*, 2nd ed. (Philadelphia: Jewish Publication Society, 1999).

Religion and Environmental Responsibility

1. Javier C. Hernández, "In China, a Religious Revival Fuels Environmental Activism," *New York Times*, July 13, 2017.
2. *M. Avot* 6:2. "Horeb" is another name for Sinai (see, e.g., Deut. 4:10–15).
3. Exodus 5:17–18.

Judaism as Counterculture

1. Hearing the universal, and thus personal, nature of this call is at the heart of the famous story of Rabbi Shne'ur Zalman of Liady and his jailer recorded in Martin Buber, *Tales of the Hasidim* (New York: Schocken, 1947), 268–69.
2. RaSHI's comment draws on passages in b. Taanit 20a and b. Sanhedrin 104a.
3. For a comment on the meaning of "whiteness" in the view of Jewish tradition, see above in the essay "All about Being Human" regarding Miriam's punishment for speaking against her dark-skinned sister-in-law.
4. American Jews on the left generally tend to paint all the settlers with a single brush, not noting the varying attitudes toward their Arab neighbors that have begun to spring up among them. While I remain completely opposed to the settlement project, as I have been since 1969, I do recognize the good intentions of people in Tekoa and elsewhere, seeking to change the behavior, and not only the image, of the settler population.
5. The Universal Declaration of Human Rights was authored and supported, in significant measure, by Jews in the early postwar years, as has been shown. See, for example, James Loeffler, *Rooted Cosmopolitans: Jews and Human Rights in the Twentieth Century* (New Haven: Yale University Press, 2018).
6. Y. Nedarim 9:4, 30b.
7. M. Sanhedrin 4:5.
8. B. Berakhot 58b.
9. B. Yebamot 60b–61a.
10. Sifrei ba-Midbar 69:2, famously quoted by RaSHI in his comments on Genesis 33:4. About the correct text and interpretation of this source, see Martin Lockshin, "'Esau Hates Jacob': But Is Antisemitism a *Halakha?*" *The Torah*, https://thetorah.com/esau-hates-jacob-but-is-antisemitism-a-halakha/.

11. B. Shabbat 88a.
12. Kohelet Rabbah 7:13.

Wandering Jews

1. Abraham Saba, *Tsror ha-Mor*, beginning of *parashat massaʿey*, and the influential Lurianic collection edited by Meir Poppers, *Likkutey Torah, parashat massaʿey*.
2. See also the discussion above in "Sukkot" in this volume.
3. B. Megillah 29a. In the following, I am much influenced by the work of Jerusalem scholar Biti Roi in her book *Ahavat ha-Shekhinah: Mystika u-Poetika be-Tikkuney ha-Zohar* (Ramat Gan, Israel: Bar Ilan University Press, 2017).

Scholarship Is Not Enough

1. Originally published in *Luaḥ Ha-Arets* (Tel Aviv, 1945), 94–112. Available in English translation in Gershom Scholem, *On the Possibility of Jewish Mysticism in Our Time and Other Essays*, ed. Avraham Shapira, trans. Jonathan Chipman (Philadelphia: Jewish Publication Society, 1997), 51–71.
2. See the story about R. Menaḥem Medel of Vitebsk, "At the Window," in Martin Buber, *Tales of the Hasidim* (New York: Schocken, 1947), 179; and compare Menachem Kallus, *Pillar of Prayer* (Louisville, KY: Fons Vitae, 2011), 195, n. 1095.
3. This is my own translation from his Hebrew text. Scholem, *On the Possibility of Jewish Mysticism*, 52.
4. See Shai Secunda, *The Iranian Talmud: Reading the Bavli in Its Sasanian Context* (Philadelphia: University of Pennsylvania Press, 2014).
5. In differing ways, Paula Fredriksen and Daniel Boyarin have taken leading roles in this scholarly enterprise. See also the recent book by Michael Rosenberg, *Signs of Virginity: Testing Virgins and Making Men in Late Antiquity* (Oxford: Oxford University Press, 2018).
6. This describes Raphael Mahler's views on Hasidism in *Hasidism and the Jewish Enlightenment: Their Confrontation in Galicia and Poland in the First Half of the Nineteenth Century*, trans. Eugene Orenstein et al. (Philadelphia: Jewish Publication Society, 1985), but applies also to Louis Finkelstein's original treatment of the rabbinic period in *The Pharisees: The Sociological Background of Their Faith* (Philadelphia: Jewish Publication Society, 1938), printed by the same publishers in a third revised edition in two volumes in 1962 and 1966, where the orientation was changed significantly.
7. This applies, of course, both to Gershom Scholem's *Sabbatai Ṣevi* and to my *Tormented Master*. I have in my possession a handwritten letter from Scholem, warning me against excessive use of psychoanalytic categories in discussing historic figures!
8. The influence of psychoanalytic theory is particularly notable in this field, reflected especially in the writings of Elliot Wolfson and Ruth Kara-Ivanov Kaniel.
9. See my "Shekhinah, the Virgin Mary, and the Song of Songs: Reflections on a Kabbalistic Symbol in Its Historical Context," *AJS Review* 26:1 (2002): 1–52;

Peter Schäfer, *Mirror of His Beauty: Feminine Images of God from the Bible to the Early Kabbalah* (Princeton: Princeton University Press, 2002). On Islamic parallels and influences, see Paul B. Fenton, "Judaism and Sufism," in *The Cambridge Companion to Medieval Jewish Philosophy*, ed. Daniel H. Frank and Oliver Leaman (Cambridge: Cambridge University Press, 2003), 201–17. All of these contributions were criticized by some as overly speculative when first published, but now seem to have gained acceptance.

10. For this reason, I feel that seminaries and other Jewish communal institutions play a vital role in nourishing the Jewish future, and that is why I have made so much of my career within them.

11. Hayyim Nahman Bialik and Yehoshua Hana Ravnitzky, *The Book of Legends: "Sefer Ha-Aggadah"; Legends from the Talmud and Midrash*, trans. William G. Braude (New York: Schocken, 1992).

12. Think especially of his *Yamim Nora'im*—translated as *Days of Awe* by Maurice T. Galpert, with an introduction by Arthur Green (New York: Schocken, 1995)—and *Atem Re'item*, available as *Present at Sinai: The Giving of the Law*, trans. Michael Swirsky (Philadelphia: Jewish Publication Society, 1994).

13. The first volume of this work, which includes substantial introductions as well as selections arranged thematically and translated into Hebrew by Fischel Lachover and Isaiah Tishby, was published in Jerusalem by Mossad Bialik in 1949. See Isaiah Tishby, *The Wisdom of the Zohar: An Anthology of Texts*, trans. David Goldstein, 3 vols. (Cambridge: Oxford University Press, 1989).

14. Steinsaltz completed his work on his edition of the Babylonian Talmud in 2010, the same year in which Koren in Jerusalem became his exclusive publisher. It is available in Hebrew in twenty-nine volumes; the English translation (the "Noé Edition") is projected to be complete in forty-two volumes.

15. *The Zohar: Pritzker Edition*, 12 vols. (Stanford: Stanford University Press, 2004–17); Tzvi Mark, *The Complete Stories of Rabbi Nachman of Bratslav* [in Hebrew] (Tel Aviv: Miskal, 2014).

16. Perhaps these two terms may serve as renditions of *ruah* and *neshamah*, which the Zohar (3:25b) claims can be acquired only through *talmud torah*.

17. The kabbalistic source is in R. Ezra of Gerona's *Sod 'Ets ha-Da'at*, translated by Gershom Scholem in his essay "*Sitra Aḥra*: Good and Evil in the Kabbalah," in his *On the Mystical Shape of the Godhead* (New York: Schocken, 1991), 56–87; see esp. 65–71.

18. Y. Shekalim 2:5, 11a teaches that you should picture the teacher standing before you when you recite a Torah teaching that has been passed down; see also Nachman of Bratslav's *Likkutey MoHaRaN*, 1:192. Compare also Joseph B. Soloveitchik's description of the experience of learning as involving the sages of the past coming to join him "all in my little room, sitting around my table" in his *And from There You Shall Seek*, ed. David Shatz and Reuven Ziegler (Hoboken, NJ: Ktav, 2008), 145.

19. On the value of *ḥevruta* learning, see Elie Holzer with Orit Kent, *A Philosophy of Havruta: Understanding and Teaching the Art of Text Study in Pairs* (Boston: Academic Studies, 2013). For its application specifically to Talmud study, see Jane

Kanarek and Marjorie Lehman, eds., *Learning to Read Talmud: What It Looks Like and How It Happens* (Boston: Academic Studies, 2016). Note also the remarkable work being done by Benay Lappe in her SVARA Yeshiva in Chicago.

20. For example, Ya'akov Yosef of Polonne, *Toledot Ya'akov Yosef*, vol. 2 (Jerusalem: n.p., 2011), *parashat aharey mot*, 623. See also Joseph Weiss, "Torah Study in Early Hasidism," in *Studies in East European Jewish Mysticism and Hasidism*, ed. David Goldstein (London: Littman, 1997), 56–68.

21. Levi Yizhak Bender, *No'am Siah*, 3 vols. (Jerusalem: n.p., n.d.).

Dear Brothers and Sisters

1. See my essay on this subject in *A New Hasidism: Branches* (Philadelphia: Jewish Publication Society, 2019).

Jewish Mysticism and Its Healing Power

1. In rabbinic sources, the act of religious defiance is called by the curious name "casting words upward" (b. Berakhot 31b–32a), something like throwing stones to break God's windows. On this aspect of rabbinic theology, see also Anson Laytner, *Arguing with God: A Jewish Tradition* (Northvale, NJ: Jason Aronson, 1990); and Dov Weiss, *Pious Irreverence: Confronting God in Rabbinic Judaism* (Philadelphia: University of Pennsylvania Press, 2017). Here I see myself throwing things at the void, confident that this is not a vain exercise.

2. B. Rosh Hashanah 16a.

3. Taking *refa'enu* as though derived from *r-f-h*, "soft," rather than *r-p-'*, "heal."

4. Understanding *tamu* as related to *tam* or *tamim*, "simple" or "whole," rather than "concluded."

5. Of course, the hasidic sources—and none more so than R. Levi Yizhak of Berdychiv—are especially fond of the seemingly contradictory words in b. Mo'ed Katan 16b: "The blessed Holy One issues a decree, and the *tsaddik* nullifies it." I have to read this "nullification" (*bittul*) as the sense that a *tsaddik* has the equilibrium to show us how to accept things as they are, without feeling that the hand of heaven is turned against us.

6. Arthur Green, *EHYEH: A Kabbalah for Tomorrow* (Woodstock, VT: Jewish Lights, 2003), 156–57.

7. See discussion in the essay "Scholarship Is Not Enough" elsewhere in this volume. For the Franz Kafka reference, see "Paradise," in his *Parables and Paradoxes* (New York: Schocken Books, 1961), 29–34.

8. From his "Tale of the Seven Beggars." Translation from my discussion in *Tormented Master: A Life of Rabbi Nahman of Bratslav* (Birmingham: University of Alabama Press, 1979), 301.

9. This longing is the "narrow bridge" of which R. Nahman speaks in the passage (*Likkutei Moharan Tinyana*, no. 48) whose words (slightly altered) have now become a well-known song. See also the remarkable teaching by R. Menahem Nahum of Chernobyl on Jeremiah 31:3 ("From afar Y-H-W-H appears to me"),

translated in Arthur Green et al., *Speaking Torah: Spiritual Teachings from around the Maggid's Table* (Woodstock, VT: Jewish Lights, 2013), 2:177–78.

10. I have translated part of this teaching in my *EHYEH: A Kabbalah for Tomorrow*, 127–31.

11. The reader is referred to a more extended discussion in my book *EHYEH: A Kabbalah for Tomorrow*, especially the chapter on the *sefirot*, 39–60. A more academic presentation is available in my *A Guide to the Zohar* (Stanford: Stanford University Press, 2004), 28–59.

12. In hasidic language, we are here engaged with the three "uppermost" (translated into "innermost") levels of mind, called *ḥokhmah, binah, da'at*.

13. These are called *netsaḥ* and *hod* in the kabbalistic system. *Hod* is most often read in the hasidic sources as a shortening of *hoda'ah*, recognition or grateful acceptance.

14. *Yesod* and *malkhut*, the loci of gender identity and sexual expression within the human self, hence primal "giver" and "receiver."

15. On this journey from esotericism to relationship-based healing and teaching within the history of early Hasidism, see my treatment in "The Hasidic Tsaddik and the Charism of Relationship," in *Essays in Honor of Moshe Idel* (Jerusalem, 2021).

My Own Jewish Education

1. On R. Zalman and his relationship to Chabad, see my interview with him, now published in *A New Hasidism: Roots* (Philadelphia: Jewish Publication Society, 2019).

My Rabbinate

1. S. Y. Agnon, *Days of Awe*, with a new introduction by Arthur Green (New York: Schocken Books, 1995), 22.

2. See my essay "*Da'at*: Universalizing a Hasidic Value," in *Religious Truth: Towards a Jewish Theology of Religions*, ed. Alon Goshen-Gottstein (London: Littman, 2020).

3. See "Personal Theology," in my *The Heart of the Matter: Studies in Jewish Mysticism and Theology* (Philadelphia: Jewish Publication Society, 2015), 345–58, also available on my website http://artgreen26.com.

4. Y. Nedarim 9:6.

Index